Cuban Fire!
Stan Kenton..................T-731

In the Wee Small Hours
Frank Sinatra................W-581

High Society
Original Soundtrack...........

Gypsy! · Hollywood Bowl
Symphony Orch..............P-8342

More Harry James in Hi Fi........W-712

Ray Anthony Plays for Dream Dancin

Music to Change Her Mind
Jackie Gleason...............W-632

Guy Lombardo in Hi Fi...........W-738

The Piano Style of Nat "King" Cole

The Long-Player Goodbye

Also by Travis Elborough

The Bus We Loved: London's affair with the Routemaster

THE LONG-PLAYER GOODBYE

The album from vinyl to iPod and back again

TRAVIS ELBOROUGH

SCEPTRE

First published in Great Britain in 2008 by Sceptre
An imprint of Hodder & Stoughton
An Hachette Livre UK company

2

A CIP catalogue record for this title is available from the British Library

ISBN 978 0340 93410 4

Typeset in Sabon by Hewer Text UK Ltd, Edinburgh
Printed and bound in the UK by CPI Mackays, Chatham ME5 8TD

Hodder & Stoughton policy is to use papers that are natural,
renewable and recyclable products and made from wood grown in
sustainable forests. The logging and manufacturing processes are expected
to conform to the environmental regulations of the country of origin.

Hodder & Stoughton Ltd
338 Euston Road
London NW1 3BH

www.hodder.co.uk

For Emily

ACKNOWLEDGEMENTS

On the inner sleeve of his 1979 LP *Exposure*, Robert Fripp declared himself 'indebted to all those who took part in the hazardous series of events culminating in this record, and several who do not appear but helped determine the final shape.' And faced with this blank page, I feel much the same about this book. In an ideal world, the acknowledgments, aping the dedications that appear on another album cover (The Chocolate Watchband's *Inner Mystique*) would probably give the Yellow Pages a run for their money. But in the interest of brevity, and to conserve valuable paper for the unruly narrative and, on occasions, jolly pictures that follow, I'll try to be succinct.

First off, I'd like to thank the can men of Clissold Park, who inadvertently helped to inspire this book. Their seemingly unwavering devotion to frighteningly strong lager and The Waterboys' folk rock opus *Fisherman's Blues*, an album that over the course of one summer a year or three back they played, tirelessly, over and over again on a portable boom box, set in motion a few thoughts about the LP. These thoughts (something along the lines of, 'God, what would it actually be like to have just the *one* album?') were hardly any more profound than clutching a handful of those salmon-coloured 500 quid bills during a game of Monopoly and saying, 'imagine if this was real', but my ever-patient agent, Nicola Barr, felt there was something in them. And so, to our immense gratitude, did Helen Coyle at Sceptre, whose enthusiasm for the book and forbearance during a missed deadline or two, and a, not insubstantial, manuscript and research depleting hardrive failure, has been unsurpassed throughout. I'd also like to thank Henry Jeffreys, Brett Woods, and, really, everyone else at Sceptre and Hodder for their work on the book without whom, etc . . .

I am also immensely grateful to all the people, from fellow gig-goers and record bin browsers to journalists and musicians, whose opinions I sought while writing this book. And Louis Barfe in particular, for kindly passing on a transcript of his interview with Hugh Mendl.

Much of the groundwork for this book occurred in the racks of record shops, and while my wallet would possibly have been fatter, this volume would have been much thinner without the aid of Flashback and Haggle on Essex Road, N1; On the Beat on Hanway Street, W1T; Beanos of Croydon; Records aka Collections in Lewisham and Waxfactor in Brighton. And in fond memory of Reckless Records and Totem Records. Needles and Spins in cyberia, *http://www.needles-and-spins.co.uk/*, assisted in keeping the turntables turning.

The staff at the British Library in St Pancras and in Colindale more than amply helped me in my quest to avoid writing the actual book by spending any allotted time reading back issues of *Gramophone, Billboard, Music Week, High Fidelity, Disc,*

Downbeat, *Melody Maker*, *NME*, *Record Mirror*, *Vox* and what have you and raiding their sound archive on the grounds that it was 'research'. The staff at the London Library in St James, similarly, kept me supplied with books on the folk revival and a wifi friendly googling environment.

I have tried hard to avoid lists in this book but turning to personal notes of thanks to friends, colleagues, and souls who have been nice along the way, I see no other option than to just pile in with a few names and seek forgiveness from anyone I have inadvertently missed out. So here goes: Ian Jack, Andrew Martin, Sukhdev Sandu, Ian Sansom, Steve Jelbert, Andrew Holgate, Eithne Farry, Frances Wilson, Chris Roberts, Andy Miller, Declan Clarke, Rachel Bailey, Essie Cousins, Gwendolen MacKeith, Cathcrine Taylor, Katrina Dixon, Senay Sargut, Michael Knight, Donna Blackburn, Simon Hughes, Eugene Wolstenholme, Guadalupe Nunez-Fernandez, Pam Berry, Stephen Troussé, John Noi, Dusty Miller, Louise Campbell, Nick Rennison, Nick Tucker, Paula Byerly Croxon, Angela Penhaligon, Ashley Biles, Gail Lynch, Sarah Wasley and Karen McLeod and, breaking with that for a bit, special extra thanks are due to Gail O'Hara who took my author shot, and Mike Jones who produced some of the excellent photos inside. And Lauren Wright, Alex Mayor, Nick Parker and Josh Lacey, for listening, reading and generally enduring more of my rambling nonsense than is good for any sane person.

Which leaves space, just about, to thank my folks for being my folks and for buying a stereogram way back when, and Emily Bick, whose beauty, astonishing mind and love I am honoured by every day.

CONTENTS

A man would simply have to be as mad as a hatter
To try to change the world with a plastic platter
– Todd Rundgren, *An Elpee's Worth Of Toons*

Most artists, I tell you, grateful for an LP, cos a 45 like little
slug from a gun, but the LP like a rocket launched, long-
distance missile that shoot far.
– Dillinger, quoted in the *Rough Guide to Reggae*

Parents should always be careful what they say. 'Try not to
scratch the surface of the LP,' mine advised. And like its near
siblings, 'don't run in corridors', 'always look both ways before
crossing the road', 'never accept sweets from strangers', 'eat the
meat' and (a little later) 'have a half and make it last', to this day
it remains lodged in my brain.

I can picture the scene now. I am about four and poised before the
stereogram, the hulky wooden box resembling a coffin that dominated our lounge. The soundtrack from *Oliver*, odds on, is clasped
in my overeager hands. ('Please, sir, I want some more . . .')

'Try not to scratch the surface of the LP,' my mother gently
but firmly states, once again.

Loading the disc on to the spindle. Triggering the autochanger so that it lets out a spud-gun *ping*. And waiting,

1

patiently (very impatiently, actually), while the tone arm jerks into life and, shuddering like a clockwork marionette, deposits itself on the edge of the disc with a biscuit-crunch bump. These simple procedures, her admonishment implies, are fraught with possible dangers. Spinning this wheel is a game of chance. Nothing is entirely certain. One false move and it could all go horribly wrong.

Was it any surprise, then, that in my childish imagination, putting on an album was soon equated with conducting major heart surgery, defusing a bomb or cracking an exceptionally fiendish safe? So overdeveloped were my fantasies that sometimes it came almost as a surprise (and a disappointment) that a black disc, sleek and shiny as liquorice, opted to play Shirley Bassey's 'I Capricorn' rather than spontaneously explode.

But, in a way, nearly anything seemed possible, probable even. These LPs possessed strange magical powers (as well as an irrepressibly pixyish ability to skip and generally misbehave[1]). Two parts Darth Vader to one part Tupperware, they looked foreboding and yet comfortingly domesticated. Their snug cardboard sleeves, bearing cheery images of woolly-jumper-wearing groups, car-coat-clad crooners and be-hatted cockney flower girls, cloaked the mysterious dark arts of sound. Just how did so much stuff . . . so much noise . . . fit into those tiny, tiny grooves? The enchantment was instantaneous. This scratch was an itch that was never going to go away.

---

1 Okay, Ron Moody and his h-dropping juvenile charges could be trusted to deliver 'Consider Yourself' and 'Where is Love' etc. pretty flawlessly time after time. But Tom Jones' 'The Green, Green Grass of Home', on the other hand, appeared to be tirelessly intent on improvising as it went along. Such was the range and variety of skips and jumps it produced, no single play of this LP ever seemed to be the same. If I'd known then what jazz or turntable-ism was, I would have concluded that this was it. Probably.

Lolling about on the fibrous purple carpet, repeatedly playing album after album, my imaginary friends Benson and Hedges beside me, I'd idle away hours enraptured by the witchcraft of it all. Attempting to decipher the hieroglyphic codes contained on their covers, matching faces to voices and songs to the typed lists on the back, were games that easily bested such trivial pursuits as Happy Families and dull old Snap.

In comparison with the handful of tawdry singles we had (Boots Randolph's 'The Shadow of Your Smile', anyone?), most dressed in tatty, pictureless, paper singlets, LPs gave you . . . well, more of everything really. More to hear. More to look at. More to enjoy. (More to be annoyed by, if you were that way inclined.) But more, even, than the sum of their individual parts.

As a matter of fact, my parents owned only a dozen or so LPs. And all of those were stored away in a slot inside the stereogram – a compartment that was so diminutive that it tacitly said, you'll-not-be-wanting-more-than-twenty-of-these-fellers-now-will-ya? Accordingly, new albums arrived with the infrequency of comets. Their appearances normally coincided with birthdays, wedding anniversaries and religious festivals and generated equally brief flurries of excitement. Like the greetings cards that often accompanied them, they vanished surprisingly quickly. I almost considered it my duty to resurrect these seemingly forgotten discs from the stereogram's crypt, this land of the audio undead. Looking back on it now, I can see that what I took for neglect was possibly closer to respect. My parents merely saved them, as with Sunday best, for special occasions. And the last thing they really needed was for me to ruin what precious few discs they had. I didn't, and my enthusiasms were indulged, but like most children I wanted it to be Christmas or a birthday – exciting, essentially – every day of the week. I couldn't understand why anyone wouldn't want to play their LPs every single day. I still can't, perhaps.

At friends' and relatives' homes and at school, I was gradually made aware of the mean gruel I'd been subsisting on, as doors, usually made of smoky grey glass and attached to steely hi-fi cabinets, opened to reveal LPs of previously unimagined oddness and sophistication. Records whose sleeves were bewildering, disturbing enough on their own. What did a skull need with oxygen or oxygene? How on earth could a band of eighteenth-century fops acquire electric guitars and headphones? This man shaking hands was obviously on fire, why had no one dialled 999? And, to make it worse, a bloke on the back in a bowler hat was missing his face . . . and sections of his limbs . . . LPs of singing wallet-swipers were eventually abandoned and never spoken of again. Soon enough there would be other fish to fry, but the wonder and that sense of preciousness would not fade.

All of this came swimming back to me only the other day, as I sat on a bus next to a young girl. Glancing over, I saw Lilliputian album sleeve after album sleeve whizzing by on the screen of her iPod. Here was what previously would have been the collection of a lifetime for many, housed in something little larger than a fag packet. The distance travelled from the cumbersome lounge furniture of my youth to the nano-technological present suddenly seemed painfully large – and tremendously exciting.

Even typing these words now on a laptop that itself holds several thousand songs (and is effectively a mini-recording studio and pressing plant), the rigidity of that recent past and the paucity of its options are hard to avoid.[2] I grew up obsessed with music, spending whatever spare money I had on albums.

2 Lavishing one's affection on vinyl today is, after all, only another consumer option. For a while my own aesthetic choice did have the added bonus of being cheaper, but alas no longer . . .

When I was younger, these records owned me as much as I owned them. They shaped (skewed?) every aspect of my life, from the friends I had and the clothes I wore to some of the books and films I sought out. (The sight of the sunburst orange of a CBS label, the tangerine of RCA, the vermilion of Polydor, or the rather sickly lemon yellow and grotty green of Harvest are enough to bring forth eidetic memories of cider- and weak lager-laced teenage gatherings and a hundred languid wet afternoons in rented rooms long vacated.) I gave up smoking only after calculating that I could afford another album a week with the money I'd save. But most people I knew back then, avid muso types included (Hello Aidan! Hello Steve! Hello Phil! Hello Sue!), probably possessed less music than can currently be stored on your average mobile phone. The idea of actually making and releasing an album, while not entirely unthinkable, still seemed a distant prospect in the extreme. Less might have been more, but it was also less. But what now looks like limitation was once, of course, liberty. Before the LP arrived, the longest record you could buy or make lasted just over four minutes, wore out after around seventy plays, shattered if dropped, and subsequently went on to spend much of its retirement 'voicing' that snapping sound in chocolate-bar adverts.

This book is an attempt to step back and consider – to remember, to celebrate – just how radical the LP was in its day. Because the long-playing vinyl record really did change . . . everything. Forget iPods, MySpace and the Internet, for a moment, anyway.

The LP revolutionised the way music was produced, packaged, marketed, sold, purchased, listened to and performed.

It offered unsurpassed levels – and lengths – of recorded sound.

It gave punters more music per dollar than had ever been offered before.

It put complete classical symphonies, collections of songs,

shows, film scores, plays and field recordings within easy reach of millions.

It persuaded musicians of all stripes to forge sustained artistic statements that continue to be cherished soundtracks to everyday lives.

It provided a canvas for an entirely new visual language to blossom.

It inadvertently spawned the 7-inch single.

It encouraged a legion of enthusiastic amateurs to enter the record game.

It ushered in life-shattering experiences in sound.

It supplied the obsessive with something to obsess about.

It forced you to buy a handful of tracks you didn't really want . . . but, hey, what were you going to gripe about otherwise? House prices?

It allowed levels of indulgence practically unequalled in any other artistic discipline. (You make that sound like a bad thing?)

It brought back music from the dead and the dormant.

It supplied the twentieth century with a social and cultural record that is the equal of the movie camera.

It tempted millions to try drugs, sleep with strangers, sport weird hairstyles and abandon perfectly good college courses and careers to embark on non-conformist journeys of self-discovery.

It speeded up divorces, ended relationships, split families and estranged friends, siblings, parents and children.

It has given some remarkably talentless people long and financially remunerative careers.

It has led to madness, deafness, premature baldness and incontinency . . . probably.

All the same, it may not be long before we say goodbye. Because right now we stand at a pivotal juncture with the LP and what it bequeathed: our understanding of the album. In a relatively short period of time, what was until recently the unquestioned moneymaking – and creative – engine of the music industry has in essence broken down. Its obituary has already been penned in some quarters.

Having lasted for sixty years, the long-player can at least take comfort from being astoundingly, if at the time rather lazily, well named. This is a book about the LP and *those* years, if you like.

Think about what's happened in the last six decades. When the LP was born in 1948, the average life expectancy of a working man was fifty-seven. Sliced bread was only bettered by Bing Crosby and Alfred Hitchcock's *Rope* was quite the daring new thing at the cinema. The LP arrived at the point when post-war austerity was giving way to affluence and an era of unprecedented leisure and technological advancement – the kind of technological advancement that we largely take for granted – beckoned.

The LP survived, and sometimes thrived on, huge emerging shifts in social mores. God was lost, and television, frozen food, drugs, more reliable contraceptives and holidays abroad were found. Sexual, political and musical revolutions were sent spinning. And such innovations as the 7-inch single, multi-track recording, stereo sound, the eight-track cartridge, modern jazz, easy listening, rock 'n' roll, soul, progressive rock, funk, reggae, punk and techno all came barrelling along. The album has weathered the cassette, the compact disc and the fall of communism in turn.

These days, the songs and covers of some LPs are so familiar they feel practically arc welded into our collective consciousnesses. Peter Blake's collage for The Beatles' *Sgt. Pepper's Lonely Hearts Club Band* recently took its place beside Concorde and the Spitfire in the BBC's *Great British Design Quest*. The sleeve of *Abbey Road* has been parodied almost as frequently as the songs on it have been covered, while the group's so called *White Album* formed the basis for a play staged at Nottingham's Playhouse Theatre. Less reverentially, in 2004 Danger Mouse treated the LP to a 'mash-up' with Jay-Z's *Black Album*.

Pink Floyd's *Dark Side of the Moon*, itself the recipient of a speaker-rumbling reggae tribute LP (*Dub Side of the Moon* by the Easy Star All Stars), became the first album to spend a total of 1500 weeks on the American Billboard chart. To date the album is believed to have sold in excess of 40 million copies worldwide. And new entrants seem to be inducted into a burgeoning pantheon of 'classic albums' all the time. The BBC and VH1 continue to broadcast programmes charting the creation of such supposedly seminal long-players as *Disraeli Gears* and, erm, *Stars* by Simply Red. Meanwhile, the press and Internet message boards all hum with opinions about new releases and reappraisals of lost masterpieces and unfairly neglected gems.

In a move that has clear parallels with the rise of the 'director's cut' phenomenon in film, established recording stars have also shown a greater willingness to return to past albums and 'restore' them in line with their original intentions; however dimly remembered those might be after years of unresolved artistic enmity, narcotic abuse and critically derided forays into poetry. Failing to heed its title, Paul McCartney remade *Let It Be*, stripping it of the lavish Phil Spector overdubs that simultaneously cloaked and glaringly drew attention to the bitter infighting that dogged the album's protracted creation in 1969.

Finally, though, MP3s, downloads and iPods have cracked open any notion of the album as a linear, (awkwardly) unalterable whole. The domestic listener is currently freed from the physical constraints, the existential thingy-ness of the album as an object. The ability to accrue a ragbag of different songs on our computers and iPods has – much as the LP itself once did – irrevocably altered how we think about, acquire and listen to music. And how in turn music in the future will be composed and consumed.

The LP, lest we forget, was developed as a commercial property first and foremost. The album would not have lasted without a money-paying audience who remained as enamoured of the medium as the musicians, engineers, entrepreneurs, record companies and outright crooks were keen to continue exploring (and exploiting) its possibilities. At quite an astonishing rate of knots, digital downloading has, of course, turned much of that on its head.

For the time being, the semantics of the LP remain: people still talk about making albums, regardless of whether they are really only referring to uploading a clump of tracks to a website. The album continues to represent a creative benchmark to which millions aspire. One to which the public, having provided *X Factor* star Leona Lewis with the fastest selling debut album in the UK in November 2007, can still buy into. For the moment, at least . . .

But online music sites have been very good at being able to offer instant and cheap (if not free) aural gratification. These days, we can have an album beamed to our computers or phone within seconds of its release (if not earlier). And rather like junk food, such easy fodder leaves us ever peckish for more. While this has led to people discovering hundreds, thousands, of new albums and artists they might never have found otherwise, the more general tendency, encouraged by iPod playlists and per song pricing, has been for albums to be consumed in the manner of small children nibbling away at sandwiches and leaving the crusts. Instead of being gobbled up/ suffered in their entirety, albums are snacked upon and filleted for a handful of tracks.

Lou Reed can sternly huff and puff (as he once did on the rear sleeve of his 1989 outing *New York*) that his album is 'MEANT TO BE LISTENED TO IN ONE 58-MINUTE (14 SONGS!) SITTING AS THOUGH IT WERE A BOOK OR A MOVIE' until he is blue in the face. Jocular exclamation marks and block capitals will do him little good. His missive doesn't appear on the iTunes blurb for the LP and each one of those 14 SONGS! can be popped out individually, like a pill from a pack, for just 79p a go.[3]

In this savage new dog-eat-dud-track audio jungle, nothing is truly sacred. And why should it be? No one needs to pretend to enjoy all (any?) of *Trout Mask Replica* ever again. But if iPod users are following the example set by Dylan 'Bye, Bye Ringo' Jones in his book *iPod, Therefore I Am*, then Starr's vocal contributions to The Beatles' catalogue are likely to be proving expendable, which seems more of a shame.[4]

3 Lou presumably had programmed the album for CD . . . and was twitchy back then about punters hitting the 'random' button, or flipping over to the radio for the latest news on the Knicks game, in between numbers about AIDS and recession-ravaged Manhattan.

4 Ringo fanatics, however, are able as never before to respond in kind. The Beatles' story can be told anew with Lennon, McCartney and Harrison recast as the tunesmiths and session men behind an all-singing, all-drumming, all-acting Scouse superstar. With Starkey centre stage, an ingenious new pop narrative can emerge, one that seamlessly progresses from 'Boys' and 'Matchbox' to his solo masterwork *Ringo* – an LP that, incidentally, on its release in November 1973, *Rolling Stone* magazine, no less, concluded 'in atmosphere . . . the most successful record by an ex-Beatle. It is not', they believed, 'polemical and abrasive like Lennon's, harsh and self-pitying like Harrison's, or precious and flimsy like McCartney's, but balanced, airy and amiable.' Unfortunately for Ringo, Paul McCartney's *Band on the Run* was released less than a month later. It went on to walk off with *Rolling Stone*'s Album of the Year and in Britain became the biggest-selling LP of 1974.

Asked recently about downloading, the musician David Byrne commented that, 'The sad part is, I guess, a lot of songs don't grab you right off the bat. But they grow on you, and you don't have a chance for that to happen if you're only going to download the things with the big hooks. Sometimes, the quieter or the subtle song is the one that gives the counterbalance to the loud and brassy one that preceded it. There's a balance. There are shadings of personality that this band is coming forward with. Life isn't just about parties.'

But the trend is now well advanced and in March 2007, the *New York Times* noted that 'sales of albums, in either disc or digital form' had 'dropped more than 16 percent' while 'individual songs, sold principally through iTunes, continued to rise'. One industry insider told the paper, 'I think the album is going to die. Consumers who have had iPods since they were in the single digits are going to increasingly gravitate toward artists who embrace singles'.

Later in the year, Ash was one such group that announced it had committed itself to a 'singles only' record deal. And both Prince and Ray Davies chose to give copies of their new albums away with newspapers while Radiohead opted for a pay-what-you-like download for their latest opus – discovering, in the process, that paying nothing at all was many people's preferred option. (Though they profited handsomely from those who did.)

In some respects, things have almost gone full circle to the pre-LP era when people collected individual songs and did much of their listening via the radio; spinning from station to station until they found something to their taste. The earliest albums were simply sets of 78s stored, like photographs, in binders – the term was first applied to a four-disc package of Tchaikovsky's *Nut-cracker Suite* in 1909. The phrase rather nicely conveys the idea that these were keepsakes, things you might cherish. And like a photograph, a record is really a little sliver of the past we get to enjoy again, one that accordingly becomes irreversibly entwined in our own memories.

Looking at a family photograph album, only a month or so back, I was struck by how few snaps were there and how bad many of them were. They'd been taken and, even if dreadfully out of focus, kept to remember the occasion. Now, of course, with digital cameras and mobile phones, we take pictures all the time, load them up to flickr and email them round. The glut can make individual shots seem less essential than when we only used one roll of twenty-four in a year. But who can go back to that?

Music is in much the same situation. In 1973, only around 5,000 albums were released; in 2005 it was in excess of 44,000. Everyone has more music than ever before but it's valued very, very differently. When our options were fewer, our grooves were deeper but narrower too. With three television channels, the radio, the record shop, music papers and local library as the main sources of information, our commitments were more intense. Clannish even. Perhaps sometimes a little blinkered.

For a while in the early Noughties, advertisers and politicians frequently alluded to an iPod generation in press releases and speeches. Presumably this was to appear 'with it' and in the hope that some of the iPod's apparent 'nowness' would rub off on them or their products. Nevertheless, as a reflection of a con-sumerist era of political consensus rather than ideological tribal loyalties, where eclecticism continues to be valued over the specific, the focus group and the blog over the expert, the iPod *was* a remarkably neat fit. It offers soundscapes shrivelled to palatable soundbites and allows musical tastes to be presented with a 'whatever' twirl of the dial akin to a judgement deflecting rising inflection. The enormous appeal of all of this to the audio addict and the dilettante are clear enough: the avid collector can have everything at their fingertips; the not-really-bothered don't have to bother with the stuff they don't like.

With an iPod, iTunes, e-Bay and so on, we are free to thumb through music's back pages, helping ourselves to what takes our fancy with gay abandon. We have been released from the tyranny of critics and the mocking sneer of the rock-snob record-shop till jockeys. Internet sites like MySpace have encouraged us to have a go ourselves. Despite this, one of the first scientific studies on downloaders conducted by Dr Adrian North at the University of Leicester concluded that the sheer ease of obtaining music these days was making us, if anything, more apathetic about it. The report found that 'the accessibility of music has meant it is taken for granted and does not require a deep emotional commitment once associated with music appreciation'. Dr North declared that for his subjects at least, music had 'lost its aura' and was 'seen as a commodity'.

In the face of these advances, to purposely listen to LPs on vinyl could seem dangerously close to an act of deliberate historical re-enactment, like putting on a stovepipe hat and pretending to be a Parliamentarian pike carrier at weekends. But what if less really is more? The sheer ubiquity of semi-disposable music has started to produce some peculiar rearguard actions. Sales of vinyl LPs have, for instance, been growing. In October 2007, even the Internet retailer Amazon.com began selling vinyl albums and a range of record players. Though, tellingly, consumers are often having it both ways. The independent record label Matador is not alone in supplying a coupon for MP3 downloads with every new 180-gram vinyl LP they sell.

Live performances too, have caught a dose of LPitis. Where performers might spend months or years, decades in a few instances, diligently perfecting an album in the studio, it was extremely unusual, impossible sometimes, for a group to present an LP in full on the road. The 'gig' was, and continues to be, prized for its variety and spontaneity, that *je ne sais quoi* blend of something old, desperate attempts to try out new material on the punters and a couple of influence-acknowledging or vaguely ironic 'something borrowed's for good measure. A formula so winning that it provided artists and record companies with lucrative spin-off live LPs and for decades kept a nefarious industry in bootlegs afloat. And, as album sales have dipped and illegal downloads flourished, it has become a far more reliable and financially rewarding stream of income than recordings for many artists – hence Prince's willingness to loose his new disc to the *Daily Mail* in 2007.

But the live concert has also recently become an acknowledged vehicle for acts to mount symphonic performances of their 'classics'. The Stooges, Dinosaur Jr, Sonic Youth and Belle and Sebastian have all dusted down *Funhouse*, *Bug*, *Daydream Nation* and *If You're Feeling Sinister* respectively over the last couple of years – with Belle and Sebastian and Sonic Youth subsequently making recordings of their performances available. (The devoted can, therefore, effectively buy LPs of LPs, as it were.)

Jolly as these concerts are, they too appear to prove that we can no longer be trusted with our own albums any more. To be assured we won't fiddle with running order, bands seem to have to physically play the LP for us. Artists and audiences at these concerts all appear locked into mutual bouts of nostalgia for the days when everyone felt a greater obligation to listen to every track at home – an obligation that iTunes and chums have helped to dash. In this light, these gigs appear more like wakes, or gatherings of speakers of some soon-to-be extinct tongue that their own offspring might never learn, than anything else.

* * *

LPs, books, films and plays are often described as iconic. But of all these cultural commodities, this seems particularly true of albums, where millions were bought literally as representations of (usually) secular musical saints. Like a piece of the true cross, the album could be an object of veneration for the believer, a physical instantiation of one's faith. The catechism of the vinyl LP involved a complex series of rituals over sleeves, sides played, needles, fluff and cloths, that were only enhanced by the scents of the record (rather waxy) and cardboard (woodlouse dampish, if anything) that mingled with the actions like incense.

This book, accordingly, comes to praise, rather than bury, the album. It is an unashamedly rhapsodic, if highly partial tour of the LP's life and times, from a lifelong fan who accepts, in principle, that it may not be around for ever. (Albums in whatever format will survive as long we want them and as long as people are prepared to make them. But the cultural and commercial forces that for decades sanctioned their ongoing creation do at this juncture appear severely imperilled.) It nevertheless looks back to the days when there was literally everything to play for, and people were still taking note of these newfangled sleeves. An era when we took the time to listen with pleasure all the way through – even if that was only because there was bugger all else to do and flipping between songs was trickier.

The LP was as arbitrary a construction as any. It was often less than what we expected. Or, worse, sometimes more than we needed. Yet the sense of cohesion the format alone bestowed is, or was, enormously appealing. However illusory it might be, we crave order, along with a sense of purpose, in our everyday lives. No less so in art or commerce. LPs were a chance to commune with and express our commitment to someone else's imagination, no matter how tawdry, for a while. Just as we yearn to read novels that take us out of ourselves, or that speak to us directly, an album was a chance to become entangled in a narrative.

LPs are bound up not just with history but with so many of our own histories. We all make our own record collections as we move through life. Paul Williams, reviewing *(The Kinks Are) The Village Green Preservation Society* LP for *Rolling Stone* in 1969, wrote: 'I've played it twice since it arrived here this afternoon, and already the songs are slipping into my mind, each new hearing is a combined joy of renewal and discovery. Such a joy, to make new friends!' Who hasn't thought of songs on a particular album as a set of companions, at some time or other? And LPs can be rather like friends. We fall out with them. We grow up and move on. We lose contact and find new ones. And then, years on, renew our acquaintance, only then remembering why we fell out in the first place. And fascinating as my coming to terms with the Psychedelic Furs' 'difficult' third LP is, or the weeks when Steel Pulse's *Handworth Revolution* or Schoolly D's *Smoke Some Kill* or The Feelies' *Crazy Rhythms* were never off the turntable are, this book is not intended as any kind of personal story. Nor is it any type of critical guide, though anecdote and opinion, naturally, rear their ugly heads from time to time. It is an attempt to tell a broader social story: LPs do not exist in isolation – they need consumers as much as producers, after all.

In keeping with the format itself, there may be bits you want to skip, the odd duff track, bad cover version or indulgent instrumental; it will on occasions jump, probably peter out just when it seemed to be getting interesting, or elsewhere go on for far too long.

When people asked me if I was including such-and-such an LP, the insanity of trying to talk about LPs at all was driven home again and again. Usually I'd find I wasn't, and no attempt at completeness has been made. This is a magpie's book, one that owes an enormous debt to the shiny stuff from many other earlier tomes. The reasons some albums or events are mentioned veer from the wilfully arbitrary to the breathtakingly callow. It only barely scratches the surface of the LP, but what more can anyone do? That is what they are designed for. And to listen to an LP is to acknowledge our mutual decay – at its end we are both older and neither of us will get those forty minutes back again. What greater tribute can there be than to lift up the needle and play it from the beginning one more time?

Chapter One
SPEED WARS

On 18 June 1948,[5] Columbia Records invited members of the press to a suite in the Waldorf Astoria on Park Avenue to attend a demonstration of a 'Revolutionary Disk Marvel'. Around forty journalists, grizzled fedora-wearers who had seen the Edison Diamond Disc come and go in their time, filed into the hotel, more eager to escape the heat and indulge in Columbia's hospitality than to witness a revolution. Once inside, they were addressed by the company's president, Edward Wallerstein. Wallerstein was far and away the most conspicuous of the Columbia bigwigs present that day, since he stood flanked on one side by a stack of conventional 78s and on the other by a

5 *Billboard* has a report filed from New York on 19 June 1948 that refers to the demonstration as having taken place 'yesterday', making it 18 June. Wallerstein in *High Fidelity* gives the date as 20 June and others have reprinted this, but I am inclined to go with *Billboard* since the issue in question was published on 26 June.

stack of 101 'long-players' – the name the company had chosen for its new microgroove vinyl record. Each stack, the journalists were informed, represented equal amounts of music. The 78s teetered some 8 feet high; the long-players – LPs – stood at a mere 15 inches.

Wallerstein delicately extracted a 78, a classical 'Masterwork' in the firm's acclaimed range, from the tower and proceeded to play it. After four minutes the record stuttered to an end, as was usual, midway through the first movement. In a gesture mined for maximum theatrical effect, he then bent down and picked an LP of the same symphony off the top of the other pile. Placing the 12-inch disc on a special adapter unit hooked up to an ordinary phonograph, he set the needle on its way, stood back and let sound fill the room for the next twenty-two and a half minutes.

When the music was finally over, a moment of stunned silence was instantly replaced by a hubbub of questions from the floor. Having exhausted their enquiries, the reporters fell upon the complimentary cocktails; some needing three or four just to reassure themselves that they'd been sober during the actual demo. Several maintained that they had hardly been able to believe their ears.

This marvel was the fruit of years of technical spadework. Looking back on that momentous demonstration twenty-odd years later, Wallerstein maintained that 'the critics were struck not only by the length of the record but by the quietness of its surfaces and its greatly increased fidelity. They were convinced that a new era had come to the record business'. Yet new eras, especially in the record business, never arrive quite so neatly. The LP, despite its self-evident merits and a critical thumbs up, would meet considerable opposition, entrenched habits, and a rival format in its first and distinctly unsteady steps towards any kind of widespread acceptance. In 1948, it was by no means certain it would prevail, let alone endure for sixty years.

Pottering happily along at around seventy-eight revolutions per minute since its invention by the German-American Emile Berliner in 1888, the gramophone record, though modified significantly over time, had, after all, seen off its near contemporaries and faced down many new contenders. It had weathered two world wars, prohibition, a stock market crash, the Depression, talking pictures, jazz and the radio. Chucking the old 78 speed out seemed rather churlish, ungrateful even. Would the record-buying public stand for it? 1947 had been a bumper year, with $204 million worth of records sold in the States alone. Were these newly purchased discs to be rendered instantly obsolete? As things stood, even owners of the earliest gramophone discs could, needle-ravaged grooves permitting, still play their ancient treasures on the latest machines. History and the mores of over 12 million Americans who owned conventional record players appeared stacked against the 33 1/3 LP.

And there had been long-playing records before. Edwardian Londoners, hardly shy of novelty, had found the Neophone Company's 21-inch discs charming enough in 1904. Offering a full eight minutes of playing time per side, they certainly lasted longer than the other discs and cylinders around. But to what end? The sheer effort of playing these hulking great monsters undermined any other benefits to be obtained. Within two years they were gone. Others had similarly tried and failed.

For all of its microgroovery, Columbia's disc, or disk, struck some as eerily familiar. Hadn't Columbia's chief competitor, RCA Victor, in fact produced plastic 33 1/3 rpm records similar to this in 1932? And where were they now? Probably adjusting to new identities as salad servers or bubble gum dispenser casings, their brief days as audio equipment long, long gone. And, with an irony that wasn't lost on some industry insiders, Edward Wallerstein, the man currently championing this revolutionary marvel at Columbia, had axed those very discs as a Victor employee. 'When I became general manager of the Victor Division of RCA in 1933', he recalled, unapologetically, 'my first act was to take them off the market.'

His decision was made on entirely pragmatic grounds: the Depression and the radio had left the record business in poor shape – only 6 million records were sold in America in 1932, down from 104 million records in 1927. And while these RCA discs, made of a special vinyl compound called Victorlac, might have worked fine in themselves, 'The pickups available at the time', Wallerstein maintained, 'were so heavy they just cut through the material after several plays.' Customer complaints were so numerous, he felt he had no choice. Wallerstein himself never lost faith in the idea of a longer-playing record. Described by one contemporary observer as possessing 'a mind like a steeltrap and a temper – when roused – like a good-natured grizzly bear with gutaches', Wallerstein drank RCA's bitter experiences in. After persuading William Paley, the urbane Ivy-League educated CBS radio mogul, to buy the American Record Corporation, Wallerstein moved to head up Columbia's record division in January 1939. When the ball started rolling on a longer-playing record at Columbia, he was around to ensure RCA's mistakes were not repeated.

*   *   *

In a world where a mobile phone is capable of holding several thousand songs, the scale of the obstacles that needed to be overcome to make the first LPs is hard to fully appreciate. And harder still not to regard as all a bit quaint, since it would take Columbia's lab-coat-clad boffins nearly nine years to achieve their goal. The discs, arguably, presented the lesser of their difficulties.

Until 1948, the principal ingredient in all records pressed was shellac, a resin secreted by Asian tree insects. Rather like pectin in jam, it's the principal gelling agent in the record, each individual 78 being comprised of a highly toxic mix of shellac, carbon black (hence the colour) and an array of abrasive fillers such as emery powder and limestone. (Reserves of the latter in Indiana resulted in the state becoming the centre of American record production.) The fillers, there to ease the erosion of grooves by heavy steel needles, are what give shellac 78s that distinctive crackling hiss.

The precursor to the vinyl eventually used in LPs was Bakelite, a synthetic plastic developed by Leo Baekeland in 1907. By 1930, the Union Carbide and Carbon Company had refined Baekeland's Bakelite to produce an extremely durable but malleable polyvinyl acetate they christened Vinylite. Experimenting with this material at RCA Victor's Camden, New Jersey lab, Jim Hunter, the company's chief engineer, had come up with a version that looked extremely suitable for gramophone records. It was tough enough to allow narrower grooves to be cut into its surface, increasing the number of lines per inch and therefore paving the way for a slower, 33 1/3 rpm longer-playing record. Unlike shellac, which was heavy and extremely brittle, this stuff was light and by comparison very durable . . . unless your customers spun it into motion on a turntable and insisted upon applying weighty pickups to it, then it did rather come a cropper – which was rather unfortunate, since that was all most of its first consumers could do when the breakthrough in lightweight tone arms was still to come.

The choice of 33 1/3 for Victor's new vinyl disc was, incidentally, far from arbitrary. Following extensive research into sound for the Vitaphone Film Company in 1927, the Bell Laboratory scientist Dr J. P. Maxfield had hit upon this speed while trying to reach a compromise between the size of a record needed to match an eleven-minute film reel and the noise distortion it gave off. Maxfield's work led to the speed becoming standard in the film and radio industry.

It is, therefore, a mark of Wallerstein's considerable foresight that in 1939, while everyone else in the record business – Victor included – continued to master their discs at 78 rpm, he insisted that each recording session that Columbia undertook should simultaneously be backed up on 16-inch 33 1/3 blanks.

But if the outbreak of the Second World War now temporarily derailed any plans for an LP, the conflict provided the greatest impetus to the development of vinyl records. With the Japanese occupying Malaya, supplies of shellac dried up. The situation became so grave that at one point American consumers were forced to return old shellac discs before they were allowed to buy new ones. It was possibly fortunate, then, that an all-out recording ban orchestrated by the American Federation of Musicians' president James Pertillo over royalty payments from jukeboxes and radios practically silenced the nation's studios from August 1942 until November 1944. However, under a deal brokered between Pertillo and the Armed Forces Radio Network, recordings for the US military in what became known as the 'V-Disc program' were exempted from the ban.

Since shellac was in short supply and was in any case too fragile to be shipped into combat zones, more robust polyvinyls were substituted. And a hardy spring-loaded turntable with replaceable steel needles to play them was created especially for the program.

More than 8 million V-Discs were eventually distributed around the globe between October 1943 and May 1949, taking to the Allied troops such delights as 'Blintzes Bagel Boogie' by Peanut Hucko and His Men and 'Ooh, Hot Dawg' by Gene Krupa and his Orchestra, as well as unique recordings by Fats Waller, Duke Ellington, Count Basie, Ella Fitzgerald, Tommy Dorsey, Frank Sinatra, Dinah Shore and Benny Goodman. Though still running at 78 rpm, V-Discs were capable of handling six and a half minutes per side, as opposed to the maximum four minutes twenty seconds of a conventional shellac 78. Their success served as an invaluable pointer to the viability of a longer-playing vinyl record for the industry, since RCA Victor and Columbia were both involved in the V-Disc program.

Among those who at this stage would probably have viewed a longer-playing record with little enthusiasm were the musicians and studio engineers. Recording techniques, such as they were, required performances to be 'cut' live on to a lacquer master disc. Entire sides were therefore completed in one take. If anybody made an error, the whole thing had to be started from scratch. Even for seasoned concert professionals, playing for four minutes under these conditions was hard work. The possibility of having to keep going at it for twenty could only have filled all concerned with dread. Once again it was technology, in the form of magnetic audiotape, hothoused in the crucible of the Second World War that would provide the solution to these difficulties.

John T. Mullan, an America GI with the Signal Corp stationed in Britain in 1944, was astonished to hear German radio stations playing concert quality music throughout the night. 'Hitler', he remembered surmising, 'could, of course, have anything he wanted. If he wanted a full symphony orchestra to play all night long, he could get it. Still', he reasoned, 'it didn't seem very likely that even a madman would insist on live concerts night after night.'

In Germany later in the war, he discovered how such broadcasts were possible when he came across a highly advanced 'tape machine' that until then had belonged to Radio Frankfurt. The first tape recorders, using wire and of limited fidelity, had been developed back in the 1890s. But it wasn't until 1928 that the German chemist Dr Fritz Pfleumer perfected and patented a working method of applying metallic oxide to strips of film or paper. Six years later, BASF and AG were able to unveil the first 'proper' commercial tape recorder – the Magnetophon – at the German Radio Exhibition. These machines, finessed by Nazi engineers throughout the war, had gone on to provide Goebbels with a valuable weapon in his propaganda arsenal, allowing him to saturate the airwaves with pre-recorded speeches and music.

Mullan, impressed by what he had heard, now wasted no time in shipping this machine home to California, dismantling it into thirty-five separate packages to overcome postage restrictions. He was not alone. Similar booty was liberated by Allied troops when they captured Radio Luxembourg in 1944. Bing Crosby, who was, according to Mullan, 'a very casual person' who resented 'the regimentation imposed by live broadcasts' was one of the first performers to take advantage of the serviceman's tape recorder. Crosby employed Mullan to tape and edit his weekly radio shows for ABC in 1947. Impressed, Crosby became the driving investor in the small Ampex company, which launched their own range of machines, closely modelled on the Magnetaphon, the following year.

Their arrival on the market, virtually coinciding with that of the LP, proved more than fortuitous. Without tape, creating LPs was – and would have continued to be – a laborious process. Many of the earliest LPs were simply old 78 recordings bolted together. This had to be done in real time, with the engineers completing a delicate replay race, passing on from one 78 disc to the next while a 33 1/3 master chugged along, logging it all as the single side of an LP. In his memoir *Putting the Record Straight*, the Decca records producer John Culshaw offers a vivid account of the 'nightmare' of 'assembling' LPs in this way:

> If a work occupied, say, ten 78 rpm sides then in all probability five of them would take up one side of an LP, and the problem was to get a smooth crossover from one 78 rpm side to the next. I stood there with a score and began a countdown during the last thirty seconds of a side and then shouted 'Drop!', at which point one engineer would fade out the side that had just ended while another, with luck, would lower the pickup on the beginning of the next side. If anything went even slightly wrong there was nothing to do but go back to the beginning, and as every LP had to be cut at least twice in case of an accident during processing at the factory it was a tedious and frustrating business.
>
> To this day I cannot hear Bartok's Concerto for Orchestra or Rimsky-Korsakov's *Scheherazade* with any pleasure, because I was satiated with them during these dubbing sessions; indeed, if I catch one of them inadvertently in the concert hall, it is all I can do to stop myself from leaping up and shouting 'Drop!' as each familiar joining point approaches.

Thanks to Wallerstein's canny foresight, Columbia, with their store of 16-inch 33 1/3 rpm recordings, therefore had a considerable head start on their competitors when it came to mastering LPs. But while their 16-inch discs ran to around eleven minutes, nearly three times the length of a 78, Columbia's cutting team – chief engineer Bill Savoury, his assistant Paul Gordon and the musical producer Howard Scott – still had to go through the same irksome business of dubbing one record after another to form the company's very first LPs. (As it was, an error in the cutting room rendered their first thirty transfers worthless, and they had to start the whole process from the beginning.) Tape swept aside all of this, allowing recordings to be edited and shaped as never before. Its versatility has led many to speculate that had Columbia not upped the ante on a vinyl long-player, a consumer tape system could well have seen off shellac – and records as we know them – in the 1950s, raising the distinct possibility that the album as we know it might never have emerged.

One of the biggest issues that had to be addressed was exactly how long a long-playing record should be. Eighteen months after the Second World War, this matter continued to vex the Columbia research team under the supervision – at least officially – of Peter Goldmark, though his precise contribution to the project remains a matter of enormous dispute.

In his self-aggrandising memoir, *Maverick Inventor: My Turbulent Years at CBS*, the Hungarian-born scientist responsible for the first, if eventually unviable, colour television system, maintained that he was the driving force behind the LP. The chapter dealing with the creation of the vinyl album is titled 'The LP Caper or the Case of the Missing Fuzz' and like the rest of the book is written in a pseudo hardboiled prose. Goldmark waxes lyrical about electrical engineering as if were he a score-settling Chandler gumshoe recalling all the lowdown cases he's solved. 'The phonograph', he writes, 'was still murdering Horowitz, Toscanini and above all Brahms, and I felt somehow compelled to stop this shellac killer in its tracks.'

The letter 'I' studs the text like cloves in a ham, and on balance the book seems to owe more to Norman Mailer than Philip Marlowe – although when he casually mentions that he always loathed symphonies on 78s because listening to them was 'like having the telephone ring at intervals while making love', it is Swiss Tony from *The Fast Show* that unavoidably springs to mind.

It is here, though, that Goldmark claims to have proposed the idea of a long-playing record to Wallerstein in 1945 and to have received short shrift: 'He listened to me patiently for exactly three minutes,' Goldmark wrote, 'put an arm around my shoulder, and suggested in a fatherly manner that I should drop the entire project and do something in the television line instead.' This rebuff, obviously, drove Goldmark 'harder to ferret out a way to accomplish what Wallerstein . . . believed was impossible.'

Goldmark's memoir was published in 1973, by which point Wallerstein had been dead for three years and was unable to counter his version of events. However, in an interview in 1969, not published until 1976, Wallerstein poured scorn on Goldmark's contribution. He 'didn't do any of the work,' the Columbia boss stated. 'No one man can be said to have "invented" the LP, which in any case was not strictly speaking an invention, but a development.' The one person Wallerstein did single out for special praise, in what he stressed was always 'a team effort', was Bill Bachman. Bachman was a former General Electric engineer, and it was his work for Columbia on a heated stylus and lightweight pickup that Wallerstein contended was crucial to so much of what followed.

What isn't in dispute, however, is that it was Wallerstein who settled the length of the LP. Presented with prototypes lasting between seven and twelve minutes in length, Wallerstein repeatedly complained: 'That's not a long-playing record.' Asked by a somewhat exasperated William Paley, who was pumping hundreds of thousands of dollars of the company's money into the scheme, to explain 'what in hell *is* a long-playing record?', Wallerstein spent a week timing works in the firm's classical repertoire and came up with a figure of seventeen minutes per side – roughly the length of Beethoven's 'Eroica'. 'This would enable', he believed, 'about 90 per cent of all classical music to be put on two sides of a record.'

An LP to Wallerstein's exacting specifications was finally complete by the autumn of 1947. Playing for a full twenty-two and a half minutes per side, this 'microgroove' disc was capable of holding 224 to 300 grooves per inch as opposed to around ninety on a normal 78. The electronics firm Philco in Philadelphia were engaged to manufacture a player for the discs. Here, again, Wallerstein's experiences at RCA served him well. In the early 1930s, when it looked as though radio would bury the gramophone record for good, RCA had launched the Duo Jr, a disc player specifically designed to plug into any radio set. Sold at cost, it proved popular and remarkably effective at steering consumers back toward records. Philco were charged with coming up with an LP unit along almost identical lines. Priced at $29.95 (later dropped to $9.95), the Philco LP adapter could be fitted to any standard gramophone player (or radio), allowing prospective customers to sample the new technology without breaking the bank or losing their ability to play 78s.

Though optimistically billed as 'unbreakable' by Columbia, the playing surface of vinyl records, free of the limestone fillers and God knows what else that went into shellac discs, were more susceptible to damage. It wasn't that they were much more delicate – they were sturdier in many respects – it was just that any minor scuffs were no longer hidden by the ambient grind of needle and disc as they went about the usual *danse macabre* on the turntable. If LPs were stacked up in the same basic kraft paper sleeves used for 78s, it was found that the new discs emerged noticeably marked, and those marks were clearly audible when the disc was played. It was obvious that a fresh kind of packaging would be needed. Wallerstein turned to Alex Steinweiss.

Back in 1939, Alex Steinweiss had made a novel suggestion. The twenty-two-year-old art director for Columbia responsible for designing the advertising paraphernalia (booklets, show cards) that accompanied the label's new releases, Steinweiss had been struck by the crushing dullness of the records themselves. Whereas his posters and ads employed bold typefaces, striking colours and ingenious motifs along contemporary European modes, the 'albums' he was promoting tried their best to resemble the dustiest tomes in a library. Boxed collections of three or four 78 records, these albums were usually dressed in tan brown covers with cod-leather binding, and ersatz gilt lettering if you were really lucky. From time to time an old master got pasted onto the front, but this was pretty rare. Steinweiss felt this was terribly wrong and put forward the then radical idea that more visually arresting packaging might help them to sell more records. Although at first Columbia baulked at the extra expense, Steinweiss was eventually given a handful of covers to trial. His first, for *Smash Songs Hits* by Roger & Hart, featured an illustration of a glitzy theatre awning, a brilliantly succinct visual representation of the Broadway numbers it contained. Steinweiss's picture covers were an immediate success. Sales of a Masterwork recording of Beethoven's Ninth Symphony, previously clothed in a plain binder, rose 894 per cent when it was reissued with one of Steinweiss's illustrated jobs. Eschewing portraits, his compelling graphic style defined the medium for

31

a decade, attracting imitators across the board; however, in 1948 he would bequeath an even greater legacy to the history of music and the visual arts, by inventing the LP sleeve.

Experimenting with cardboard and paper, he hit upon a dapper square outer jacket. His 'sleeve' protected the vinyl record from everyday wear and was capable of carrying an eye-catching 'front' image, while informative details about the artists or the recording could be printed on the back. His cover was simple, practical, functional design at its best. The only snag was getting someone to invest in the $250,000 equipment needed to churn the things out. The LP was an untested, unknown format. There was no guarantee of success, and as yet, no one outside Columbia's labs could play or listen to them. In the end, nepotism saved the day, with Steinweiss's brother-in-law apparently finding a printer willing to take the job on.

The first LP – ML4001, Mendelsssohn's Concerto in E Minor for Violin and Orchestra, Op. 64, Nathan Milstein, violin, with Bruno Walter conducting the Philharmonic Symphony Orchestra of New York – fell into the world, clad in a predominantly aquamarine cover enlivened by black lettering on a bold white corniced graphic that was possibly intended to be a Greco-Roman plinth, but which most commentators took for a tombstone. If it was an oblique comment on the fate of the 78 or Columbia's arch-rivals RCA it would be woefully premature, for neither were going to roll over without a fight.

Some two months before the LP's official press launch, in what was clearly intended as a conciliatory gesture – one that with any luck would ease the transition to the new format – William Paley invited RCA President David Sarnoff and his leading men over to CBS's offices on 799 Seventh Avenue to see the 'new developments' Columbia were working on. Sarnoff, who as a newly arrived nine-year-old Russian Jewish immigrant had helped to support his family selling Yiddish newspapers on the Lower East Side, was a force to be reckoned with. Known at his own insistence as The General, since being so honoured for his war work by Roosevelt, he had risen from a junior telegraph operator at Marconi to become the visionary force behind America's predominant radio and recording company. Ruthless, dictatorial and not a little bit vain about his own achievements, Sarnoff was thrown entirely off balance by what he saw and heard of the LP that day. Falling into an apoplectic rage the instant the demonstration was over, in the words of CBS's Howard Scott, he 'chewed out his entire staff in front of Paley'. Regaining his dignity enough at least to appear to consider Paley's offer of a licensing deal whereby Columbia would press LPs for RCA until their own plants were up and running, Sarnoff hauled his team away as soon as was politely possible. Back at RCA's headquarters in the Rockefeller Center, the tongue-lashing began again in earnest.

The launch of the LP came and went, with RCA keeping a dignified silence on the issue in public; in further private discussions with Columbia they maintained their money was on magnetic tape. Columbia by this point had abandoned any idea of licensing deals and was offering the technology free to any label that wished to run with the format, a policy that was intended to encourage its widespread adoption as quickly as possible. *Billboard* newspaper ('The World's Foremost Amusement Weekly') followed the progress of the LP closely, astutely observing that it could 'quite conceivably change the buying attitudes of collectors and delegate present modes of purveying recorded classical music to limbo'. In June 1948, at a time when record sales appeared to be 'running 15–30 per cent lower' than the previous year, it reported that dealers across America

reputedly saw 'the 33 1/3 innovation as a hypo' and that 'phonos' had 'been void of sales-spurring gimmicks since the widespread adaptation of the record changer'.

By the late summer of 1948, the first fourteen of an initial catalogue of '101 records, covering 325 compositions' appeared. Of this 101, seventy were classical – the Masterwork recordings of Bach, Beethoven, Brahms, Prokofiev and Khatchaturian; twenty were 'light classic' or 'show score', with items like *The Chocolate Soldier*, *Grand Canyon Suite* and the original cast recording of *Finians's Rainbow*; leaving eleven in the 'pop field' – of which *Frank Sinatra Sings*, *Harry James Favorites*, *For You Alone* with Buddy Clark and *Dinah Shore Sings* were deemed the highlights. Twelve-inch discs went on sale at $4.85, while the 10-inches sold for a dollar less at $3.85. In the classics, they represented particular value for money. The Ormandy-Philadelphia Orchestra's recording of Tchaikovsky's

Fourth Symphony, for example, now available on a single 12-inch LP, cost $7.25 on a five-disc 78 'album'.

If dealers had, until then, felt the absence of 'sale-spurring' phono gimmicks, they were soon assailed by one. By that December it became apparent that RCA were not, it seemed, going to be adopting a 33 1/3rd system – one, lest anyone forget, they'd left for the dogs in the 1930s. Nor did they believe people were ready to abandon the disc for tape. With an rpm that to all the world appeared to have been conjured up on the back of a fag packet by simply subtracting 33 from 78, RCA were going with 45[6]. 7-inch vinylite 45. That Sarnoff would prefer to roll out another format rather than admit his company had lost the initiate speaks volumes about his bloody-mindedness. This was, after all, 'a record with no long-playing feature whatsoever', as Joe Caida, who broke the story in *Billboard*, put it. Summing up the situation as he saw it, Caida wrote:

> So it boils down to this. No matter what anybody says or writes, the record business as of early spring 1949 will have three types of records available to consumers: 78, 33 1/3 and 45. The 15–17 million people who now have 78 rpm players will be able to buy records for their machines. Those who buy 33 1/3 players will be able to get records for their machines, those who decide they want 45 rpm records will be able to buy such disks and the players for them.

For consumers and the industry as a whole, who had cheerily bumbled along with the one speed of disc for years, this was a

6 It was actually based on another Dr Maxfield calculus. As befitted something pressed in sleek vinyl, the 45 was referred to as Madame X at the R&D stage – a codename that even then would surely have held good for some 'teaser girl' in high heels from the pages of *Eyeful*.

sudden and bewildering profusion of formats to take in. A month before RCA's new records were due to hit the shops, Columbia unleashed a series of press ads to bury the challenger under the banner: 'What's All This About a "RECORD WAR"?' announcing that 'The Long-Playing Record is here to stay' and backing up their claims by pointing to the '2 million LP records' sold and the '600,000' LP players installed in American homes so far.

The precise benefits of the rival RCA system over the 78, let alone the LP, did seem rather mixed. A tough, compact vinyl record, it was certainly much better in terms of sound quality than a 78. RCA had also excelled in making their new discs desirable objects by initially pressing them in a range of 'sparkling identifying colors': red vinyl for classical, midnight blue for light classics, green for country and western hillbilly, yellow for children's, sky blue for international, cerise for 'race' or R & B and black for pop. However, carrying around four minutes of music per side, they relied on consumers buying music in the same manner they always had.

With popular music, that continuity held enormous benefits, especially for jukebox manufacturers who'd struggled to find a use for a sprawling twenty-two-plus-minute-long disc. (One firm, Aireon, had produced a jukebox capable of carrying the Columbia 33 1/3, but as they told *Billboard* in April 1949, there had been 'little interest displayed in the unit to date'.)

However, in classical music, a Rubicon had really been crossed with the LP. As much as RCA extolled the convenience and storage benefits of the 45, boasting that more 'than 150 single records or 18 symphonies fit in one foot of bookshelf space', it didn't alter the fact that those symphonies were still in bite-sized chunks. In an effort to counter this, RCA had designed their discs to work with a special automatic changer, onto which a pile of 7-inches could be stacked and released at 'Trigger Action Speed'. ('Five Ball Novelty' pinball was another big new thing at that time.) *Contra* Caida et al, their adverts maintained that the 45 music system actually offered 'more than 50 minutes of music without need of attention. And it's just the music the listener wants when he wants it. It can play up to ten records with speedy, silent, hardly noticeable changes.'

But who were they kidding? An 'album' on 45 came on four or so 7-inches. Whereas a pop single might have side one and side two, to sequence, say, a symphony with the autochanger required side one to be backed by side eight, side two with side seven and side three with six, and so on. The listener, therefore, had to place the discs in the right order with the right sides up to achieve the same effect as playing one side of an LP. And then there was the 'hardly noticeable' whirr, clunk and flop of the autochanger between each movement.

Aware that they had (a) underestimated the lengths to which Sarnoff would go to avoid conceding ground to Columbia and (b) overlooked the pop market, Columbia produced a 7-inch 33 1/3 single. And so 'The Battle of the Speeds' rumbled on, and in the ensuing confusion record sales dived, slipping to $157,875,000 by the end of 1949. Record buyers were playing wait and see, baulking at the expense of buying players to cope with the variety of speeds. Faced with little other choice, manufacturers cannily began retooling their models to cope with all three. That summer, however, a major victory was won when the National Association of Music Dealers came out in favour of the LP, and in addition to Mercury, Cetra-Soria, Vox and Concert Hall, English Decca (London) and American Decca all committed to the LP.

In a decisive coup, Columbia had acquired the rights to the original cast recording of Rogers and Hammerstein's *South Pacific*, which they released as a 78 album and an LP. The latter was the ideal medium for such a popular two-act Broadway show, and if any single record put the LP into the average American home in 1949 it was *South Pacific*. (If in the musical Joe Cable could woo Liat 'in approximately 12 seconds', as Emma Brockes notes, then forty minutes was surely time to fall in love with an LP.)

The opera singer Ezrio Pinza, a longstanding RCA Victor artist enjoying popular acclaim for his part in the show, signed a new contract with Columbia. He wasn't alone: Thomas Beecham was another defector. Convinced that their careers were being stifled by RCA's resolute determination to ignore the longer format, other conductors and classical musicians followed suit.

After mounting a massive last-ditch advertising and publicity campaign for the 45, costing around $2 million, the distinguished conductor Arturo Toscanini, a close friend of Sarnoff, prevailed upon the RCA head to think again about the LP. 'I don't remember', Wallerstein (surely disingenuously) recalled, 'having any particular interest in RCA's announcement on January 4, 1950 that it was making available its "great artists and unsurpassed classical library on new and improved Long Play (33 rpm) records".' That same year, nevertheless, Columbia began issuing 45 rpm 7-inches, its own 33 1/3 7-inch disappearing from view in about 1951.

RCA was estimated to have lost $4.5 million in the period it held out against the LP. Its format, though, survived, and became the preferred speed for pop. With the LP cleaning up in the classical and adult market, the 78's death warrant was signed, sealed and delivered in America. By the middle of the 1950s it was virtually extinct. In Britain, however, the old speed held out. Its champions there even mounted one last futile stand against this 'damned Yankee LP'.

One of the most vocal critics of the format on British shores was Compton Makenzie, the comic novelist and founder of *Gramophone* magazine. Using *Gramophone*'s editorial pages as his soapbox, he fired off an eccentric and jingoistic salvo against the LP in April 1950. It 'amuses me', he wrote, 'how some English collectors wish for the LP record, but do they realise what sort of tiger it may turn out to be?' Explaining away the LP's success in the States, he maintained: 'It's something *New*, and that is what appeals to the American mind, regardless of its merits'. Continuing in a similar vein, he observed: 'You will very often read in American periodicals how the LP record sounds so much better than the regular "78" – of course it would when it is compared with the smooth surface to a rather indifferent, rough and noisy surface. But to compare the difference with a surface the English companies give us, well that's an entirely different matter!' In conclusion, and putting his weight behind the status quo, he believed that 'English record manufacturers . . . need not fear to any extent, the long-playing, the "45" or any other size or shape the American companies may offer.'

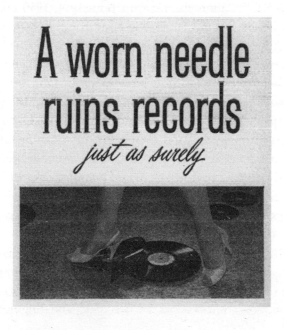

The two leading English record companies – Decca and EMI – were actually among the first European manufacturers that Columbia had shown their LP to. Both companies, according to Wallerstein, had been impressed. But EMI had close ties to RCA and stalled, finally, choosing to become the most obdurate defender of the 78 in the UK. It would be 1952 before EMI released an LP, a decision that would cost the company dear. Decca on the other hand, led by Ted Lewis, threw itself into LP production for the American market – Culshaw's arduous transcription work was undertaken specifically for US releases. Decca's Full Frequency Range Recording system (a by-product from wartime submarine reconnaissance research for the navy), and the 'London' records brand had a strong following in the States. By waiting until June 1950, by which time the Stateside speed war was over, Decca was able to prepare a good range of LPs and players for the UK market. Its cheapest player started at just £9.

By July, the company had released fifty-three LPs in Britain. A set had by now found their way to MacKenzie, along with one of the company's Deccola record players. It was time for the *Gramophone* man to eat some humble pie. 'I have been able to listen to the first lot of discs issued at leisure and as often as I wanted,' he reported. And after such extensive research was happy to reveal that 'the needle makes hardly a whisper on the Vinylite'. Of '*The Mikado* on two 12-inch discs, overture and all', he was stunned to meet 'seventy minutes of music with three moves from one's chair to turn it over!' Offering a rather different finale on this occasion, he admitted, 'I am glad that I am able to salute this gramophone advance without mystery . . . these LP Decca discs are jewels.' Two years on and *Gramophone* would be urging EMI 'to break the LP ice'.

Even in the UK, it seemed, 33 1/3 was here to stay.

Chapter Two

FOUR SEASONS ON TWO SIDES

The LP could not have picked a finer moment to be born. In comparison to what had passed before, the 1950s were to be an age of astonishing material affluence, especially for Americans who had finished the Second World War in a considerably better situation than their European allies. After magnanimously funding the rebuilding of the continent under the Marshall Plan, they duly set about colonising its consciousness, as the German filmmaker Wim Wenders once put it. With an almost uncanny prescience, the decade's unabashed consumerism was heralded by the arrival in the States of the Diner's Club credit card in 1950. As the Cold War grew ever frostier, the impetus to consume gained a political and moral angle as a demonstration of the superiority of the West's economic system. Higher wages, shorter working hours, longer holidays, better houses, cars, washing machines and television sets were to be the spoils of the Military-Industrial Complex and something to keep Reds at bay.

But if The Affluent Society, as Galbraith dubbed it in 1958, was an acquisitive one, it was simultaneously inquisitive and anxious. Living, as it did, under the constant shadow of 'the bomb', and guided by the newly emergent mass media, its mores and its ideas about status depended increasingly on peer group pressure rather than traditional sources of authority. The sociologist David Reisman in his book *The Lonely Crowd*, first published in 1950 and an unexpected bestseller in paperback three years later, outlined an account of this shift. Reisman argued that the character of the then rapidly growng suburban middle class was shifting from 'inner-directed' people who gained lifelong unwavering ideals and aspirations from their elders and betters early on, to 'other-directed' people, 'sensitised to the expectations and preferences of others'. In the heavily simplified version of Reisman's theory that did the rounds in the 1950s, the 'inners and outers' joined 'the us and them', 'is he, isn't he?', 'good and evil', 'raw and cooked' 'Tom and Jerry', 'Martha and Arthur' badinage of every cocktail party going. When what the novelist Richard Yates called 'the elusive but endlessly absorbing subject of Conformity' cropped up, Holden Caulfields young and old could be relied upon to rail against the perceived 'phoniness' of the 'other'-directed world.[7] But what Reisman identified was that while making the populace beholden to their infantilizing dreams of the good life, the new media empires of the advertisers on Madison Avenue and the television networks were nevertheless expanding horizons and ambitions. As a result, society as a whole was becoming less static and far less provincial.

7 Tellingly, Reisman's title appears in Bob Dylan's 'I Shall Be Released', a song to be found on Joan Baez's album of Dylan covers, *Any Day Now* (1968) and *Music from Big Pink* (1968), a long-player of ersatz head-to-the-hills Americana from The Band, Dylan's predominantly Canadian backing group.

In short, an irrepressible spirit of entitlement to both material betterment and a kind of socially useful intellectual self-improvement was in the air. Home ownership, travel and higher education, all once the preserve of the few, had become much more widely accessible. The GI Bill in America and the formation of the Welfare State and the passing of the Butler Education Act in Britain allowed greater numbers of people to learn for longer and to take up places at university.

Of course the LP and the multi-speed diamond stylus gramophone player – now marketed as a 'hi-fi' – immediately joined the ranks of those other domestic consumer desirables the Frigidaire and the range-top oven. But as commodities went, the LP, much like the paperback book, was unduly suited to inform as well as entertain a post-war generation who in matters of leisure were often of a faintly autodidactic or social-climbing disposition. Those whose curiosities had been piqued, say, listening to BBC Radio's *Third Programme*, the corporation's stalwartly Reithian arts and music network established in September 1946, now had the purchasing power and the leisure time to seek out similar recordings on, say, an LP from Nixa – a company founded in 1950 to license many American classical long-players for British release. If the condescension of record department staff worried them before, they could now order 'unbreakable' LPs 'very safely by post' – as an advert for Murdoch's on Tottenham Court Road in *Gramophone* assured would-be customers in August 1950.

These were, after all, boon years for hobbyists, with thousands now possessing the space, time, money and opportunities to indulge a whim for watercolour painting, hot rodding, interior decorating, gourmet cooking or morris dancing as they saw fit. Naturally enough, LP collecting and 'hi-fi' soon became legitimate hobbies in their own right. The pages of *High Fidelity*, one of several audio-buff magazines catering to this burgeoning enthusiast market in the 1950s, brimmed with adverts for build-it-yourself amplifier kits and concealing cabinets for the DIY enthusiast or budding gadgeteer to construct at home. Usually these were illustrated with a line drawing of a pipe-smoking, Daddie's sauce-bottle picture-perfect dad tinkering about with what looked frighteningly like a scaled-down model of a nuclear cooling tower, as junior and a busty wife gazed on in rapt amazement at his endeavours.[8]

Record collecting, obviously, was not new in itself. Just a year prior to the LP's launch, a volume entitled *How to Build a Record Library: A Guide to Planned Collecting of Recorded Music* was published. This too was far from the first, and certainly not the last, guide of its kind, but in it the broadcaster and writer Sigmund Spaeth saluted a breed of 'new music lovers'

---

8 Though possibly of little use if your own kit still lay in bits on the kitchen table, Junior was by now in bed and the busty wife was threatening to ram a valve into an orifice at an angle that would have brought tears to Dr Kinsey's eyes, there was an LP specifically aimed at the more befuddled hi-fi DIYer, boasting the talents of Mr Magoo.

Magoo in HiFi achieves, for the 1950s, impressive levels of meta-textuality, offering as it does both an audio chronicle of the myopic cartoon character's 'misadventures while trying to build a do-it-yourself hi-fi set' and 'a practical demonstration of true high fidelity' in one. Predictably, the finished article is less fun than you'd hope and can hardly have been great shakes back then either. As far as the high fidelity demo goes, in reality the listener is treated to a couple of whooshy low-to-high sweeps through the frequency range on a New Orleans-esque jazz number on side one, an effect that now might, at best, just about be capable of inducing mild pangs of nostalgia in an aged ham radio fan. And since Magoo's whole schtick is visual, his stock-in-trade the mistaking of bears for nephews ad nauseam, on audio the jokes pall pretty fast. Significantly, his services are dispensed with completely on a musical Magoo suite that occupies side two.

who he claimed were 'literally "at home with music".' To Spaeth, these *souls* possessed 'a fundamental sincerity and honesty of taste, which was not always true of the specially trained and privileged [concert-going] connoisseurs of the past who had been taught that music was a duty rather than a pleasure, an evidence of culture and social superiority, perhaps even a burden to be borne with dogged determination'. Whereas the radio 'dialer' was at the mercy of haphazard programming, those who bought records and listened to them were, in his view, thrusting, bull-by-the-horn-grabbing individualists who laughed in the face of 'duty', 'chance', 'or coercion of any kind'. Unconcerned about being 'seen in the company of other music lovers', 'the typical record fan' bought what they liked or that which was recommended to them 'by trustworthy authorities'. (People like Spaeth, obviously. If they really were buying *just* what they liked they wouldn't need the book.)

The fact that they 'willingly paid' for this 'recorded music' spoke for itself. Despite this they were, he maintained, 'careful' about what they added to their musical libraries and did not 'deliberately' clutter up their houses 'with albums that represented a hypocritical pretense' rather than their 'actual taste'.

Self-serving flim-flam consciously intended to butter up any would-be purchaser of the book it may have been, but at its core, Spaeth was insisting that the record buyer could exercise as much discernment, and in some respects, greater discernment, than the concert-goer of old. Listening at home on records, instead of being the second best option, could be a preferable experience. Such a view and the notion of building a record library of one's own gained an enormous currency with the LP.

Shellac discs had, in effect, only ever been semi-permanent objects. Ignoring their basic fragility, their average lifespan was still only between seventy-five and 125 plays. It was easy literally to play an album to death. Better sounding, longer, cheaper, lighter, durable, and storable, the LP made purchasing and collecting records a far more viable and, ultimately, worthwhile proposition for the average Joe and Jane. But it was their playing time and *the sleeve*, allowing for entirely new, ingenious combinations of sounds, printed text and illustrations that would dovetail perfectly with the needs of the epoch. Here was a society that was more prosperous, spending a greater amount of time at home and as hungry for knowledge as it was for luxury and fun – and all three of these factors would commingle in unlikely ways on many a swishly packaged LP.

Looking back on the earliest years of the format, the cultural historian Jacques Barzun, who in the 1950s had likened its development to 'the Renaissance rediscovering the ancient classics and holding them fast by the means of the printing press', argued that what recording on LP 'accomplished was to greatly enlarge the musical repertory and to make it known to thousands of unassuming people as yet untouched by the opposing prejudices of Hear Nothing and Read Nothing'. These newcomers, he believed, 'wanted to know'. And they 'got to know the music by playing the disc and they got the habit of reading about music by scanning the commentary on the back of the jacket.'

The record buyer, as Barzun noted favourably, faced a wealth of releases as the expanded format put complete symphonies and operas oh so neatly into the record racks. The tide of new records became so frenzied that as early as February 1951, the editor of a seasonal catalogue routinely issued by The Gramophone Record Shop in New York apologised to its customers for failing to keeping pace with their stock. 'Due to the current flood of LP releases, it has been impossible', they confessed, 'to listen to more than a mere portion.'

The musicologist Timothy Day calculates that in the first decade of the long-playing disc alone, 'a greater amount of recorded classical music and a greater range of musical repertory was brought into the home than in the entire history of recording during its first century'. Among them were the first complete recordings of Mahler's Third, Sixth and Eighth symphonies, Bach's St Matthew Passion, Bruckner's Third and Sixth Symphonies and Strauss's *Elektra*.

During the second decade, John Culshaw at Decca, with George Solti conducting, would achieve the previously untenable feat of recording Richard Wagner's *Der Ring des Nibelungen* in its entirety, and in stereo – a mammoth project of enormous technical and musical ingenuity that would take seven years to complete and see a Swiss peasant, discovered to be in possession of a suitably Teutonic fifteen-foot alpine horn, flown to Vienna to contribute to the recording session of *Die Walküre*.

By Culshaw's own estimation, to have attempted *The Ring* on 78s 'would have required something like two hundred and twenty-four sides, or one hundred and twelve records'. On LP, Culshaw was able to smuggle the whole of the Rheingold onto six sides, *Die Walküre* and *Siegfried* onto ten sides each, and *Götterdämmerung* onto twelve – making nineteen records for the entire cycle with a playing time of over fourteen hours.

It wasn't just that more music could now be recorded. The vastly expanded possibilities regarding listening in the home would in turn drastically transform the 'popular' classical repertoire, as formerly neglected strands of music and works by major, minor and long-forgotten composers, previously thought impracticable for the auditorium and/or the 78, were gradually ushered, over time, into the mainstream. In the earliest years of the format, some of the records that left the most lasting impression on the classical canon in the long term came from small independent labels.

Columbia's decision to offer to the technology for free, and to press LPs that did not compete with their own output for a nominal fee, meant that a number of hi-fi and musical enthusiasts entered the record business. Armed with cheapish Ampex and Magnechord tape recorders, giant breeze-blocks encrusted with knobs and spools, these evangelists for a range of causes, from early music and madrigals to fallow chamber pieces, pursued their aims as pioneering amateurs, in the noblest sense of the word. Often they cared little about monetary reward. Several, such as Overtone Records of Connecticut, for instance, were closely aligned to university music schools, in their case Yale, and were buoyed by philanthropic funds and patient subscribers, and oxygenated by notions of scholarship.

Music from the baroque period, under-represented by the major companies and requiring smaller ensembles to record, was to enjoy a spectacularly fertile revival on LP. While they certainly had their devotees, until then several of what are popularly regarded today as leading composers languished as little more than file-under-Bach footnotes of the baroque age. Much as John Webster's plays are overshadowed by those of Shakespeare, these concertos and symphonies were chiefly enjoyed by a minority, and then mostly for the purpose of enhancing an understanding of their better-known contemporaries.

Antonio Lucio Vivaldi, and one of the most ubiquitous pieces in the entire baroque firmament, *The Four Seasons*, is a case in point.[9] Until 1942, when Bernardino Molinari and the St Cecilia Academy in Rome offered up their loose and histrionically romantic interpretation, neither *The Four Seasons* nor any of Vivaldi's other compositions had ever been recorded before. And

9 It is surely almost impossible to listen to Vivaldi now without believing you are on the phone and spending what feels dangerously close to four *full* seasons on hold.

The Four Seasons wasn't tackled again until the dying days of 1947, when the American violinist Louis Kaufman, perhaps more famous for his contributions to hundreds of Hollywood scores, undertook the recording for the Concert Hall Society Inc., a tiny outfit formed just a year earlier that then specialised in limited edition pressings of 'unknown' classics for musical connoisseurs.

Kaufman worked from midnight until the early hours of the morning to complete the sessions before (yet another) musicians' union ban kicked in on 1 January 1948, and under the baton of Henry Swoboda, he corralled an assortment of players from the New York Philharmonic through the concertos in Carnegie Hall on the last four nights of the year.

Kaufman's *Four Seasons* – and Kaufman *had* doggedly tracked down the most complete version of the score he could find, so he deserves full credit for restoring the work to us – was initially released as an album of 78s. But since Concert Hall's co-founder, David Josefowitz, was both a conductor and a scientist with a PhD in plastics, the society was one of the earliest converts to the new format – and it managed to establish a not insignificant foothold in the classical LP market, thanks in part to Kaufman's *Four Seasons*. Toasted by Howard Taubman in the *New York Times* in October 1948 as 'an early and delightful experiment in program music', as an LP, *The Four Seasons* was greeted with a universally rapturous reception. A critical and commercial success, it was awarded the prestigious Grand Prix du Disque in France two years later. (Its historical significance was acknowledged, somewhat belatedly, when it was inducted into the Grammys 'Hall of Fame' in 2002.)

More recently, Jeremy Eichler of the *New York Times* has gone so far as to argue that 'its distance from a freshly tainted German Romanticism', together with the genuine 'lightness and transparency' of the music 'made it perfectly suited to American life in the post-war decade of the 1950s'. Its basic theme (a yearly cycle) has a universal human appeal, as Eichler, among others, has noted. But one can't overlook the out-and-out novelty factor that the recording must have held for 1950s listeners. Here was a musical exploration of the passing of time on a disc whose temporal bounds allowed it to be listened to in two poignant cycles: one given over to birth and bloom, the other to decline and death. With a baby boom in full swing and Truman greenlighting the hydrogen bomb, these issues, as ever, were not without their contemporary resonances. Without wishing to be trite, it is, after all, a concept LP – the baroque progenitor of The Pretty Things' *S. F. Sorrow* and the ripe *quattro formaggio* of Yes's *Tales of Topographic Oceans* in crystalline strings. (Equally, it is not surprising that with the arrival of the CD in the 1980s, when the chance to listen to the cycle as one uninterrupted whole became a reality, its fortunes rose once again.)

A less directly ideological reason why music of the baroque period also chimed with 'American life in the post-war decade' was that much of it had been composed for intimate settings. The LP put *hausemuzik* back into the home. Where the delicacy of baroque instrumentation was often lost on wax masters and scratchy 78s, tape recording and noise-free vinyl was the ideal foil to a musical form where clarity and sonorousness is essential and could most readily be discerned at home on the lounge hi-fi, a post-work, pre-prandial Tom Collins in hand. After all, 1950s Americans, along with their peers in Britain, *were* spending a larger percentage of their leisure time at home. And with good reason: by the end of the decade, 60 per cent of American families owned their own homes, and those homes were, increasingly, in the suburbs, with 33 per cent of Americans living in what the census bureau defined as 'suburban areas' by 1960.

The sophisticated suburban diner tucking into a Tuna Potato Chip Casserole conjured from the pages of *The Betty Crocker*

Picture Cookbook, the publishing sensation of 1950, could, if they so wished, do so to the tinkling accompaniment of baroque *tafelmusik* that Vivaldi, Handel and Mozart had specifically written to help their rich patrons digest pheasant on feast days.

As a choirboy, Joseph Haydn had sung in the requiem mass held for Vivaldi after his death, and he was another dormant composer whose fortunes were to be revived in the 1950s by a small band of admirers and the LP. The recordings undertaken by the Haydn Society, one of the most audacious if financially wilful of the independents, continue to be revered for bringing the full oeuvre of the composer to greater public prominence.

The Society's foray into recording was the brainchild of H.C. Robbins Landon, a Boston University music student, who since hearing the eighteenth-century Austrian composer's music in high school had been filled with a proselytising zeal to convince the world of Haydn's genius. Aided and abetted by a legacy from his uncle, and utilising an indulgent aunt, society members, talented friends and the cash-strapped city of Vienna's wealth of musicians and facilities, Robbins Landon and his acolytes embarked on a scheme to eventually commit all of Haydn's compositions to vinyl. No mean task, when prior to 1950 only twenty-five of over a hundred of his symphonies had made it near a producer's microphone.

Their endeavours were championed by *Gramophone*'s American correspondent, Harold C. Schonberg in February 1950. Reporting on the Stateside 'LP craze' for the magazine's English readers, he wrote:

> At present, the most ambitious recording achievements derives from the Haydn Society of Boston, which has just issued seven hitherto unrecorded Haydn symphonies on three L-P discs. Jonathan Sternberg is the able conductor, the orchestra is

named the Vienna Symphony Orchestra (not to be confused with the Vienna Philharmonic), and the symphonies are Nos. 1, 13, 28, 31, 44 and 48. All are wonderful music: fresh, spirited, melodic, and – as always with Haydn – so beautifully worked out. British collectors would do well investigating these discs. Information can be obtained from the Haydn Society, 30 Huntington Avenue, Boston 15, Mass.

But while its records attracted favourable notices and its order book was seldom empty – a much-admired edition of the 'Nelson' mass sold well – its grand ambitions finally outstripped its means and the Haydn Society dwindled into bankruptcy in 1956 'after a long struggle with chronic insolvency', as *High Fidelity* magazine tactfully put it in February 1957.

The torch for Haydn would pass on, with the majors picking up the option to record his symphonies, but the Society's fate was a common one in an epoch when have-a-go optimism and a voracious audience for new records led to dozens of short-lived new labels entering the field. Even those who could not afford the expense of advertising their discs could take their place alongside their elders and betters in the pages of *The Schwann Long Playing Record* Catalog – *the* LP bible. Schwann's Catalog was started in October 1949 by William Schwann, a Boston record-shop owner who became so infuriated by his failure to locate an LP for a rather persistent customer that he started cobbling together a list of all the available long-players. Surmising that other local dealers might face similar difficulties, he canvassed opinion and immediately amassed an order for 5,000 copies. His first issue was a densely typed twenty-six-page booklet that looked as though it had been reproduced with a potato. It listed 674 works by ninety-eight composers from a mere eleven record labels. By 1953, Schwann had relinquished the shop to concentrate entirely on the catalogue. Nearly a decade after the LP's arrival, his 100th *Catalog* was being shipped to thirty-seven countries around the globe and had swelled to include 19,830 works by 718 composers from some 303 labels and was accruing over 400 recordings a month.

Particularly in its infancy, but also far beyond it, Schwann was the lifeblood of small independent labels. A little like MySpace for the bedroom techno bod today, Schwann provided a one-stop shop window for their wares, especially if their wares weren't in many, or indeed any, shops, and the label was a one-record unit run by a sousaphone fanatic from his garage in Des Moines. As Schwann told *Business Week* in 1954, 150 or more of the smallest companies he featured subsisted purely on orders acquired via his organ. Without him, he believed, they would not exist at all. Schwann's canny scheme of marking recently deleted items with a black diamond frequently rekindled demand, and in turn led to LPs then being re-pressed.

Schwann's success and the pivotal role of his catalogue illustrates the fresh ways in which consumers could obtain their records following the arrival of the LP. Traditional outlets, usually radio and gramophone player dealers, could stock larger ranges of recordings. But a new breed of entrepreneurs, known as 'rack-jobbers', seemingly on better terms with Frank Bettger's *How I Raised Myself from Failure to Success in Selling* (a bestseller of the time) than Arthur Miller and Willy Loman, began acting as intermediary sales agents for record companies, taking LPs into drugstores and supermarkets.

In his memoir, *As It Happened*, Columbia mogul William S. Paley claimed that the idea of creating an in-label club to sell records direct by mail had come to him when he initially acquired the company back in 1939, but 'then the weight and the fragility of the old shellac records made it impractical'. This could, perhaps, have been the case, but again, partly out of necessity, it was the independents rather than the majors who seized the potential of record clubs and selling LPs by mail. Concert Hall, for instance, started their Musical Masterpiece Society in 1950. By contrast, The Columbia Record Club would not be launched until 1955.

The quality of the LPs – mysteriously 'not available in the shops' – from some of the less reputable mail order clubs was variable to say the least. Shoddy patch-ups from old 78s abounded to begin with, but others, utilising lesser-known orchestras, often from the backwaters of Europe, were soon on hand to provide decent enough editions of the standard classics at rock-bottom prices. Many of these clubs were directly aimed at self-improving musical neophytes. Music-Appreciation Records, run by the American Book-of-the-Month club, offered subscribers 'who enjoy good music but are aware, too often, that they do not listen to it with complete understanding and appreciation' discs that boasted a famous piece of classical music on one side with an exposition of it on the other. By 1955, record clubs accounted 'for about 35 per cent of the total dollar of all classical LP records sold in the US'. The majors countered in kind with Columbia, and two years later, RCA Victor setting up clubs of their own and slashing their high-street prices. In Britain, Decca responded to the challenge with a new bargain-bin label, Ace of Clubs, that was intended, as its name implied, to 'ace' the clubs by providing a flow of cheap but reputable subscription-free releases in the shops.

The dilettante or full-on classical buff, it could be argued, had never had it so good. However, at least one serious critic and an early admirer of the LP, Roland Gelatt, expressed his disquiet about the sheer volume of releases and the ease and cheapness with which music could now be purchased. Writing in *High Fidelity*, Gelatt maintained that the world was being 'dulled by a glut of merchandise' and that records were 'considerably less cherished objects' and no longer listened to with their 'former devotion and absorption' – a criticism that has obvious parallels with the current situation of the album and MP3s. Having spent two successive evenings listening to new recordings of *La Sonnambula* and *Der Rosenkavalier*, Gelatt reflected that two decades ago 'either of these sets would have constituted the chief opera issue of an entire season'. They would have been savoured 'without competition for months' and 'acquired . . . in instalments, act by act, to spread the expense'. Today, he believed, they represented 'pebbles in an avalanche'. Back in 1940, when 'Alban Berg's Violin Concerto, played by Louis Krasner and the Cleveland Orchestra under Rodzinski', remained 'the only twelve-tone composition to be found on domestic records', Gelatt contended, he and his peers 'had learned those six four-minute sides by heart'. Nowadays, any young person interested in the twelve-tone idiom had over three hours of difficult listening scandalously easily at their disposal since the complete works of Anton Webern were available on eight LP sides. Was this stuff being ingested as thoroughly as in the more leisurely days of 78 rpm? Of course it wasn't.

FREE!
ON THIS AMAZING OFFER
THIS EXTRAORDINARY
High-Fidelity Recording of
MOZART'S
Symphony No. 14 in A Major

LP
33-⅓
RPM
Long Play

Why, when you could 'buy two Mozart piano concertos on LP for the price of a dinner in a not very fancy restaurant' was it any wonder that record buying had become, in Gelatt's view, 'a far more casual affair . . . than it was in pre-LP days'? Cognitive senses once kept at the peak of mental agility by continuously having to switch discs at unlikely intervals in longer pieces were getting flabby. Gone, too, was the creative stimulation of choosing a programme of one's own music, as indolent LP buyers let record-makers dictate their listening itineraries – and, accordingly, forced them (and still do . . .) to accept junk they didn't really want or like in order to obtain what they did.

If all of this wasn't horrid enough, modern recording techniques used to produce the damned things were making musicians and conductors increasingly lazy. Here, Gelatt reserved his ire for what he termed 'the malefactions of magnetic tape', and again it was 'the ease and cheapness of tape recording' that was producing a corresponding decline in rigour. Musicians no longer approached recording with their former professionalism; instead they bumbled into the studio with a 'we can repair it later' attitude that was symptomatic of a falling-off in standards in general. The 'challenge of the unpatchable wax blank [tape's predecessor]', Gelatt argued, 'stimulated a musician to do his utmost'.

At the time, the practice of 'patching' or 'splicing' together different performances in a single piece or movement was immensely controversial. Opinion in the classical world, especially, was heavily polarised. There were those who believed it gave the listener the chance to experience a kind of über-recording that was truer to the score and to the conductor's and musicians' own desire for perfection. In 1958, Wilma Cozart Fine, for example, strove to replicate the battle-crazy conditions Tchaikovsky himself had originally envisioned for performances of his 1812 Overture. To achieve the desired effect, Fine superimposed recordings of the cannon at the West Point Military Academy and the bells at the Harkness Tower in New Haven onto the score performed by the Minneapolis Symphony Orchestra and the University of Minnesota Brass Band.

There were, however, those who looked upon splicing as a Frankenstein's monster, virtually the audio equivalent of eugenics or some similarly unattractive form of selective breeding. Gelatt, as you might guess, was not a fan: 'Does anyone imagine', he asked, 'that this artificial tape-splicing results in a truly convincing performance?'

Tape-splicing had really just reignited longstanding questions about authenticity that had bedevilled recording since its infancy. One of the earliest record 'producers', Fred Gaisberg, likened his art to taking 'sound pictures'. His point-and-shoot approach to the task was not unlike the tripod-wielding smudgers of his day. Every effort was made to capture the performer as they *really* were, but the limitations of acoustic recording imposed aesthetics of its own. Just as the exposure rates of primitive photography meant sitters had to keep rigid to avoid blurring, mongrel orchestral arrangements and unorthodox instruments never used outside the studio were needed to keep things audible on wax.

The sound or, more accurately, the experience that Gaisberg and his immediate heir, Walter Legge, hankered after was that of the concert hall. But the home and concert hall are, it goes without saying, very different listening environments. The effect of listening to a record in a concert hall would still not be the same as listening to a live concert in the same space (there would probably be a lot less coughing and shuffling around in the seats, for a start). In any case, to make a record sound *as* good as hearing a live concert – which again is different from, say, a *recording* of a live concert – might, like additives in processed foods, require a degree of studio trickery to convince the senses.

With better technology, first electric microphones and then tape, to hand, Legge grasped this more fully than his predecessors. A perfectionist, he also believed that new recording methods gave him the opportunity to refine performances and so improve upon the average concert outing. 'My declared principle in recording', he wrote, 'was to make records which will sound in the public's home exactly like what they would hear in the best seat in an acoustically perfect hall.' But the word 'exactly' is a toughie: after all, can there ever, objectively, be such a thing as an 'acoustically perfect hall'? And what, and where, would the ' best seat' in it be? I am different from you. I hear things differently. My home is different from yours. My record player is different from yours etc., etc. You get the idea.

Legge was not, as it happens, a huge fan of 'splicing' willy-nilly, by all accounts preferring to record several takes of significant passages, then run with the best of each, cut and paste fashion. But he did like a splice if, in his view, it provided a means to construct something more 'convincing'. In August 1953, Legge spent the first of what would become many subsequent summers at La Scala in Milan, convening with Maria Callas to record Italian operas. When Callas had been pointed out to him a year or so earlier, Legge recalled: 'she was massive, shabbily dressed in a nondescript tweed coat, and her walk had the ungainly lurch of a sailor who after months on rough seas, was trying to adjust himself to terra firma'. But in Callas he had met an ideal collaborator, one he judged 'as avid to prove and improve herself as any great artist I have ever worked with'. A crash diet and a new wardrobe, along with the febrile performance she gave for him that summer as Tosca in what Legge would later cast as their 'immortal contributions through records to the artistic history of our time', established Callas as La Diva *par excellence*.

In the sessions for *Tosca*, undertaken during sweltering temperatures Milan hadn't known for a decade, Legge, evidently inspired, gave full reign to his exactitude. He made Titto Gobbi, who was singing the role of Baron Scarpia, repeat all of his first-act music over thirty times, 'changing the inflections and colours even on individual syllables' until he was satisfied. To create the sense of distance required to make Tosca's entry sound 'convincing' in this (still) mono recording age, Callas's three calls of 'Mario!' were done separately, 'each one nearer the microphone – and spliced together later'.

Left with 'miles of tape' to sort through to come up with the finished master to press the LPs, he asked the conductor Victor de Sabata to assist him with the selections. According to Legge, de Sabata is supposed to have replied: 'My work is finished. We are both artists. I give you this casket of uncut jewels and leave it entirely to you to make a crown worthy of Puccini and my work.'

A line any self-respecting minor baddie in a James Bond movie would kill for, I am sure you'll agree. But one that for all its intended flattery seems to hint less at respect for Legge's talents than utter exhaustion with the whole process.

To men with Gelatt's view of tape, however, Legge would always be beyond the pale for his involvement in a recording of Wagner's *Tristan and Isolde* with Kirsten Flagstad a year before, which saw rank accusations of outright fraud being made. Flagstad was widely considered the greatest Wagnerian soprano of her generation (less of a niche accolade in the 1930s), but in 1952 she was fifty-seven and her voice, while regarded by many to be at its mature peak, had deepened slightly. Legge's wife, Elisabeth Schwarzkopf, was therefore hired to deputise the high Cs in act two, with Legge choosing to splice them in but opting to keep schtum about it, a deception that was quickly detected and caused much brouhaha.

For the Canadian pianist Glenn Gould, such 'creative cheating', as he called it, was only to be applauded. The quality of a recording, not its authenticity, was the only criteria that mattered to him. But then Gould was made for and *by* the long-playing record. His cult, his worldwide fame were built upon, and perpetuated by, his debut LP – *The Goldberg Variations* – and he quoted with admiration the opinion of one Toronto musicologist that the long-playing record had 'come to embody the very reality of music'. It certainly came to embody *his* reality of music: he disliked what he referred to as 'the non-taketwoness' of the concert stage so much that he took the then unheard-of step of renouncing it entirely in 1964. On aesthetic grounds, he retreated to the studio for the rest of his career.

From his steady diet of tranquillisers to his prediction that the public concert would die and his fervent hopes that 'a new kind of listener' able to actively re-edit any recordings they bought would emerge, Gould was a genuine technological optimist in an era when dreams that 'one day lunch will be a pill' loomed large. In contrast to the Flagstad and Schwarzkopf fiddle, where what you got was Schwarzkopf instead of Flagstad, Gould used 'the splendid splice' to give people what they wanted – which was more idiosyncratically Glenn Gould-like Glenn Gould stuff.

Indeed, the public appetite for uniquely Gould-like stuff formed from the instant *The Goldberg Variations* was released. The story of this LP's creation, widely circulated in the press, was pivotal in establishing Gould as a star. The story emphasised Gould's personality, a personality that addressed the home audience directly in the self-penned liner notes on the back of the album. His image (not Bach's) appeared on the original front sleeve in a series of thirty-odd contact sheet snapshots taken during the recording sessions – one for each variation. Gould is pictured playing, gesticulating at scores, running blurred hands through the air, engaging in intense conversations with shirt-sleeve-clad engineers and tinkering with open pianos, gazing at their ribby innards like a lion contemplating second helpings of a wildebeest's carcass. Part musician, part mad scientist, he was a tousle-haired, piano-playing whizz kid on the loose in Dr Quatermass's (audio) lab.

This already impressive consumer package was augmented by an extraordinary press release, and since virtually all accounts of Gould and *The Goldberg Variations* can only ever paraphrase it, it's practically impossible to improve upon.[10] Here it is in full:

---

10 I tried, but really, trust me: 'Gould wasn't sure if New York was his kind of town, or if it ever would be, pounding the sidewalks, a heavy muffler on . . .' It all got a bit Woody Allen in Manhattan from then on.

Columbia Masterworks' recording director and his engineering colleagues are sympathetic veterans who accept as perfectly natural all artists' studio rituals, foibles or fancies. But even these hardy souls were surprised by the arrival of young Canadian pianist Glenn Gould and his 'recording equipment' for his first Columbia sessions. Mr Gould was to spend a week recording one of his chief specialties, Bach's *Goldberg Variations*.

It was a balmy June day, but Gould arrived in coat, beret, muffler and gloves. "Equipment" consisted of the customary music portfolio, also a batch of towels, two large bottles of spring water, five small bottles of pills (all different colors and prescriptions) and his own special piano chair.

Towels, it developed, were needed in plenty because Glenn soaks his hands and arms up to the elbows in hot water for twenty minutes before sitting down at the keyboard, a procedure which quickly became a convivial group ritual; everyone sat around talking, joking, discussing music, literature and so forth while 'soaking' went on.

Bottled spring water was a necessity because Glenn can't abide New York tap water. Pills were for any number of reasons – headache, relieving tension, maintaining good circulation. The air-conditioning engineer worked as hard as the man at the recording studio control panel. Glenn is very sensitive to the slightest changes in temperature, so there was constant adjustment of the vast studio air-conditioning system.

But the collapsible chair was the Goldberg (Rube) variation of them all. It's a bridge chair, basically, with each leg adjusted individually for height so that Glenn can lean forward, backwards or to either side. The studio skeptics thought this was wackiness of the highest order until recording got under way. Then they saw Glenn adjust the slant of his chair before doing his slightly incredible cross-hand passages in the *Variations*, leaning in the direction of the 'cross.' The chair was unanimously accepted as a splendid, logical device.

Gould at the keyboard was another phenomenon – sometimes singing along with his piano, sometimes hovering low over the keys, sometimes playing with eyes closed and head flung back. The control-room audience was entranced, and even the air-conditioning engineer began to develop a fondness for Bach. Even at record playbacks Glenn was in perpetual motion, conducted rhapsodically, did a veritable ballet to the music. For sustenance he munched arrowroot biscuits, drank skimmed milk, frowned on the recording crew's Hero sandwiches.

After a week of recording, Glenn said he was satisfied with his recording stint, packed up his towels, pills, and bridge chair. He went round to shake hands with everyone – the recording director, the engineers, the studio man, the air-conditioning engineer. Everybody agreed they would miss the cheerful 'soaking' sessions, the Gould humor and excitement, the pills, the spring water.

'Well,' said Glenn as he put on his coat, beret, muffler and gloves to venture out into the June air, 'you know I'll be back in January!'

And so he will. The studio air-conditioning engineer is getting ready for the workout.

The public bought it and him. Or vice versa. Released in January 1956, Gould's recording of Bach's *Goldberg Variations* became Columbia's bestselling classical LP. On 12 March, *Life* magazine profiled the 'Music World's Young Wonder' with a double-page photo essay, and a month later, the 'frail loose-jointed Canadian with a bumper crop of light-brown hair' was declared one of *Glamour* magazine's 'Men We'd Like to Meet'.

Witty in interviews, eccentric in his habits, the wearer of ordinary business suits on stage, Gould was the tortured genius for his times; *The Goldberg Variations* appeared almost contiguously with the arrival of Miltown, America's first psychotropic wonder drug, and William H. Whyte's *The Organization Man*, a potent critique of white-collar life. Not since Shelley (and perhaps not again until Morrissey) had hypochondria been playing so well. Even the choice of the *Variations* themselves, an esoteric opener for a pianist's recording career as far as his label was concerned, came to be seen as inspired and in the course of events became weighted, not unreasonably, with psychological import, given their historical association with sickness. According to legend, and it is only a legend, Bach was commissioned to write the *Variations* in 1741 as a musical palliate for a Russian envoy to the court of Saxony. The envoy suffered from appalling neuralgia and liked to have his harpsichordist, one Johann Gottlieb Goldberg, play him soothing ditties when he could not sleep at night. As the story goes, the envoy was so pleased with the *Variations* that he gave Bach a golden goblet filled with a hundred Louis d'or for his efforts. (Hans Christian Andersen, eat your heart out.)

First recorded on the harpsichord by Wanda Landowska in 1933, the *Variations* were rarely performed and little known before Gould. Its fortunes and Gould's (who would return to the *Variations* in the months before his death in 1981) depended on a whole new consumer market for serious music whose listening habits, desires and aspirations were unthinkable before the arrival of the LP.

Chapter Three

CUNNING LINGUISTS AND EXTENDED PLEASURES

When Thomas Edison, who famously had an ear as tinny as one of his own cylinders as far as music was concerned, dreamed up the phonograph, he primarily saw it as a device for recording the spoken word. And while the LP had been, effectively, tailor-made for classical music, the extra playing time was quickly utilised for records of dramas, poems, stories and speeches – by the end of the 1950s, the British firm Argo would be embarking on what became a seven-year project to put all of Shakespeare's plays on LP.

Just a cursory glance at the wares offered in what is called the 'Diction' category of a catalogue issued by The Gramophone Record Shop in February 1951 confirms the boggling range of non-musical LPs on offer. We find *The Bhagavad Gita* with 'chants Read in English and Sanskrit by Dr M. P. Mahadevan & Swami Nikhilananda'; *Spoken and Broken English* by George Bernard Shaw from the Linguaphone language firm; *Then Came*

War: 1939, a 'dramatised account of the events leading to the beginnings of hostilities in 1939 with actual excerpts of speeches by Chamberlain, Daladier, Hitler, edited by Elmer Davis'; and *Prelude to Pearl Harbor* – four LPs offering 'on-the-spot recordings of events leading up to World War II and the Pearl Harbor attack'.

The preponderance of documentary history discs here can be largely attributed to Edward R. Murrow, the radio and television broadcaster whose campaign against Senator Joseph McCarthy was dramatised in the film *Good Night, and Good Luck*. In 1948, Murrow had narrated *I Can Hear It Now*, an album that interwove political speeches and *verité* recordings to provide an aural chronicle of the 1930s and 1940s. A version had been released on 78s but as an LP, this then highly unusual recording became a major commercial hit, as listeners immediately warmed to the chance to hear the story unfold as it would on a normal radio show, and it triggered a vogue for similar records.

As Goddard Lieberson, the urbane head of Columbia Records during the 1950s, subsequently noted, what the long-playing record really succeeded in doing was to transform the average living room into a scene of cultural activity, bringing 'the university lecture hall, the theatre and the concert hall into the intimate possession of many who had never known them'. In the process, to his mind, it established 'a new consciousness in the art of listening'.

By the same token, it might also be said that it established a new consumerism, a development in which Lieberson himself played no minor part. A shrewd businessman, composer, linguist, record producer and suave man about town, his original cast LPs of the Broadway musicals *South Pacific*, *Gentlemen Prefer Blondes*, *My Fair Lady* and many more led – or more accurately created – the field, and most remain on sale to this day.

Lieberson had greenlighted the Murrow record and, in 1950, he made the first LP recording of a stage play – a production of George Bernard Shaw's *Don Juan in Hell* on two discs directed by Charles Laughton. The following year, he recorded a fully realised studio version of George and Ira Gershwin's 'folk opera' *Porgy and Bess*. He restored, with Ira's help, sections of the libretto never previously staged and stunned hi-fi fans with an array of drama-enhancing sound effects – most notoriously, rolling crap-game dice in the opening act (a novelty that wears thin after a while). That same year, he commissioned Noël Coward to revise, and revive, his musical comedy *Conversation Piece* for LP ('I must beware of this modern medium. Long-playing records can spell tedium', Coward, the play's narrator, drolly opines at the start of the disc). In addition to this he would eventually put on microgroove such uncompromisingly high-brow offerings as Samuel Beckett's *Waiting for Godot* and, on the music front, the complete works of Schoenberg and Stravinsky conducting his own music, before the general public.

Ironically, the one venture of Lieberson's that did not fare quite so well was his luxurious Literary Series. Here he perhaps overestimated the amount people were willing to pay in bulk to listen to the likes of Aldous Huxley reading the introduction to *Brave New World*, extracts by Christopher Isherwood from his *Berlin Diary* and Edna Ferber chatting about 'The Gay Old Dog'.[11] Although sumptuously trussed up in a well-tooled leather case and complemented by a weighty booklet containing

11 Possibly little read today, Edna Ferber was a member of Dorothy Parker's 'Vicious Circle' and one of America's most popular novelists in the 1920s and 1930s. The musical *Show Boat* is based on her 1926 novel of the same name. Lieberson recorded a revival of the show for a 78 album in 1946 and again on LP in 1962.

a fetchingly ponderous essay by Irwin Edman on 'The Writer as Reader', this twelve-LP set still cost nearly $100 in 1954. The Audio Book Company of Los Angeles, by comparison, was offering an 'Audible Edition of the New Testament' that lasted twenty-three hours and eleven minutes for $20 on twenty-four records.

It could possibly be argued that in the face of the competition, Lieberson's set looked rather vulgar to bookish types, who, let's face it, can be rather contrary about the gaudiness of their possessions. Caedmon, a small concern founded by Barbara Cohen and Marianne Roney, a pair of bright, poetry-loving young Hunter graduates, was then one of the leaders in the literary field. Cohen and Roney had made an LP of Dylan Thomas reciting his verse two years earlier, a production that had required the girls to spend some weeks stalking the Welshman around New York. Their persistence paid off, and the album, *Selections from the Writing of Dylan Thomas – READ BY THE POET* (including 'Fern Hill', 'A Child's Christmas in Wales' and 'Do Not Go Gentle into That Good Night'), was followed by LPs of readings from Seán O'Casey, Archie MacLeish, Eudora Welty and Osbert Sitwell. With tactile cardboard covers bearing abstract designs that one critic likened to summer dress prints and loquacious notes penned by the girls themselves, Caedmon records looked like offerings from a New England poetry press, a factor that no doubt contributed to their popularity among thoughtful bibliophiles and the like.

This opportunity to personalise your airspace, the ability to fill twenty-minute segments of time with your chosen uninterrupted sound as only radio had previously allowed, was the LP's greatest asset. But while it meant that there was an opportunity to listen more attentively for longer – an opportunity many seized with gusto – there was, correspondingly, plenty of scope and a vast appetite among the public, it emerged, for stuff you could bung on and all but forget about.

Well, not quite.

It could be argued that it is the deliberate unobtrusiveness of background, light, mood or champagne music, as one of its leading practitioners, Lawrence Welk, called it, that many find so offensive. The meek are as likely to get bullied as they are to inherit the earth; their unassuming gentleness, their urge to slink into the background, their willingness to please others, acts as a hair-trigger to the Flashmans and Gripper Stebsons of this world. And there's inevitably something about a musical oeuvre that forever strives for emollience, for niceness, for the path of least resistance, for . . . *easy* listening, that often sticks in people's craws.

Characterised on the whole by languid tempos, tinkly piano melodies, parping muted horns, ethereal choruses of ba-ba backing singers and strings buffed to flashgun gleams, 'easy', depending on your palate, was either as exquisitely crafted and delightfully fluffy as a soufflé, or as sickly and insubstantial as candyfloss. But as a genre it blossomed quite exponentially, quite unexpectedly, on microgroove, and with lasting effects across the board.

Hearing its influence on dance-band music, one *High Fidelity* columnist in the 1950s wrote: 'The appeal is moving away from the feet to the ears. This may be blamed on the records: people are listening sitting down. Violins are being added . . . and brass is becoming softer. Smoothness is increasingly evident in the arrangements.'

It wasn't only a matter of 'sitting down' or 'smoothness', though. What the LP really unleashed was the utility of 'light' music – whether that was its ability to soothe or, in more up-tempo form, to invigorate. Industrialists pumping muzak into their factories and broadcasters like the BBC, whose daily *Music While You Work* programme the British Government had considered vital to the war effort, were already masters in this sonic art of manipulation. But now themed LPs like *Reveries for Languid Lovers* or *Melodies for a Lazy Afternoon*, unfairly dismissed by at least one contemporary critic as 'recorded sleeping pills', allowed consumers themselves to pick whole records that matched, or helped them to create and sustain a mood, just as they might scatter cushions, dim the lights and pull the drapes in their new ranch-style homes.

The derisory phrase 'aural wallpaper', mildewed and peeling with age as it is today, was so acute precisely because it mocked the relationship between background music and interior décor that musicians and record companies themselves were using to sell mood music LPs. If Erik Satie first proposed the notion of *musique d'ameublement* in 1920, the phenomenon reached its apogee some thirty years later when record purchasers were encouraged to think of their discs as pieces of furniture. Which in a 'books do furnish a room' way, they obviously were. But on LPs like The George Shearing Quartet's *Velvet Carpet*, the worlds of *Better Homes and Gardens* and the *Melody Maker* collided. Shearing's LP, in particular, promised music that was 'as smooth and polished as old mahogany', and furthermore offered to provide its buyers with 'a vast velvet carpet of harmony'.

But in essence, if you really felt like listening to something to send you to sleep after a hard day at desk and Rolodex, or you were a languid lover in need of a twenty-minute burst of tryst tunes (that *was* as languid as it got), or possessed a sudden hunger for melody and a spare afternoon to laze away (and hell, it was the 1950s, you couldn't waste it googling your own name) then there was an attractively picture-sleeved LP out there for you somewhere. Probably.

The man credited (or blamed) for the rise of this phenomenon was Paul Weston. An arranger for Tommy Dorsey, Bing Crosby, Dinah Shore, Jo Stafford (his wife) and (later) Ella Fitzgerald, and the first director of A&R at Capitol Records, Weston created the 78 album *Music for Dreaming* in 1945. Slack, smooth and gentle, it set the pace for a series of popular albums on LP: *Music for Dreaming*, *Music for the Fireside*, *Music for Romancing*, *Music for My Love*, *Music for a Rainy Night*.

Ploughing a similar thematic furrow in the UK was George Melachrino. A fixture in BBC dance bands from the 1930s onwards, and during the war the leader of the British Band of the Allied Expeditionary Forces and the Orchestra in Khaki, Melachrino turned his attention to film composition on civvy street before hitting his stride with a line of bestselling 'Music for Moods' LPs for RCA Victor. The formula, syrupy orchestration with bags of closely harmonised strings, was unwavering to say the least. Reviewing the Melachrino Orchestra in their early 1950s heyday, *High Fidelity* felt it only fair to admit: 'They pour their mellifluous ointment on the hoariest chestnuts around'. And Melachrino's 'string' and 'orchestra' ensembles perpetuated the package long after his bizarre and untimely death in 1965 (he drowned in a bath at home). Inaugurated with the pleasant, if lachrymose, *Music For Dining* in 1954 (a record that claimed to 'add that little bit of extra seasoning that turns an ordinary supper into an adventure') the catalogue ran to such confections as *Music for Relaxation, Music for Reading, Music for Courage and Confidence, Music to Help You Sleep, Music for Daydreaming, Music to Work or Study By* and *Music for Romance.* Marginally more explicit was his *Music for Two People Alone,* 'something to make a nice hour of being alone together just a little bit nicer'. An LP of knee-trembler assisters ('Blue Room', 'Embraceable You', etc.), its efficacy as an aphrodisiac was probably only improved by the lack of lyrics on a version of the Pollack/Lew/Webster number two, 'Cigarettes in the Dark' ('Gone is the flame and the spark, leaving just regrets and two cigarettes in the dark).

For Melachrino's audience, though, cigarettes were synonymous with sex. Peggy Lee could sing 'Don't Smoke in Bed' as a parting shot to a lover on her debut long-player, *Rendezvous With Peggy Lee,* but anti-smoking advocates remained in the minority in 1952.[12] (Although the first article connecting cigarettes to increased rates of cancer by Dr Evarts A. Graham, a surgeon at the Barnes Hospital in St Louis, had been published two years earlier.) A study of Hollywood films from the 1950s conducted by scientists at the University of California in 2004 found there were 'an average of 10.7 incidents of smoking per hour'. In the fashion of the day, most of those smoking were wealthy, good-looking and obviously getting laid. If you were never alone with a Strand, then a pack of twenty and a flip-top lighter certainly did you no harm when trying to strike it lucky.

The image of two cigarettes smouldering in an ashtray, a smudge of lipstick on the filter end of one, their owners evidently

---

12 Twelve years later, however, Melachrino's producer Ethel Gabriel would mastermind the Living Strings LP *Music to Stop Smoking By.*

elsewhere and otherwise engaged, was a potent one and much used throughout the decade. Often coupled with a pair of half-empty wine glasses, you didn't need to be Dick Tracy to put the pieces together.

Today Jackie Gleason would probably be visited by a health and safety official and lectured about promoting smoking in a poorly fireproofed dwelling whilst under the influence of alcohol. But back in 1952, his suitably 'smoky'-sleeved long-playing debut *Jackie Gleason* presents *Music for Lovers Only* pushed enough buttons to sell over 500,000 copies. The liner note helpfully set the scene. 'A wisp of cigarette smoke in the soft lamplight, the tinkle of a glass, a hushed whisper . . . and music for lovers only.'

Gleason, a roly-poly, boozy, comic actor, was once memorably described by *Time* as looking 'like a big basset hound who had just eaten W. C. Fields'. The star of the long-running TV sitcom *The Honeymooners*, he was credited, on his own album, with an ability to delight 'his audiences with wonderful transitions from loud buffoonery to touching pantomime'.

What he could not do, though, was read a word of music or play any musical instrument. But Gleason, a 'from dirt' former Bushwick pool hall ace (he played his own shots in the film *The Hustler*) had already overcome greater obstacles. A self-made, university-of-life kind of guy, he fancied himself as something of a *sui generis* conductor and composer. Convinced, as he saw it, that if Clark Gable needed background music to help him woo his leading ladies in the movies 'then surely the poor slob in Brooklyn did too', he hired the arranger C. Dudley Jr and the Dixieland jazz cornet player Bobby Hackett to bring his vision of a slob seduction disc into being.

While the sleeve may have coyly referred to 'your most relaxed listening moments', Gleason adopted less bashful terminology when trying to rouse what he believed had to be suitably sensual performances from the musicians he employed. 'It's five a.m. and you see her body outlined through her dress by the streetlight and you get that "Mmmmmm, I want to come" feeling' was a widely reported direction he gave during one recording session.

Music for Lovers Only was to be the first of over forty *Jackie Gleason* presents . . . LPs, and arriving just before the second Kinsey Report and *Playboy* magazine in 1953, his vast output fulfilled a complementary role in this ongoing sexual revolution, servicing the John Doe in his cups with an easy to hand, easy on the ear, audio marital aid. And as photographs of blousy, come-hither strumpets, usually in need of having their cigarettes lit, gradually became something of a given on Gleason sleeves, in times of real desperation, the artwork was probably able to offer certain solitary consolations of its own . . .

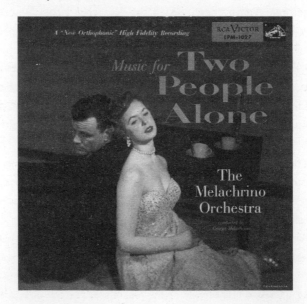

Lover's Portfolio, an LP for 'listenin', sippin', dancin' and lovin'', came with the added bonus of a set of cocktail recipes on the back cover. Presumably this was to assist would-be Romeos to intoxicate their Juliets into submission or drown their sorrows if they failed. And really, any dame who allowed 1956's *Music to Change Her Mind* to be cued up on the turntable in front of her could scarcely have been in need of the LP in the first place. But then who knows what horrifically unreconstructed mating rituals were going on in Brooklyn at that point. The borough was about to lose the Dodgers to Los Angeles; perhaps the area's male population, struck speechless by this imminent calamity, were simply unable to articulate their desires by any other means.[13]

Among the most bizarre records Gleason ever made, however, was *Lonesome Echo*. Tapping the same ripe, and at that time prevalent, line in pseudo-Freudian psychoanalysis as Alfred Hitchcock in film, the LP was a musical journey into memory and the unconscious. Again there was a bit of a trend for these on-the-couch albums in the 1950s – in an advert for The Sauter-Finegan Orchestra's *Under Analyse* LP, Eddie Sauter and Bill Finegan were said to 'psychoanalyse some big band hits of the past, and come up with stunning new musical treatments'. But Gleason's effort had the added bonus of a cover by Salvador Dalí. Elucidating his understanding of the project, Dalí informed listeners that:

The first effect is that of anguish, of space, and of *solitude*.

Secondly, the fragility of the wings of a butterfly, projecting long shadows of late afternoon, reverberates in the landscape like an echo.

The feminine element, distant and isolated, forms a perfect triangle with the musical instrument and its other echo, the shell.

13 Was the track 'All By Myself' on this record a sly nod to a possible plan B?

Which may or may not explain why a butterfly perching on an anorexic totem pole (or its own tail, perhaps?), a woman wearing what could be a snakeskin dressing gown, a giant mandolin, a snail and a stone monolith, all standing in a desert, wound up on the sleeve.[14]

'This is music that says relax . . . close your eyes . . . remember to listen to the lonesome echo . . .' a liner note elsewhere soothingly advises (Relax? Don't do it?). Whatever message this bricolage conveys about egos, ids, sexual repression, penis envy and Oedipal complexes is never entirely clear, or possibly never clearly intended.

The maudlin arrangements it contains of 'Deep Purple', 'Come Rain or Come Shine', 'There Must be a Way', 'Dancing on the Ceiling' – heartstring-tugging mandolins and domras to the fore – most readily suggest that if the unconscious lay anywhere for Gleason, it was in Pasquale Scognamillo's Italian restaurant on 56th Street. Given his gargantuan appetites for drink (Scotch by the loch), food (two flying saucer-sized pizzas at a sitting, Chinese dinners for four for breakfast) and sex (showgirls by the chorus line), it easily could have done. That the album sold well probably said much the same about the record-buying public . . . which could also go some way to explaining the then popularity of Annunzi Paolo Mantovani.

*　　*　　*

I have something of a pet theory about LPs in charity shops, which is that while they can and do supply reams of fascinating data about the rise and fall of musical trends and formats, the

14 In the late 1950s Gleason went through a brief phase of using his own 'abstract' paintings – an ochre Rorschach blotch and a pinky blue triangle respectively – on the covers of *Rebound* and *That Moment*, implying that possibly an 'Oh God, even I could do better than that' momentum had built up in its aftermath.

shifts in status of artists as their records slide from ubiquity to obsolescence (oh, happy day it was when copies of *No Jacket Required* and *Brothers In Arms* started turning up in Help the Aged shops in the early 1990s), they also tell us (or did for a long time anyway) that Mantovani and his peers (Frank Chacksfield, Percy Faith, Bert Kaempfert, Ray Conniff, James Last, et al) once bestrode the world as musical colossi.[15] Which, though probably truer than we'd like to admit, now seems unimaginable – and odd.

If, for example, some peculiar meteor were to strike the earth, triggering an even more bizarre apocalyptic event that wiped out at a stroke most of the globe's population and every LP ever made, except those stored in charity shops (bear with me on this: it's something to do with the uniquely awful window displays – wonky dummies clad in previously unimaginable combinations of man-made fibre outfits and figurines of small children with dogs – deflecting the vinyl-, cassette-, CD- and iPod-melting radiation), then future civilisations would be forced to conclude that *Hawaiian Album*, *Silk and Steel* and *Strictly Mantovani* were the acme of this lost world's musical achievements.[16] And who is to say they wouldn't be right? To achieve this level of market penetration, if you'll forgive the jargon, is to reach the pinnacle of popular arts in a mass-media age.

Still, the fact that so many people are willing to relinquish these LPs so readily, a spot of easy-come, easy-go listening, hints that Mantovani and co. only ever enjoyed a less than pivotal

---

15 For this to work, you have to exclude the Oxfam shop on Kingsland Road in Dalston, a *Wunderkammer* of the strangest records, CDs and tapes ever made, let alone subsequently dumped.

16 Try it with books and you'd end up with a literary canon whose ur-texts were by Desmond Bagley, Leon Uris and Robert Ludlum.

place in their former owners' lives. There's nothing wrong with that, either. But viewed from this perspective, this impermanence then seems built in at the start. Inevitable; expected; welcomed, even, by both parties, like a mutually fulfilling fling or one-night stand, say. Or a done deal, a case of: 'Look, you're not really sure about music, are you? Tell you what, mate, buy this – these tunes are quite popular at the moment, and it'll do the job for a bit. You can stick it on when guests come round.'

Naturally there are thousands of other reasons why LPs end up in charity shops: deaths, house clearances, lack of space, lack of a record player, lack of a receipt with an unwanted present, boredom, laziness, hatred, revenge, a sense of embarrassment at possessing a copy of *Popped In, Souled Out* when you are trying to cut it as a from-the-cradle hardcore techno DJ, charity, feng-shui downsizing, etc., etc.

However, a sentimental part of me wonders how easy it is to give up something you once loved deeply, even if you no longer love it. I am a hoarder, though, so maybe I don't count. I have never, to my knowledge, given away any records, CDs or tapes that I've bought. Not even records I never ever liked. Not even records I have never ever played more than once or twice. Not even records I have never ever played at all, like the bag of Bert Kamperfert LPs I found in a skip on my road. The compulsion to hoover up such items, and I admit it is a compulsion, stems from an urge to give these records a caring new home. In charity shops I often find myself buying the most forlorn-looking LPs, not out of some highly developed sense of kitsch, but because I feel sorry for them. I respond emotionally to abandoned records in the way others might to orphans, stray dogs or lone gloves on walls. I am incredulous. I can't believe someone could have been so thoughtless as to toss them aside. It's worse with records I *do* like. I currently own at least four copies of Michel Legrand's *Brian's Song: Themes and Variations*. It's one of those 'easy' LPs that invariably turns up in charity shops. The cover is an unappealing pub ceiling yellow, and there's a less than flattering pen and ink portrait of the bespectacled composer, pianist and soundtrack supremo on the front. And yet, each time I encounter it, I am outraged that anyone could be so stupid as to have parted with their copy. It's a masterpiece of its kind. Everyone should have one, I think to myself, while prodding that familiar sleeve. The bass lines on that record – cue in beardy session-guy with a pipe, scampering up and down the fret boards as if his life depended upon it on the title track– are worth the admission price alone. Scandalised on behalf of Michel and co. that their efforts are going unrewarded, I am compelled to buy it. Thereby depriving someone else of the joy of discovering it looking rather mangy and forlorn in a goodwill bin, as I did myself the first time round. But, I reason, at least if I buy it, I can be assured it will finally be appreciated. Or that it'll make a great present for someone I like who *will* surely cherish it later on . . .

However, given the huge number of Mantovani LPs in charity shops, and that so much of his music is so astonishingly unexceptional – it is exceptional even in the field of easy for being so astonishingly unexceptional – did anyone ever truly love Mantovani? Millions purchased, listened, liked and enjoyed his records, sure.

And then, after a while, gave them away.

*   *   *

The son of the principal violinist for Toscanini at La Scala, Mantovani was born in Venice in 1905. His family moved to England when he was seven and the young Annunzio made his professional debut in a restaurant in Birmingham at the age of fifteen, a beginning that seems all the more apposite considering his recordings became a mainstay in steakhouses and checkered tableclothed, candle bedecked bistros across the Western hemisphere for over twenty years. Even patrons of Nelson's wine bar in the Radio 4 soap opera *The Archers* tippled on Liebfraumilch and grazed on open sandwiches to the strains of Mantovani. Like the calorie-rich, stomach-churning fare these establishments then served (Duck à l'Orange, Scallop Supreme, Baked Alaska and Chicken à la King), which in the 1950s was probably as much a reaction to the lean years of powdered eggs and butterless cakes as anything else, Mantovani's music was elaborately concocted and leaned towards the processed and the sugary. His 1953 hit 'Elizabethan Serenade', a tune written by the maestro's long-standing multi-talented arranger Ronald Binge to honour Elizabeth II's accession to the throne, is Coronation Chicken in woodwind and rich strings: sickly sweet, glutinous, cloying but fiendishly moreish all the same.[17]

What Mantovani brought to the table, to prolong the culinary metaphor, was something 'nice' for the hi-fi, and the lustre of modernity. For millions — and he was the first artist to sell a million stereo LPs in America — his records were part and parcel of what living in a drip-dry, polyester world was meant to be like. Along with the suburbs, nuclear power, instant coffee and frozen orange juice, his LPs were safe, clean and synthetic. The hallmark of Mantovani was *that* 'cascading strings' sound. And it definitely is a *that*, in a 'stop, hey, what's *that* sound', sort of *that*. It's such a *that*, in fact, that it is *the* 'Mantovani Sound'. A sound that is instantly recognisable for sounding intensely unnatural and yet all the blander for it, rather like sliced white bread or Kraft cheese. The strings on

17 Binge was also responsible for the irresistible 'Sailing By', the theme to Radio 4 and light music's answer to 'The Lark Ascending', if ever there was one.

his records, whisked into a fondant by Binge and the Decca engineer Arthur Lilley, who removed all the baffling and deployed up to nine microphones to achieve the reverberating 'wall of schmaltz' effect required, are immediately overwhelming, then merely incessantly stultifying.

Hearing Mantovani is to be put in mind of strip-lit ice rinks and supermarkets, albeit strip-lit ice rinks and supermarkets of a kind last seen in around 1974. This is not because his music, or stuff that sounded like it, was played in Silver Blades and/or Liptons, which it was. But for the plushness of the arrangements, it's shiny and sterile with a curiously glacial beauty if anything. There's a majesty in that blandness that now seems positively avant-garde – the world in which Mantovani was 'normal' is long, long gone. If anything, it's a mystery that his albums don't sound more interesting today than they do. Other LPs do. They just don't. And the bugger kept up the routine for over fifty – and with the odd exception, heroically samey – instrumental LPs, a slush pile of trend-chasing show tunes, love songs, popular standards, and the odd quasi-classical speaker filler.

Mantovani's LPs, though, spoke to a generation for whom recorded sound retained a sense of novelty, adventure, glamour and hope that we've become largely inured to. This was a generation getting the hang of things, who demanded and bought LPs to show off their hi-fis – a phenomenon that only increased with the arrival of stereo LPs in 1958.[18] (Perhaps the best

18 The bandleader turmed record producer Enoch Light reaped enormous rewards in the early days of stereo with his *Persuasive Percussion* LPs. These albums of popular light tunes, first produced in 1959, featured heavily embellished arrangements that were specifically mixed so that the instruments cantered from speaker to speaker, drumming (quite literally with bongos and maracas) the LP's stereo-ness over and over into the brain.

analogy, at a stretch, would be the modern craze for ring-tones of popular songs. The thrill is in the machine's ability to reproduce the tune in its own inimitable, if awful, sonic range.) They were happy to listen with simple wonder rather than prejudice to some of the most unusual (and hokey) records ever produced for pleasure. As a contemporary tagline for RCA maintained, what was often desired was 'New Experiences in Sound'. Those sounds could, apparently, be the Guckenheimer Sour Kraut Band on *Music for Non Thinkers* – 'the album to end all German band albums. A riot of out-of-tune favourites for brassy, bouncy hi-fi fun!' Or Billy Mure's Super-Sonic Guitars playing *Fireworks* – 'a dazzling, colorful musical display'. Or Oscar Brand singing 'Old Time Bawdy Ballads' to the accompaniment of 'Dave Sear and his banjo'. Or *Tokyo Flight*, an LP of 'zany, Oriental sounds from the mighty Wurlitzer 5 Manual Pipe Organ by the inimitable George Wright'. And so on. As star turns go, some of the acts on these LPs would have struggled to hold their ends up against the blind xylophonists and piano-playing birds in Woody Allen's *Broadway Danny Rose*, but these LPs were entertainment and spectacle in the fine vaudeville tradition, a tradition then being undone – done in, arguably – by television and to a lesser extent the hi-fi.

Pitching up somewhere between *Variety* and *Holiday*, a lively subgenre in this terrain was the travelogue LP. In *The Slide Area*, Gavin Lambert's sly Hollywood novel, a blind multi-million-airess who yearns to make one final jaunt around the globe is duped by her two parsimonious nieces. Unwilling to squander a cent of their precious inheritance, this avaricious pair resort to faking the journey, ingeniously using gramophone records, heaters and fans to carry out the deception in the woman's Californian mansion. Outlandish as their scheme appears, in the

1950s there were plenty who willingly chose to use hi-fis and LPs to embark on remarkably similar trips from the safety of their Parker Knoll armchairs.

The jet age, ushered in by the maiden flight of The De Havilland Comet from London to Johannesburg in 1952, had landed. While only a privileged few could afford it to begin with, the idea of international travel had gripped the popular imagination. For American ex-servicemen who had spent parts of the war on the continent or in Asia, the rest of the world seemed less remote than it had done. Soon, cheaper flights and a booming economy meant foreign holidays were a reality for many Americans. As Tom Wolfe has commented, 'the reason American tourists became a byword for vulgarity in Europe was that suddenly there were working-class Americans going abroad. There had never been such a period before . . . astonishing amounts of money had come into ordinary people's homes'. Those who couldn't afford the fare, or just preferred to travel vicariously, could slip a copy of Ted Heath and His Orchestra's *A Yank in Europe: The Compositions of Raymond Scott* onto the turntable. Easing off with a quick '*bonjour*' to the Lady of the Riviera and an amble around the Garden in Versailles, the LP presents a whistle-stop, geography-defying tour that encompasses Supper At the Savoy, Nightfall in Venice, a Nightclub in Sorrento, the opening chorus at the Folies Bergère, a Train Ride in the Alps, the Blue Grotto in Capri and, finally, winds up in London Airport.

There were literally hundreds upon hundreds of similar LPs. Budding Ernest Hemingways, a schooner of sherry or a flagon of tequila on the go, could sample a Death in the Afternoon in their den with The Brave Bulls' *La Fiesta Brava: Music of the Bullfight Ring* – an LP that came complete with a twenty-four-page booklet of bullfighting posters to flip through as the drama unfolded before the ears. Those seeking less fiery temperaments and climes could always try Jim Fassett's *Scandinavia: A Portrayal in Sound*. 'From Norwegian wolves through multi-lingual Stockholm guides, to the great bells and ivory organ of a Danish castle, these are sounds to set one packing his bags (if he can), or wishing he could (if he can't).'

Paris, which in the early 1950s was filling up with tourists and another round of literary-minded American ex-pats – a generation (including George Plimpton and co.) more financially loaded than lost this time round – continued to hold enormous appeal as a destination for the romantically inclined. *I Love Paris*, an LP commissioned from the then twenty-two-year-old Michel Legrand by the Francophile George Avakian at Columbia, said it all, and in 1954 made the young Frenchman a star. Comprised of a suite of fifteen Parisian-themed instrumental vignettes ('I Love Paris', 'Mademoiselle de Paris', 'Paris', 'Under the Bridges Of Paris', 'Paris In The Spring', 'Paris Canaille', 'April In Paris', 'Under Paris Skies', 'Paris, Je T'Aime', 'Á Paris', 'The Last Time I Saw Paris', etc), the pieces were arranged so that they segued unendingly into one another. The listener could, therefore, enjoy two sides of seamless, accordion-inflected, gently jazzy French music.

Despite sporting a cover with a photograph of a Parisian market porter who was as grotesque as a Notre Dame gargoyle and, courtesy of a large melon perched on his shoulder, seriously hunchbacked, the album went on to sell a staggering 8 million copies worldwide. In America the appetite for this disc and, by extension, a Paris of ripe onion soups, spindly loaves, smoky Left Bank bistros, and picturesque and 'free-spirited' grisettes, proved insatiable. The LP served as a mere aperitif to a banquet of other album-length meditations on the city from Legrand – *Bonjour Paris*, *Paris à la Hi Fi*,

Rendez-vous à Paris and *The New I Love Paris* – and spawned a host of imitators.

One Johnny-come-after LP, *My Paris*, by André Colbert and His Golden Violins, claimed to have been brought especially from France 'for those who know Paris (and wouldn't consider a musical portrait of an outsider)' and 'the Yank who can only make the trip in his fancy – which, if less satisfactory, is also less expensive. In either case, here is the real stuff, the real music of Paris – romantic melody that can never be copied'.

Less pretentious, if no less authentically French produce was available from the accordionist Jo Basile, later to compose the music for the Magic Roundabout animation. *Accordion de Paris*, an LP of 'Romantic French café rhythms – each tenderly weaving their own enchantment with all the captivating nostalgic Paris magic', admirably showcases Basile's virtuosity at the instrument. But its impressive sales could scarcely have been damaged by a sleeve that matched the basest fantasies ever to enter the head of a sex-starved GI in Pigalle on twenty-four-hour leave. A potent blend of national and sexual leitmotifs that at one time in the 1980s a cultural studies student could probably have winkled a pass-grade thesis out of, it was adorned with an image of a beret-clad accordionist serenading a scantily dressed mademoiselle. Musician and girl, both smoking, are positioned in front of a red and white check clothed table, on which stand a wine bottle and two half-empty glasses. The girl is dressed in a bumble-bee black and yellow striped vest top that has long abandoned any pretence of struggling to contain her ample charms, and a narrow blue skirt with a long slit up the side. She has one leg, gartered and shod in a pinky-red stiletto, raised up on a pale blue chair. Her head, partially enveloped by a plume of cigarette smoke, is thrown back, her eyes are half closed, and she fondles her own knee in an ecstatic swoon as a rather bow-legged Mr Music looks and, as far as we can tell, plays on.

Ooh là là.

Neither Basile nor Legrand restricted themselves to their home turf. Legrand voyaged on with *Holiday in Rome*, *Vienna Holiday*, *Castles in Spain* and *Legrand in Rio*. (*Time*, less than impressed by Legrand's sojourn in Austria, pronounced his LP 'A major atrocity that should cause Vienna to break diplomatic relations with Paris'.) Basile, armed with an overlapping itinerary (did they exchange holiday snaps?), forged *Acordion d'Espana*, *Accordeon Di Roma*, *Cafe Italiano*, *Viennese Waltzes* and *Rio with Love*.

Their choice of destinations was by no means arbitrary and mirrored the pleasuring preferences of the smarter American sets. A whiff of musty hotel safe and fresh Guardia di Finanza ink emanating from the well-travelled passports of, say, Dickie Greenleaf and Freddie Miles in Patricia Highsmith's *The Talented Mr Ripley* is palpable here. Italy, the setting for much of that particular novel's action, loomed especially large in the 1950s. A glamorous holiday destination for rich Yanks, it was fast becoming the source of a range of stylishly modern consumer goods. ('The post-war *ricostruzione*', as Stephen Bayley has written, 'was defined by design'.) Having funded its post-war redevelopment, America provided further financial assistance by generally falling in love with Pucci 'Capri pants', dinky espresso coffee cups and raffia-coated bottles of Chianti – at least once they had been safely filtered through the Hollywood prism of *Roman Holiday*.

Italian-Americans, of course, were also one of the largest ethnic minorities in the United States and presented a ready-made audience for LPs of Italian songs and, importantly, full-length operatic works – the Italian-American Cetra-Soria label, which specialised in imports of Italian operatic recordings was among the earliest converts to the new format. The 1950 census found 1,427,145 Italian immigrants and 3,143,405 American-born people of Italian parentage were living in the country. However, the whole point of the travelogue LP was to be transported in comfort to some other place, some other world. They were in the business of vending *la difference* – and no castanets were clickier than they were on *¡Juerga Flamenco!*, no yodelling yodellier than on *A Touch of Tyrol* or *Swiss Mountain Music*. Accordingly, when these audio explorers ventured to the 'exotic east' or the 'dark continent', they went, for the most part, as Great White Hunters in search of local colour and traded on the same stereotypes as *King Solomon's Mines* or a Tarzan movie.

However, just as cod-Freudian psychology was a perfect means to sell an LP of shag-pad schmaltz to the discerning young bachelor, so the rising academic discipline of cultural anthropology lent a patina of seriousness to the off-the-shelf primitivism of LPs like Les Baxter's *Ritual of the Savage (Le Sacre du Savage)*. Appearing a couple of years before Levi Strauss's *Tristes Tropique,* the French title seems an especially nice forward-thinking touch. Baxter was a prolific writer, performer, producer and arranger – throughout the 1950s and 1960s his 'whistling' theme sent the canine wonder Lassie off on her weekly adventures with disused mineshafts and trapped farmhands. A gifted pianist and tenor sax player, he sang in Mel Torme's Mel-Tones, worked with Bob Hope and Abbott and Costello on radio, and on record with Nat King Cole. In 1948 he collaborated on an album of proto-space-age pop with the light-classical composer Henry Ravel. Entitled *Music out of the Moon*, its otherworldliness was enhanced by some off-kilter orchestration, with Baxter utilising just a choir, a single cello, a French horn, a rhythm section and a Theremin played by Dr Samuel J. Hoffman – a man previously called upon to add this electronic instrument's distinctive quivering metal detector tones to the soundtracks of *Spellbound* and *The Lost Weekend*. The album became the first to be issued in all three (i.e., 78, 45 and 33 1/3) formats – and the first long-player to have a full-colour sleeve.

Just prior to *Ritual of the Savage*, an LP its creator proclaimed a 'tone poem of the sound and struggle of the jungle', Baxter had produced the debut album by Yma Sumac. An Incan princess blessed with feline cheekbones, a voluptuous figure and a four-octave vocal range, Yma had taken the New York and Borscht Belt cabaret circuit by storm. Despite persistent rumours that she was a housewife from Brooklyn called Amy Camus who'd gaily applied a mirror to her original name, Sumac was actually a Quechuan and had moved to New York from Lima in 1946 with her musical director husband, Moises Vivanco, so that they could further their careers. Signed to Capitol in 1950, her 10-inch *Voice of the Xtabay* LP includes such gems as 'Accia Taqui' ('Chant of the Chosen Maidens'), 'Wayra' ('Dance of the Winds') and 'Choladas' ('Dance of the Moon Festival'). Although written, for the most part, by Vivanco, Baxter's hand sits heavily on the tiller. The orchestration is riddled with hammy flourishes (pounding tom-toms, swoopy strings and cartoon-pratfall marimbas) that somehow conspire to make Sumac's dramatic yelps and operatic trills seem about as native as Johnny Weissmuller's jungle calls. Still, they're no less thrilling for that.

Unhindered by the presence of any indigenous peoples, Baxter was able to let his imagination run wild on *Ritual of the Savage*. A trip to an Africa only ever visited by Allan Quatermain in an adventure story never penned, the LP is awash with knocking congos. Personifying the 'exotica' genre Baxter 'willed into being', it's a primordial travelogue that presents a package safari of this remote interior from 'Busy Port' to 'Quiet Village'. It concludes with a chance to hear the tribesmen undertake 'The Ritual' – a primitive religious rite that in the transfer from mud hut to hi-fi mysteriously acquired the involvement of a full string section sawing away.

Here's the album that young America has been asking for...

SKINS!

a bongo party with Les Baxter

Verisimilitude was never Baxter's forte; his genius was to steal and remodel on Western lines – as one sleeve-note scribe conscientiously explained: 'Travel – an adventurous search for new sounds, new music – has become a part of Les's life. He studies primitive music constantly – understanding and absorbing the instruments as well as the music and in this way using his "finds" as a part of *his* "natural vocabulary"' (my italics, but you get the drift). On his next effort, *Tamboo!* (the Haitian Creole word for drum), the names of the songs ('Havana', 'Maracaibo', 'Oasis Of Dakhla', 'Tehran', 'Rio') read like the stickers on a suitcase belonging to a seasoned reporter for *Life* or *National Geographic*. Sonically, however, this LP would probably imply that the hack in question could not have ventured much beyond the hotel bar and filed his copy, gonzo-style, on the basis of a couple of compelling, half-cut exchanges with a local trinket vendor.

'Simba' is one of the album's real joys, providing you are willing to overlook the absolutely shameless use of every 'dark continent' cliché going. Wedding a low-voiced, incomprehensible tribal chant to a rumba beat with the undulating pace of an elephant caravan, it is two minutes and forty seconds of stock footage safari. Baxter wrote the number for the Arthur Murray Dance Studio, who were developing a routine inspired not by Africa itself, but by the British film *Simba*. A sensationalist account of the then recent Mau Mau uprisings in Kenya, it starred Dirk Bogarde and was marketed in the US under the dubious banner 'White Heat Exploded in Green Hell!' (You don't even want to see the poster . . . Or arguably the movie itself.)

Baxter's commercial heirs, Martin Denny and Arthur Lyman were, if it was possible, even less bothered about matters of authenticity than he was. Denny, whose bestselling albums *Exotica*, *Hypnotique* and *Afro-Desia* were described by *Time* magazine as being 'labeled like bargain-counter perfumes', told one interviewer: 'My music has always been like fiction, no authenticity; I didn't want to make African music – I only wanted to suggest how African music might sound.'

Since Denny and Lyman established themselves at The Shell Bar in the purpose-built Hawaiian Village resort on Oahu, a venue where garlanded diners routinely swigged blue drinks and accepted any dish topped with a slice of pineapple as genuinely Polynesian, it was perhaps inevitable that they were on freer terms with reality than their peers. In presenting Honolulu in hi-fi, an unspoilt paradise that was otherworldly but easily accessible, Denny, Lyman and co. rode a wave of interest in all things Hawaiian that foamed into a Tiki craze as the island prepared to join the Union in 1959.

Lyman, Denny's vibesman until he branched out alone, was born on Kauai and had a Hawaiian mother, but he was a consummate professional who knew light entertainment was his trade and was content to horse around impersonating a macaw or a gibbon if the musical mood 'sent' him. A spin of Lyman's *Taboo* album, an LP that sold nearly 2 million copies, confirms that that was quite often. Promising the 'primitive superstitions of an island volcano woven into eerie, lush, tropical sounds', the LP brims with conch shell honks and chiming Balinese gongs. Woodblocks tap as though manned by angry Ouija board spirits and percussive corrugated gourds click away like keys winding up alarm clocks. But it is the caterwauling of exotic birds and the yawp of bullfrogs, varmints and cheetahs that are hard to shake off. Lyman and crew plug every gap on the record with the noise of some fantastical Waikiki menagerie.

This gimmick had its basis in Denny and Lyman's original Hawaiian Village stage act. One evening a bullfrog in an artificial pond beside the bandstand began croaking along to the songs. The group responded by co-opting the amphibian's interruptions into the set, jiving with it, ad-libbing a few 'ribbits' and wild bird calls of their own to liven up the show. The blue drink and pineapple crowd bought it and Denny made it a regular feature of the act and a signature of his many recordings.

If Baxter, Denny and Lyman approached their armchair exploring lightly – and the only zombies likely to be summoned up by Lyman's 'Bwana A', Denny's 'Jungle Drums' or Baxter's 'Voodoo Dreams' were those that came in highball glasses – others had more serious anthropological intentions. Not that this meant they weren't averse to ringing some of the same sensationalist bells if it would shift another copy or three. Reviewing the lively sounding *Voodoo* LP by Emy de Pradines and the Haiti Danse Orchestra, a first-rate album of authentic Haitian folk music, *High Fidelity* groused, 'the title of this disk is a misnomer; only about half this disc . . . has any connection with Voodoo religious ritual'.

De Pradines was the daughter of a Haitian poet and a folklorist of repute who also recorded an LP of original méringues. Her endeavours, along with those of the African-American dancer Katherine Dunham, an initiate of a vodun cult and curator of the *Afro-Caribbean Songs and Rhythms* LP, and the American field recordist Henry Coulander, were invaluable in raising the stature of Caribbean music in the States and beyond. However, some of the most extraordinary recordings of 'ethnic' music to emerge on LP in the 1950s hailed from an audio nut based in Stamford, Connecticut. Emory Cook was an audiophile's audiophile. And there were a lot of them about back then – the fact that *Time*, in its profile of the man in 1954, felt willing and able to slip in a quote about demonstration records that ran, 'We've put 20,000 cycles on disks when everybody was crowing about reaching 15,000', without the need for further clarification, says here was a society at ease with hertz.[19]

A professional sound engineer and inventor, with a commendation for war work on radar at Western Electric and fresh methods of grooving vinyl to his name, Cook was an evangelist for the second sense who became the high priest of hi-fi and a pioneer of stereo recording – though he mocked his competitors for peddling 'high fidoodledy'. Hearing, as he told the *New Yorker* in 1956, was 'always being kicked aside in favor of sight', and in 1950 he founded Sounds of Our Times (later simply Cook Records) with the intention of doing something to rectify that bias. Convinced he could produce records that sounded better than anyone else's, he sought to prove it by rendering the

19 Nope, I have no idea what they are either.

ordinary in uncanny detail. The steam trains of Harmon and Peeksill, New York, a once everyday but soon to be extinct, species, were one of his opening subjects. A few rainy nights with a tape recorder or two in the shunting yards gave birth to the *Rail Dynamics* LP – a toccata of clanking metal and tooting whistles that was almost as unnerving in its fidelity to the 'real' thing as the Lumière brothers' cinema-clearing film' *L'Arrivée d'un train en gare de La Ciotat* had been in its day. (Okay, not quite. It confused a few lapdogs, probably, but no one was ever reported fleeing from an audiophile cocktail party fearing that they were in the proximity of a runaway train.)

Trainspotters don't, on the whole, do the big picture; detail is what interests them – the numbers, the timetables, the engine types – you name it. Mystifying as it might seem now, Cook astutely judged that there were legions of hi-fi fanatics of exactly the same mind, i.e. obsessives for whom the minutiae of recorded

This is it! Men

The record that has everything!

COOK'S TOUR OF HIGH FIDELITY runs a brilliant gamut from the highest fidelity to the lowest comedy ever recorded! Dream stuff, organ, sounds from the subconscious, nocturnal predators, do-it-yourself soap opera! You've heard exotic sounds, but never anything so broad range, wonderful, party provoking! If your dealer's out of stock, insist that he order this for you pronto! COOK'S TOUR OF HIGH FIDELITY 1079 12" LP $4.98

sound was uniquely fascinating. Thus he catered specifically for the kind of audio bores who would, well, 'shiver in ecstasy over a tingling triangle while hardly noticing whether the music [wa]s a symphony or a psalm', as *Time* put it.

Pandering to the goofiest needle junkies with records of chiming music boxes, Cook wasn't shy of breezy jokes, toe-curling puns or girls in polka-dot bikinis when it came to titling, marketing and sleeving his LPs. *The Compleat in Fidelytie*, 'the ultimate high fidelity demonstration record', was touted as 'something to frighten everyone'. *Burlesque Uncensored*, an LP of 'saucy comedy sketches and bawdy music' recorded in Minsky's theatre in Newark, was stag party titillation cum social science and billed as 'a bare-faced documentary'.[20] But there was a serious purpose behind the jokes. Cook wished 'to preserve something; a performance, a situation, a sound, an emotion' with each and every one of his LPs – whether that was crashing waves and the blast of the West Quoddy Head horn on *Voice of the Sea* or the rambling theories of Buckminster Fuller on *Buckminster Fuller Speaks His Mind*.

It was, in a way, his complete lack of interest in 'named' musicians – the people others often took for granted were 'interesting' – and a love of 'curious "found" sounds' that disposed him to hunt out street performers in Trinidad and Antigua, who were, of course, wonderful to listen to and almost as cheap and easy as trains to record. Steel bands, whose instruments initially derived from the oil barrels that flooded

20 Those who equate the Elektra record label with the output of counter-cultural groups like Love, The Doors and Earth Opera, are probably less aware that in the 1950s, the label did a roaring trade in LPs of smutty songs. *Every Inch a Sailor* by Oscar Brand, one Elektra offering popular with seadogs young and old, was summed up by *Time* as a 'largely unprintable tour through the racier passages of Navy mythology'.

into the Caribbean with American troops during the Second World War, were Cook's biggest 'discovery' – please note the inverted commas. His LPs *The Brute Force Steel Band of Antigua, B.W.I.*, *Beauty and the Brute Force* and *Steel Band Clash* popularised the musical form in America. And Cook's stake in Trinidadian Calypso became so large that he set up a pressing plant in Port of Spain, producing records for both the American and Caribbean markets – what was exotic to one was to the other homegrown, the ordinary made extraordinary and the extraordinary familiar; all, of course, only possible through this magical medium, the LP.

Chapter Four

BLOWING HOT
AND COLD

The French philosopher Jean-Paul Sartre once observed that freedom is the heaviest burden. I like to envisage Sartre reiterating this remark in a smoky Left Bank jazz club, Le Tabou on the rue Dauphine, possibly, peopled by intense, beard stroking painters and gamine *jeunes poétesses* in ballet shoes and black polo-neck jumpers *à la* Juliette Greco or Audrey Hepburn in *Funny Face*. For if existentialism, the intellectual credo that Sartre famously bequeathed to the canon of Western thought, can be said to have had a soundtrack, that soundtrack was surely jazz. Visiting the music joints on 52nd Street in New York after the war, Sartre himself wrote that the bebop performers there spoke to 'the best part of you, the most unfeeling and most free'.

Yet Sartre's maxim – the one about heaviness, not the one about bebop, that is – also sums up the central dilemma jazz faced as it adapted to the long-playing record. Utilising the format, jazzers were able to take greater liberties, pushing the music in directions that some to this day believe ultimately destroyed it as a popular art. But if the LP did help break jazz – and it is an *if* – it also assisted in invigorating it. It provided an ideal canvas for the exploration and communication of ideas and emotions, immortalising performances and concepts that might otherwise have vanished into the ether. As the jazz critic Whitney Balliett/ wrote in *The Sound of Surprise* in 1959, 'by destroying the arbitrary time limitations of 78-rpm recordings' the LP record 'suddenly encouraged any number of new musical approaches simply by making room for them'.

At the moment of the LP's arrival, modern jazz, much like existentialism, seemed to be engaged with keenly felt desires among some for greater individualism, freedom, spontaneity and authenticity in the face of an emerging and homogenising mass media. The stress on unconscious improvised horning in jazz and its African-American origins placed it outside the debased realm of European rationalism that had led to the gas chambers at Auschwitz. In America, its vibrancy and the seeming alienation of its innovators – largely by dint of their race – from conformist 'mainstream' society was especially appealing to the restless college dropouts who initially formed the Beat Generation. In *Hustlers, Beats and Others*, his jivey period study of hipsters and pool sharks, Ned Polsky maintained that: 'In so far as most beats, whites and Negroes alike can be said to have a dominant intellectual interest, it is jazz music.'

A parallel transatlantic tribe to the existentialists, the Bohemian libertarian Beats not only listened to jazz but also utilised it in their novels, poems and booze-and-Benzedrine- loaded performances. Jack Kerouac, the *de facto* high priest of the movement, deliberately imitated the fluttery lines of the saxophonist Lee Konitz in his 'spontaneous' prose. Called to explain this method of composition, he once described it as: 'Blowing (as per a jazz musician) on subject image'. And, subject matter (saxophonist Lester Young) aside, it's hard to imagine lines like 'Lester droopy porkpie hung his horn and blew bop lazy ideas inside jazz had everybody dreaming' being composed without some exposure to jazz and/or marijuana (jazz cigarettes), though probably both would be necessary.

Jazz is the binding component of *On the Road*, which is, for most, the defining novel of Beat. It has been suggested that even the narrative's looping structure mimics jazz forms – though given the book's protracted coffee-aided composition, redrafts and substantial edits, this could be more by accident than design. However well intentioned, there are passages in that *roman à clef* about black musicians that now appear as racially condescending as the compliments visiting minor royals used to pay African leaders about their teeth. 'Man do you imagine what it would be like if we found a jazzjoint in these swamps, with great big black fellas moanin guitar blues and drinkin snakejuice and makin signs at us,' Sal comments at one point, rather as if he were discussing encountering a lost tribe of headhunters instead of citizens of the same country.

Told retrospectively, much of *On the Road* looks wistfully back to 1947 and 1948 and the pre-LP era of bebop jazz. In one evocative scene, Sal's charismatic road buddy Dean Moriarty (Kerouac's real life pal Neal Cassady) performs a kind of ceremonial dance while listening to a new jazz 78. 'They ate voraciously as Dean, sandwich in hand, stood bowed and jumping before the big phonograph, listening to a wild bop record I had just bought called *The Hunt* with Dexter Gordon and Wardell Gray blowing their tops before a screaming audience that gave the record fantastic frenzied volume.'[21]

21 Illustrating the frustrating limitations of the format, the complete edition of this particular performance, a toot for toot, tenor-sax-on-tenor-sax battle that was an early example of an on-the-spot concert recording, was spread over four 78s.

After *On the Road* had made him a phenomenon, an event for which Kerouac was almost catastrophically ill prepared, the self-proclaimed King of the Beats groused that everyone in America was 'a slave to the Deepfreeze and the hi-fi'. However, while awaiting a verdict from the publisher Harcourt Brace on the very first draft of *On the Road* in 1951, Kerouac had written a letter to Neal Cassady outlining a more audio-friendly future: 'Ah shit man I think I'll just go to Mexcity and build me a topflight pad & relax in coolness, kicks, food, mistresses, main once-a-week etc. heh? Get me an LP record player & great LP Charlie Christian album.'

When *Life* magazine belatedly ran a piece on Beat on 30 November 1959, it was accompanied by a photograph of a couple of models, dressed in his 'n' hers black turtlenecks and sandals, posing in a well-equipped Boho pad. There beside the appropriate Beat books, a coffee pot, a set of bongos and a marijuana plant, were LPs by Miles Davis and Charlie Parker. And when fellow Beat traveller William Burroughs once quipped that after 1957, '*On the Road* sold a trillion Levis and a million espresso coffee machines', he could easily have bunged in a hundred thousand jazz LPs.

For however much Kerouac later grumbled that the Beat generation was destroyed when it became 'common property of the commercial cultural world', his novel was a mass-market product.[22] One that offered a compelling and accessible off-shelf vision of hip – a vision that proclaimed jazz, along with hoboing across America with a loquacious thrill seeker[23] as the acme of cool. His disciples may not have bought the jazz he loved, or bought jazz at all ('the ingestion of drugs became official . . . and even the clothes style of the beat hipsters carried over to the new

22 There were also, of course, LPs of Kerouac's live readings.
23 The dynamic duo rode again, as it were, in 1977 when Tom Waits chose to channel their zappy exchanges for 'Jack & Neal/California Here I Come' on his album *Foreign Affairs*.

rock 'n' roll youth', he wrote dispiritedly in *Esquire* in 1958) but the symbolism, i.e. that certain records were hip, wasn't lost on them. And in the age of the LP, where stylish album sleeves could be left out on coffee tables to send out the right signals, lots of jazz that would once have been heard probably only in a few obscure New York clubs was much more accessible to anyone, whoever or wherever they were.[24]

By the time the LP rolled up, jazz, in various guises, had had over thirty years of life on record – and it was the records, those 78 discs, that had helped to carry the music out of the brothels of Storyville and the downtown Chicago speakeasies into the 'respectable' world at large. But while the Beat generation could feast on more varieties than ever before, courtesy of the LP, jazz's relationship with the recording medium and the mass market was long and complicated.

24 By 1963, arguably all of Kerouac's worst fears were realised, for Tom Wolfe was able to report that: 'Intellectuals, generally, no longer take jazz seriously . . . it has all been left to little training executives with their first apartment and a mahogany African mask from the freeport shop in Haiti – let me *tell* you! – and a hi-fi.'

In one of the most apocryphal stories of an idiom beset by apocryphal stories, Freddie Keppard of the Original Creole Orchestra, the first jazzer ever approached to cut a disc in 1915, turned down the offer from the Victor Talking Machine Company. Keppard, known as the 'king' of the cornet players in his native New Orleans and among the earliest bandleaders to take that southern city's exuberant musical style onto the northern vaudeville circuit, reputedly declined because he feared others would be able to 'steal his stuff'. Keppard was a chronic alcoholic who died of TB in 1933 at the age of forty-three. Though he did eventually cut some 78 sides ('Stock Yard Strut' and 'Salty Dog') with his Jazz Cardinals in Chicago in the 1920s, Keppard's Original Creole Orchestra never recorded. Alongside another legendary New Orleans figure, Buddy Bolden, a trumpeter who lost his marbles nearly a decade before gramophone companies came sniffing around, the Original Creole Orchestra provided jazz with one of its most abiding tenets, namely that the best stuff was to be heard in the heat of the moment and usually evaded the recording horn. A tenet, as we shall see, that perversely was only bolstered by the LP.

The honour of becoming the first jazz artists on record passed to The Original Dixieland Jass Band; a group of Johnny-come-lately honkies, who those in the know, then and since, judged less 'original' than their peers. What these Orleanians did have in their favour, however, was a whiter shade of pigment and a residency at Reisenweber's Restaurant, a fashionable eatery on Eighth Avenue and 58th Street.

Ushered before Victor's recording equipment one afternoon in late February 1917 – a few short weeks before the Russian Revolution and America's entry into the First World War – the ODJB gamely honked through two numbers: 'Livery Stable Blues' and 'Dixie Jass One-Step.' The former is a musical riot of clownish barnyard impersonations, presumably popular among their restaurant patrons for encouraging diners to splash out on the steakier items on the menu, and the latter is a foot twitcher which probably assisted them in working off any gastronomic excesses on the dance floor afterwards. When the songs came to be pressed up on a two-sided 78, the disc was categorised as 'jass' on the label. The record went on to sell over a million copies, and in doing so lent F. Scott Fitzgerald an age to write about.[25]

As Keppard had suspected, though, records did allow other musicians far from the hot joints to 'cop' the riffs and construct new jazz records of their own. For the most part, live jazz continued to dance to the beat of the dancers. But numbers that in the heat of a club and following the demands of customers keen to keep hoofing might stretch on for ten choruses or more, on record were curtailed by the medium to three or four minutes. Studio work could be liberating, but it forced jazz musicians to think compositionally in as-long-as-it-takes-to-boil-an-egg tranches. Fascinatingly in the light of Kerouac, when Francis

25 Did any other popular musical genre have an age? Rock and roll had its years. Folk had a boom, blues a revival and psychedelia a period . . . but jazz . . . the word alone practically demands the unearthing of a cocktail shaker and the donning of spats or a beaded dress. Versatile enough to escape those initial trappings, jazz did, of course, have the added advantage of having a proper noun that could be turned into a verb (jazzed, jazzing or jazz up), an adjective (jazz hands, jazz pattern) and a useful collective noun for a set of similar things (all that jazz), in a manner that would always frustrate the universal adoption of, say, rag or honky tonk (but also worked in swing's favour). According to the nearest dictionary to hand, the first use of the word 'jazz' dates from 1909, and is thought to originate from black American slang for a 'strenuous activity . . . particularly sexual intercourse' – a meaning that persists today, in a slightly debased form, in the phrase 'jazz mags', a British colloquialism for porn.

Newton (aka Eric Hobsbawm) was looking for a convincing metaphor to describe the punchier, poppier jazz sounds of the 'Chicago records' from the 1920s, he reached for Hemingway and Fitzgerald. A Chicago side, like 'Home Cookin'', he argued, was 'Hemingway prose-style translated into jazz'.

But the constraints of the 78 had a profound knock-on effect for jazz as a whole and attitudes towards recording: think of a teenager, chafing at being prised into a suit for an older sister's wedding, and you're in the right 'You're messin' with my style, man' ballpark.

Naturally, there were those who rebelled against the restrictions of the format. As early as 1929, Duke Ellington was using both sides of a 10-inch for 'Tiger Rag'. Emboldened by its success, two years later he annexed two 12-inch sides for 'Creole Rhapsody'. In 1935, 'Reminiscing in Tempo' enveloped four 10-inch sides. Recording the lengthiest jazz piece ever to appear on standard 78 rpm disc, the Duke's 'Black, Brown and Beige' gobbled up four 12-inch sides in 1944. Dexter Gordon and Wardell Gray's *The Hunt*, which so excited Neal Cassady, was another example of a multi-disc jazz record.

It is perhaps rather surprising, then, that the LP did not, by all accounts, result in an instantaneous explosion of twenty-minute jazz noodling on disc. Ellington, understandably, was quicker off the mark than most. His 12-inch LP, *Masterpieces by Ellington*, recorded in December 1950, contained just four tracks, three vastly expanded interpretations of his early hits 'Mood Indigo', 'Sophisticated Lady' and 'Solitude', and 'The Tattooed Bride', a majestic and ambitious new piece that was nearly twelve minutes long – all quite exceptional for a studio recording at the time. It was live recordings like *The Hunt* – made far easier after the arrival of magnetic tape – that really opened many jazz musicians' ears to the temporal possibilities of the LP.

Along with Charlie Parker, Lester Young, Dizzy Gillespie, Thelonious Monk and Miles Davis, Dexter Gordon was at the forefront of the bebop style, that 'grand wild sound' Jack Kerouac adored and that had kicked against so many jazz conventions.

Spearheaded by Charlie Parker, bebop, or just bop, had evolved in the 1940s, partly as an antidote to the crowd-pleasing showmanship (demeaning minstrelry, as they saw it) that was demanded in popular big band swing. It originated in performances of small, off-the-cuff, after-hours ensembles at dining clubs like Minton's in Harlem. Here the musicians were able to luxuriate in the freedom to please themselves, sparring with one another like boxers to achieve greater feats of musical excellence. Heavy on improvisation, bop was difficult music and difficult to play. Weaker musicians could, and would, be blown off stage. Here, audiences, lesser mortals of debased tastes, were expected to listen, not dance. Miles Davis, notoriously, used to turn his back on the punters as he played, all the better to commune with his brothers on the stump. Inscrutable, cerebral, voraciously thirsty for knowledge and experience, the bop musicians cultivated tastes that ran from atonal, contemporary classical music, Afro-Cuban rhythms and heroin, to goatee beards, heavy-rimmed specs and berets. These sartorial flourishes were subsequently adopted by the admiring and wannabe Beats – by 1955, *Downbeat*, one of the leading jazz periodicals, was carrying ads for bebop glasses ('Be Smart, Wear the Original Be Bop . . . with clear or tinted lenses . . . complete with leatherette case $3.95). The novelist Thomas Pynchon, reflecting on his own Beat affectations around this period, recalled that: 'Like others I spent a lot of time in jazz clubs, nursing the two-beer minimum. I put on hornrimmed sunglasses at night. I went to parties in lofts where girls wore strange attire.'

The other mainstay of bop was heroin, a drug that did quite a bit of work – freeing up inhibitions, honing a type of fearless concentration – all the while ensconcing those who indulged in it even deeper in a beyond-the-squares clique. (Interviewed on Radio 4 in November 2007, saxophonist Sonny Rollins likened drugs to a family bond, something like: the clan that does smack together, stays together.)

Though he tried (ineffectually) to discourage others from following his example, Charlie Parker seemed to blaze a trail for the artistic pinnacles that could be scaled on the drug. A user from the age of fifteen and dead by the time he was thirty-four,[26] Parker inadvertently became the Pied Piper of smack. Wherever 'Bird' blew his horn, and he blew it like no one else, a trail of bop junkies were sure to follow. But for all its sonic innovations (and the hour-bending drugs), the key documents of bebop and the 'hard bop' and 'cool' jazz that immediately followed it were stored on 78 rpm, and, tune for tune, hardly bothered the listener for more than three minutes at a time. Though plenty of listeners found three minutes of it troubling enough as it was.

To begin with, the Dial label pressed a measly 300 copies of Charlie Parker's very first long player, *Bird Blows the Blues*, advertising this 10-inch to the bop faithful in the classifieds of *Downbeat* magazine in 1949. A gander at the timings on the 148 Charlie Parker studio sessions anthologised on the CD *The Complete Dial Recordings* gives 'Out of Nowhere' at 4.07 as the longest number he ever mustered for the label on wax; the majority clock in at well under that time. Similarly, Miles Davis's immaculately restrained *Birth of the Cool*, recorded in 1949 and 1950 still as a batch of 78 sides for Capitol, was not collected together and issued on vinyl until 1953, and then only as a

26 Parker died on 12 March 1955, Kerouac's thirty-third birthday.

complete 12-inch LP in 1957. Whatever sound barriers it broke, and there's a tuba and a French horn on it, for God's sake, it did so with remarkable brevity. None of the tunes featured on it exceed three minutes by more than seventeen seconds.

At the very outset of the LP, many jazzers who might have wanted to chew the fat for longer were often simply at the mercy of the technology to hand. Blue Note, a tinpot unit formed by two fans, Alfred Lion and Frank Wolff were, for instance, still using disc (rather than tape) masters in 1949. They didn't release their first microgroove discs until 1951, and again those were made up of earlier 78 recordings: their second LP, the woozy brilliance of Thelonious Monk's *Genius of Modern Music*, was a 10-inch pulled together from his first sessions for the label.

As with the classical music scene, though, it was canny enthusiasts who were responsible for much of the production of jazz on LP,[27] a trend that was given an unexpected boost by a curious anomaly in the law. Copyright legislation in the US did not, technically, cover records. There was therefore nothing to prevent anyone pressing up an LP from a batch of shellac discs. Well-meaning jazz aficionados – reacting to what they saw as the sluggishness of the majors – and out-and-out pirates alike gleefully exploited this legal loophole. For a brief while, a slew of unauthorised and unofficial LPs flooded onto the market. In what proved to be a decisive case, Columbia and Louis Armstrong filed a suit against the aptly named Jolly Roger label for putting out LPs that were flagrantly assembled from crinkly old Armstrong 78s. Jolly Roger was run by Dante Bolletino, a twenty-three-year-old record collector from Manhattan. Bolletino had used RCA's 'custom pressing department', the facility

27 In Britain, there was a greater time lag, with many jazz albums continuing to be issued on 78 into the 1950s. The leading jazz paper, *Melody Maker*, did not start to review LPs in its pages until 20 October 1952.

that churned out LPs for dozens of small companies, to make his records. He'd even had the audacity to get the firm to press up LPs that were pirated from Armstrong's own recordings for RCA. Columbia, aware of the gap in copyright law, fought and won its case by arguing that Bolletino was infringing their property rights and trading on Armstrong's name without permission.

Jolly Roger and its ilk subsequently disappeared, but their brief existence underlined the hunger for old jazz on new LPs. For some, this was purely for nostalgic reasons, a yearning for records heard but never owned, or bought and lost, or on shellac, loved away by playing. For others, it was down to basic incomprehension of bebop's successors, with their idiosyncratic time signatures and discordant chord sequences. But there was also a growing feeling that jazz was long enough in the tooth to have a lineage worthy of serious devotion and study. By the mid-1950s, Leonard Feather's *Encyclopedia of Jazz* and the *Hugues Panassié-Madeleine Gautier Guide to Jazz,* two of the first serious books to pore over the roots and branches of jazz had appeared. More controversial was a four-LP *Thesaurus of Classic Jazz* – a compendium assembled by the critic Richard Du Page and issued by Columbia that did not include a single black musician in its vista.

What is perhaps important to remember is that the concept of the reissue jazz album and in fact the jazz album itself were relative novelties – only dating, in fact, from March 1940. It was then that George Avakian persuaded the Decca label to let him record and release as a proper 'album' set six 78 sides with Eddie Condon and Pee Wee Russell, two veterans from the 1920s Chicago jazz scene whose names are best not uttered around stoned adolescents. In the same year, Avakian began running the 'Hot Jazz Classics' line for Columbia – the first regular series of reissue albums ever produced, and the blueprint for any and every vault-clearing compilation or dug-from-a-crate golden oldie LP since. Before that, jazz had mainly floated around on single 78s, and many early masters were out of print and unobtainable. It was therefore understandable that a substantial sector of the LP market should be devoted to what the jazz critic Frederick Ramsey Jr first dubbed 'recapturing', in his *Guide to Longplay Jazz Records* in 1954. Meaning 'the transferring to the new speed or groove anything from the past held to be worth salvaging, saleable, or of exceptional aesthetic or historical significance', 'recapturing', according to Ramsey, was one of two distinctive types of jazz recordings that became available in the first five years of the LP. The second was the rather more amorphous grouping he dubbed 'on with the living', which was everything else by 'both new and established artists'. Here, though, Ramsey argued that 'major companies didn't always respond to the latest and best of the younger, lesser known artists, and credits smaller companies for taking advantage of the new technology and jumping in to fill the gap. '[W]e owe them', he wrote in 1977, 'a debt for capturing many great performances that might otherwise have gone unnoticed, and certainly never recorded.'

A by-product of all this, and 'perhaps not so clearly perceptible at the time', he also later concluded, was that 'the new technology was making many facets of jazz widely available. This prodded new assessments of the music, which was already under academic scrutiny'.

Now as then, though, some of the most intense arguments about the music raged not among academics but among ordinary fans. '[F]or the true fan', Francis Newton wrote in *The Jazz Scene*, 'jazz . . . is not merely to be listened to, but to be analysed, studied, and discussed.' Conjuring up an image that with a tweak could be easily reapplied to a patchouli-drenched gang of prog-rock devotees in the seventies, or a bunch of indie nerds clutching their latest purchases from Rough Trade today, he continued: 'The quintessential location of the fan is not the dance hall, the night club, or even the jazz concert or club, but the private room in which a group of young men play one another records, repeating crucial passages until they are worn out, and then endlessly discuss their comparative merits. For every jazz fan is a collector of records within his financial means.'[28]

The collecting of jazz records was not, of course, restricted solely to men. Dora, the female protagonist of Iris Murdoch's 1958 novel *The Bell*, is a former Slade School of Art jazz-head. 'As a student she grew plump and peach-like', Murdoch writes, 'and had a little money of her own, which she spent on big multi-coloured skirts and jazz records and sandals.'

Debates of baffling complexity over the origins and directions of jazz certainly raged, usually among men, in the pages of *The Record Changer*, a monthly magazine for record collectors, stuffed to the gills with essays and letters that ranged from the gauchely fanatical to the nit-pickingly purist. *The Record Changer*'s major selling point was a classified section of baffling length and obscurity.

With a readership for whom reissues were articles of faith and sacred texts rolled into one, it had followed the RCA–Louis

---

28 Newton (Hobsbawm) was writing in Enland, where thanks to a Musicans' Union ban on visiting American groups that lasted until 1956, the only way to hear the real jazz deal, if you like, was on record. The promoters of a concert given by Humphrey Lyttelton at the Winter Garden Theatre, Drury Lane in November 1949 were even prosecuted for breaching the ruling after the American jazz musician Sidney Bechet, in the audience on the night, joined Lyttelton's troupe on stage for a few numbers.

Armstrong bootleg debacle closely. Its coverage of the trial had unintentionally left RCA hands with the impression that its editors, Bill Grauer and Orrin Keepnews, were keen to lease neglected items from its vaults and the label contacted the magazine about cutting a deal. The idea hadn't previously crossed their minds, but not ones to look a gift horse in the mouth, the pair signed on as independent producers at RCA and founded a new label that they named Riverside, after the magazine's Manhattan telephone exchange, to handle reissues of Armstrong, Ma Rainey and other 1920s recordings from companies like Paramount. Excited by newer developments, they moved into contemporary jazz in 1954, putting out the LP *Cole Porter in a Modern Mood* by pianist Randy Weston and the following year signing up a rather down-on-his-luck Thelonious Monk, who would record some of his most acclaimed albums – *Brilliant Corners,* for example for the label.

Riverside was just one of a new breed of dedicated jazz labels including Contemporary, Pacific, Blue Note and Prestige, run by jazz lovers for jazz lovers, that were able to operate reasonably competitively because of the LP. Tape recorders soon cut recording costs and allowed such labels to stage impromptu sessions in nightclubs – a phenomenon with lasting consequences for studio and concert jazz. Since these companies they were usually run by fans, they also understood their audience and took the opportunity to address them as knowledgeable peers from the backs of carefully designed sleeves.

The man who probably had most to do with altering the scope, style and packaging of jazz on (and off) LP in the early 1950s was Norman Granz, one of the pioneers of concert recordings. A film editor on the West Coast, Granz was a record collector and jazz fan with impeccable liberal leanings who began organising a series of free-wheeling jazz concerts for desegregated audiences at the Philharmonic Auditorium in Los Angeles in July 1944. The Philharmonic called time on the concerts two years later, but the formula was reprised – and the name kept – as a successful touring and recording package with a roster that in its thirteen-year lifespan would include Ella Fitzgerald, Louis Armstrong, Count Basie, Charlie Parker, Billie Holiday, Oscar Peterson, Stan Getz, Art Tatum, Dizzy Gillespie and Lester Young.[29]

The concerts enjoyed a deeply symbiotic relationship with the Jazz at the Philharmonic albums, furnishing Granz with the raw material for the live records, with the records in turn plugging the tours as unique live events (the record giving enough of a flavour of the evening to make those missed it yearn to have attended). Alternatively, for those lucky enough to have been present, there was an option to bore visitors rigid with a running commentary of the evening in question as the disc ticked along. The tours probably wouldn't have been as successful without the albums, and vice versa, thus 'Jazz at the Philharmonic' stands as a nascent musical superbrand, one eventually afflicted by the same attendant problems with ubiquity, overproduction, quality control and the vagaries of musical fashion as, say, the Ministry of Sound. A persistent criticism of the LPs was that taken one after another, they did get rather monotonous. There was something of a tendency for each jam session recorded to conclude with similar rounds of overexcited, climatic honking, which fresh and wildly infectious as it may have seemed in the concert hall, and perhaps on

29 Dizzy Gillespie once observed that 'the importance of the Jazz at the Philharmonic is that it was the original "first class" treatment for jazz musicians'.

hearing the very first LP, did rather pall by the fifteenth album in a row.[30]

The first Jazz at the Philharmonic album was filed on transcript discs and came out on 78 in 1945 – two years before Gordon and Gray's *The Hunt*. Neither the musicians nor the audience were aware that a record had been planned. What 'sent' the album's buyers was the preservation of solos, fluffs and all by Gene Kupa, Illinois Jacquet and Charlie Ventura that would have evaporated otherwise. (Nat King Cole also played piano at the gig, but to avoid jeopardising his contract to Capitol, appeared pseudonymously as Shorty Nadine on the album, a ruse that fooled no one but satisfied the etiquette demanded. Guesting on records by the likes of Stan Getz, Lester Young and Buddy Rich, King used the names Sam Schmaltz, Lord Calvert, Eddie Laguna, Nature Boy and The King, a moniker so laughably transparent that it makes the bluesman Muddy Waters' alter ego Dirty Rivers look head-scratchingly cryptic.) Not everyone saw this a positive development – the jazz critic Joe Goldberg later complained that it was 'an artificial means of retaining that which was never meant to be permanent', which, while true enough, is a little bit like grumbling that photography has ruined real life. However, just as photography changed painting, with these recordings able to capture the untameable, previously impermanent spirit of the likes of Buddy Bolden or the Original Creole Orchestra, a line had now been crossed – making that

30 Though I suppose there must have been many who bought the albums for those finales and waited with bated breath for them with each new release – ears cocked in rapt anticipation on that first listen – who would have been thrown into utter despondency if something they'd come to rely on, a certainty as familiar, steadfast and comforting as an Agatha Christie mystery, failed to materialise and, for example, the ensemble had chosen to wrap up the LP with some delicate wire brush drumming . . .

untameable sound all the more valuable. The Jazz at the Philharmonic LPs, now recorded on tape and released on 10-inch vinyl, were able to ferry 'real' unfettered spontaneous jazz to the punters while (most) studio recordings remained, or so the logic went, icy Xeroxes. The urge to replicate that unfettered spontaneity in the studio would become overwhelming.

The success of the Philharmonic LPs and concerts established Granz both as the leading jazz impresario of his day and as one of the most innovative producers of LPs around, in the studio as well as in the field. By 1954, Granz was head of two labels, Clef and Norgran, and was responsible for over 200 long-players. Realising that the presentation could be just as important as the music, he employed the illustrator David Stone Martin, who frequently designed covers for *Time* magazine, to create the sleeves of his albums. Martin's style, blotchy, antic Chinese ink line drawings, embellished with simple daubs of colour, looked fresh, *moderne* and witty. Figures, jostling instruments, light bulbs and hands were recurring Martin motifs that caught the *joie de vivre* of the (often live) performances that these LPs contained.

Not content with a being a label boss, Granz became Ella Fitzgerald's manager. He oversaw her most creative and commercial period by orchestrating a series of Songbook albums in which the vocalist surveyed a songsmith's compositions for the course of a whole LP – a concept that Louis Armstrong and his producer George Avakian at Columbia had already broached with their 1954 tribute album to W.C. Handy and its follow-up, *Satch Plays Fats* (i.e. Armstrong plays Fats Waller). Not all of Granz's commercial instincts reaped artistic jewels, however, and among the most controversial was the teaming of Charlie Parker with a string section presided over by Mitch Miller – a combination that from this distance could be a post-modern joke, the jazz equivalent of a mash-up of Jimi Hendrix and Mantovani. ('We deplore this castration' was Ramsey's Long-play Guide's view.)

The Philharmonic LPs, though, were widely emulated, and Columbia scored a massive hit in 1950 with a then unique LP of a 1938 concert recording by Benny Goodman. By 1950, the swing style of jazz embodied by Goodman, 'The King of Swing', was on the wane in dance halls, but the release of the clarinettist and bandleader's *Famous 1938 Carnegie Hall Jazz Concert* on a double LP set triggered a renaissance of swing in the home. Married-with-kids former jitterbuggers and lindyhoppers were able to party like it was 1939 all over again. And since post-war Americans married earlier and had more children at an earlier age than at any point in the twentieth century, there was a large audience looking to recall those carefree days. Furthermore, if plotlines of the era's sitcoms were to be believed, a double LP was probably cheaper and easier to obtain than the babysitter needed for concert-going or dancing.

The Goodman concert record was among the first LPs to amass sales of a million and remains in circulation to this day. What made it so unique on release was that it had been pieced together on tape from a set of radio-style acetate transcript discs taken during the show on 16 January 1938. The concert marked the first time 'jazz' had been performed inside the august environs of Carnegie Hall. On the night, Goodman had pulled out all the stops: the set included a genre-affirming musical canter through Twenty Years of Jazz, and Goodman lead his own entourage, Count Basie, and a host of stars from Basie's and Duke Ellington's bands on an array of raucous whooping jams. On 'Sing, Sing, Sing', the number appears all but over (the audience burst into what is audibly intended to be their final applause) when suddenly, from the ashes, pianist Jess Stacy sparks up a whole new solo, to a chuckle from Goodman, that carries the song along, extending it to a full twelve minutes in total – four minutes longer than a version recorded on two sides of a 78.

That Stacy's solo did not become 'just a dim, hardly creditable memory' was down to the transcript discs that made the LP possible. Lasting for 8.45 minutes each, they were kept running in sequence on two turntables throughout the evening as a single mike relayed events on stage to CBS's radio studio. Virtually the whole concert was therefore in the can. At the end of the night two copies of the transcripts were made; one batch was filed in the Library of Congress, the other sat festering in a cupboard in Goodman's home until his daughter Rachel reputedly excavated it some eleven years later. Goodman then sensibly had them transferred onto tape.

What the Carnegie LP owner was able to savour at leisure, as never before was concert quality swing jazz – all the improvs, the works. The LP's colossal sales soon meant that other similarly aged acetate transcript and concert recordings from Tommy Dorsey, Louis Armstrong and Artie Shaw were dusted down and put out on LP, with a second album of Goodman's performances from 1937–8, *Jazz Concert No. 2*, following in 1952. That same year saw two 10-inch LPs of Woody Herman's 1946 Carnegie Hall show hit the racks, which were received with particular interest among jazz fans, since Herman's repertoire and line-up during that period bridged a gap between pre-war swing and 1940s bop.

Nevertheless, it's somewhat typical that it was Glen Miller, the WASP swinger who had the least to offer in terms of live performance 'spontaneity', who profited most from the concert-recording phenomenon. Three volumes of his grindingly tidy unreleased radio broadcasts – and it could just be a matter of unshakeable WWII associations, but his arrangements always seem to reek ever so slightly of Brasso and parade ground spit and polish – flew off the shelves when they were issued on LP in 1951. Miller, last seen clambering aboard a small plane bound for France one foggy afternoon in December 1944, then went on to enjoy a huge revival that culminated in a Hollywood biopic in 1954. Cornball of the highest order, *The Glen Miller Story* starred James Stewart as Miller. The film revealed or invented that the bandleader eschewed the marital bed to spend his wedding night jamming with Gene Kupa and Louis Armstrong in a 'hot jazz' club. Given the frigidity of so much of what he committed to wax, one can only ponder the state of Miller's subsequent sex life, and his weedy posthumous efforts only gave further succour to the long-held notion that 'proper' jazz wasn't to be heard on traditional 'studio' recordings, where its wings were well and truly clipped.

The general public's fondness for the 'live music' LP was shared by jazz musicians themselves, who on the whole believed that they played at their best when in front of an appreciate crowd of cats.

An LP like the 1951 *Jammin' at Rudi's*, for example, a fly-on-the-wall recording of a jam session by Conrad Janis and his Tailgate Jazz Band at the critic Rudi Blesh's New York apartment, was sold on the meagre basis of containing, at nine minutes, the longest version of 'When the Saints Go Marching In' ever pressed. And while that might be reason enough for some to wish that microgroove vinyl had never been invented, it indicated the growing prevalence of discursive jazz recordings.

What was being sought out was a sense of the fleeting inspirations of the moment. The on-the-spot LP, though obviously an artifice, gave a feeling of unmediated intimacy between the musicians and the listener. It was a seductive deception, with much collusion on both sides. A few years later, Duke Ellington's *At Newport* concert album, the biggest-selling LP of his entire career, was in fact almost wholly recreated in a New York studio when it was discovered that the live tapes weren't up to the job.

Nonetheless, 'live' LPs were certainly in tune with a prevailing mood for greater emotional 'truth' in artistic performances. Improvisation, the lifeblood of jazz since its infancy, was on the loose in Italian neo-realist cinema, the action paintings of Jackson Pollock, the method acting of the studio and Marlon Brando and, of course, in the spontaneous bop prosody of Jack Kerouac and the Beats. The world was speeding up with the proliferation of cars, roads, aeroplanes, new buildings and energy-saving devices. Television and adverts flooded the senses with images and information. Daily life became freer, cleaner and more efficient, but also far more anxious, kinetic, disjointed and disorientating. It was this busy, often exciting, absurd and frightening universe that artists, actors, designers, writers and musicians were trying pin down, and that sociologists and psychoanalysts, with their abstract expressionist Rorschach's inkblots, were desperate to understand.

Okay, people bought live jazz LPs for lots of reasons, many of which had nothing to do with post-war alienation or repressed sexuality. The music on the record bopped, bebopped, swung, cooled or sent them daddio; it had a neat cover; it would impress some gamine *jeune poétesse* in ballet shoes and a black polo-neck . . . But there were parallels between the live jazz LP and the more general belief – based on half-digested Freud and those inkblots – that the slip and the off-guard remark could be more revealing than a measured, calculated response: that feeling was more important than thinking. Live LPs, to a degree, were legitimising the publication of ephemeral works in progress, with first drafts and unfinished or one-off musical sketches frequently thought superior to 'finished' versions. A number of Charlie Parker out-takes and on-the-spot recordings which otherwise would not have seen the light of day appeared on LPs after his death, and were cherished because they were felt to have caught something of the intensity missing from his official releases. These were the holy relics, after all, of a man who was now canonised as a bebop saint.

For modernists wanting to move things on, the relative ease with which a pulled-together-then-and-there set could be taped and parcelled out into the world on LP opened up a range of possibilities. Practically every faintly progressive artistic discipline in the early 1950s got the bug for 'workshops'. Jazz was no exception. And whereas live LPs, even of the often thought-provoking Ganz Philharmonic ilk, had been about entertainment – a gaudy souvenir of a concert you hadn't attended – their function as musical manifestos were seized by the likes of Charlie Mingus. 'This is a Jazz Workshop Album!' announces the rear cover of *Mingus at the Bohemia* – a live LP recorded at New York's Café Bohemia. 'We are not presenting these concepts with the feeling that they must be used as is', the listener is later advised. 'Instead we are presenting them as a record of our developments in Jazz.'

Mingus would carry the workshop concept into the studio on his next LPs, *Pithecanthropus Erectus* and *The Clown*, but the 'nothing written' and 'never played the same twice' working methods of the Café date – right down to an improvised poem by Jean Shepherd on *The Clown*'s title track – remained the same. The open-endedness of one form, to an extent, was freeing up the other, as musicians like Miles Davis, among others, now consciously strove to emulate live dates in the studio: recording late, dimming the lights, extemporising as the vibe grabbed them.

Davis's recording *modus operandi* – the one-take session – was grounded in a musical aesthetic as ornate in its justification if simple in practice as Kerouac's I'll-load-up-on-coffee-and-type-prose pose. It was fortuitously in sync with the thrifty practices of Prestige, the independent company he signed to in 1951. Prestige, briefly New Jazz, had been founded only two years earlier by Bob Weinstock, an affable jazz-head that the kindly would describe as niftily entrepreneurial, and the less kindly as anything-to-save-a-buck cheap. Weinstock began selling jazz records in the classifieds of *Record Changer* when he was still in short pants. At twenty, he recorded and released a disc by an ensemble headed up by the saxophonist Lee Konitz (one of Kerouac's heroes and a member of the Davis nontet who recorded the *Birth of the Cool* sides) and the pianist Lennie Tristano. A performer who had dates with Bird and Gillespie to his credit, Tristano was a bit of a jazz Lee Strasberg. A tutor to Konitz, Wayne Marsh and Billy Bauer, he established his own 'School of Jazz' in New York. Blind since infancy, he was preoccupied by the notions of feeling and spontaneity in music and led sorties into the territory of improvisation in the fag-end of the 1940s that were subsequently tagged and emulated a decade later as 'free jazz'.

Weinstock therefore got the ball rolling with artists who dealt in of-the-moment brilliance. What gave Prestige its cachet – apart from snapping up the not inconsiderable talents of Sonny Stitt, Stan Getz, Coleman Hawkins, Eric Dolphy, Sonny Rollins, John Coltrane and, of course, Davis – was the self-evident 'honesty' and 'spontaneity' of the often shonky discs it released. After all, how could anything that sounded that ropey not be 'real'? As Ira Gitler, writing on the sleeve of a Prestige LP of Miles Davis and Sonny Rollins sessions, explained: 'I appreciate a well-integrated performance but will always prefer moments of sincere-emotion jazz with mistakes to the slick product which is too often palmed off as jazz today. Whether it be old jazz or new, I guess I'm kind of a *purist*.'

Whether it was down to purity – a desire to allow these musicians to emote, untrammelled by the fetters of squaresville entertainment industry norms – or to save Bob a few bob, Prestige didn't, for instance, believe in rehearsals. Well, certainly not on company time and money, anyway. The desired effect was a facsimile of a sweaty late-night club session; an action painting in hi-fi with Weinstock remaining pretty hands-off about the unevenness, slashes and drips of the finished results.

In his history of Prestige's rival Blue Note Records, Richard Cook contrasts John Coltrane's sole LP for the label, *Blue Train*, with that of Coltrane's output for Prestige in the 1950s. *Blue Train* currently performs the same palate-training function in popular music as Woodpecker cider once did for teenage drinkers: it is an album consumed by those looking for an 'in' on jazz but who are perhaps uneasy about the genre. As a place to start, it's easier going than, say, some of Coltrane's other (later) recordings (the dizzying forty-minute cacophony of 1965's *Ascension*, for instance). But it is also far less interesting than Coltrane's hauntingly beautiful 1964 album *A Love Supreme*.

The deal to lay down the *Blue Train* album was agreed casually, with a handshake, nothing signed, when the saxophonist wandered into Blue Note's Lexington Avenue offices on the off chance of blagging a couple of their Sidney Bechet LPs. Though shortly afterwards Coltrane committed to Weinstock and Prestige, he chose to honour the arrangement.

A Blue Note LP is almost instantly recognisable by its artwork – the one-colour tints, bold typography and cropped black and white portrait treatments that their house designer Miles Reid deployed on their jackets are now so iconic they feel drilled into the visual lexicon. The care lavished on the covers was only an outward manifestation of the attention paid to the record itself.

The company's LPs, and *Blue Train* is no exception, were almost always cut after two days of paid rehearsals. It has, in Cook's estimation, 'a polish and precision' unmatched on any of Coltrane's (never paid to rehearse) Prestige LPs – though he concedes 'there is a sense of impeccable routine about the music'. Even the title track was tidied up, with Kenny Drew's piano solo spliced in from a different version of the song. Such nips and tucks were usually impossible in Weinstock's house – not because they were considered breaches of musical integrity as such, though they probably were, but because the producer rarely kept alternative takes and had the miserly habit of respooling and recording over any below-par performances to preserve valuable tape.

Similar concerns over economics intriguingly had completely the opposite effect on the West Coast jazz svengali Richard Bock and the Pacific Jazz imprint he created to release LPs by the Gerry Mulligan Quartet. Seeking to minimise expenditure, he drove stock to retailers himself and recorded at a sound engineer friend's pad to save on studio bills. To overcome a fairly green Chet Baker's shortcomings as a soloist, Bock would cut and paste his fumbled efforts together to achieve a convincing enough replication of inspired jazzery for viable commercial release.

Another West Coast luminary, Dave Brubeck, was more in line with Weinstock's get-it-while-it's-hot (or 'cool', more accurately) philosophy, with several of his live albums sounding for all the world as if the pianist himself was spinning from keyboard to tape recorder to press stop, pause or record. Which in some instances he was – or nearly, anyway. Lanky and bespectacled Brubeck studied classical composition under Darius Milhaud at Mills College in Oakland, California, but had been performing as a professional jazz pianist since he was a teenager. Under Milhaud's influence, Brubeck came to the conclusion that jazz improvisations could be as valid for him as the improvisations in toccatas and fugues had been for Bach. He formed an experimental Jazz Workshop Octet with fellow students in 1948. Following the addition of saxophonist Paul 'Martini Smooth' Desmond in 1951, a slightly less avant-garde but musically omnivorous Brubeck Trio finally expanded – after some stops, starts and a surfing-induced spinal injury – into a quartet, and went on to gain notoriety for their sets at the Blackhawk Club in San Francisco and at The Haig in Los Angeles. Unusually for that time, Brubeck then took his music back to school, embarking on a circuit of college tours that eventually established campuses as the Quartet's premier stomping grounds and students their most loyal early fans.

While further endearing them to their college faithful, *Jazz at Oberlin*, an LP of the Quartet's date at the Oberlin Conservatory of Music in Ohio on 2 March 1953, also served as an artistic and commercial breakthrough. It was the original blueprint to a concert album subgenre that would go on to spawn The Who's rocking-the-redbrick *Live at Leeds*. The LP captured the Quartet warts, grunts, chuckles, magnetophone squelches and all, floating through dreamy, loose percussive interpretations of 'These Foolish Things', 'Stardust' and 'How High the Moon'. An intoxicated audience, meanwhile, can be heard roaring and tugging on their pipes and scarves in VU-needle-baffling shows of appreciation that are partially lost to both the moment and the acoustics of the hall.

Refresher courses in academic home taping were quickly supplied; with Brubeck's *Jazz at the College of Pacific* and the plusher *Jazz Goes to College* LPs immediately building on the success of Oberlin. In 1954 the pianist became only the second jazz musician to grace the cover of *Time* magazine (the first was Louis Armstrong).

Brubeck had cut his first sides ('Indiana', 'Tea for Two' and so on) for local jazz hobbyist label Coronet, before teaming up with Max and Sol Weiss to release the *Jazz at Oberlin* and *Jazz at the College of Pacific* LPs on Fantasy – a new San Francisco Bay Area-based venture in which he supposedly had a casting stake.

But the terms of his agreement turned out to be punitive enough to require a further five cheapie 'live' or impromptu Brubeck albums of varying line-ups and quality to be produced after he hopped to Columbia for his *Time*-sanctioned *annus mirabilis*.

Around this same period Miles Davis was in a similar bind, but without demeaning Brubeck's second-drawer LPs, what emerged from Davis's contractual wranglings was a good deal more scintillating. At the 1955 Newport Jazz Festival (the second time the event was staged), a rejuvenated Davis, having weaned himself off smack, stole the show with an astonishing solo during a jam session of 'Round Midnight' with the tune's composer, Thelonious Monk.

George Avakian of Columbia discarded previous reservations and approached Davis about recording for the major. Davis's contract with Weinstock and Prestige, however, had four albums to go. Cutting a deal that brilliantly combined an adherence to legal formalities with cheap-to-produce unfettered post-bop expressionism, Davis and a quintet composed of John Coltrane, Red Garland, Paul Chambers and Philly Joe Jones, booked themselves into a studio on two separate days in 1956 and motored through enough material to fill up four LPs. A total of twenty-four extended numbers were put on tape, Davis calling up the tunes just as he would during the Quintet's residency at the Café Bohemia in Greenwich Village that summer. There were no second takes. Stumbled beginnings on 'You're My Everything', Davis's instructions to the group, his horseplay with Weinstock and engineer Rudy Van Gelder all went into the bubbling pot. Prestige was able to eke out the release of the resulting *Cookin'* ('that's what we did – came and in cooked', as Davis put it), *Relaxin'*, *Steamin'* and *Workin'* LPs until 1961, by which time Davis had galloped on to pastures modal and was presenting *Sketches of Spain*, a soaring near-classical LP based on

Rodrigo's *Concierto de Aranjuez* for guitar and orchestra and arranged by Gil Evans.

Davis had reconvened with Evans, the Canadian-born dot-fixer and creative foil on the *Birth of the Cool* sessions, for his second LP for Columbia, *Miles Ahead*. The arrogant title underlined the progressive direction he and Evans were scoping out with the aid of a budget generous enough to stump up for nineteen musicians on the record. The decision to provide Davis with a bigger backing band came from Avakian. It was taken with the express intention of expanding Davis's potential audience. In the publicity campaign for his first Columbia long-player, *Round About Midnight*, much had been made of the phrase 'The Relaxed Horn of Miles Davis'. Elsewhere, the trumpeter was busy being championed by the label as 'the unofficial headmaster of relaxed trumpet playing'. 'He seldom goes in for frantic effects', was another punter-assuring, look-he's-nothing-like-the-late-Bird, honest, line it put out. Davis hadn't, however, kicked the skag merely to fade into obscurity, and the palate of woodwind and brass that Evans put together for *Miles Ahead* put Davis firmly centre stage as the lead voice on an album comprised of a suite of ten songs that included Brubeck's 'The Duke'.

Perhaps carried away by its sonorousness, Columbia unveiled a crass scheme to sleeve the LP with a kind of mood music cover bearing the image of a winsome blonde dame on a boat. 'Why'd you put that white bitch on there?' Davis reputedly, and not unreasonably, asked. The cover was dropped, but it was revealing of the label's desire to court an audience of white wannabe hipsters who might dig Dizzy and dream of Dinah, but who would always love Lucy in the end.

Evans' 'Blues for Pablo', included on *Miles Ahead*, was also recorded by Hal McKusick on his *Jazz Workshop* LP – one of a series of 'workshop' albums inaugurated at RCA Victor in 1956 by the A&R man Jack Lewis. Evans himself played piano on George Russell's *Workshop* LP, and it was Russell who now profoundly altered the kind of music Evans, Davis and John Coltrane would go on to play and record. Triggered in part by a conversation with Davis some years before, Russell published a book in 1953 entitled *The Lydian Concept of Tonal Organisation* in which he advocated improvising on a single 'mode' or scale instead of the traditional chord progressions, a theory aimed at liberating the jazz soloist from the ever-diminishing pool of variations available in the latter. Russell put his ideas into practice on his *Workshop* album, and this LP in turn spurred Evans and Davis to explore modalities in their own recordings, Evans introducing Davis to classical pieces that utilised model themes by Bartok and Ravel, whose 'Concerto for the Left Hand and Orchestra' the trumpeter became infatuated with.

'Milestones', the eponymous track on the next album, marked the first fruits of Davis's experimentation with things modal that would coalesce into *A Kind of Blue* – an LP that near enough played itself into being in nine hours in the spring of 1959. Though Evans had been presented with some ideas for the record, Davis held no rehearsals before either of the two recording sessions. The assembled musicians (Cannonball Adderley, John Coltrane et al) were handed charts containing the barest open-ended sketches of what were scarcely songs at all, so the fact that they then insouciantly set about wrapping up all five numbers in a single take – or two, when it came to the North African-tinged 'Flamenco Sketches' – remains nothing short of jaw dropping. The results were so startling, some of the pauses in between Davis's spare phrasing every inch as hypnotic as the two-note riff on the opener 'So What', that it was nearly forty years before anyone noticed that side one was half a tone sharp. But then that's what happens if you try something so new.

However, the avant of *Kind of Blue* sounded deceptively guarded when lined up beside Ornette Coleman's jarring and audacious *The Shape of Jazz to Come*, released just a couple of months later. If *Kind of Blue* was melodious, smoky and self-evidently brainy, it was nevertheless a little like eavesdropping on a conversation about existentialism in a late-night diner: pleasurable enough over a coffee, even if you didn't understand a word of what was being said. *The Shape . . .* , on the other hand, was more akin to having the ghost of mad Bohemian Joe Gould there in your booth, chewing your face off, panhandling for dollars, forking up ketchup, impersonating a seagull in your ear.

Coleman, whose favoured instrument was a dinky white plastic alto sax, coined the word 'harmolodic' to describe his music. Plenty doubted it should be called music at all. What Coleman did was to extend the parameters of spontaneous improvisation beyond what had previously been thought feasible, desirable even. In his harmolodic jazz, every individual member of the group was free to contribute whatever they wanted to, whenever they wanted to. No single player was subordinate to any other and all the elements of a composition – the rhythm, melodies and harmonies – were of equal importance to the end form. That end form sounded like chaos to some but there was beauty and melody, admittedly of a strange kind, lurking amidst the (apparent) insanity for those who chose to seek it out. After releasing in quick succession a run of albums whose titles (*Something Else!!!*, *Tomorrow is the Question!*, *Change of the Century*, *This Our Music*) were as provocative (prophetic?) as their contents incendiary, Coleman recorded the LP *Free Jazz* on 21 December 1960.

Subtitled a 'Collective Improvisation' and played by a double quartet, Coleman's regular henchmen (Don Cherry, Charlie Haden and Ed Blackwell), joined by Freddie Hubbard on trumpet, Eric Dolphy on bass clarinet, Scott le Faro on bass and Billy Higgins on drums, it was comprised of a single thirty-six-minute long track. This bold exercise in sustained making-it-up-on-the-spot art embodied such a temporal leap that it had to be chopped in two to be accommodated on a 12-inch LP. Freedom on this scale can be giddying, and there are moments on *Free Jazz* when the players, obviously feeling a tad vertiginous, audibly give themselves up to something approaching convention for ballast. Like the Jackson Pollock splatter painting on its original cover, the album has lost the power to shock. It has gained a greater coherence in the wake of the freer 'free jazz' that surfaced in its aftermath, and today it seems free but not wilfully feckless or entirely impenetrable; more *Ulysses* than *Finnegan's Wake*, say. And while it is not Coleman's best album, nor perhaps his most influential, its impact meant that neither jazz nor the LP would ever be quite the same again. Coleman's great leap, followed later by Albert Ayler, Archie Shepp and Pharoah Sanders, left large sections of the public behind.

The poet and jazz fan Philip Larkin, reflecting on the innovations Coleman and his heirs had wrought, later declared jazz 'a popular art no more'. They had, he reasoned, made jazz 'self-conscious, artistically as well as socially', and the drift into chromaticism ('the language of the minority artist') had starved listeners of foot-tappers, love songs or simply tunes to whistle. This, he argued, explained 'the recent and extravagant vogue for "beat music". It doesn't take much imagination', he concluded, 'to see that this is where the jazz impulse, the jazz following, has migrated. This is where the jazz following has migrated. This is where the jazz public has gone, and even where jazz has gone, for this music, rock and roll, rhythm and blues, or just plain beat, is for all its tedious vulgarity nearer jazz than the rebarbative astringencies of Coleman, Coltrane and the late Eric Dolphy.'

It wouldn't, of course, be long before, as Thomas Pynchon noted, 'Beat prophets were resurrected and people started playing alto sax riffs on electric guitars', for while rock might have gained the upper hand, and its legendary urgency, jazz would never really lose its cool. All those LPs from this golden creative period, some as immaculately pressed as a three-button suit to this day, would see to that.

But that kind of timelessness takes time, and in order to thrive, you need to be considered out of date – at least for a while. As the teenage narrator of Colin MacInnes's novel *Absolute Beginners* says: 'Now, you can think what you like about the art of jazz – quite frankly, I don't care what you think, because jazz is a thing so wonderful that if anybody doesn't rave about it, all you can feel for them is pity: not that I am making out I understand it all – I mean certain LPs leave me speechless.'

Hmm, is that supposed to be a good thing? Perhaps it's time to move on and explore the father of the concept LP . . .

Chapter Five
TO BE FRANK

When Frank Sinatra died in 1998, Gore Vidal estimated that 'half the population of the United States over the age of forty were conceived while their parents were listening to his records'. He said 'records', but I think we can assume he meant LPs, since between 1955 and 1959 Sinatra spent longer than anyone else on *Billboard*'s album chart – a total of 450 weeks. Where a quick two and half minutes with an oily haired truck driver's 7-inch might have satisfied what were being called teenagers, grown-ups bought albums and romanced in the comfort of their own homes. (It was for this reason that 'most LP buyers hardly noticed the creeping emergence of rock and roll' as Atlantic records producer Gerry Wexler recalled in the early 1970s.) If Elvis Presley had more number one singles – fifteen – on LP, Sinatra enjoyed greater dollar sales throughout the decade.

But then Sinatra made buying LPs a worthwhile expense. He organised his albums like shows, choosing and arranging the running orders of the songs with the meticulousness his more dubious associates were alleged to deploy in heists. And if the thought of dusting up a complete album around a mood was already in the air, no popular singer before Sinatra executed the idea with as much care or verve. Still, while others might have been happy to hang their hat on a mood, Sinatra went all out for full-blown concepts, sustained expressions of thoughts and feelings, and in the process became, in the film critic David Thomson's words, 'the first great exponent of the long-playing record'. From 1955's *In the Wee Small Hours* onwards, his LPs were adult pleasures, and often ones best savoured lingeringly, repeatedly, and late at night with company – or failing that, a carton of Kents and a bottle of whisky.

While Sinatra recordings were among the very first crop of pop long-players Columbia released in 1948, it was this album (along with an Oscar for his portrayal of Angelo Maggio in the eve-of-Pearl-Harbor drama *From Here to Eternity*) that established the pattern for his mature artistic output and resuscitated his nearly dead career. The story of Sinatra's rise, fall and revival is a three-act marvel so unbelievably spectacular that it could have been penned by Robert McKee (and, in true Hollywood fashion, the original tale would be undone for a time by trend-chasing sequels replete with increasingly, eventually embarrassingly, youthful female romantic leads – the whole franchise eventually being brought back to life, after a short break and a rest, when all of a sudden it started to make some kind of glorious sense once again).

For a man later so finicky about everything from the monographs on his slippers to the deportment with which he walked across a casino lobby, Sinatra's entry into the world in a cold-water flat in Hoboken on 12 December 1915 was undignified in the extreme. Presumed stillborn, his neck and left earlobe were damaged by the forceps used by an impatient doctor to yank him from the womb. Sinatra bore the scars all his life. The only child of Italian immigrants in an Irish-Italian neighbourhood where Catholicism made the Sinatras' proto-Maoist unit an outright rarity, his boyhood was lonely. He was left in the care of his grandmother while his ambitious mother, Dolly, dipped chocolate by day and panhandled for the Democratic Party at night. Meanwhile his dad, Marty, a washed-up boxer turned fire captain, manned the local station at all hours. Before becoming entranced by Bing Crosby, the young Francis excelled primarily at stoop sitting and gazing into space. During his many years of fame, Hoboken old-timers, dragged up by journalists with the regularity of cement-booted bodies from the Hudson River, could always be relied upon to give a smattering of anecdotes about a forlorn-looking young Blue Eyes sizing up the action from afar. ('Ya knew he wassa plannin' somefink big, but . . . Little Frankie . . . An angel, the apple of his mother's eye, always with the smartest pants . . .' and so on.)

Sinatra would channel that loneliness into his work, gradually becoming in song, much as Edward Hopper was in paint, twentieth-century America's pre-eminent exponent of doomy romanticism and urban isolation. Though less noir on those bobby-soxer-pleasing, pre-Ava Gardner 78s ('I'll Never Smile Again', 'Saturday Night Is the Loneliest Night of the Week', 'All or Nothing') the needy sexuality, vulnerability and loneliness was always there, an underlying factor in his winsome, leg-humping, puppy-dog charm. A singer with the Harry James Big Band until he was lured away by the more successful Tommy Dorsey, then finally took the risky decision to go solo, Sinatra's period of estrangement from his original audience was a necessary process for both parties to grow up and move on together again. And it was vital to the singer to gain a larger constituency of male fans, who before then had mostly regarded this

enchanting girlfriend/wife/sister/mother/aunt/grandmother charmer with envy and suspicion rather than admiration.

The scrawny-framed crooner, who at 5 feet 8 inches and 130
pounds sometimes appeared in danger of collapsing under the
weight of his own bow-ties, had only enhanced his appeal to girls-
next-door everywhere by marrying his teenage sweetheart – as
millions did in a time of war. Throughout the 1940s, Sinatra's
progressive politics and his highly principled and unparalleled
public stance on racial equality were radical and not without
controversy. Pathetically, the simple refusal to expunge his name
of its ethnicity, as his contemporaries Frankie Laine (Francesco
Paolo LoVecchio) and Dean Martin (Dino Paul Crocetti) had
done, was in itself a bold move for the time. Laying out Dorsey for
an anti-Semitic remark, slugging a waiter in a Southern restaurant
for refusing to serve a black musician in his band and championing
Sammy Davis Jr, Sinatra never stinted from fighting the good
fight. His views, though, which cost him audiences in the South,
kept pace with the rhetoric of a nation committed to defeating
fascism, on foreign shores at least. In 1945, he made the ten-
minute propaganda short, *The House I Live In*. Filmed stepping
out of the studio for a quick fag, Sinatra spies a gang of kids
taunting a Jewish boy. Outraged that this could be happening on
American soil, while all right-thinking and non-4F category
excused men were off fighting Hitler, he intervenes, growling:
'Look, fellas, religion makes no difference 'cept to a Nazi or
somebody as stoopid' (or words to that effect . . .).

However, when the Senate Committee on Un-American Activities started snooping around the entertainment industry in the late
1940s, Sinatra was top of their hit-list. The singer would be labelled
a communist in no less than twelve hearings. The charge was never
officially substantiated. He was, however, frequently denounced as
a red in Hearst's newspapers, and a few unfortunate photographs

of Sinatra carousing with figures from the organised-crime world found their way into print. Far more instantaneously damaging to his fanbase, however, was leaving his wife and their three kids for the screen siren Ava Gardner. Sinatra already had a reputation as a womaniser, having previously dallied with Lana Turner, but this act was the final straw and wrecked all the happy-ever-after romantic conventions many of his devotees, now themselves married or going steady, clung to in their own lives. Sinatra's adultery was looked upon as a personal act of betrayal, a dream-trampling affront to their collective values. Or at least that was how the newspaper columnists chose to report it. In any event, fans gave the blue-eyed boy a wide berth, dropping him as speedily and unflinchingly as Daisy cast aside Gatsby.

Floundering about in the wilderness, his personal life in turmoil, Sinatra then suffered the indignity of losing his voice. Silenced for forty days and forty nights, he returned to the studio to be confronted by an incarnation of the devil.

Over the years, Sinatra said quite a lot about Mitch Miller and none of it was ever complimentary. Miller's principal crime in Sinatra's eyes was to do his damnedest to kill off his singing career, a charge that although it carried a certain let-he-who-is-without-sin hypocrisy about it, wasn't without foundation. Running into one another in Las Vegas a decade later, Miller extended his hand in greeting, a gesture he evidently hoped might broker some kind of reconciliation between them. His olive branch was rebuffed. 'Fuck you! Keep walking,' was Sinatra's pithy rejoinder.

As an A&R man at Columbia, then later as a bestselling recording artist in his own right, with a string of truly dreadful top-ten *Sing Along with Mitch* LPs to his credit, Miller was living proof that no one ever lost money overestimating people's capacity for bad taste in the 1950s. A virtuoso classical oboist with a Mephistophelean goatee beard, Miller was the king of the novelty song. 'You've got to work out a gimmick that'll get people's attention and hold it', he informed *Time* in 1951. And setting the tone for so much of what would follow, he scored his earliest pop hit in 1949 with 'Mule Train' for Frankie Laine – a faux western number laced with enough cracking whips to keep regulars at Torture Garden happy for a month. Subsequent Miller gimmicks involved equipping Dinah Shore with six cater-wauling bagpipes, and foisting a harpsichord on Rosemary Clooney. The results were depressingly popular with the public. Though Miller openly vouched 'I wouldn't buy that stuff for myself', plenty of others did, and in his first eighteen months at Columbia, pop sales increased by 60 per cent.

With his own hit rate falling like a stone, but still under contract, Sinatra had little choice than to now and again accept, with gritted teeth, the material Miller gave him to record. One of Miller's specialities was to take hillbilly or country numbers and give them a pop twist, two of the more successful and admirable examples being the belter Frankie Laine's recordings of Hank Williams' then little-known 'Hey Good Lookin'' and The Singing Rage, Miss Patti Page's song 'The Tennessee Waltz'. Sinatra duly found himself hoeing down with a washboard on 'Tennessee Newsboy'. The nadir, however, came when Sinatra was persuaded to perform a canine-themed love duet with Dagmar, a curvaceous blonde TV star famed for perching on high stools in low-cut dresses. No one emerges from 'Mama Will Bark' with any dignity, least of all the listener, and hearing that voice – *the* voice, as it were – caress the syllables of a line that runs 'It was the dog-garnest thing you ever heard' and then barking like a dog as Dagmar tunelessly drawls 'But Mama will spank' is a soiling experience, I can tell you. It feels like being the unwilling voyeur of a humiliating sex game that no one is bothering to pretend to enjoy.

The cruelty of it all is made a million times worse when you discover that while this catastrophe was on the A-side of a single, 'I am a Fool to Want You', a ballad delivered due to his messy personal circumstances with the emotional candour of the confession booth, languished on side B.

Entreaties to record 'She Wears Red Feathers (And a Hula-Hula Skirt)', 'There's a Pawnshop on the Corner in Pittsburgh', 'Pennsylvania' and 'Feet Up (Pat Him on the Po-Po)' were cold shouldered, and Miller increasingly bypassed Sinatra in favour of his new protégé, Guy Mitchell. In 1952 Sinatra was finally dropped by Columbia; his radio show was cancelled; the film *Meet Danny Wilson* flopped and Universal Pictures chose not renew an option on a second Sinatra feature; and his agent released him. In Sinatra-speak, Endsville loomed.

Sinatra would have to die for his sins before undergoing a

resurrection, and while the death was on screen, in *From Here to Eternity*, it did the job. A new contract with Capitol records, signed before the film's release and under the condition that Sinatra paid for his own recordings, also proved fortuitous. The switch to Capitol brought Sinatra together with the label's young, up-and-coming arranger Nelson Riddle, albeit initially against the singer's wishes. Riddle, though unaccredited, had scored Nat King Cole's 'Mona Lisa' and would go on to arrange Cole's *Unforgettable* LP, as well as others for Cole and Peggy Lee. Riddle and Sinatra would go on to collaborate on nine Capitol albums, including many (*Only the Lonely, Songs for Swinging Lovers*) that are viewed as the finest in the Sinatra – and popular music – canon, however dubious such collective nouns are.

Though more exuberant albums (*Come Swing With Me*) would follow with Billy May, and more maudlin ones (*Where are You?*) with Gordon Jenkins, from the outset of their collaboration Riddle seemed most capable of sourcing the soul of Sinatra. Or at least the soul that he wanted to bare to the world – that of the weathered lover and bipolar tippler, exuding chutzpah or affecting self-pity by turns. Typically, the chutzpah Sinatra was pictured on LP sleeves in states of Look-at-Me-Ma ecstatic joy, trilby hat at a jaunty angle and tie loosened. On *Songs for Swinging Lovers* he appeared as a kind of cupid to a dancing and romancing couple, so content with the state of the world, it seemed, that he was willing to let a pen and ink representation of him gurning like a jug-eared orang-utan loose upon the record-buying public. The other Sinatra, however, was to be found despondently hanging about beneath lampposts at ungodly hours, or sitting alone in bars, gazing into whisky glasses as if the secrets of the universe, or better still the phone number of a brunette with a nice set of pins, could be fathomed in their malty depths.

In all of these roles, he was a consummate method actor, only recording after 8 p.m. to maximise the lustre of his voice and drawing on events in his own life for sustenance. If he sounded palpably lost on 'In the Wee Small Hours' or 'Only the Lonely', then it wasn't unreasonable for audiences to assume that the recently departed Ava or a spat with Lauren Bacall were to blame . . . or perhaps to be credited. In many respects Sinatra accelerated and popularised this pseudo-psychological trend – to a point popular singers, much like Hollywood actors until newfangled questions of 'motivation' arose, hadn't really been expected to care about what they were saying, only to pretend and to sing the lines well.

According to his biographer, Norman Harris, it was this quality that drew the footballer Bobby Charlton to Frank Sinatra after the Manchester United air crash in Munich in 1958. Grieving for the loss of his teammates and racked with survivor's guilt, the emotionally taciturn Charlton had sought solace in Sinatra's records. Charlton, Harris maintains, 'knew of the special meaning in Sinatra's songs, that the man had been been down and got himself up and when he sang in the vein of "Only the Lonely" he made it sound so believable. Bobby bought all of Sinatra's LP records, and Sinatra remained the man he would have given anything to meet.'

As Charlton's reaction suggests, Sinatra's Capitol LPs in particular were prized for their autobiographical honesty. Some were not infrequently read as open letters to whoever it concerned.[31] His final album for the label, *The Point of No Return*,

31 Billie Holiday had admired Sinatra's 'suicide' LP *Only the Lonely* and it is similarly difficult to distinguish art from life on her last (and for some still deeply distressing) albums *Lady In Satin* (1958) and *Billie Holiday* (1959). The arranger Ray Ellis later recalled: 'We started to pick the songs [for *Lady in Satin*] and I didn't realise that the titles she was

recorded as a contractual obligation, was one of his most conceptually mischievous – an entire LP of kiss-off songs. In 1957, the year of Ava and Frank's divorce, his records ping-ponged between the wheedling of *Where Are You?* and the carefree 'fuck you' of *A Swingin' Affair*, where he manages to seem deliriously happy on an all-out weepie like 'No One Ever Tells You' and fittingly sardonic on Rodgers and Hart's 'I Wish I Were In Love Again'. Since he released six LPs in that year alone, he could go with whatever mood took him – and Frank, I think it's reasonable to say, was on speaking terms with moods.

What had really made Sinatra such an unusual singer to start with was his phrasing. Beginning partly by emulating Tommy Dorsey's trombone playing, the vocalist had perfected a method of breathing so he could bend and sustain notes. This allowed him to interpret songs in a unique fashion using his voice emotively with the aid of the microphone, much as the lead instrumentalist in a jazz band might do ('I discovered very early that my instrument wasn't my voice,' he once said. 'It was the microphone . . . You have to learn to play it like it was a saxophone'). He learned to converse with his audiences when many of his early peers were still bellowing like Shakespearean dagger-carriers of old.

With the LP as his stage and Riddle, May et al as the dramaturges, Sinatra was able to flavour not just a single song

picking at the time were really the story of her life'. Song choices apart, the travails of her dissolute life are painfully audible in the hoarse register in which she sings here. Lady Day's rasping and pickled tones sound, if anything, all the more harrowing for Ellis's silken string backing. Rather than plastering over the cracks, his lachrymose strings merely highlight the wooziness of her diction. That she had to be physically held upright by her friend Alice Vrbsky to complete the sessions for the final album, lends a poignancy that is almost unbearable to her rendition of 'Don't Worry About Me'.

but a whole cycle, constructing a broader tale through a carefully considered accumulation of songs and performances. Though Sinatra himself had to all intents and purposes invented the 'standards' repertoire – reworking and incorporating popular 'classics' into his sets and record releases – the idea, as he told Robin Douglas Home in 1962, had stemmed from Tommy Dorsey, who Sinatra recalled with every show 'played, paced . . . [and] planned every second from start to finish'. Having decided on a theme or package for an LP, and settled on which songs to record, Sinatra would himself 'put the titles of the songs on twelve bits of paper and juggle them around like a jigsaw puzzle until the album [was] telling a complete story lyric-wise'.

While Sinatra remained committed to this mode of construction, success and his own hubris would slowly come to diminish both the range and consistency of the 'stories' put out on LP under his name. The lapel-grabbing, slappy, happy Sinatra, the magnanimous, if mercurial, Rat Pack party host and bester of tieless hoodlums in lounge bars, gradually seemed to edge out the more introspective Sinatra. The rot arguably started to set in when the *soi-disant* chairman of the board, frustrated with his share of the financial spoils at Capitol, jumped to form his own record company, Reprise.

If the new label's name meant to 'play again', then his old one was quick to spot the similarity between a then-forthcoming Sinatra album and a Capitol predecessor. Gunning for battle ever since Sinatra had launched his venture with a trade campaign that promised 'A newer, happier, emancipated Sinatra . . . un-trammelled, unfettered, unconfined . . . on Reprise', Capitol slammed a suit on the singer. Their charge was that *Swing Along With Me* 'closely resemble[d] in concept, type of repertoire, style, accompaniment and title an album already recorded by Sinatra and released by Capitol under the title of "Come

Swing With Me" '. Reprise was eventually ordered to retitle the LP – it appeared as *Sinatra Swings* – and the enmity between the labels would only increase when Capitol began clearing out their vaults, flooding the market with Sinatra LPs.

Sinatra weathered the storm, though he eventually had to sell Reprise to Warner Brothers. And having seen off the first wave of rock 'n' roll, a genre he called 'The most brutal, ugly, degenerate, vicious form of expression it has been my displeasure to hear', the singer entered the Swinging Sixties . . . well, swinging, with *Sinatra's Swingin' Session!!!*, *Come Swing With Me* and *Sinatra Swings* being joined by *Sinatra and Swingin' Brass* in 1962. Holding court at the mob-connected Sands Hotel in Vegas in the early 1960s, Sinatra and 'The Clan' (Peter Lawford, Joey Bishop, Sammy Davis Jr and Dean Martin) looked invincible. A universe where dames weren't broads and snap-brimmed hats, cufflinks and bourbon on the rocks were not the epitome of style was impossible to imagine. In John Kennedy they spied a future president in their own image – though the Catholic playboy evinced a worrying disdain for those snap-brimmed hats.

Seizing the chance to wield real political influence, Sinatra acted as a pimp to the Democrat, in every sense of the word. He introduced the roving-eyed senator to his main extramarital squeeze, Judith Campbell, recorded a special version of 'High Hopes' for Kennedy's 1960 campaign with lyrics that ran 'Everyone is voting for Jack / 'Cause he's got what all the rest lack', and organised the president's inaugural gala.

But then came the debacle over JFK's official visit to California. Kennedy, on the advice of his mafia-baiting brother Bobby, chose to forgo Sinatra's hospitality – and the helipad the singer had purposely installed in his Lake Tahoe retreat to accommodate the president's aeronautical whims – and stayed with the more respectable (and Republican) Bing Crosby in Palm Springs instead.

It was a rebuff Sinatra never forgave, and one that sent him rightwards into the arms of Nixon and then Reagan.

As the 1960s marched on, though still able to pick up Grammys for 'Stranger in the Night' and the album *The Man and His Music* in 1966, Frank became the victim of shifting demographics. Where previous generations had, on the whole, aspired to act and dress like their elders and betters, the baby-boomers were sure there was more to life than possessing over sixty hairpieces, and wanted something to call their own. Among suburban wife-swappers, croupiers, bartenders, waiters, semi-professional golfers, taxi drivers and anchormen on regional television stations, Sinatra's cachet would never diminish, but the natty cardigans he sported for *Nice 'n' Easy* and the highball-fuelled japes had him pegged as tragically Dad. In Oedipal fashion, as the father of the concept LP in popular music, it was perhaps inevitable that as successors stumbled into this genre in the 1960s they would wish him old hat, if not actually dead.

Sinatra's insistence on doing things *his way*, so compelling in the 1940s, '50s and early '60s, would produce some jarring moments when he tried gamely to keep abreast of contemporary pop mores. The Sinatra of *Cycles* in 1968 was on a mission to get a bit more 'with it' and tackled Joni Mitchell's 'Both Sides Now' and Glen Clampbell's 'By the Time I Get to Phoenix' and 'Gentle on My Mind'. But in the latter, Sinatra insisted on singing the more grammatically correct 'gently' in the final bar, almost as if he were offering an admonishment to the modern world for letting such slovenliness pass unnoticed before. The cover image – Sinatra seated in a pose reminiscent of Rodins *Thinker*, the fingers of his left hand pinching the bridge of his nose – carries the impression of despairing boredom with the finished results, rather than quiet contemplation.

His antipathy to this kind of folk rock material was further exemplified by a tongue-in-cheek cover of Simon and Gar-funkel's 'Mrs Robinson' on his next LP *My Way* – whose Jacques Brel-penned title number would go on to become a bar-room anthem and, once it had been invented, a karaoke perennial. Unwilling to take the Lord's name in vain, Sinatra replaced 'Jesus' in Paul Simon's original lyric with 'Jilly', a less than sly nod to Jilly Rizzo, the meat-fisted patron of a watering hole at Eighth Avenue and 52nd Street that was famed as Sinatra's home from home whenever he was in Manhattan. To most people under the age of about twenty-five, this fuddy-duddy namedropping stuff was about as welcome as a guest at a graduation party uttering the word 'Plastics'. When the western-inflected *Watertown* – a much more questing record, and 'a love story' concept LP composed by Bob Gaudio of the Four Seasons and the singer-songwriter Jake Holmes, whose 'Dazed and Confused' was busy being pilfered by Led Zeppelin at the time – missed the *Billboard* top 100 in 1970, Sinatra, seeing the writing on the wall, chose (briefly, as it happened) to retire.

Though some would probably not have cared to admit it, Sinatra had opened the door to the very ideals of artistic integrity and emotional expression in popular music that were now in effect putting his career on ice for a while. Most importantly, of course, he'd taught the everyday audiences and mainstream performers to think in terms of LPs.

Chapter Six

AND NOW FOR SOMETHING COMPLETELY DIFFERENT . . .

It became fashionable in the 1990s to describe comedy as the new rock and roll. Still, it was fashionable in the 1990s to describe installation art, cooking, football, interior decorating and even rock and roll (certainly as practised by bands of chippy northern lads with electric guitars) as the new rock and roll. What, presumably, commentators were hoping to convey was that these activities could inspire the same daring excitement as when 'Rock Around the Clocks" appearance in *Blackboard Jungle* rendered no cinema seat in South London safe again. But back then, when rock and roll was new, comedy was . . . well, almost the new jazz.

Almost.

Bear with me – it really is all to do with the LP. Honest.

At the dawn of the 1960s in Britain, *Beyond the Fringe* was celebrated for inaugurating a fundamental shift in comic consciousness – a break, splint and reset for the nation's funny bone. Kenneth Tynan, reviewing the show for the *Observer* in May

1961, wrote, 'future historians may well thank me for providing them with an account of the moment when English comedy took its first decisive step into the second half of the twentieth century'. What made this satiricial revue so startling when it opened at the Edinburgh Festival in August 1960 was the witty irreverence with which it laid into the sacred cows of British life. The war, the then serving Prime Minister Harold Macmillan, the Church of England, all got a jolly good ribbing. And from four Oxbridge graduates who performed this demolition job while dressed in cardigans and flannels, the mufti of sensitive young men with novels to write and possibly sherry parties, CND meetings and trad jazz concerts to attend.

The show, which moved to the West End and eventually Broadway, spawned The Establishment club and triggered a short-lived craze for satire, with *Private Eye* magazine and BBC television's *That Was the Week That Was* soon bringing up the rear.

Significantly, though, while only a limited number of people could ever see the show – and far fewer still ever managed to wheedle their way into the oversubscribed Establishment club – Peter Cook, Dudley Moore, Alan Bennett and Jonathan Miller's performances were available on a Parlophone LP.[32]

The theatre critic Michael Billington, who as a student was fortunate enough to attend *Beyond the Fringe*'s opening night, only recently recalled that: 'The jokes spread among the

---

32 Moore, a gifted pianist, also recorded a series of jazz albums with the bassist Pete McGurk and drummer Chris Karan as the Dudley Moore Trio. They weren't funny, just jazz. Rather good small combo jazz, actually. Definitely streets above your standard wine-bar outfit. Moore's playing, which owed something to Oscar Peterson, is breezy, full of subtle little fills and neat digressions when tackling 'Baubles, Bangles and Beads' or working with a bossa nova rhythm on the self-penned 'Pova Nova'.

young, there was a long-playing record of it, and I remember going to parties where people would put on the LP . . . Because of that show, a whole generation was enfranchised and liberated.'

We could quibble over that last point, but if we accept it for now, then using admittedly unforgiveably dodgy logic, we could also be moved to argue that an entire generation was therefore enfranchised and liberated, not by the show itself, but by the LP of the show. Because it was the LP, after all, that enabled a greater number of young people across Britain to learn and circulate the jokes amongst themselves.

Owning this LP or playing this LP to your friends, or being in the presence of this LP while it was being played, in Billington's youth obviously held a certain cachet. As, we can imagine, did remembering to laugh in the *right* places and perhaps occasionally pre-empting the odd punchline, or echoing the jokes as you might when singing along to a favourite song, just to make plain to everyone else present as it played that you *knew* this LP *intimately* – exhaustively, even.

We can easily picture reverential listening sessions that are only a stone's throw, albeit with prevailing winds, from the description Francis Newton gave of earnest young jazz fans in 1959, (already pilfered for chapter four, if you skipped that one): 'a group of young men play one another records, repeating crucial passages until they are worn out, and then endlessly discuss their comparative merits'.

It's a pretty transferable image, admittedly, but surely what Billington's young peers liked was the sense that this was *their* show. That their parents, their elders and betters, the vicars, dons and crippled Second World War flying aces pilloried in it might not get it, or would at least express their mild disapproval. In actual fact, both the Queen and Macmillan went to see *Beyond the Fringe* and even the *Daily Mail* bigged up it as 'a sensation'. *Never Mind the Bollocks* it was not.[33] But it was young, fresh, smart and did represent a challenge to the tame variety show comedy that still dominated things then. Their only obvious predecessors on these shores were the Goons on BBC radio, who used zany catchphrases, surrealism, silly voices and ingenious sound effects to tremendous comic and quite socially subversive effect; LPs of their sketches were adored by future monarchs and Beatles alike.

One of the most famous routines from *Beyond the Fringe* was Peter Cook's pastiche of a political address by Harold Macmillan. In it he portrayed Macmillan as a mildly senile old duffer,

---

33 Forget raiding Johnny Rotten's Gunter Grove flat and arresting Malcolm McLaren for hosting a boat party on the Thames, if the establishment had really wanted to take the sting out of punk rock in 1977 they should have sent the Queen on an official visit to the 100 Club, replaced the commemorative 50p Jubilee coin with a safety pin, instantly adopted 'God Save the Queen' as an alternative national anthem and fitted all the corgis with spiky studded collars and dyed their fur bright green.

probably happier in a dusty library than attending to matters of high office, a portrayal Cook toned up rather then down on the night that the Prime Minister himself was in the audience.

In the key part of the sketch, Macmillan's supposed decrepitude is contrasted with the vim of President Kennedy – a metaphor for the state of their respective nations.

'I then went to America', Cook as Macmillan maintained, 'and there had talks with the young, vigorous president of that great country, and danced with his lovely lady wife. We talked of many things, including Great Britain's role in the world as an honest broker. I agreed with him, when he said no nation could be more honest, and he agreed with me, when I chafed him and said that no nation could be broker.'

Boom boom.

But America, at that moment, had made great strides in satirical humour too. As American radio and television had become dominated by sponsors, whose timidity in the 1950s far surpassed that of the BBC, a new breed of comic performer had sprung up, largely outside the mainstream media. And a weapon in their arsenal, for that very reason, had been the LP.

In a way, the commercial demands of American broadcasters that comedy should be 'for everyone', or at best not be offensive to the advertisers' idea of 'everyone', had inadvertently served as a catalyst for a new type of comedy that didn't bother to seek widespread approval. In fact in most instances, it was quite the reverse. The point was underscored by *Time* magazine's decision to label them The Sickniks and pronounce comics like Mort Sahl, Lenny Bruce and Shelley Berman 'a symptom of the 20th century's own sickness'. 'What the sickniks dispense', it wrote in July 1959, 'is partly social criticism liberally laced with cyanide, partly a Charles Addams kind of jolly ghoulishness, and partly a personal and highly disturbing hostility toward all the world.'

Many of these new, often college-educated comics, had started performing in small clubs and coffee houses frequented by students, sometimes in between equally outré jazz acts and Beat poets. Bypassing the usual showbiz venues and the restrictions demanded by radio and television networks, they were able to reach beyond their minuscule live circuit audiences by releasing their routines on LP. And a rather unlikely pioneer, Tom Lehrer, was among the first to blaze the sicknik trail.

Lehrer's forte – and if anyone had a *forte* it was definitely Lehrer – was the musical parody or the satirical song. A genre that in the 1950s, while capable of the odd acid sting in Noël Coward's manicured hands, more often than not resulted in mud rhyming with blood. Lehrer was rather different, injecting a much-needed dose of perversity into the form.

He was only ever an extremely reluctant performer and to this day remains comedy's Bartleby – preferring not to do his comic songs. For him, the LP was the ideal piece of technological kit, providing him with both the access to a wider public and a convenient barrier that could be erected to keep troublesome concert work at bay.

Lehrer started singing his comic songs at parties as an under-graduate at Harvard. 'Fight Fiercely Harvard', a frat-boy baiting spin on college sporting chants that brought the unlikely ex-clamations 'jolly', 'goody' and 'peachy' to the touchline, remains one of his most characteristic numbers. Though the subject matter of his songs would step well beyond the meagre concerns of the campus quad, the polite repartee and jovial fug of Massachusetts's common rooms, damp tweed and pipe tobacco, was a major component of his act – when he deemed to perform it. Addressing his audiences in the clipped tones of a don bemused by the idiocy of the contemporary world, Lehrer concerts were grounded in the tradition of the college smoker and would always carry the air of a wayward seminar about them. (The periodic table and the nineteenth-century mathematician Nicolai Ivanovich Lobachevksy would supply the meat for two of Lehrer's songs.)

Lehrer was part Cole Porter and part Mr Chips and his satirical ditties, whether he was mocking the Catholic Church in 'The Vatican Rag', Southern racists in 'I Wanna Go Back to Dixie', the boy scouts in 'Be Prepared' or American foreign policy in 'Send in the Marines', were compelling for being conveyed to the strains of tinkling ivories and with unwavering urbane civility. Lehrer was always more Broadway than Bowery – when he was a boy musicals had been his first love and he attended a summer camp with Stephen Sondheim – but the topicality of his lyrics meant that he came to the attention of the left-leaning folk journal *Sing Out!*, despite mocking beardy Old Smokie-singing types in 'The Folk Song Army', 'Clementine' and 'The Irish Ballard'.

Nevertheless, his songs were still deemed too 'crude' for radio and no recording companies appeared interested – not that he seemed to try especially hard to approach either with his wares at this stage. And so figuring that he had enough material and enough of a following in the Cambridge area to chance the expense, Lehrer cut his debut LP himself in January 1953 – making him one of the first, if not *the* first, singer-songwriters to successfully pull off the DIY bag. Booking himself into a Boston studio he found in the Yellow Pages, *Songs by Tom Lehrer* took around an hour and $15 to record. Pressing up 400 10-inches for $700, he hawked them to stores around the university. These first pressings carried the address of his college digs on the sleeve, as well as informing the curious that Lehrer 'earns a precarious living peddling dope to the local school children and rolling an occasional drunk'.

> NOTE: Although we have tried, by using a different cover, to delude you into thinking otherwise, this record contains exactly the same songs as the 10" LP SONGS BY TOM LEHRER (LF 1311). This one, though, has been padded out with Mr. Lehrer's allegedly droll commentary on the songs as well as some rather cloying audience reaction. These additions are quite unnecessary, but they enable us to charge more.

As many of his customers were students who carried the record home with them during spring and summer breaks, sharing the comic delights of their marvellous new purchase with their peers, news of the LP spread from campus to campus. Lehrer began receiving orders from Ivy Leaguers across the States. His album quickly became a cult item among American college kids, with those in the know initiating novices and ever afterward dropping his lyrics into conversations, as others would restage sketches from *Beyond the Fringe* or, later, Monty Python, or recite Derek and Clive's lines from *Withnail and I*. (*Songs by Tom Lehrer* would not be released in the UK until 1959, when he toured the country and the record was played in its entirety on the BBC. Prior to that, imported copies of the album, passed around like samizdat pamphlets, nevertheless ensured that Lehrer attracted a similarly loyal following among students here.)

At the point when the LP went into its third pressing, Lehrer did ask several major labels about taking the record on. All, apparently, passed. One executive at RCA confessed that they weren't prepared to risk adding such a controversial LP to their list in case it brought about a boycott of the cookers and fridges they also sold. (Rock 'n' roll, eh?)

Lehrer resigned himself to carrying on alone, and, content to let the LP do the talking, he continued to perform infrequently. Between 1955 and 1957, when he was drafted and worked on classified military projects, he was out of action entirely. When he emerged from the army, he was bemused to discover that his LP was still selling. Not only that, but he was now in demand from the same nascent college concert circuit that was playing host to Dave Brubeck and folk acts like Odetta and the Kingston Trio.

While never a contender for James Brown's (self-bestowed) crown as the hardest-working man in showbusiness (Lehrer mustered a mere sixteen concerts in 1958), he nevertheless gave up academia and spent the next three years touring. The distaste for the rigmarole of life as a jobbing performer would surface soon enough, though. In 1957, aged twenty-nine, he told *Newsweek*: 'I wouldn't want to do this all my life. It's okay while I'm still an adolescent.' After recording a live album at the Sanders Theatre in Harvard (*An Evening Wasted With Tom Lehrer*) and a 12-inch studio album (*More of Tom Lehrer*) in 1959 and giving a series of 'farewell' concerts at the Royal Festival Hall in London and a final concert in Glasgow on 2 July 1960, Lehrer scuttled back to grad school at Harvard. He surfaced again some four years later to contribute songs to the American version of *That Was the Week That Was*. The material from this period formed the basis for one final album, *That Was the Year That Was*, released in the same year that J.D. Salinger published his last story in the *New Yorker*. Apart from the odd Democratic fundraiser for McCarthy (Eugene not Joseph) in the early seventies, rather enigmatically, Lehrer pretty much disappeared from view . . . unless you were fortunate enough to be doing a maths course at MIT, or, later, Santa Cruz . . .

Around the time that Lehrer was dutifully posting the earliest batches of his LPs to the satirical song-starved, Mort Sahl, a twenty-four-year-old graduate of the University of Southern California, was making his first appearances at the hungry i club in San Francisco. Taking to the stage tieless, in a V-necked pullover and slacks, and wielding a rolled-up newspaper in his right hand, Sahl gave the impression of a man hurrying to find a picnic table devoid of wasps. What he would swat, in fact, night after night in mordant, staccato spun monologues was . . . well anyone and anything that was banal, corny, crooked and pompous in Eisenhower's America. As you can imagine, he was never short of things to say.

A million miles from the staid, gag-driven 'Take, My Wife, Please!' song and dance comedy routines that still prevailed, Sahl peppered his iconoclastic diatribes with the argot of Beat (chick, drag, gasser, cool it, bug, dig, weirdo). A contributor to the jazz magazine *Metronome*, he was closely aligned to the 'cool'

Californian jazz set. He toured the colleges with the Dave Brubeck Quartet and was a close friend of Brubeck saxophonist Paul Desmond – until Desmond's relationship with Sahl's first wife rather soured things. He wrote the liner notes for one of Desmond's albums (*The Paul Desmond Quartet with Don Elliott*) and his own LPs were released on the jazz labels Fantasy (home to Brubeck and co.) and Verve, founded by Norman Granz.

In keeping with the concert format of Granz's *Live at the Philharmonic* and Brubeck's college LPs, Sahl's first LP, *Mort Sahl Iconoclast: The Future Lies Ahead* was a straightforward recording of one of his evening shows at the hungry i (the 'i', incidentally, stood for 'intellectual'). It was the first 'live' stand-up comedy LP ever to be released when it appeared in 1955.

Sahl's fanbase, as *Time* reported in 1960, was 'narrow and his appeal . . . anything but universal'. In contrast with his contemporary Shelley Berman, a comic whose chief shtick was holding improvised imaginary telephone conversations with (unheard) interlocutors on stage and whose Sahl-endorsed albums sold over a million copies, his first four LPs sold a modest, if still bestselling, 125,000 copies. In his rather caustic memoir, *Heartland*, Sahl commented that Berman's records 'sold like magazines, and mine sold more like books'.

But his influence was vast. Every new round of jokes against President Eisenhower, Vice-President Nixon et al on each new LP were instantly quoted in magazines across America. And Sahl paved the way for a new school of comics – including Berman, Bob Newhart, Jonathan Winters, Mike Nichols and Elaine May – whose material would be satirical, personal, way-out, wacky or, as far as some were concerned in Lenny Bruce's case, sick and obscene, and were frequently most readily heard on LP.

There had, of course, always been funny records, but in line with the vaudeville tradition, songs rather than sketches or routines predominated. Noël Coward's concert revue LP *Live at Las Vegas* was, for instance, a bestseller in the mid-1950s. But what Sahl and Berman's records did was to create a whole new sit-down audience for stand-up comedy, as it were. Prior to that, record companies had assumed that LPs of jokes would quickly outstay their welcome. What they hadn't anticipated was the arrival of a type of comedy that was sophisticated enough to bear repeated listening. The range of references or allusions used sometimes made this necessary, if not mandatory, even to 'get' the in-jokes. Coupled to this was the enormous cultural capital to be gained in this epoch from knowing routines by these hip gun-slinging comedians by heart. And you'd have to give the LP more than a cursory play to hear everything that a comic said.

Also, records, as Bruce's biographer Albert Goldman commented, 'got comics into places they could never reach, like the college dorm or the Bohemian Beatnik pad'. As such, listening to this brand of comedy communally on record began to enjoy a kudos really previously only accorded to jazz among the young, the with-it and the happening.

In September 1960, *Playboy*, in a piece headed 'Hip Wits Disc Hits', presented a comic order of ceremonies that suggested 'serving up Nichols and May with cocktails, the Mort Sahl on disc for dinner, followed up by Lenny Bruce with the cognac' to produce 'a sort of do-it-yourself night club with a bill of entertainment that no single club in the country can match'.

But Sahl's career would stutter in the Kennedy era. At Papa Joe's request, he had penned (unpaid) a steady stream of jokes for the Democrat during his campaign for office. But his refusal to give the blue-eyed boy or his brother, Bobby, an easy ride once elected tested the patience of those who somehow believed the battle for a liberal America had been won. Having made political leaders a subject fit for satire in the US, he had to sit back and watch Vaughn Meader's timid Kennedy parody album, *The First Family*, sell 7.5 million copies in 1962, while his more astringent *The New Frontier* (released on Sinatra's Reprise label) withered on the vine. (Sahl's first line on the album was: 'Here we are on the New Frontier – Cuba!') If Meader's career suffered a fatal blow with Kennedy's assassination – as a mark of respect shops pulled copies of his LPs from their shelves and all his nightclub bookings were cancelled at a stroke – then Sahl's was no less devastated by his own preoccupation with the events in Dallas that day. An early dissenter from the official line that Lee Harvey Oswald was the lone gunman, he joined Jim Garrison, a district attorney in New Orleans, on a crusade to expose a political conspiracy behind the murder. Openly scornful of the findings of the Warren Report, he tried to ram home the absurdity of this Byzantian document by quoting lengthy and obtuse chunks from it in his live act. As riveting as chewing the fat about the CIA, gunmen and grassy knolls was, audiences responded to this by leaving in droves. In 1965, he earned just $13,000 – down from an estimated $600,000 at his peak just a few years earlier – and what had been a steady flow of LPs dried up. He issued just a single LP (*Anyway . . . Onward*) under LBJ and did not bounce back on record until *Sing a Song of Watergate . . . Apocryphal of Lie* in 1973.

Whereas Sahl has had the satisfaction of outliving many of his enemies, detractors, imitators, and fairweather friends and fans, Lenny Bruce was not so lucky. The main recipient – target if you like – of *Time*'s sicknik tag, Bruce died at forty, bankrupt and a junkie, in 1966, after spending the last six years of his life fending off obscenity charges and multiple arrests for possession of narcotics. A living embodiment of the joke 'Just Because I'm

Paranoid, It Doesn't Mean They Aren't Out to Get Me', Bruce had something of a persecution complex. But then he suffered some rather complex persecutions for a comedian ('He died', Phil Spector once commented, 'from an overdose of police').

Bruce was raised by his mother, Sadie, a bit-part actress who did comic turns in low-rent vaudeville fleapits and burlesque clubs to which young Lenny was invariably dragged along. Growing up among the carnival folk who, backstage at least, spoke and did as they pleased, would prove an invaluable education for a comic who would grow notorious for the saltiness of his tongue. As would a hitch in the merchant marines and years on the grimiest rungs of the showbiz ladder, often with his wife Holly Harlowe, a stripper-singer he met in 1951 – the same year he also fell head over heels for smack. First treading the beer crates as a standard Borscht Belt gag-monger, Bruce gradually pulled off the trick of putting the unfettered talk of single mothers, bored stagehands, casting-couch hardened showgirls, sailors in bunks, dopehead jazzers and loquacious barroom philosophers on stage. And Bruce was a spieler, first and foremost. To paraphrase Eliot, he do-doed on the police in different voices. Though less overtly (party) political than Sahl, his rangy surreal routines, which became increasingly autobiographical, left no social, sexual, racial hypocrisy unprobed. Organised religion was a speciality, with the Catholic Church in particular being something that did not endear him to the agents of the law who were mostly of Irish Catholic origin in places like Chicago and New York. To *Time* in 1959, he was the sick peddler of 'vicious barrage', who in their view 'merely shout[ed] angrily and tastelessly at the way of the world'. With around $100,000 a year from his nightclub dates and sales of the LPs *Interviews of Our Times*, *American* and tipping his hat to the sicknik label, *The Sick Humour of Lenny Bruce*, 'the most shocking comedian of our time' was laughing all the way to the bank.

By February 1961 he was performing to a full house at Carnegie Hall – the spoils of which were later released on a posthumous LP set. However, 1961 was also the year that things started to go wrong for Bruce. He was arrested for narcotics' possession that September, though the charges were subsequently dropped, but hauled in again just a month later for breaking the state of California's obscenity code after using the word 'cocksucker' in his act at the San Francisco Jazz Workshop. Representing a landmark for freedom of speech and First Amendment rights, he eventually won his case – blithely celebrating this Pyrrhic victory on his next LP, *To is a Proposition; Come is a Verb*. The law would be back and further arrests meted out for obscenity in Los Angeles, Hollywood Chicago, Miami and New York – where his work was deemed illegal for violating 'contemporary community standards' and for being 'offensive to the average person' – along with a slew of arraignments for drugs.

Where controversy had once been good for business, nightclub owners fearing for their licences now fought shy of Bruce. On some nights he was so loaded he could barely hold the mike; in any case, the comedian appeared to be losing his sense of humour. Comedy goers looking for titillation in the form of blue words and black humour frequently received white powder-powered citations from his ongoing legal battles. 'I'm not a comedian, I'm Lenny Bruce', he once told a reporter, and towards the end, this was, unfortunately, painfully near the mark.

Two months after giving his last performance at the Fillmore West in San Francisco, where he played with Frank Zappa and the Mothers of Invention, Bruce's prone naked body was discovered in the bathroom of his Hollywood Hills home on 3 August 1966. He'd overdosed on morphine; a syringe was still in his arm. The police, suddenly covetous of press freedoms, allowed photographers to snap the dismal scene. A genuine obscenity, masquerading as news, thereby made it onto front pages around the world.

Throughout the following summer, the so-called Summer of Love, reissues of Bruce's LPs found new ears as the counterculture – ever prone to defining themselves by buying things – claimed him. His face stared out at stoned hippies everywhere from the cover of that year's must-have LP, the Beatles' *Sgt. Pepper's Lonely Hearts Club Band.* The comic who, on a trip to Peter Cook's satirical Establishment club had been deported from England in 1963 as an 'undesirable alien', was sneaking into respectable abodes everywhere at the bidding of a group who, as loveable moptops, had signed to a label famous for its comedy records and were still being produced by a man who'd made LPs with the Goons and, naturally, *Beyond the Fringe*

Chapter Seven

BEAT LESS

A music journalist friend of mine once vowed to write a book where the Beatles were relegated to a monstrously serpentine footer that crested along the bottom of every single page. It could then, he believed, be marketed as the only study of British popular music where the Fab Four appeared as a footnote. As you may have guessed, I am something of an admirer of the footnote, and would have dearly loved to have thought of this. Although his book has yet to see the light of day, I value the friendship too much to nick the idea. But in essence it captures the oil slick of ink that it's virtually mandatory to devote to the Beatles when writing about pop – and never more so when considering the album.

To think of the Beatles is, as often as not, to think of a Beatles LP.

The LP-ness of the group is at the core of their identity – a component as essential as the number four. Liverpool. Those boots. The hair. George Martin. This is, of course, to be retrospectively wise. But during the band's lifespan the mere phrase 'Beatles LP' did enjoy a kind of privileged, totemic existence. To use those words was to conjure up a Platonic form of pop, one with which few rival practitioners could be compared or contrasted. (Reviewing the *Roger the Engineer* LP in 1966, *Disc* magazine stated: 'In their own quiet and highly individual way the Yardbirds have sprung something of a mini-Beatles on us with this album.') Simultaneously, the phrase was utilised as a mnemonic deployed – lazily, usually – by commentators, novelists, poets and judges keen to encapsulate, or castigate, the times that were a-changin'.

And not without good reason, on both counts. Beatles LPs were, after all, biannual events and such recurring fixtures of the holiday season that you could turf the decorations out of the loft to their release dates. Commenting on *Rubber Soul* on 24 December 1965, the *Financial Times* felt duty-bound to warn its readers, in a tone that mixed weary disdain with a knowing complicity, that whether they liked it or not, this latest Beatles LP was 'bound to be forced' on them 'sometime this Christmas anyway'.

In Britain, over a period of just seven years, there were officially twelve studio LPs: a set of recordings including a fistful that it would be hard to argue didn't raise expectations of what a 'pop album' was or should strive to be like, at least in the orthodox collective critical consciousness. These were LPs that musically, and equally importantly, visually, tinkered about with the idiom. Not uniquely so, obviously, but nevertheless they were discs that, for good or ill, encouraged others to do the same. They also, to the lingering chagrin of many, continue – sometimes unfairly – to eclipse others simply by dint of having been made . . . Yawn, put another record on by . . . the Beatles.

Rather like Shakespeare's plays, they occupy a seemingly unassailable position in the culture at large, one that naturally enough requires the occasional debunk. However, to say, as commentators periodically are wont to do, that pop took a wrong turn with the Beatles, is to be living comfortably beyond their times and fully armed, as much by a process of continual osmosis, with the spoils of their legacy. To fully understand the impact of the 'Beatles LP', we need to go to its roots: England, 1963.

As Paul McCartney's official biographer Barry Miles has observed, 'it requires a leap of the imagination to return to the innocent days of 1963, when the Beatles recorded and released their first two long-playing albums'. In many respects, England in 1963 remained a country lodged in the 1950s. It was only eighteen months earlier, for instance, that EMI stopped production of 78 records in the UK, by which time the format had long been consigned to the dustbin in the United States (though they lingered in India, South Africa and the Philippines, and consequently rare Indian pressings of Beatles' singles on 78 do a brisk trade among collectors). And while LP sales in America had already overtaken those of singles by 1960, it would be 1968 before this occurred in Britain. Until the Beatles, for many people in this country LPs constituted substantial and exotic purchases – though with an uncanny synchronicity that could not have harmed sales of their first two albums, the reduction in 1963 of purchase tax on all records from 45 per cent to 25 per cent rendered them increasingly affordable to British consumers. However, in the film *Billy Liar*, released that summer and starring Tom Courtenay as Billy Fisher, an undertaker's clerk with an often tenuous grip on reality, their simple plural could still serve as a potent euphemism for gone-to-the-dogs modernity.

Cornered by his elderly boss, Councillor Duxbury, Fisher deftly forestalls questions about a stash of pilfered Christmas calendars concealed in newspaper by passing off the bundle as a set of 'gramophone records' or 'LPs'. The individual letters of the latter phrase are heavily stressed, pronounced as if Fisher were speaking to a small child and they duly work their intended magic. Faced with such a technological marvel of the modern age, Duxbury is off, set swiftly adrift in a litany of half-remembered bygone things (male voice choirs, chapels, trams) that chunks of 12-inch vinyl and their ilk have heartlessly cast aside in the name of progress . . .

Okay, I am exaggerating the significance of the scene, though elsewhere in the picture, among an array of signifiers that mark Julie Christie as a liberated 'with it' contemporary kind of girl (including an ability to swing a tartan duffle bag insouciantly while skipping across a zebra crossing, hitchhiking, agreeing to have sex in a municipal park and flat hair), is the nonchalant I'll-give-it-a-whirl way that she readily agrees to do a stint on the classical desk in a hi-fi shop . . . but while *Billy Liar* is fictional, as a snapshot of the world into which the first Beatles LPs tumbled, it is rather revealing.

Shot on location mainly in and around Bradford and heavily influenced by the French new wave and *cinéma vérité*, it captures a northern metropolis – and a nation, no less – hurtling towards a future of high-rise towers, plastic coffins, supermarket shopping and suede shoes. A newly affluent country being perked up by gleaming Wimpy burger bars – all chrome fittings, formica tables and plastic tomato-shaped ketchup dispensers – presided over by lippy, beehive-hairstyled platinum blondes. Dustys with grease-stained menus, if you will. Eateries where the sizzle of cheeseburgers and the hiss of a frothy coffee machine would forever be complemented by the sounds of Shadows-style electric guitars 'ding a ding ding dinging' from a tranny on the counter.

But despite these innovations, resolutely it remained a land where nice girls apparently 'didn't' until they were married (and adverts for free family planning pamphlets in the *Melody Maker* during the period carried the proviso that applicants confirmed: 'I am or am about to be married'). Tearooms serving elevenses to the strains of live piano and strings valiantly went about their business as if Ivor Novello or Eric Coates were expected in at any moment. Popular tunes were rationed, and only begrudgingly doled out to housewives on the request shows of the BBC's *Light Programme*. And the conclusion to a working week, for the majority of provincial youngsters, consisted, as it had for their parents, of a Saturday night shindig at the local Roxy, where a full dance band might well be knocking out a conga as if Desi Arnaz remained the height of musical fashion.

As though in a bizarrely prophetic urge to fulfil Larkin's adage that sexual intercourse began in 1963, sex is everywhere in *Billy Liar*. This is the Lawrentian north, after all: a region that since Alan Sillitoe's *Saturday Night and Sunday Morning* and the Lady Chatterley trial had become a byword for unfettered, earthy promiscuity.[34] But while the sex in *Billy Liar* is upfront and down to earth, it is dealt with far more casually than before. No truculent lathe operator impregnates a workmate's wife here.

Billy, in turn, is not a 'Whatever People Say I Am, That's What I'm Not' angry either. He's a daydreamer and an unlikely lothario. When the adult world gets too much for him, he retreats into fantasy. Far from putting childish things away, once married he yearns to preserve a green-doored playroom where he and his wife (while evidently enjoying full conjugal relations elsewhere) will spend wet afternoons messing about with model trains and paper uniforms. (And all of this four years before Sgt. Pepper, I hear you say . . .)

Here he (and Liz) sum up a pivotal change in the early 1960s, as exemplified by the Beatles, where to be young (and preferably working class and/or northern) was not only bliss but *the* most desirable state. And where the mores of culture were being reshaped, from top down to bottom up. (As the Rolling Stones manager Andrew Loog Oldham put it, '1963, and the 60s as we knew them began'.) The fashion designer Mary Quant, herself widely if mistakenly regarded as 'classless', was on a similar wavelength, expressing her own distaste at the idea of growing up: 'To me,' she confessed, later, 'adult appearance was very unattractive, alarming and terrifying, stilted, confined and ugly. It was something I knew I didn't want to grow into. I saw no reason why childhood should not last forever. I wanted everyone to retain the grace of a child, so I created clothes that allowed people to run, to jump, to leap to retain this precious freedom.'

---

34 It would take that summer's Profumo scandal, with its prime southern locations, call girls, Russian spies and Westminster politicians to finally kill off the north's stranglehold on morally compromising sexual relations.

The Beatles, who would spend hour upon hour leaping about for the cameras in the coming years, were perfectly in sync with their times. They were rather androgynous in appearance, working class and northern. 'This working-class explosion was all happening,' Paul McCartney recalled in 1997, 'and we were very much part of it. Making it okay to be common . . . we were the wacky chappies from up north.' Their influence was so pronounced that on 22 June, the *Melody Maker* advised its readers that THE WAY TO SUCCESS IN THE POP WORLD in 'our classless country' was to 'get an ACCENT'.

Just as the Northern Wave films of Tony Richardson and John Schlesinger spoke about sex frankly, so did the Beatles. The standard conventions of 'Love' in song were adhered to, tiresomely on occasion, but there was an honesty that had been rare in British pop before them. The first Beatles LP, only confirming Larkin's thesis, opens with the unambiguously sexual 'I Saw Her Standing There'. The first lines: 'Well she was just seventeen/ You know what I mean' put the 'her' of the title safely over the age of consent (you *know* what I mean?). Their fondness for personal pronouns nevertheless established a chummy rapport with their young audience, just as the throwaway 'my friend' in 'Can't Buy Me Love', may, as the music critic and Beatles discographer Ian MacDonald has contended, have summed up 'the casual etiquette of coolly unromantic new age'.

But as a contemporary writer in the *Sunday Times* identified, while 'sexual emancipation' was 'a factor in the phenomenon' there was 'none of Presley's overt sexual attack, nor for that matter any of the "smoochy" adult sensuality of Sinatra' about the group as such. Their sexuality, in line with Quant's dollies, was, carefree and distinctly modern.

By a cunning coincidence, when he's not looking for modern love, skirt-chasing fantasiser Billy Liar is also part of a songwriting duo, Crabtree and Fisher. Their composition 'Twis-terella' (cue chorus: 'She doesn't have a fellar') is a lame big-band attempt to piggyback on the early sixties dance craze – a craze then being mined to the point of exhaustion by Chubby Checker in a series of diminishingly interesting elbow-dislo-caters ('The Twist', 'Let's Twist Again', 'Twistin' USA', 'Slow Twistin'', 'Don't Knock the Twist', 'Twist It Up', 'Teach Me to Twist', 'Twistin' Around the World', 'It's A Mad Mad Twist My Masters', 'Twist Me Over Baby And Do Me From Behind', etc).[35]

But then *everybody* was doing the Twist – from Sam Cooke ('Twistin' the Night Away') and Joey Dee and The Starliters ('Peppermint Twist') to King Curtis and His Noble Knights ('Soul Twist') and Cyril Stapleton and His Showband ('Come Twistin''). Even Ray Charles, whose R&B songbook had pro-vided the Beatles with a good deal of source material, and whose irrepressible 1962 *Modern Sounds in Country and Western Music* LP did as much as anyone to shake up American music's multi-racial map, was lumbered with a Twist LP. His former label, Atlantic, opportunistically bundled up some of his choice sides, 'What'd I Say' (a Merseybeat staple) and 'I'm Movin' On', on *Do the Twist with Ray Charles*. (In 2005, Jools Holland, for whom it was the first Ray Charles record he'd ever owned, recalled that it 'was a crazy record: it had instructions on how to do the twist on the back of it, about how you dance and where you put your feet'.) The Beatles, with their spirited recording of Medley and Russell's 'Twist and Shout' on their debut LP, were not immune either.

The Twist phenomenon exemplified the degree to which, in the wake of rock and roll, high school fads, gimmicks and attention-

35 Okay, I made the last two up, but really . . .

grabbing novelty held sway in the early 1960s. According to George Melly, one of the more significant after-effects of the Twist craze was an increase in dancing to records, and in turn the rise of discotheques, as traditional nightclub bands *à la* Billy Liar's were unable to master the reedy attack and volume of a crunchy, heavily amplified 45.

Naturally enough, the Beatles were viewed – and treated – as another passing fad, though writing in the *Melody Maker* on 9 February 1963, Chris Roberts declared that 'a hefty shot of their exciting music is just what the meandering pop scene needed'. For starters, there was Liverpool. Those boots. The hair. George Martin etc., etc. At the outset, the latter's track record of producing discs for comedians – the Goons and Peter Sellers, Flanders and Swann, and Bernard Cribbins, among others – led to them being erroneously, albeit briefly, cast as another of Martin's novelty acts by senior executives at EMI. One suit, upon hearing the band's name, is reputed to have asked, 'Is it really Spike Milligan disguised?'

The comedy records were nevertheless an inestimable factor in the group obtaining their contract. The band, Lennon in particular, were huge Goons fans, and humour rather than music proved the inaugural bonding point between producer and musicians when they met for the first time in Studio Two, Abbey Road on 6 June 1962. Famously, a quip by George Harrison about not liking Martin's tie helped to transform the outcome of this audition, establishing a jokey rapport that persuaded the Parlophone man that, raw as they were, this group had 'something'. He would later state that though 'very bubbly people' and 'great fun to be with', at that stage he thought they were 'rotten composers'. But before any of this, manager Brian Epstein had been advised to visit Martin in his offices in Manchester Square by Syd Coleman of the music publishers Ardmore & Beachwood, precisely because he'd had some success 'with the most unlikely recording acts'. And with rejections from Pye, Philips, Decca, and Columbia (EMI's pop wing) at that juncture, the Beatles looked a *most* unlikely recording act.

Dick Rowe, the A&R man at Decca, has been immortalised for rejecting the Beatles with the demeaning 'guitar bands are on their way out, Mr Epstein' – a line he himself may never have uttered. (Since he signed Brian Poole and the Tremolos instead, a group who showed no noticeable shortage of long-necked stringed instruments, it's debatable.) And leaving aside, for the moment, what possible motives Epstein and his beatsters could have had for publicly humiliating someone who'd dismissed them so callously, his words (or whoever's they were) can nevertheless be taken, salt to taste, as a barometer of the general received opinion about the direction of pop within the British record industry at the time.

The pop industry continued to be a singles- and song-led business – teenagers, its target market, were not expected, nor thought readily able to afford, to buy LPs. The supply and demand of tunes and artists were policed in Britain by many of the same light entertainment merchants that had run things since the war. After the initial shake-up and rattle of American rock 'n' roll, pop business as usual had resumed and hoards of indistinguishable and often undistinguished off-the-peg pop singers roamed the British charts with virtual impunity during this period. And heaven I am sure it was to be alive, if you were a short-armed fatty on Denmark Street, a clutch of tearjerkers about 'Darlin's', 'Angels' or 'Johnnies' to peddle in your sweaty palms.

For any pop performer wanting to extend their career beyond a few brief months in this viperous climate, diversions into more grown-up material and/or legitimate showbiz were not merely prudent but near enough mandatory. And this is the path that Brian Epstein certainly had in mind for the Beatles and pursued with more mettle – or more success – with Cilla Black, the Cavern coat-check girl turned singing sensation. Asked about the follow-up to her number one hit 'Anyone Who Had A Heart' in the *NME* in March 1964, Cilla said: 'It'll have to be upbeat. Real w*ild* R&B if I can get away with it. I love that. And I'd like to do a calypso and blues. Oh, I'd love to do all kind of way out stuff if they'll let me.' The 'if they'll let me' says it all, and it was not quite to be, though Cilla, of course, went on to enjoy a long and fruitful chart and light-entertainment career.

Lennon and McCartney implicitly understood the score, although they themselves were ultimately able to reject such a trajectory. In their first interview for the *NME* printed on 15 February 1963, both expressed a burning desire to write a musical. Quizzed elsewhere, they repeatedly presented themselves as old-school songsmiths for hire, telling journalists that they'd 'written about 100 songs' – though they modestly conceded 'some of them are rubbish, of course'.[36] Helen Shapiro, the sixteen-year-old belter of 'Please Don't Treat Me Like a Child' and 'Walking Back to Happiness', on whose national tour the group spent the opening months of 1963 performing fifth on the bill, was one of the very first singers upon whom they tried (unsuccessfully) to foist a ballad.

The nation's indigenous rock stars had, in any case, always tended to veer towards the motherable. Larry Parnes, British pop's original Svengali, dubbed 'Mr Parnes, Shillings and Pence' by Fleet Street, prided himself on his ability to turn out boy-next-door stars that British teenagers, evidently a nervy breed back then, could identify with. After successfully transforming Thomas Hicks, a toothy mop-haired boy from Bermondsey, into Tommy Steele – 'England's answer to Elvis' – Parnes equipped a line of gawky kids with volatile-sounding names and (often) fleeting appearances in the hit parade.[37]

By 1963, Steele himself, in keeping with Parnes' master plan, was doing panto and inflicting cockney music hall numbers on

36 At the peak of Beatlemania, Paul McCartney tried to snare Frank Sinatra with one of his compositions. Somewhat unfortunately, given its intended singer's history, the number was entitled 'Suicide' and Ol' Blue Eyes – assuming it to be a joke at his expense, apparently – rejected it out of hand.

37 Parnes' professional exploits, along with his fondness for housing an ever-replenished bevy of young male hopefuls in his Cromwell Road pad, were derided by Peter Sellers in 'So Little Time' on his Martin-produced *Songs for Swinging Sellers* LP. 'These boys stay here willing because to them I'm . . . I'm almost a second father, we enjoy a very beautiful relationship, beautiful, Miss Lisbon,' Major Ralph Ralph, the sketch's horsetrader-turned-pop-impresario tells a bemused interlocutor. The Beatles had their own brush with Parnes when they were hired as the backing band for Johnny Gentle, on a desultory tour of north-east Scotland in May 1960, where singer and group frequently came to blows.

the general public. Billy Fury the genuine rocker in Parnes' 'stable of stars' and the first British artist of that ilk to furnish an entirely self-penned LP, *The Sound of Fury* (1960), was telling *Disc* that he intended 'to make an album of spirituals and jazz'. In the wake of the Beatles, a retreat from music altogether and into the sanctuary of his aviary would, alas, follow.

And then there was Cliff Richard and the Shadows.

Curl lipped and oil quiffed, Richard offered a far more compelling brand of Elvis impersonation than Steele ever did. 'I copied him quite consciously,' he stated in 1973. 'When people told me I looked like Elvis it was the biggest compliment they could pay me.' Difficult as it is to believe today, Richard was considered so salacious in Britain in 1958 that the *NME* denounced his appearance on the TV show *Oh Boy* as 'hardly the kind of performance any parent could wish their children to witness'. The perception (or misperception) of Richard as a teenage wildcat was not limited to these damp islands, either. In a series of photographs taken in Berne and Zurich by Karlheinz Weinberger during the late 1950s, Cliff's face adorns belt-buckles and leather jackets worn, with evident pride, by members of Switzerland's nascent Hell's Angels – The Lice-Infected Ones or 'die Verlausten', as they were known.

When Norrie Paramor came to record Cliff's debut album, *Cliff*, for Columbia at Abbey Road in February 1959, he taped it live over two nights in front of a specially invited audience of 200 fans – a move that was clearly intended to harness all the giddy potency of Richard 'sending' the kids. Either that or it was a heartlessly cynical exercise to guarantee that at least 200 people went out and bought the record. In any event, four years later George Martin, himself keen to siphon some of the Beatles' on-stage effervescence, briefly considered recording 'Please Please Me' under virtually identical conditions. 'I am thinking of recording their first LP at the Cavern Club,' he informed *Disc*. 'If we can't get the sound right then we might do it somewhere else in Liverpool, or bring an invited audience into the studio. The Beatles told me they work better in front of an audience.' The scheme was deemed impractical in the end. And as is well documented, Martin plumped instead for getting the group to blast through a set of their live standards almost as if it were a show, recording ten songs for the album in one thirteen-hour session on 11 February 1963.

Basking in the newly acquired fame that such recordings had afforded him, Lennon would take some relish in telling Michael Braun that Cliff 'was everything we hated in pop'. And as well he might, though back in Liverpool in 1958, he and McCartney had devoted several hours to mastering the guitar intro to 'Move It', Richard's barnstorming debut. But then Cliff the outrageous rocker had not lasted long. By his second LP, *Cliff Sings*, Richard was already tackling string-drenched ballads and exuding a distinct whiff of wholesomeness. Respect for the fans. Sobriety. The formative childhood years in India. A subsequent impoverished, if genteel, adolescence in Cheshunt. A passion for study, hard work and a novel sultana- and coconut-laced meat dish, obliquely referred to as 'a curry'. These became the dull, recurring and distinctly patronising leitmotifs of Cliff interviews – and full-blown Christian evangelism, Eurovision and tennis was still to come.

The one-time teenage delinquent in the 'social issue' picture *Serious Charge* (1959) was now starring in full-colour musical comedies. And full-colour musical comedies to boot where he was depicted saving youth clubs from the clutches of rapacious property developers. Or personally avenging de Gaulle's veto of Britain's entry into the common market by setting up profitable Anglo-American tourist ventures on the continent.

For a while, the public lapped it up: *Summer Holiday* was the second biggest general release at the UK box office in 1963. So did the music press: on 16 February 1963 *Disc* pronounced the soundtrack album to *Summer Holiday* 'a landmark . . . in recording history'. Flagging up the Bachelor Boy's unequivocal move into the mainstream, they declared 'Cliff's best and the best of the whole set, is "A Swingin' Affair" . . . It literally is a swinging affair on all counts, moving along on a solid instrumental raft provided by Stanley Black and the ABS Orchestra. This calibre of material and interpretation puts Cliff within sight of the Sinatras, the Grecos, and Damones of the pop singing world.' Solid instrumental rafts? Vic Damone? Frank Sinatra? This was enough to cause Swiss bikers to choke on their muesli. 'It became', Cliff conceded many years later, 'very, very "family", for me.'

To most then, rock 'n' roll appeared commercially on its uppers. George Martin purposely excluded the Beatles' covers of Little Richard and Chuck Berry from *Please Please Me*, though they were staples in their Cavern shows, presumably on the grounds they were old hat. Berry, at that point, was languishing in prison. Eddie Cochran and Buddy Holly were dead – though both continued to exert a considerable influence from beyond the grave.

Holly was a singer who Lennon and McCartney continued to revere, the gangly, bespectacled Lubbock rocker having established the inspiring precedent of writing many of his own numbers on the 1957 album *The "Chirping" Crickets*. 'We started in the Buddy Holly days', John Lennon informed *Disc* in February 1963, 'when everyone thought they could turn out simple songs like his and we've been writing ever since.'

Others, however, even at this late date, sought rather more fiendish schemes to harness the dearly departed Holly's muse for the contemporary pop market. In May 1963, in the week the Beatles *Please Please Me* album straddled the top spot, a position it would hold for the next thirty weeks until finally being bumped by *With the Beatles*, the Buddy Holly LP *Reminiscing* was released. Compiled from old demo tapes with fresh backing tracks by The Fireballs spliced on by Holly's estranged producer Norman Petty, it was heralded as the apogee of studio wizardry in its day. Elsewhere, it was castigated as a money-spinner of dubious legitimacy and taste.[38]

Meanwhile, in his studio above a shop on the Holloway Road, Joe Meek, the independent record producer whose preoccupations with the otherworldly extended to masterminding 'Telstar', the Tornados' ethereal sounding wasp-in-a-jam-jar hymn to the first global communications satellite, and wandering around churchyards at midnight to tape mewling stray cats, regularly conferred with Holly via a Ouija board.

Holly, it must therefore be assumed, sanctioned the producer's 'Tribute to Buddy Holly', a hit for Mike Berry and The Outlaws in 1961 despite a ban by the BBC. Along with the Cochran-inspired 'Just Like Eddie', a solo vehicle two years later for Heinz Burt, the bottle-blond Tornados bass player who Meek had groomed for stardom. That Heinz possessed scant musical abilities and couldn't really sing did nothing to diminish Meek's faith in his protégé. Sadly, 'Just Like Eddie' would be Heinz's only hit; two weeks after it entered the top twenty, the Beatles' 'She Loves You' performed a blitzkrieg on everything that had gone before it. As a character in Jake Arnott's novel *The Long Firm* ruefully observes: 'Something new was happening but Heinz definitely wasn't it.'

Notoriously, Meek subsequently derided the Beatles as 'a bunch of noise copying other people's music' – a charge that holds some

---

38 'Free as a Bird', a single that the then remaining three Beatles recorded in 1995 with John Lennon vocals culled from a old demo tape caused similar bellyaching. 'It's a purely commercial exercise devoid of musical enthusiasm, youthfulness or any of the other qualities the Beatles used to possess', was the pop pundit Jonathan King's verdict.

water. The group were, and McCartney remains, fairly open about borrowing from songs by black artists they liked – work by Ray Charles, Smokey Robinson, The Marvelettes and the Shirelles were favourites – and as well they might. But the stream of far rarer American R&B records that Liverpool sailors imported were also key. Largely built on (invidious) trade with Virginia, Liverpool is the closest city to the Americas and up until the early 1960s, it remained one of the few places where such records could be easily heard and bought. Motown did not have a proper English distribution until 1963, the same year that Pye began to issue recordings of American blues label Chess, home to Chuck Berry, in the UK. The 'blackness' of the Beatles' sound led to the *Melody Maker* dubbing them 'the boys from Nashpool' and their fidelity to black music was actually saluted by Little Richard. 'Man, those Beatles are fabulous. If I hadn't seen them I'd never would have dreamed they were white. They have a real authentic negro sound.'

And initially passed over by Capitol Recording, the first Beatles records – and their first album, *Introducing the Beatles* – were released in the States on the small black-owned Vee-Jay label.

That the Beatles were widely described as an R&B band by the British press in these early months of fame tends to get overlooked, the phrase being more regularly associated with the wave of 'blues' groups – Blues Incorporated, the Graham Bond Association and the Rolling Stones – that emerged in parallel to the Merseybeat scene in London at that time.

The Rolling Stones' subsequent public image – truculent where the Beatles were cooperative, etc. – was coupled with a repertoire that was thought by some to be more 'authentic' because it stuck much closer to – in other words, was directly copied from – black American blues (the inherent contradictions of this notion always rather escaped the purists). But where the Beatles managed against the odds and their backgrounds to achieve respectability, the Stones against the odds and their backgrounds managed to gain notoriety for being disreputable – much of this down to the concerted efforts of their manager Andrew Loog Oldham, who, in his *Clockwork Orange*-esque sleeve notes for their second LP, exhorted the cash-strapped to roll blind beggars for the 'bread' to buy the record.[39]

Muddy Waters toured England in 1960. And in 1962, an American Folk Blues Festival package had toured Europe, with the Rolling Stones pitching up to see John Lee Hooker, T-Bone Walker, Sonny Terry and Brownie McGhee when it arrived in London. But in the way that rock tribute acts first sprang up in gig-deprived Australia, the early Rolling Stones and many of their cohorts existed merely to pay homage to the Chicago blues in the absence of the real thing. The Stones were even named after a Muddy Waters song, and their creative imitation was intended as an honest and proselytising form of flattery. 'We wanted to sell records for Jimmy Reed, Muddy, John Lee Hooker,' Keith Richards recalled in 1989. 'We were disciples – if we could turn people on to that, then that was enough. That was the total original aim.'

And it was the ownership of a stash of rare blues LPs that was crucial to the Stones' formation in the first place. Richards, an academic wastrel, had, much like Lennon, been able to stave off entry into the dreary nine-to-five world of work by enrolling at Art School. At Sidcup School of Art, the former choirboy and Dartford Ted fell in with a group of likeminded students who worshipped blues players like Big Bill Broonzy. One morning, on his commute to college, Richards happened to step into the same railway carriage as Mike Jagger, a distant local acquaintance from primary school days who was then en route to the LSE. It is

39 The notes caused the longed-for outrage. Mrs Gwen Mathews of the Bournemouth Blind Aid Association called on their record company, Decca, to change the offending cover, a request they happily complied with.

unlikely they would have exchanged anything except wary glances of recognition had Jagger not been carrying, rather ostentatiously, a pile of imported blues albums under his arm. Richards spied 'four or five albums' by 'Chuck Berry, Little Walter, Muddy Waters'. For those few in the know in England then, this was an enviable hoard of American musical booty. Compelled, as members of a secret religious sect might be, to address a fellow acolyte, Richards struck up a conversation with Jagger. Their exchange ended cordially: Keith invited Mike to come round for a cup of tea, and Mike in turn suggested Keith should tag along to a rehearsal of a little blues group he'd put together with Dick Taylor, a mutual friend, later of the Pretty Things. And the rest, as they say, is now worth more than the GDP of some small nations.[40]

40 Stones founder and guitarist Brian Jones was a no less conspicuous consumer of blues albums, and brought one especially influential LP into the group's mix – Robert Johnson's *King of the Delta Blues Singers*. In an arc that rather sadly ended up mirroring Jones' own brief life, Johnson had died in his late twenties and in murky circumstances. Long purported to have sold his soul to the devil for a mastery of the guitar that even terrified a young Muddy Waters, Johnson was poisoned by a jealous husband, a wronged woman or a bitter rival, or some combination of all three, very probably. In the spicier versions of the Johnson legend, on the night in question, the guy with the horns and the tail had simply called in to collect on his deal, and the twenty-nine sides of plaintive, devilish blues Johnson left behind should never be played on full moons. Selections from these crumbling and much-sought-after 78s from 1936 and 1937 were belatedly gathered up and issued by John Hammond at Columbia on an LP in 1961. Hammond gave a copy of the album, *King of the Delta Blues Singers*, to Bob Dylan. The LP duly wound up on the cover of *Bringing It All Back Home*, but not before Dylan had sucked long and hard on the marrow of Johnson's oeuvre, as, naturally enough, would the Stones, and another Johnson devotee, Eric Clapton. None of which should be held against Johnson himself, naturally, nor put you off getting this LP.

All of this borrowing needs to be understood in the context of England then, a far less multicultural and cosmopolitan country than it is now, and an unthinkingly racist one in lots of ways – the number one album in Britain for Christmas 1962 was the truly egregious *On Stage With the Black and White Minstrels*. This 'blackface' variety television show then attracted 16.5 million viewers in Britain each week. (In 1961 it walked away with the Golden Rose of Montreux and the Press Award as the 'World's Top TV Show'.)

But it does seem something that at least Paul McCartney was aware of. On the eve of their first American tour, his chief worry was that they would be surplus to requirements, in a way that they clearly weren't in the then overwhelmingly monocultural UK. 'What are we going to give them', he is reported to have asked Phil Spector, 'that they don't already have?'

If Buddy Holly, Eddie Cochran's and Joe Meek's tragedies were that they died too soon, in the early 1960s, Elvis Presley looked seriously in danger of outstaying his welcome. Shorn of his sideburns, a Samson blindly following his manager 'Colonel' Tom Parker's orders, the King had been knocking out one teeth-grindingly dreadful movie after another since leaving the army in 1960 – to the horror of many former admirers. John Lennon pointedly took the opportunity to liken Elvis to Bing Crosby when the Beatles were guests on television panel show *Juke Box Jury* in 1963. The matter obviously needled Lennon. During a far from easy encounter between the group and singer at Elvis's Bel Air home in August 1965, Lennon irked Presley by demanding to know why he didn't go back to making rock 'n' roll records. Elvis reputedly blamed the tightness of his moviemaking schedule.

That the accompanying soundtrack LPs from Elvis's pictures did reasonable business arguably played a bigger part in stymying the quality of his musical output than the execrable movies themselves. An entire album of original material that Presley had recorded in Nashville in May 1963 as a follow-up to the previous summer's *Pot Luck* LP, was, for example, quietly shelved by Parker. The Colonel had surmised, not unreasonably, that if they could make money from half-baked toss like *Girls, Girls, Girls*, then soundtracks really *were* where it was at. (These Nashville recordings, on the whole squandered as fillers on various soundtrack discs and as B-sides, were finally reunited and issued as *The Lost Album* in 1990.)

To be fair to Parker, he was only in step with the market. The week that *Please Please Me* was released in the UK, *Girls, Girls, Girls* stood at number three in *Melody Maker*'s top ten album chart. Of the other nine entries, a further three were soundtrack LPs: *West Side Story*, *South Pacific*[41] and at number one *Summer Holiday*.

The Beatles own foray into the genre, *A Hard Day's Night*, released the following July and the only one of the group's albums to be comprised solely of Lennon and McCartney songs, itself speaks volumes about the medium's prosperity then. In a grave lapse of judgement that illustrates just how little EMI and Capitol thought of the Beatles' long-term prospects, neither company ring-fenced soundtrack albums in their contracts with the group. United Artists, discovering this loophole, pounced. Walter Shenson, their appointed movie producer in London, was told bluntly: 'We need a film for the express purpose of getting a soundtrack album. Just make sure that there are enough new songs for a soundtrack album and don't go over budget.' So, in

---

41 From the autumn of 1958, the soundtrack of *South Pacific* topped the British album charts for seventy consecutive weeks and actually regained the spot in 1961 and 1962, thus spending a total of 115 weeks – i.e. over two years – at number one.

essence, the film was a loss leader for a record. The utter skinflintery of the project was further underlined by the decision to film in black and white to pare costs down to the barest minimum. From this unlikely combination of con-tractual negligence and thrift arose a film of genuine and lasting import.

Kicking off with THAT chord, a G eleventh suspended fourth where every ounce of 'driiiinnnnnnnng' buzzes from the strings, *A Hard Day's Night* instantly announced itself as a very different beast from the usual pop fare. Intermittently zany but shot with the same cut-and-dash realism as the Northern Wave pictures (in the opening sequence on the station platform, Norm, with his carton of milk, could almost be picking up a baton left by Tom Courtenay at the end of *Billy Liar*) director Richard Lester adeptly portrayed the insane bustle of the Beatles' daily lives. Wilfred Brambell, playing Paul's (pretend) Irish grandfather, delivers the most knowingly acute line in the entire picture when he complains: 'I thought I was supposed to be getting a change of scenery and so far I've been in a train and a room, and a car and a room and a room and a room and a room.' (Similarly, the film's French title, *Quatre Garçons dans le Vent*, which translates literally as 'Four Men in the Wind', lacks the buoyancy of the English Ringoism, but as a reductive summary it is curiously bang-on.)

The script was the work of Alun Owen, the author of the gritty Liverpool-based TV drama *No Trains to Lime Street* and a seasoned hand on the BBC's *Z-Cars*. He diligently shadowed the group on the road to prepare for it. Using a broad brush, Owen chose to stress the individual personalities of the Beatles, fixing forever more the notion that John was the acid wit, Paul the amorous charmer, George a doleful romantic and Ringo . . . well, he was pure Ringo, comic Scouse gold from his fisherman's cap to his pointy toed boots. These were flavours-upped Beatles, MSG moptops, and over time the band would come to feel typecast by these cinematic alter egos. But then, as the critic James Miller has written, an overwhelming factor in the Beatles' instantaneous appeal was that they had always 'seemed like four characters in search of a play'. From this vantage point, Owen often seems amusingly prescient. 'It'll be wine, women and song all the way once he gets a taste for it', Brambell (again) says of the future alcoholic, Starkey. And in an exchange between the two chief songwriters about whether to enter a first-class carriage on a train that hints at debates in the studio long to come, it is McCartney who pushes on through, telling the reluctant Lennon, 'Well, I don't care, I am going to broaden my outlook'.

That Lennon and McCartney had written all the music for the accompanying LP was an innovation that did not go unnoticed. In keeping with a policy agreed after the phenomenal success of *Please Please Me* of avoiding padding out albums with songs that dutiful fans might already own, several numbers featured on the actual soundtrack ('I Wanna Be Your Man', 'She Loves You', 'All My Loving', etc.) were omitted. In addition to the six new numbers in the film, the fecund Lennon and McCartney supplied seven more for the English LP (and rest assured, we will come to the difference between their English and their American long-players anon).

On a baser level, for a paltry layout of $560,000, the flick netted United Artists a cool $13.5 million. Kids from Bognor to Idaho were denouncing anything unsavoury as 'grotty' – an Owen neologism formed from the mistaken belief that it was Liverpool slang for 'grotesque'. Roger McGuinn, soon of The Byrds, was so impressed by the fancy twelve-stringed guitar he saw George Harrison playing in the film, he went out and bought one, setting one or two things in motion. The Monkees had been presented with a blueprint to exist.[42]

The film succeeded in consolidating the group's already substantial cultural capital. Andrew Sarris, the film critic of the *Village Voice*, toasted it most memorably as 'The *Citizen Kane* of jukebox musicals'. And if the Beatles represent a tipping point in pop in the 1960s, it is regarding the degree to which the critical establishment bothered to take them seriously. In a lengthy and hilariously florid assessment of their wares for *The Times*, William Mann wrote that:

> The slow, sad song about 'That Boy', which figures prominently in Beatle programmes, is expressively unusual for its lugubrious music, but harmonically it is one of their most intriguing, with its chains of pan-diatonic clusters, and the sentiment is acceptable because voiced cleanly and crisply. But harmonic interest is typical of their quicker songs too, and one gets the impression that they think simultaneously of harmony and melody, so firmly are the major tonic sevenths and ninths built into their tunes, and the flat submediant key switches, so natural is the Aeolian cadence at the end of 'Not a Second Time' (the chord progression which ends Mahler's 'Song of the Earth').

Such musicological considerations were probably entirely lost on most screaming fans in 1963 – and mocked by Lennon who to his dying day claimed he thought Aeolian cadences were 'exotic birds'. If asked, the screamers would probably have agreed with Maureen Cleave, who felt that 'without a doubt the Beatles' most

42 Reflecting on the Monkees in his review of *Sgt. Pepper* in *The Times* in May 1967, William Mann wrote : 'I suspect that their songs were written by a computer fed with the first two Beatle LPs and *The Oxford Book of Nursery Rhymes.*'

exciting musical moment is when they throw back their heads, shake their furry hair-dos and go "Oooooooohhhhh" like a train'. And who could blame them for that? But Mann's piece, among others like it, bestowed an air of intellectual respectability upon the Beatles that by extension made them more readily acceptable to society at large. As George Melly notes in *Revolt into Style*, '[T]heir first two LPs were to be seen lying about in quite smart drawing rooms'.

Unlike the often empty prattle of their near contemporaries, they didn't condescend or insult the intelligence of their fans. They came across, and were frequently described, as 'bright young men'. Like much of their audience, they were children of the 1944 Butler Education Act, working(ish)-class lads who'd had the benefits of a secondary education – and in Lennon's case an all-important spell at art school, that great crucible of British pop. (Though in actuality McCartney, a classic autodidact, would be the group's prime culture vulture. 'I'd rather stay at home when I'm not working', Lennon admitted in 1963, 'but Paul goes out to Harry Secombe and *Lovely War*. I suppose I *should* like those things, but I just don't.')

Their verbal wit and love of Goonish puns won them plaudits far and wide. Confronted by an insouciance bordering on hipster cool, even ardent jazzers, people like the *Melody Maker*'s Bob Dawbarn, turned out to be willing to give them the time of day. In an op ed headed 'Why I Dig The Beatles', Dawbarn confessed that while it was 'not art with a capital A', he believed the Beatles to 'have given pop music a gaiety and a zest that vanished with the old music halls'.

If it wasn't 'art with a capital A' as yet, by their second long-player, *With the Beatles*, which had chalked up an unheard-of 250,000 advance orders in the UK, the group was looking consciously arty. The matching collarless suits tailored by Dougie

Millings – who, incidentally, kitted out Cliff Richard and Tommy Steele – remained firmly in place on stage. But for the cover of this disc, a grainy monochrome picture of the fabbers wearing subdued expressions and black polo-neck jumpers, gave off a serious 'Pass Me Those, Bongos, Man', Left Bank or Greenwich Village vibe.

The man responsible for emphasising, or re-emphasising, the Beatnik in the Beatles was Robert Freeman, a photographer with previous form in the jazz world. Some three and a half years earlier, pictures of a flat Lennon was sharing with his art school buddy Stuart Sutcliffe on Gambier Terrace in Liverpool had, after all, appeared in a *Sunday People* exposé headed 'The Beatnik Horror'. Whatever Beatnik leanings the group had had at home were only enhanced in Hamburg by their friendships with a trio of local art students, Astrid Kirchheer, Klaus Voorman and Jürgen Vollmer. If their gruelling four-sets-a-night, seven-nights-a-week stints at the Indra and Kaiserkeller clubs of the St Pauli red light district were the making of them musically, then the 'French-style' forward combed hair and modish sartorial flourishes came directly from Vollmer and Kirchheer. Freeman was shown some of Kirchheer's black and white photos of the group in Hamburg, and specifically asked to come up with something similar.

The cover was a substantial and formative victory over their record company for the group. Marketing executives at EMI had tried to veto the image, describing it as 'shockingly humourless'. Which, compared to the four boys grinning on a balcony sleeve of *Please Please Me*, where the band could easily have passed for grateful council tenants in a publicity photo for slum clearance tower blocks, it was.[43] But in winning the day, they bequeathed

43 The building in Angus McBean's portrait was in fact EMI's offices, but whatever its failings, I think we can all count our blessings that George Martin's preferred venue, the insect house at London Zoo, was barred to them.

an immediately imitated an era-defining image. 'Among the vulgar fairground barking of the LP covers of the period', George Melly believed, it 'had the dramatic impact of a bomb in a bouquet of multi-coloured gladioli.' Such intrinsic artiness could be readily understood by affluent middle-class fifth formers, for whom 'pop' per se had not previously seemed that impressive.

This trend clearly annoyed more conservative commentators. Writing in the *Daily Express* in the month of *With the Beatles'* release, Robert Pitman expressed his dismay at the effect the group were having on the youth of the nation (and, quite bizarrely, on a hobby George Orwell had once cast as quintessentially English, in particular). 'The Beatles influence on schoolboys is also sad', he remarked. 'No longer does their hope of a fortune lie in finding a rare issue in a packet of assorted stamps. Even in prep school they are busily buying electric guitars and drums instead.'

Prior to this, prep school boys, if popular music held any fascination for them at all, would probably have erred toward trad. This form of back-to-the-roots New Orleans revivalist jazz had grown up in response to the increasing sophistication/incomprehensibility (delete according to taste) of so-called 'modern' or 'cool' jazz, a genre pioneered by the likes of Charlie Parker, Dizzy Gillespie, John Coltrane and Miles Davis (see chapter four). In this country, trad's leading champions in the early 1950s were old Etonian and guardsman Humphrey Lyttelton, Ken Colyer and Chris Barber, all of whom held court in the 100 Club on Oxford Street. Its most fervent devotees tended to be drawn from the beardy, brillo-pad-haired and tweed-jacket-sporting types then found in art schools and in the newly ascendant red brick universities. (Lucky Jim is a trad man, as is *Look Back in Anger*'s Jimmy Porter.) But the idiom perversely underwent a second wind after the Aldermaston CND march of 1958. Acker Bilk, a clarinettist from Somerset who wore waistcoats and bowler hats, and whose taste for high Victorian showmanry and cloudy cider knew few bounds, rode the maudlin 'Stranger on the Shore' to number one in the United States in 1961. But in the process he arguably, and thankfully, sowed the seeds of trad's ultimate destruction by boring the living bejesus out of everyone concerned.

Bilk had performed at the Cavern Club, in its infancy purely a jazz venue, on numerous occasions and shared a bill with the Beatles on a Mersey 'River Boat Shuffle' back in 1961. His success with a version of 'A Taste of Honey', the title song from Tony Richardson's film of Shelagh Delaney's northern drama, resulted in the song's McCartney-sanctioned but unwarranted and immensely tiring two-minute spot on *Please Please Me*. But then trad, for all its faults (and they were legion) had, largely by accident, spawned a musical craze that was the catalyst for the Beatles and virtually every other self-respecting figure in British pop in the 1960s: skiffle. And fortunately for you, dear reader, its brief boom had everything to do with the length of an LP.

Hugh Mendl was the young producer at Decca who first spied the commercial potential of London's burgeoning trad jazz scene. On 13 July 1954, he herded Chris Barber and his band into Decca's studio at 165 Broadhurst Gardens, London NW6, fully intending to cut a rip-roaring 10-inch LP that would be the aural equivalent of any boozy night at the 100 Club. His masters at Decca had, albeit reluctantly, furnished him with £35 to do the job on a strictly 'no royalty' basis (two words that would haunt Lonnie Donegan to his grave).

Four tracks down and it became painfully apparent that the Chris Barber Band, as Mendl, with supreme understatement, explained to Billy Bragg some forty years after the event, 'did not have a very big repertoire'. At a loss at quite what to do next, the band ambled off to the Railway Hotel next door and imbibed a pint or two of Merrydown cider, *the* tipple of choice in trad circles. Suitably restored, the group trooped back into the studio and polished off 'Merrydown Rag', a brand-new number that an hour or so in the pub had miraculously willed into being. And marvellous it was, with Monty Sunshine's clarinet insistently twittering away like a bluebird on a cotton picker's shoulder as Pat Halcox, Ron Bowden, Jim Bray, Lonnie Donegan and Barber himself gamely chugga-chugged along on cornet, drums, double bass, banjo and trombone respectively.

Clocking in at three minutes and eighteen seconds, though, it left Mendl over six minutes short of a full 10-inch. Jim Bray, bored and nursing a prodigious thirst, sloped off into the night. Others soon followed. Heads were scratched until, in the spirit of these thrifty make-do times, rationing only having ended nine

days earlier, Donegan finally suggested that 'a bit of skiffle' might do the trick.

Emerging from the American South around the depression and reputed to derive its name from the amateur groups who played at the 'rent parties' poor tenants often held to rustle up money for their landlords, skiffle was a loose, shuffling folk blues with a infectious clip-clop beat. These were songs about prisons, railroads, mining disasters, smoky mountains, conditions on farms etc., usually knocked out on a guitar and accompanied by whatever else could be found, reflecting the genre's panhandling origins. Washboards. Broom handles. Table tops. Tea chests. Saucepans. Hair combs wrapped in brown paper. It didn't really matter. The bluesmen Big Bill Broonzy, Huddie 'Leadbelly' Ledbetter and Lonnie Johnson, from whom Anthony Donegan took his stage forename, had all recorded 'skiffle' numbers at various points in their careers. Donegan normally wailed his way through an array of these ditties in the interlude between sets, while Sunshine and the horn boys repaired to the bar to lubricate their ever-dusty throats.

Strapping on a guitar, with Barber picking up the double bass for only the fourth time in his life and the jazz singer Beryl Bryden dragged in to assist on washboard, Donegan sped through the traditional American railway ballad 'John Henry' and an old Leadbelly favourite 'Rock Island Line' – 'the story of some shady business on a railroad "which goes down into New Orleans"', as the sleeves notes on the finished LP put it.

Two takes and they were done. Released in November 1954, *New Orleans Joys* by Chris Barber's Jazz Band and The Lonnie Donegan Skiffle Group was favourably received by the trad fraternity, but didn't leave any impression on the public at large. A year slipped by.

BBC presenter Christopher Stone, however, had liked the album and aired 'Rock Island Line' on his radio show, promptly receiving a mailbag of requests to play the song again. Decca decided to release it as a single in November 1955 and it went on to sell a million copies across the globe and triggered a full-blown skiffle craze in Britain. Its simple three-chord formula and everything-bar-the- kitchen-sink sound was cheap and easy to imitate. Sales of acoustic guitars soared. Washboard manufacturers went into overdrive. At the peak of the craze in 1957 there were estimated to be over 5,000 skiffle groups in the land.

The list of ex-skifflers is vast: Tommy Steele, Adam Faith, Hank Marvin, Keith Richards, Jimmy Page, Roger Daltry . . . Paul McCartney and George Harrison were members of the Liverpool branch of the Lonnie Donegan Skiffle Club. When Donegan arrived for a season at the Empire Theatre in Liverpool, the fourteen-year-old McCartney bunked off school to greet him and secure an autograph. Harrison was a Donegan fanatic, cadging the money off his parents to see every performance at the Empire. He later recalled that 'Donegan and skiffle music just seemed made for me'. Richard Starkey, then a trainee joiner, first employed his sticks in the Eddie Clayton Skiffle Group. Lennon, who played his 78 of 'Rock Island Line' until he'd exhausted the grooves, formed his own skiffle group with mates at the Quarry Bank School – hence their name, The Quarry Men – into whose ranks, after a crucial encounter with Lennon at a garden fete in Wooton on 6 July 1957, McCartney was duly inducted.[44]

44 On 1 January 1962, the Beatles would themselves step into Broadhurst Gardens for their recording audition with Decca. Nervous and weary after a ten-hour van journey through freezing fog the previous night, the group's lacklustre performance and repertoire (on Epstein's insistence, they'd steered away from their own compositions) failed to convince Mike Smith, Dick Rowe or the ex-Shadow Tony Meehan, who produced the session, that they were worthy of a contract with the same firm as their one-time idol.

The fad was short lived, and overrun in the end by the influx of rock 'n' roll from the States. In its aftermath, though, a generation of British teenagers had picked up guitars and a proficiency in American rhythm and blues. Unfortunately, Donegan himself rather blotted his copybook. He speedily diversified into novelty, releasing such classic numbers as 'Does Your Chewing Gum Lose Its Flavour on the Bedpost Over Night?', 'Have A Drink On Me' and 'My Old Man's A Dustman'. No music hall horror or spoon-damaging cockney singalong was free from his roving attentions. And sure enough, everyone stopped paying any attention to him.

His contribution, however, was respectfully acknowledged in the *Melody Maker* on 30 March 1963. 'If you had to thank anyone for the thriving beat group scene in Britain', Chris Roberts stated, 'you couldn't do better than pick on Lonnie Donegan. Ask any young guitarist, bassist or drummer earning pounds from pop, when he started making music. Then join him in the chorus . . . "In the old skiffle days".'

With the Beatles, and especially after *With the Beatles*, a new spirit of skifflish anyone-can-have-a-go optimism was abroad. Here was a group that 'could neither read music nor write it' but nonetheless managed to churn out their own songs and had control of their own image.

In the words of one-time Beatles plugger and Rolling Stones manager, Andrew Loog Oldham, 'the Beatles changed the rules – not the rules of engagement and payment, but the total package they delivered of songs, sound, ideas and attitude made them as self-reliant as recording artists as they were on stage.'

America, encounters with a corkscrew-haired cat in a hotel room and a retreat into the studio were still to come, but even at this stage, still essentially a singles band, the group had already laid the ground rules of how pop albums henceforth could and would be made.

Well, very nearly . . .

It could be argued that it was the Beatles' success in America that gave them the *real* clout to claim artistic freedom at home, a freedom that would see them wanting to express themselves on cohesive LPs. In the States, though, Capitol Records seemed to take an almost sadistic pride in carving up their English Parlophone albums for what they blatantly regarded as the undiscerning, or perhaps more accurately, exploitable, American pop LP market. A difference in the method of calculating royalty payments in Britain and America partly explained the differences, as English LPs, on average, contained fourteen tracks and American ones only ten or eleven. But the manner in which they parsimoniously eked out tracks to keep a new Beatles album, any new Beatles album, on the market every four months looks contemptible now. From repackaged oldies (*The Early Beatles* – this is, remember, 1964) to double discs of interviews (*The Beatles Story*) and an LP with a German-language version of 'She Loves You' on it (*Something New*), from early 1964 until the summer of 1966 there seemed nothing Capitol wouldn't press onto 12-inch vinyl and sling out if they could get away with it (apart, of course, from the LPs as they were being recorded and issued in the UK).

Yesterday and Today proved to be the most abysmal example of Capitol's handiwork. A Beat music Boris Karloff, it was stitched together from the body parts of three separate LPs. The label blithely siphoned three songs off a then unfinished *Revolver* to make up the numbers. For the cover, the band, attired in Doctor Dose white coats, posed with decapitated Tiny Tears dolls and slabs of raw meat. The image horrified all and sundry, and 500,000 copies of the album were hastily withdrawn at a cost of around $75,000 to Capitol. Long after the fact, the sleeve was interpreted as a direct protest by the group at the 'butchery' of their art, but this is extremely wishful thinking.

Vee-Jay played the same game, reissuing, and reissuing the Beatles tracks they still owned on split albums with Frank Ifield

(*Jolly What! The Beatles And Frank Ifield On Stage*), double discs with The Four Seasons (*The Beatles vs. The Four Seasons*) and drumming up an interview LP of their own (*Hear the Beatles Tell All*).

But the American music industry had caught on to the spending power of teenagers much more rapidly than elsewhere and as reported earlier, by 1960 LPs were already outselling singles in the States. Though the majority of LPs continued to be aimed at and bought by adults, the impetus to crank out cash-in albums on the back of a hit single – any hit single – or a new teen trend, was therefore that much greater. Their audiences were under no illusions either; they understood the formula. Pop LPs were consumed, like those other little-piece-of-me icons in teen life, the fan magazines and the posters, as much for the pictures on their covers as for their contents.[45] Phil Spector, 'the First Tycoon of Teen', who

---

45 How many millions of Beatles LPs are there across the globe inscribed with their original owner's name? But isn't it funny how signatures on so many LPs look nearly the same? Scrupulous, yet sloppy. The studied hand indicating that the writer is still finding their way. Each letter is, perhaps, approached – out of reverence or inexperience – overly cautiously. Just as a drunk trying to pass for sober ends up with exaggerated gestures, the result is messier for trying to achieve neatness. Additional curlicues that will fade once the real business of scrawling on cheques and picking up lunches and mail kicks in are proudly on display. Like the ownership of the LP itself, though, these signatures, often touching in their naivety, are among those faltering first steps to self-definition. They are the original 'tags' marking out both personal property and emotional terrain. In reality, of course, the reason for a signature on an LP is probably fairly mundane and much more akin to attaching string to a toddler's mittens – simply a vain attempt at preventing its loss. But in these little pieces of graphito are a hundred traumatic birthday parties where three or four kids found they'd all brought the same record along. A thousand sibling squabbles and disputes. And on occasions, just a fleeting glimpse of the incaution of someone who, as they raised their pen, was sure this LP would last them a lifetime.

at the time was unleashing exquisitely whizzy symphonies on 45s that were equal to a surge of adolescent hormones or the rush of a head full of Drinamyl, had nothing but contempt for pop albums. He may, by 1964, have produced nine albums himself, but he still dismissed most as 'two hits and ten pieces of junk'.

For those who just wanted a slice of the action but weren't too worried about the label on the tin, there was an array of ersatz knock-off pop LPs available.

Lou Reed, employed on a salary of $25 a week in 1964 as a songwriter-cum-session man for Pickwick, a company that specialised in slapdash rip-off LPs for the truly undiscerning, recalled that he and three others would, 'write ten California songs, ten Detroit songs' and then 'go down into the studio for an hour or two and cut three or four albums really quickly'.

The 'original' Californian and Detroit artists themselves were hardly on less hectic schedules anyway. Deploying production methods he'd picked up while working on a Ford assembly line in Detroit, Berry Gordy's Tamla Motown label became 'the most successful Black-owned business in American history'. Utilising the in-house composing and producing team of Brian and Eddie

Holland and Lamont Dozier, and a set of crack musicians, acts like the Supremes, the Four Tops, Martha Reeves, Smokey Robinson, Marvin Gaye and Stevie Wonder had hit single after hit single, accruing fourteen number one singles between 1964 and 1967 – and what hits, too: 'Heatwave', 'Baby Love', 'I Heard It Through the Grapevine' – all of which seemed to become alarmingly popular with advertisers in the 1980s.

Although Motown sold albums – including an LP of Martin Luther King's speeches in 1963 – Gordy only ever looked upon LPs as coffer-enhancing adjuncts to singles. As a result the label kept a stream of 'skimpily baited' quickies, as the critic Robert Christagu once put it, coming right up until the end of the 1960s, when Stevie Wonder and Marvin Gaye were able to make the form their own. However, the company's habit of recycling old hits did attract some censure in the British music press.

'NAUGHTY TAMLA do get away with murder on their collection of "Big Hits" album releases', *Disc and Music Echo* observed in 1966. 'They must throw all the songs and a mixture of artists' names into a big hat, select sixteen and put out a new LP . . . Once again we get "Baby Love" (Supremes), "My Guy" (Mary Wells), "Baby I Need Your Lovin'" (Four Tops), "Too Many Fish In the Sea" (Marvelettes) and "That's What Love Is Made Of" (Miracles). Good all – but really only a new combination of roughly the same songs, with a few new ones for good measure.'

But to understand, Capitol's 'milk it for all it's worth' attitude to the Beatles, you need only to look at the career of their Stateside rivals and label-mates, The Beach Boys.

*   *   *

With a stolen Chuck Berry riff or two, warbling assimilated from a collection of Four Freshmen albums that guiding light Brian Wilson had kept on continuous rotation since buying in the mid-

1950s, and a smattering of surfer dude slang that his younger brother Dennis had picked up while idling away the summer of 1961 on the South Bay beaches of Los Angeles, the Beach Boys purposely, mercilessly, rode the West Coast surf boom that had been crested, created, by the likes of Dick Dale and the Del-Tones.

Surfing, or Surfin', as it was invariably rendered in song, was a Californian lifestyle option in need of an appropriate soundtrack rather than a pop movement per se. The bop saxophonist Art Pepper, in his stints at the Surf Club in Hollywood, was performing a little number called 'Surf Ride' as early as 1952, but it was the arrival of the risible beach flick *Gidget* in 1959 that really ignited teenage interest in the sport and its milieu. By 1961, close to 30,000 surfers were to be found loafing about on Southern California's beaches most weekends and come sundown, many of them were looking for something to dance to and, hopefully, someone to snog.

Dick Dale and the Del-Tones, who unlike most of the Beach Boys were known to surf from time to time, made their name as the 'rocking' house band of the Rendezvous Ballroom in Balboa – an Orange County venue frequented by surfers. Egged on by fellow boarders and dance hall regulars, Dale strove to create music that he believed emulated the thrill of surfing. Drawing on the tribal rhythms he'd heard on records by the jazz drummer Gene Krupa, he perfected a distinctive percussive guitar style.

Using thick-gauged strings and a plectrum, he fired off choppy rakes of notes in machine-gun staccato, and found that plugging his strat into a reverb unit resulted in a gluggy bathtub echo that made the instrument sound positively aquatic. This effect became a widely disseminated feature of the surf sound and is instantly recognisable on Dale's 'Misirlou' and records like 'Wipe Out' by The Surfaris and The Chantays' 'Pipeline'.

Although known primarily today as The King of the Surf Guitar, Dale's first album – surf music's first – *Surfers' Choice* (1962), recorded by his father in the Rendezvous, does actually contain a number of vocal tracks, including, importantly for the surf canon, the West Indian nautical folk tune, 'Sloop John B'. But Dale himself was never a particularly distinctive vocalist, and it is not surprising that instrumentals came to occupy the better part of his repertoire – and his legacy. (On *Surfers' Choice*, Dale, a huge Hank Williams fan, comes across as a bit of a hiccupy vowel-chewer and sounds positively sore-throated when tackling all-out rockers like 'Night Owl'.)

As a (virtually) non-surfing, largely vocal harmony group, the Beach Boys were something of an anomaly on the surf scene. Although from their original name, the Pendletones ('a play off Pendleton shirts, then something of a fad', according to Brian Wilson), to a studiously contrived repertoire of songs championing a white teenage world of sunkissed pleasure (cars, boards, beaches, honeys and root beer) that Wilson participated in vicariously for the most part, the group were only ever astute surf carpetbaggers. A fact Wilson himself readily acknowledged: 'Dennis had mentioned the latest fad, surfing. Both Mike [Love] and I recognised the potential in writing about a fad.' To this end, Wilson ensured their output was liberally dotted with surfing references, going so far as to tap a high school friend's kid brother for appropriate locations to use in 'Surfin' USA'.

However, perhaps all this was actually a factor in the group's primary success. Unhindered by actual hands-on boarding experience, and slightly insecure as outsiders, Brian and co overcompensated, with the result that they produced a kind of über-surf music, one so blatantly, so insistently keen to bang on and on and on about the wonders of this Californian surfing lark – almost in the manner of adolescent boys yet to lose their cherries and sex – that its infectious appeal was universal. It was so idealised, so stylised, that anyone could buy in to it – and they did.

This confounded the expectations of the group's own record label, Capitol. No doubt mindful of the 75,000 copies Dale's *Surfers' Choice* had shifted in Southern California alone within the first three months of its release, the label, 'the first big label to be located on the West Coast', nonetheless wasn't entirely sure how the Beach Boys would play beyond the Golden State. As it turned out, 'Surfin' Safari', technically the B-side of their debut single for the label, broke nationally in arid old Phoenix, of all places.

The company were, in the end, no slouches when it came to capitalising on the single, and promptly herded the group into their Hollywood studios to bang out a long-player, also entitled *Surfin' Safari*, lest there be any confusion among buyers of the hit. (A trick Parlophone, you may recall, also employed in Britain with the Beatles and *Please Please Me*). Wilson remembered that the record was completed in just 'a handful of long, tiring sessions'.

Now sure that surfing was the selling point, they made certain the album screamed surf, surf surf, down to the inclusion of a short definition of the craze for the perplexed in the liner notes: 'A water sport, in which the participant stands on a floating slab of wood resembling an ironing board in both size and shape.' On the front of the sleeve, meanwhile, the group were pictured perching on top of an antiquated bright yellow pick-up truck, parked on the shore of a sandy beach. Resplendently decked out in matching Pendleton check shirts and khakis, the group, barefoot to a man, stare in the direction of the ocean, either pointing towards the horizon or with cupped hands held to foreheads in poses of There-She-Blows, Ahoy-There-Captain rapture. They look like people dressed to go surfing. But 'dressed' is arguably the operative word: there's a single yellow and blue striped surfboard between the five of them, and Mike Love and Brian Wilson, who clutch it rather self-consciously, look distinctly uncertain about what on earth they would do with it if it ever came into contact with a liquid.

Ultimately, it's a reassuring image. In marked contrast to the sleeve of *Surfers' Choice*, where a board-borne Dale is shown journeying across a vast wave, a tanned Adonis, muscles rippling, the band exude beach-bum goofiness and bonhomie rather than sporting prowess. Mike's hair is already visibly thinning. Carl is puppy-fat chubby. This is a get-this-album, get-the-khakis, get-the-Pendleton shirt and you-too-can-be-a-surfer consumer trip. Its message is very much 'Hey, I mean, eyeball these guys – they're hardly going to mind if you leave the messy and potentially lethal business of diving into undulating water to somebody else, are they?'

And boy did it work. But fearing that the surf boom would crash, Capitol wasted no time in harassing 'The No. 1 Surfing Group In The Country', as they had taken to billing them, to come up with a follow-up. For the album *Surfin' USA*, released less than five months after their debut, a stock photo of a boarder and a couple of leftover stills from the *Surfin' Safari* photo sessions were deemed sufficient for the cover. And lacking a full complement of finished songs, in an indicative move, the album was bulked out with perfunctory instrumentals, among them unedifying covers of Dick Dale's 'Misirlou' and 'Let's Go Trippin''. Just prior to recording the album, Wilson had in fact, magnanimously, given one of his best new songs, 'Surf City', to the singing duo Jan and Dean.

A couple of former locker-room buddies, who in a parallel world might well have spent the summer months kicking sand in

Brian's face, Jan Berry and Dean Torrence were seasoned pop veterans when they met the Beach Boys on the LA gigging circuit, having scored their first hit, 'Jenny Lee', a tribute to a local stripper, back in 1958. (By 1961, Jan and Dean already had one compilation LP of 'Golden Hits' under their belts.) Spying the commercial possibilities of surf, they had embraced the bug, tackling with Wilson's blessing 'Surfin'' and 'Surfin' Safari' on their 1962 album *Jan & Dean Take Linda Surfin'*, a record whose gimmicky *ménage à trois* title and cover promised far more than it could ever possibly deliver, and watched their fortunes undergo a dramatic upturn. Armed with 'Surf City', the duo were able to scale the top of the American charts in July 1963.

By this point, the Beach Boys were finishing their third LP, *Surfer Girl* – the first Wilson would produce himself, and safely away from Capitol's lackeys, but now the third to bear a snap from the five-boys-one-board-on-a-beach shoot. The expulsion of David Marks from the group's line-up, rendered the image anachronistic by the date of the album's release that autumn but, fortuitously, called an end to this artwork parsimony.

From the very beginning, songs about cars had always constituted a good proportion of the Beach Boys' material. Capitol had actually chosen to kick off the group's tenure on the label with '409', an ode to a Chevrolet penned by Wilson and Gary Usher, in preference to 'Surfin' Safari'.

Since the late 1940s, when with the possible covert influence of forces in the American motor industry, Los Angeles' 1,150 mile-long network of public streetcars – known as Red Cars – began to be dismantled and an array of new freeways was built in their place, car ownership across the city had soared exponentially. By the time the last Red Car ran in 1961, Southern California was the well-established hub of a plethora of automotive subcultures and home to numerous tribes of dedicated young stock racers, hot rodders and customisers, whose ambits, codes and fashions rivalled, paralleled and frequently overlapped with those of the surfers. Tom Wolfe, at a Teen Fair at Burbank in 1963, observed that the surfers went in 'for one particular brand of customising', taking old wood-bodied station wagons, which they called 'woodies', and fixing them up 'for riding, sleeping and hauling surfing equipment for their weekends at the beach'.[46]

Accordingly, almost all of the leading exponents of surf music in California chose to spread their bets and diversified with the odd hot rod record. Frequently, only the presence of a roaring engine or a squealing tyre at some point during the track distinguished these offerings from the standard surfer instru-mentals, though hot rod eventually grew, as much from its marketing and consumption, into a distinct subgenre in its own right. Dick Dale was one of the quickest off the starting grid, cutting the racy *Checkered Flag* album in 1963 and *The Eliminator* the following year. In September 1963, the Beach Boys were riding high in the charts with the single 'Little Deuce Coupe', a jaunty hymn to a souped-up 1932 Ford roadster, when they got wind of Capitol's plans to issue a cheap hot rod compilation featuring Beach Boys tunes. They responded by assembling an album's worth of the car songs, returned to the studio and cranked out the men-and-motors-themed LP, *Little Deuce Coupe*. Issued a month later, it was their third long-player of the year.

Its subsequent success did no harm to Jan and Dean, whose

46 It was the railways that had, in fact, helped bring surfing to California at the start of the twentieth century. In 1907, Henry Huntington, a Los Angeles property speculator and founder of the Pacific Electric Railway, had invited George Freeth, a Hawaiian who'd done much to revive surfing on the island of its origin, to give a demonstration of his art at Redondo beach as part of the festivities to celebrate the opening of the Redondo–Los Angeles railroad.

own album *Drag City* followed hot on its tail and throttled the carburettor formula for all it was worth[47], but it lumbered Wilson with the obligation to supply yet another sequel. And so it went on and on, so that in their first four years of existence, the Beach Boys notched up ten albums.

While Wilson, the poet laureate of West Coast leisure, was working like a dog, in 1964 the writers of 'A Hard Day's Night' were in New York, meeting that most political of singers, Bob Dylan. It was an encounter that would send both parties off in

47 'For the finest reproduction this recording should', the back sleeve joshed, 'be played on a chrome reversed turntable driven by a full-blown turntable motor equipped with tuned headers.' However, one of its lead tracks, 'Dead Man's 'Curve', proved appallingly prophetic. A song about an ill-fated car race on Sunset Boulevard, it foreshadowed Jan Berry's own near-fatal smash in similar circumstances some three years later.

radically different directions (as well as Brian Wilson, in his turn), with consequences – it almost goes without saying, dear, patient reader – for the LP . . .

*   *   *

Despairing at the binary nature of human reasoning, one commentator once stated that he wished our brains had a third lobe. And in the early 1960s, the polarities of popular culture tended to be belatedly retold in exaggerated 'us and them' tropes. The off and ons of straights or squares, mods or rockers, Beatles or Stones, pop or folk, acoustic or electric, Peter or Gordon, black or white were everywhere. Life and art as it is lived and breathed is obviously never quite that neat. But until around 1965, popular music could almost be said to have happily pootled along in the two speeds of 45 and 33 rpm.

Exquisitely crafted soul and pop singles from Motown, Stax and Phil Spector, perfectly calibrated to the dance floor or the dansette record player, ran at 45, while jazz, folk and blues, usually emerging on 33 rpm and in sleeves carrying lengthy notes that blathered on about 'honesty' and 'integrity', was stuff to crack out the dried banana skins for. (Or so those who can't remember the 1960s would have us believe, anyway. Tea or cocoa and a sly Woodbine were probably the most common stimulants and/or sedatives to accompany your average British teenager's listening habits.)

Both Dylan and the Beatles were, in Ian MacDonald's words, 'then unique in being prolific enough to fill complete LPs with their own material'. But while the idea of a pop group producing an LP that wasn't simply a hit single or two and nine fillers was a comparative novelty, Dylan, coming from the folk revival circuit, was expected to speak to his audiences in LP.

In his memoir, *Chronicles*, Dylan himself recalls that he didn't want to make singles because folksingers, jazz artists and classical musicians all made LPs; records with tons of songs on and covers you could gaze at, that he believed gave more of the big picture. In comparison, he judged 45s 'flimsy and uncrystallised.'

And at the height of the American folk boom, in 1963, over 200 folk LPs were estimated to have been released in the US. Folk singers, even those with hit singles to their name, were not, as Dylan's comments suggest, in the business of having hit singles. Or even if they were, they certainly didn't publicly profess to be in the business of having hit singles. That was Frankie Avalon's concern. The price to credibility of even having a hit single, or perhaps more accurately the wrong kind of hit single could be high. Wholeheartedly committed to the Civil Rights Movement they may have been, but some never quite forgave Peter, Paul and Mary for 'Puff the Magic Dragon'.

The folk revival in the 1960s was largely an exercise in musical fantasy, where groups of college kids in coffee houses, keen to slough off the complacent, comfortable lives their parents had provided for them, pretended to be Southern sharecroppers. Or at least dressed in denim and tried to sing like them. The revival trail, which more positively succeeded in resuscitating the careers of several aged black musicians (Dock Boggs, Furry Lewis, Skip James and the wonderful Mississippi John Hurt), had been foreshadowed by the rather bland and clean-cut Kingston Trio. The Trio were three Californian graduates with an ingratiating line in striped shirts, toothy grins, winking eyes, three-part harmonies and Appalachian murder ballads. In December 1959 they enjoyed the distinction of having four albums in the *Billboard* top ten. Their style of folk – think three overeager, trendy vicars armed with banjos – was affectionately sent up by Christopher Guest in *A Mighty Wind*.

By December 1960, college students were, according to *Mademoiselle* magazine, in a 'Folk Furor' and 'desperately hungry for a small, safe taste of an unslick underground world'. In response to this appetite, a new school of folknik troubadours were looking for inspiration to an earlier generation of singers who'd suffered for their art. Their idols were Woody Guthrie, Big Bill Broonzy and Huddie 'Leadbelly' Ledbetter. Their textbooks were *On the Road* (*sans* the tricky modern jazz stuff), Alan Lomax's *The Folk Songs of North America* and issues of the periodicals *Broadside* and *Sing Out!*[48] And, as often as not, their sacred tablets were LPs from the left-leaning Folkways label.

Folkways was as much a beacon of progressive social anthropology as it was a record company. At its core was the deeply held conviction that the world could be changed for the better, reweighted in a sense, during a McCarthyite and racist era, by the sound of human creativity in all its manifestations. Calypso raps, nursery rhymes, Negro spirituals, banjo concertos, jug band rags, mountain music,[49] Polish concentration camp laments and blues shouts were all equal in the ears of Moe Asch, Folkways' founder and notoriously tempestuous guiding light.

A fundamentally non-conformist enterprise, its coffers were filled by folklorists, archivists, anthropologists, musical missionaries, idealists and out-and-out cranks who scoured the world

---

48 In the UK, copies of the latter were available in Collet's Record Shop on New Oxford Street in London, a mecca for folk fans throughout the 1960s and described by one former employee, Tony Russell, as 'probably the most diverse record store in the country' and 'a club for the musically curious, where the inquiring buyer could find discs by the Copper Family from Sussex and the Carter Family from Virginia, among a stock that embraced Bulgarian village choirs, Indian film music, the Celtic harp of Alan Stivell, the Bahamian guitar of Joseph Spence and the Nubian oud of Hamza El Din'.

49 Sadly this is essentially a type of bluegrass rather than the sounds of avalanches or volcanic eruptions. With Folkways, though, like the output of Emory Cook's eponymous unit, you could never be entirely certain.

looking for chunks of old shellac, semi-dormant musicians, poets, actors, charlatans and mountebanks to commit to vinyl.

Samuel Charters was one of a number of dedicated 'field' recordists and anthologists that included Frederick Ramsey Jr, Harold Corlander, Charles Edward Smith and Langston Hughes, who 'worked' for Folkways. ('None of us', Charters has said, 'were ever employees . . . there was never any money but we didn't care.') Moving to New Orleans in the early 1950s, when the South was essentially an apartheid nation, Charters, of American-Scottish descent but possessing a head of raven hair, would often have to pretend to be a Cherokee Indian to avoid arousing undue attention from the police when recording in black neighbourhoods. Foraging in Texas, Tennessee, Mississippi, Alabama and the Bahamas, he produced over twenty LPs for Folkways and while on the trail of the bluesmen Blind Willie Johnson and Robert Johnson, unearthed a rich and then still little-known vein of downhome Southern blues. He christened it 'the country blues' after a Dock Boggs number, the title he gave to a book in which he examined the genre, and an accompanying compilation LP. Both triggered a wave of interest in pre-war blues singers like Blind Willie McTell, Blind Lemon Jefferson, Sleepy John Estes and Tommy McClennan that, without exaggeration, helped colour the future course of popular music.

One of Charters' most significant 'rediscoveries' was Lightnin' Hopkins.[50] Hopkins had cut hundreds of sides for numerous R&B labels in the late 1940s and early '50s, several of which had

50 The vogue for unearthing obscure Southern bluesmen reached such a pitch that *Downbeat* magazine columnist Don DeMichael was inspired to write a fictional profile of a Louisville strummer he named Blind Orange Adams. Though dreamt up as a one-off spoof, Adams soon took on a life of his own, acquiring both interest from several labels and his own fan club. DeMichael eventually resorted to killing his creation off in a car crash.

sold thousands of copies in their day. But a reputation for recording many of the same songs for different companies, mostly to fund his inveterate gambling and drinking habits, and the vagaries of musical fashion had stalled his discmaking. When Charters tracked him down in January 1959, he was living in a shabby tenement in an even shabbier district of Houston and his electric guitar was in the pawnshop.

After renting an acoustic guitar (not Hopkins' preferred instrument[51]), agreeing on a fee of $300 and supplying him with a bottle of raw gin, Charters sat at the end of the bluesman's bed in a 'drab, bare room' with the intention of recording an LP. Holding the microphone just inches away from the singer's face, he set his Pentron tape recorder running. When Hopkins had briskly rounded off two songs, he stopped. With an air of obvious relief,

51 Seeing the way the winds were blowing, several electric players un-plugged and returned to their roots, redefining themselves as country blues singers, for a while anyway. In 1959 John Lee Hooker recorded the acoustic album *The Folk Blues of John Lee Hooker*. Muddy Waters, who played the Newport Folk Festival in 1960, immortalised the live album in *At Newport 1960*, and made the *Folk Singer* LP in 1964.

Hopkins went to lay the guitar aside. Charters had to explain that for the type of record they were making today, he would need more than two numbers.[52] With enormous reluctance, and only once the precise length of each side and the number of songs needed had been established, he resumed. Moving from song to song, though, and renewed by intermittent long slugs of gin, he slowly became buoyed by the experience of recording again. He sang, and reminisced, for the next three to four hours. When they had finished, Hopkins pocketed the cash and headed for the nearest bar. A copy of the album was sent to him via his local post office. It was never claimed. Soon enough, though, the LP carrying his unadorned cracked voice and ferocious guitar work into college dorms and Beatnik lairs up and down the land wove its magic. Hopkins went on to enjoy a fruitful comeback that endured for close to twenty years. He gave his last major public performance at Carnegie Hall in 1979.[53]

52 Such two-song wonder LPs as Cecil Taylor's *Spring of Two Blue J's*, Fripp and Eno's *No Pussyfooting*, et al, lay a decade and a half away, obviously.

53 Success, this time round, did little to alter Hopkins' former habits. Now solvent, he simply picked up where he left off, gambling, drinking and recording the same material for other companies whilst under a new contract to Prestige. After several albums, Mack McCormick his main producer at that label, clearly reached something of a personal impasse with Hopkins. In 1962, he chose to use the liner notes of *Smokes Like Lightnin'* to launch a swingeing attack on the musician. From the back cover of Hopkins' own LP, McCormick denounced Hopkins as 'a natural born easeman, consumed by self-pity and everlastingly trying to persuade the world that it is his valet'. Of his 'that girl gone done me wrong' persona, he wrote: 'Lightnin' sings endlessly of being mistreated by women though in fact he has been the pampered daytime pet of a married woman for fourteen years.' Warming up, he characterised Hopkins 'as loveable and yet tyrannical in the same sad way of a very spoiled child', and concluded by outlining how the bluesman had recently skipped Houston to avoid settling his sister's funeral arrangements. They did not work together again.

One area that remained contentious, and applied to Charters' *Country Blues* compilation, was Folkways' willingness to appropriate old 78 recordings without securing agreements with their original labels. Folkways saw it as a moral issue to ensure that going-to-waste recordings of historical importance were freely available.

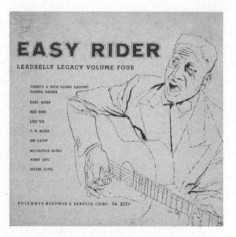

They sidestepped questions of ownership by invoking a clause in the Constitution regarding the public's right to information. It was in this fashion that Fred Ramsey's three-volume *History of Jazz* anthology had been released in 1950. The same ruse was used to rescue Woody Guthrie's 78s for RCA from limbo. They were gathered up and issued on a LP they entitled *Talkin' Dust Bowl*. (An illuminating essay on soil erosion by Ashe's brother was included in the album's notes.) Plans to get Guthrie to record a series of LPs commenting in song on contemporary events – a type of musical newspaper – alas came to nothing (but the concept was picked up by Pete Seeger, who produced two Gazette albums for Folkways, and later by Dylan peer Phil Ochs, on his debut LP *All the News That's Fit to Sing*). Guthrie, suffering from the degenerative neurological disorder

Huntington's Disease, had to enter the Greystone hospital in Brooklyn in 1956. It was here that Bob Dylan visited him in 1961. ('I missed out on meeting James Dean', he told *Village Voice* four years later, 'so I decided to go meet Woody Guthrie.')

Dylan became seriously fixated on Guthrie, adopting his repertoire, corduroy caps and Okie accent, while a student at the University of Minnesota in Minneapolis. It was also here that he was initiated into what fellow student John Pankake has called 'the brotherhood of the Anthology'. The Anthology was Folkways' *Anthology of American Folk Music*, a six-LP collection of eighty-four songs that Harry Smith had salvaged from the shellac heap of history.

To us, where every facet of the recent musical past, courtesy of YouTube, iTunes, Fopp, eBay, and so on, is omnipresent and instantly accessible, it's quite difficult to comprehend what on earth the Anthology must have sounded like when it came out in 1952. On its release, the *New York Times* complained that much of the singing was 'flat and undistinguished'.

None of the recordings was at that point very old – all were made between 1927 and 1932, so a quarter of a century earlier at the most – and many of them were carried out by such recondite outfits as Columbia, Victor and Brunswick – the EMI or the Sony, say, of their day. If we wound back the clock twenty-odd years from now, it would be a little like *Raw Like Sushi*, *Raising Hell*, *Meat is Murder* or *Candy Apple Grey* seeming to have been utterly eradicated and then suddenly reissued. Mind you, given the relative obscurity of the Anthology's contents, a closer analogy might be Vashti Bunyan's crate-dug *Just Another Diamond Day* or Lenny Kaye's *Nuggets*, the compilation of 1960s garage-sale garage band singles that was a catalyst for punk.

In Smith's view, what the Anthology offered was a taste of American music when it still retained 'some of the regional qualities evident in the days before the phonograph, radio and talking picture had tended to integrate local types'. The 'old, weird America', as the writer Greil Marcus has dubbed it (as opposed to the new, normal America). A map to a forgotten land, its coordinates were, nevertheless, all the stranger for being drawn by Harry Smith, a very weird – if at twenty-nine not especially old – American.

Smith was an odd, bearded homunculus who maintained that Aleister Crowley was his real father – Crowley's motto, 'Do what thou wilt shall be the whole of the Law', appears in the notes for the Anthology. While Smith had a voracious appetite for drugs and drink, sex was out and he found relationships with other human beings difficult. Or perhaps more accurately, other human beings found him difficult. Impossible sometimes. At his memorial in 1992, the folk singer Dave Van Ronk admitted: 'I didn't know Harry very well. I made it a point to avoid him unless I was drunk.' Smith had many talents. He painted. He made experimental films. He wrote mad, long poems. But mostly he annoyed people, wheedled for ready cash and collected things. Collecting, in the end, proved far and away his greatest art. He had a soft spot for string figures, patchwork quilts, paper aeroplanes and Kwakiutl house posts. And, of course, records.

We all probably live with dozens of vault- or collection-raiding compilation albums and delight in making our own mix tapes or iPod playlists, but Smith was the über-fan and the ur-curator rolled into one. He was a collector's collector who, much like a modern DJ, was acclaimed for sharing the fruits of his own (peculiar) obsessions – and who created an immensely covetable set of LPs.

Smith had landed in New York in 1950, penniless but in possession of hundreds of vintage 78s. An ad he placed in the wanted pages of *Record Changer* in September 1946 gives a good indication of what the Anthology would later contain:

Pre-War Race and Hillbilly Vocals. Bascom Lamar Lunsford, Jilson Setters, Uncle Eck Dunford, Clarence Ashley, Dock Boggs, Grayson and Whittier, Bukka White, Robert Johnson, Roosvelt Graves, Julius Daniels, Rev. D.C. Rice, Lonnie McIntorsh, Tommy McClennan, and many others. harry e. smith, 51/2 Panoramic, Berkeley 4, California.

Somehow Smith wound up at Moe Asch's door. By May 1952, he was putting together his Anthology in Folkways' cramped offices at 117 West Forty-Sixth Street, the process, apparently, aided by a button of Mescal that Asch would provide for him every hour or so.

A labour of love, *American Folk Music* was dictated less by the rigours of musicology as practised, equally arbitrarily really, by folklorist Alan Lomax than the whims of its compilers' eccentric tastes.

If it offers any mirror up to the 'real' America, it does so by dint of being an equally invented country. And many of those who chose to interpret it as a vision of the 'real America' then went off to invent things of their own which were similarly distant from reality, but equally beguiling.

Decanting vintage wine into new bottles, the three LPs, a trinity of 'Ballads', 'Social Music' and 'Songs', were accompanied by a booklet written by Smith that remains a master-class in creative curating. Illustrated by whimsical line drawings purloined from old music and record catalogues, it included a newspaper headline-style summary of lyrics in Smith's detailed, if idiosyncratic, discographical notes. 'Fatal Flower Garden' by Nelstone's Hawaiians, for instance, is abridged to: 'GAUDY WOMAN LURES CHILD FROM PLAYFELLOWS; STABS HIM AS VICTIM DICTATES MESSAGE TO PARENTS'. While 'Drunkard's Special' by Coley Jones is rendered as 'WIFE'S LOGIC FAILS TO EXPLAIN STRANGE BEDFELLOW TO DRUNKARD'.

Throwing together black blues, white hillbilly, old-time country, secular and religious songs, *American Folk Music* scattered hymns to God alongside tales of murdering, cheating, lying, swindling, sinking unsinkable ships, presidential assassinations and wishing to be moles in holes. Arcane and otherworldly, it acted as a cultural Trojan horse in Eisenhower's America, providing an instant, colour-blind canon for dissenters to cling to[54]. It was a trove to be raided, and percolating through the coffee houses, it became the *Book of Common Prayer* for worshippers of folk. Dylan covered six of its eighty-four tracks, creatively appropriating a few more over the years; Peter Seeger tackled thirteen and Joan Baez nine.

Only nineteen when her debut album was released in 1960, Baez was, in *Time*'s words, 'the tangible sibyl' of the modern folk scene. That first album, *Joan Baez*, composed entirely of traditional songs, stayed on the Billboard charts for almost three years. Making a principled stand, Baez vowed to release just a single album a year, rather than cash in on its success. It was a novel stance and one that probably didn't, in the end, hurt her sales. Reyneer Banham, writing in *New Society* a few years later, was moved to declare that 'some of the most durable monuments to current movements for the liberation of the person and the personality are the uncensorable LPs of Joan Baez'.

54 Recalling the political idealism that underpinned the era, Sam Charters remembered: 'We had a totally different agenda. We didn't sit around in coffee bars playing 'On Top of Old Smokey' because it was a great song. We were making an incredibly complicated political statement about why we were sitting in a coffee bar singing 'On Top of Old Smokey'. The kids like us who weren't screwed up they were listening to Bob Monroe and Frankie Lane; and Frank Sinatra and having the time of their lives. We were rejecting all of that.'

Slightly remote, politically earnest, pious almost, and an eschewer of shoes and make-up, Baez and her purling soprano, tested on the Harvard Square students, had floored the crowds at the first Newport Folk Festival in 1959. And with her lanky, dark, centre-parted hair and burlap tunics, she was to assist in shaping the outlook and sartorial mores of a whole generation of teachers. (In the opening party sequence of Malcolm Bradbury's satirical campus novel, *The History Man*, it can be no accident that a Joan Baez album is playing on the Kirks's stereo.[55]) Following Newport, Baez was wooed by several major record companies, including John Hammond at Columbia. Hammond had discovered Billie Holiday when she was just seventeen. A tireless campaigner for civil rights, he had organised the integrated 'Spirituals to Swing' concerts at Carnegie Hall in the late 1930s and that same year, he signed Aretha Franklin. It should, therefore, have been a match made in heaven, but when Baez visited Columbia's plush offices on Seventh Avenue, in David Hadju's evocative words, 'the air conditioning gave her a chill and the gold records on the walls seemed to glare like royal plunder'. She signed to Vanguard, a small company who had challenged the blacklist by releasing LPs by The Weavers and Paul Robeson. It was a firm that Hammond himself had only recently left.

Hammond's frustration at not securing Baez led him to sign another up-and-coming folk singer, Carolyn Hestor. When Hestor came to cut her first LP for Columbia, she invited a friend from Greenwich Village, Bob Dylan, to play harmonica on

---

55 Did anyone schooled in the 1970s not have a teacher with a preference for learn-by-play pedagogy and floor-length skirts who would, at the drop of a hat, pull out an acoustic guitar, strap on a capo, and break into 'Where Have All the Flowers Gone?'?

the record. At rehearsals for the album, Hammond met Dylan and . . . oh, do the math, repeat to fade.

An ex-girlfriend of mine once admitted that the very first thing she put in her suitcase when heading off to a kibbutz in Israel in the early 1980s were her Bob Dylan LPs. She knew that it was unlikely there would be anything to play them on when she got there – and indeed there wasn't. She spent six weeks living in a utility-free wooden shack, an experience that left her with a marked aversion to camping, most garden sheds and small church halls. But such was the albums' talismanic value, she couldn't countenance being without them. Dylan, it goes without saying, is a singer who almost from the beginning attracted fans who were a little obsessive – dangerously so, in some instances. Between 1968 and 1971, Alan J. Weberman, a crank with a column in the *East Village Other* paper who hoped to divine coded political messages in Dylan's now apolitical lyrics, regularly went through the singer's rubbish bins and made late-night calls to his home – which he then taped. These tapes later formed the basis of an LP, *Bob Dylan v A.J. Weberman*, released on Folkways. A threat of a lawsuit from Dylan meant it became the 'first record deliberately deleted from the Folkways catalogue', as label biographer Peter D. Goldsmith phrases it.

Nevertheless, there have been long periods, chunks of the 1970s, say, or 1985 . . . and 1986, and 1997, and so on, when Dylan himself seemed to have been inflicting upon his dearest fans some weird audio equivalent of God's trials for Job. Greil Marcus famously opened his *Rolling Stone* review of the double *Self Portrait* LP in 1970 with the words: 'What is this shit?' (But perhaps worse for any artist who sustains a long recording career after a fecund youth is the damning with faint praise: 'That new album, it's really not that bad'. Or the mealy-mouthed 'a bit of a return to form'. Or the bet-hedging 'it's at least as good as X' – X standing for an LP that nobody had a good word for when it came out, but due to utter exasperation with practically every album that followed it, and boredom with the 'canonical' works, has grown in credibility since.)

In the 1960s, of course, Dylan's LPs were quite genuinely thought to hold the answers to the secrets of the universe. But back then so was *Siddhartha*, the I Ching and *The Lord of the Rings*. Likewise, to align oneself to Dylan was to commit oneself to a consciousness-raising course in personal enlightenment. (The price of admission, sadly, continued to be drearily materialistic, bound up as it was with owning, borrowing or stealing certain objects, but being different has always had its costs.) Those who travelled with the singer as, LP by LP, he metamorphosed from a socially conscious protest singer into an electric rocker spinning intoxicating, if opaque, lines about screaming dwarfs in grey flannels and wicked birds of prey picking up breadcrumb sins, tended to believe that they themselves were higher beings – 'less hung up' than the average Mr Jones, who didn't know what was going on and continued to moan about the dearth of untreated wooden instruments.

That the wooden instrument mob felt betrayed would be an understatement. Reflecting the fanaticism of some of his English admirers, it was at a gig at the Manchester Free Trade Hall that he was denounced as a Judas for appearing with a band and an electric guitar. Everything about Dylan, after all, had appealed to those who cared most deeply. Rather like the Monty Python skit in *Life of Brian* about everyone being individuals, the more Dylan protested about being a protester and the more he told them not to follow leaders, the more they wanted him to protest and lead them to some promised land. Though the hardcore folk purists had always pegged him as a magpie for his freewheelin' approach to old tunes.

His first LP, like Baez's, was another eponymously titled job, and primarily composed of traditional songs – the only Dylan numbers on it were 'Talkin' New York', a Guthrie-esque ramble about his first trip to 'Green Witch Village',[56] 'Song to Woody', a tribute to you-know-who and 'Highway 51'. Recorded in a handful of hours over two days in November 1961, it came sleeved with a shot of Bob in a cord cap and a sheepskin coat of a style that second-division English football club managers would later adopt as their own. Like the heavily embellished biographical notes, this was first class hucksterism – Zimmerman openly posing as an untameable freight-train-jumping hobo. No one bought it to begin with. One Columbia exec called it 'a piece of shit' and at the label Dylan was openly referred to as 'Hammond's folly'. But galvanised by his politically minded girlfriend Suzi Rotolo, who he leads through a snow-covered 4th Street on the 'Startrite Kids go Beatnik' sleeve photo for *The Freewheelin' Bob Dylan*, Dylan's facility for what he later derided as 'fingerpointing songs' made him the darling of the protest movement. While he certainly cared about civil rights, and in the heat of the Cuban Missile Crisis in 1962 the imminent threat of a Third World War, Dylan's thing from the outset was creating 'songs' and writing – poems, a book and a play – rather than what we now call soundbites. Even

56 This pronunciation, and lefty folk-singing types, were roundly mocked by the Nashville songwriter Tom T. Hall in his song, 'Greenwich Village Folk Song Salesman'. In a version by Nancy Sinatra and the late, great, Lee Hazelwood on their *Nancy and Lee* album from 1968, Hazelwood at one point suddenly drawls, 'Green *Witch?*', his sandpapery baritone squeezing every drop of incredulity into this quizzical, Lady Bracknell-esque aside.

the tiresomely overexposed 'Blowin' in the Wind', a huge hit for Peter, Paul and Mary[57] in 1963, has its ambiguities. The nice-sounding chorus, viewed from a certain, albeit wonky, angle fails to supply an entirely fulfilling answer to the questions raised in the verses.

In the aftermath of his break-up with Rotolo in 1964, the decision to clamber aboard Rimbaud's drunken boat and lay down an LP in a single Beaujolais-soaked night, that despite a crack or two about the Republican senator Barry Goldwater was more poetical and personal than political, was met with outright alarm. Kennedy had been assassinated. The conflict in Vietnam was escalating after the Gulf of Tonkin Incident. China was testing its first atom bomb. In South Africa, Nelson Mandela was jailed for opposing the apartheid regime. The need for protest songs seemed more pressing than ever. Certainly the public's appetite for them did not diminish after Dylan abandoned the form. Nor, for a while, did Dylan's association with them fade. P.F. Sloan, a sixteen-year-old staffer at Dunhill Records, was presented with a copy of *Highway 61*, Dylan's first fully electric and entirely protest-song-free album, by his boss Lou Adler and told to come up with something similar. He returned a week later with ten songs – one of which was the crude but effective anti-war anthem 'Eve of Destruction'.

57 Summing up what the British trad jazzer Uncle John Renshew jokingly referred to as the 'sincerity racket', the sleeve notes for Peter, Paul and Mary's debut album are a breathtaking, stomach-churning example of faux honesty. 'Peter, Paul and Mary sing folk music', purchasers were informed. 'In your hand you hold their first album. But to be more accurate you hold a bouquet of song as fresh as the earth, and strong with the perfume of sincerity.' Who says cultural artefact as lifestyle choice is a new invention?

On *Another Side of Bob Dylan*, the title said it all; 'Ballad in Plain D', in particular, was taken as dirty-laundry-washing in public of the worst order. 'Your new songs', Irvin Silber wrote in *Sing Out!* after Newport that year, 'seem to be all inner-directed now, innerprobing, self-conscious – maybe even a little maudlin or a little cruel on occasion.'

'It Ain't Me Babe', though, with its 'No, No' refrain echoing 'Please Please Me', revealed that the singer had at least gazed beyond his navel as far as the Beatles were concerned (something that didn't exactly please Silber, either). The Beatles, meanwhile, had definitely been taking notes from the Dylan songbook. Over in Paris for some dates at the Olympia Theatre in January 1964, George Harrison carried copies of *Bob Dylan* and *The Freewheelin' Bob Dylan* he'd picked up from a local radio station back to their suite in the George V Hotel. Completely hooked, Harrison would press the LPs on the rest of the group that spring. Their effect on Lennon was immediately obvious on 'I'm a Loser', a number he wrote for their fourth LP, *Beatles for Sale*. ('That's me in my Dylan period', Lennon recalled of the song in 1980. 'Part of me suspects I'm a loser, and part of me thinks I'm God almighty.')

'The harsh, rasping haranguing voice of self-styled guitar strumming poet Bob Dylan' was soon enough championed as a 'pop' phenomenon in the British media, and Dylan presented as a rival among teenagers for the Beatles' affection. 'This, swears my seventeen-year-old son, is what the kids who used to scream at the Beatles now go for', the *Daily Mirror* maintained.

Pictured on the gatefold sleeve of *Beatles for Sale* swathed in heavy black scarves, knotty-haired and unsmiling, the Beatles themselves looked visibly tired by the rollercoaster of their own fame. The LP itself, padded out with covers (Chuck Berry's 'Rock and Roll Music', Buddy Holly's 'Words of Love'), seemed a step backwards after the entirely self-penned *A Hard Day's Night*. That expansive cover, however, made it covetable for the young fan: there was more to gaze upon and the cardboard was lovely to squeeze between your fingers as the disc revolved.

But was there, perhaps, a subtle message in that gatefold? Who needed that extra card, after all? The group who had produced it were now operating on a different plane. On 28 August 1964, at the Delmonico Hotel in New York, Bob Dylan had introduced them to marijuana.

*　　*　　*

'The great advantage of a hotel', George Bernard Shaw once observed, 'is that it is a refuge from home life.' For the Beatles, hotels, like the studio, offered a refuge from their fans. Hermetically sealed environments, hotels operate in a moral universe that is both in synergy and at odds with the world beyond its doors. Rather like drugs, the hotel gives a user a chance to play fast and loose with identities, roles and time. But woe betide anyone who expects to get breakfast after 9.30 a.m.

On his first visit to London in November 1962, a trip funded by the BBC who had cast the singer in a TV play, Dylan's 'smoking habits' caused him to be ejected from the rakish Mayfair Hotel near Berkeley Square. Cannabis was hardly an unknown quantity on the English music scene; an early sensationalist exposé of 'charge' on the London jazz circuit, Raymond Thorp's *Viper*, was published in 1956. Dylan, therefore, reacted with genuine incredulity when he discovered that the Beatles had never smoked dope. His disbelief was all the greater for having believed that there was a blatant reference to drugs in 'I Want to Hold Your Hand'. Some nine months later, when he landed in London to begin the British tour filmed by D.A. Pennebacker in *Don't Look Back* (a picture, incidently, boasting numerous scenes of Dylan hanging out in hotels), Maureen Cleave of the *Evening Standard* asked Dylan: 'Do your fans understand a word you sing?'[58] It emerged in the Delmonico that Dylan had been under the misapprehension that the line 'I can't hide' was 'I get high'. Once this little matter had been settled, and the windows and doors bolted and towels from the bathroom laid over every sill and crack, Dylan plied the Fab Four with grass. Paul McCartney was overwhelmed by the experience, wandering around the room telling everyone, 'I am thinking, for the first time, *really* thinking.'

Smoking marijuana, later augmented with LSD, soon became habitual among the group. Guarded references to it seeped into

---

58 In the same film, a group of concerned teenage girls in Liverpool admonish Dylan for the quasi-electricified 'Subterranean Homesick Blues'. 'It just doesn't sound like you, at all. It sounds like you are having a good ole laff', one complains. 'Don't you like me to have a good old laugh?' Bob asks. Their responses, after saying 'yes', are slightly inaudible, but quite movingly they seem to centre around wanting to take him seriously and worrying that he is becoming too commercialised.

their songs, its heady aroma so pungent on their subsequent LPs that the manufacturers' regular missive, 'If In Doubt Consult Your Dealer', took on an entirely new dimension. Dylan, too, would leave that encounter to embark on a fresh musical course of his own.

According to the Beatles discographer Ian MacDonald, at exactly the same time as the Beatles at Abbey Road were dragging out their acoustic guitars to record the Dylan-esque 'You've Got to Hide Your Love Away', in New York, Dylan was plugging in for the electric sessions for *Bringing it All Back Home*.

Needing, as he told the journalist Robert Shelton, 'a lot of medicine' to keep the pace, he gradually added speed and heroin to the dope and red wine, a cocktail that had him stretching space and time, mixing folk and rock, on ever-expanding chunks of black vinyl . . .

A six-minute single . . . 'Like A Rolling Stone' . . .

An eleven-minute album track . . . 'Desolation Row' . . .

Pop's first double LP . . . *Blonde on Blonde*, a record whose blurry photo cover image and opening track 'Rainy Day Women #12 & 35' in no uncertain terms exhorted its listeners to put its gatefold sleeve to only one use . . .

And then one day, like Puff the Magic Dragon, he slipped away for a year or so.

A motorcycle crash. Some rumours, naturally.

But, cliché as it is, there is nothing like absence to make the heart grow weirder. And the lack of production, a time-filling Greatest Hits compilation, a poster in the extant psychedelic style, and some silence would only send his fans back to the 'original texts' – those LPs – as they gnashed their teeth in the hope of a sign from the 'stereo micro-grooves of his soul CHARISMA', to borrow one of Toby

Thompson, an early and overly ingenuous biographer's, gushing phrases.[59]

From here on in, what Dylan didn't release started to become as important as what he did. And in the fetid, let's-seize-control-of-the methods-of-production-and-open-a-bead-shop spirit of the era, Dylan's own reluctance to release some songs acted as a spur for others to reveal to him *his* mistake.

Theses, treatises and novels – okay, one novel: Don DeLillo's *Great Jones Street* – have been written around *The Basement Tapes*. Finally officially released in 1975, though in double-LP form that still allows numerous different versions of the album to float around (a five-CD box-set of 'the Genuine Basement Tapes', for example), the LP comprised a set of songs Dylan and his backing band, The Hawks (latterly The Band) recorded

59 Each chapter of Thompson's would-be New Journalism book, *Postively Main Street*, invariably involves the word 'Gush'. No, really. 'Gushicon Two', 'the First Gush', etc., and Christ, it's unbearable. But the section entitled 'Microgush' on page 58 winningly, to my mind, does include a footnote that advises: 'Now please cue up either side one, band two of *Freewheelin' Bob Dylan* or side one, band one of *Nashville Skyline*. You know . . .' Mockable as it is, that level of gauche clubbishness seems, if only fleetingly, quite endearing from this vantage point. Elsewhere, Thompson journeys to Dylan's hometown, Hibbing, and in the local Woolworths is mortified to find that *Bob Dylan's Greatest Hits* is 'the only album of Bob's in stock'. His outrage only increases when he travels on to Crippa's, 'Howard Street's only fully-fledged music store' and finds . . . '*two* of Bob's records? *John Wesley Harding* and *Greatest Hits*. None of the fine old stuff on early albums and the north country? Neither of the folk-rock albums *Bringing it all Back Home* and *Highway 61*, the two that *crucified* popular music . . .' 'His disappointment quickly abates when he discovers that this seemingly forsaken son bought his first harmonica in the store and generally made a nuisance of himself spending hours in there listening to records and ordering way-out Hank Williams discs.

during jam sessions in the basement of the group's communal house in Woodstock. Dylan was convalescing after his bike crash at the time and since proposed tours had been cancelled, group and singer got into a routine of meeting up to play music. There they fooled around with new – and indeed old – ideas, taping the results with a portable machine. Copies of new Dylan songs that came out of these sessions ('I Shall Be Released', 'Nothing Was Delivered', 'Mighty Quinn', 'This Wheel's on Fire', 'The Million Dollar Bash') were eventually circulated among the likes of Manfred Mann and The Byrds in the hope that they might want to cover them. They did. As did Peter, Paul and Mary, Julie Driscoll and Brian Auger, and Fairport Convention.

The tapes themselves, however, remained unreleased. Copies of copies somehow drifted into the hands of two young men in Los Angeles, called 'Patrick' and 'Merlin', according to *Rolling Stone*, who 'saw it as their duty to put Dylan's songs into the hands of the people' and pressed up 8,000 copies of a bootleg double LP.

Just to add to the confusion, this LP, known due to its white sleeve and unmarked label as the *Great White Wonder*, was a mishmash of *Basement Tape* material and early taped-off-the-radio stuff. But let's not go there. Read *Invisible Republic* by Greil Marcus for that.

What it did, however, was start a cottage industry in bootlegs. It certainly wasn't the first bootleg – a term derived from whisky-running, where a boot was sometimes used to carry distilled hooch – Edward J. Smith, an opera buff and classical record producer with Allegro records in the 1950s, had taken it upon himself to issue tapes of radio broadcasts of many classic opera performances from the Met and La Scala on LP, without causing much concern or offence to artists or record companies – he once compiled a six-LP set of the 101 best versions of Rodolfo's 'Che gelida manina' aria from *La Bohème*.

But this was Bob Dylan, and the bristling-badger silence that greeted the bootleg was seen as a white dove from above. A commercial covenant was duly accepted – at least until swingeing new copyright laws were introduced in the US in 1971.

From now on, LPs were just far too important to be left in the hands of even rock gods, or so it seemed. Where pirates nowadays routinely cut entire new albums from the moorings of their release dates and set them adrift in cyberspace, this kind of free the music/power to the people malarkey remained in its infancy back then. To purchase a bootleg LP was to join an audio underground and place oneself outside the law. Like scoring, skinning up and then smoking dope, tracking down, buying and listening to these particular records offered heady illicit thrills of their own. This was word to the wise, no questions asked, plain wrappers, under the counter stuff. These albums were not coming to a Woolworths in Hibbing (or Haverfordwest, for that matter) any time soon.

On one level, to seek out a bootleg LP was to show one's contempt for whatever artistic direction Dylan himself had planned for his recording career. More seriously, perhaps, it was also to defraud the musician of a source of revenue. But on another level, to hunt down a bootleg was to prove you were a superior fan. Owners of the *Great White Wonder* were elite disciples whose thorough knowledge of the readily available set-texts of the canon was only to be enhanced by reference to supplementary LPs. For the fanatical, such recordings were the Dead Sea Scrolls and the Apocrypha in one – a confirmation of their faith and an omen of what might come.

The bootleg LP afforded a *sotto voce* conversation with the great man in comparison with the scrupulously prepared statements of the studio LPs. Contradictory as it might seem, it was the earnestness with which the latter were regarded that made the former so desirable. Having built up a relationship with an increasingly elusive Dylan via his concerts and protean albums, devotees could only hanker for greater intimacy. (And possibly something that wasn't the countrified Howdy Doody of *Nashville Skyline*.) While perhaps not in quite the same league as a Paris Hilton sex tape, an LP that its creator never intended you to hear is a chance to experience the admired at their more unguarded.

(This is pushing the point but in this respect music fans can arguably share the same hunger for something a little less polished, a little less managed as the readers of *Celebs Snapped Looking Dog Rough Coming Out of China Whites Weekly* or whatever. The ropily recorded bootleg LP and the surreptitious snap of bulging cellulite simultaneously use and expose our unease with – and relish for – the instruments of the mass media. Where we are presented with orchestrated photo spreads in magazines and newspapers, and packaged and produced LPs, practically the same kit is able to dish up to equal delight the unexpected, the tarnished and the flawed.)

That *Great White Wonder* and its clones – *Rolling Stone* in 1969 maintained that everybody was getting in on the act and that people were 'going out and buying an "underground", then pressing a few thousand copies of for themselves' – sold between 40,000 and 300,000 copies illustrates the thirst for unmediated music outside the mainstream. But we've got slightly ahead of ourselves here – it's time to reel back and consider the corresponding shifts in social attitudes that in the latter half of the 1960s saw a section of pop and its audience move from hit singles to often self-consciously 'anti-commercial' albums.

POP GOES POP!

In a symbolic moment in the mid-1960s, the clock at Victoria station in London was removed as the roads were widened, hinting perhaps at ways in which people in the eye of Harold Wilson's white-hot technological revolution would have more and yet less time. After thirteen years of Tory rule – 'thirteen wasted years' in Labour's memorable campaign slogan – Wilson's election in 1964 was heralded as a victory for a new, modern and progressive Britain at a moment when many were impatient for change. It was an age in which genuine utopianism mingled with a hungry-for-anything individualism fostered by rapid technological advances that equipped ordinary people with material goods.

But when Labour was booted out of power in 1970, chastened by industrial disputes, economic crisis and riven by internal clashes, some felt too little had been achieved and that more radical solutions were needed; others that far too much damage had been done and it was time to retrench. In this, they were in sync with the world of pop, as the giddy youthful energy of the beat boom sped on to progressive rock on LPs.

By 1964, the Rolling Stones, the Kinks and co., had enjoyed number one singles. These young guns and their fans, bowled over at having remade the charts and the media at large in their own image, must have been rather perturbed once the dust had settled some eighteen months later to look around and discover Harry Secombe and Ken Dodd swanning around the top ten. How swinging, exactly, was London when the biggest selling LP of 1965 was the soundtrack to *The Sound of Music?*[60] The record hogged the top two positions in the album charts for two whole years – from June 1965 until June 1967.

One unlikely scapegoat was pirate radio. Having broken the BBC's stranglehold of pop music on the airwaves, it was now blamed for allowing the likes of Dodd and Val Doonican to get into the charts. Kids were not purchasing as many singles as they once had because they could hear the music they liked for free on the radio. Old fuddy-duddies, on the other hand, would seemingly buy anything as long as it was sung by a middle-aged man off the telly in a spruce cardigan.

Partly triggered by the final episode of the hit music show *Ready, Steady Go*, Maureen Cleave wrote a piece for the *Evening Standard* on 29 December 1966 entitled 'The Year Pop Went Flat'. In it, Cleave argued that the pop scene that had 'diverted the general public for the last three years' was done with. Citing Val Doonican's and the Seekers' dominance of the hit parade, she maintained that its vigour, freshness and monstrous verve had gone. Chief among Cleave's other complaints was that 'pop

---

60 Okay, it does depend on your definition of 'swinging' – singing nuns and Nazis could probably out-kink the Kinks.

stars' in 1966 'floated around loving people in a patronising manner that was even more infuriating than their protest songs'. 'Paradoxically', though, she found that the records of The Who, the Beatles, the Stones and the Beach Boys, were 'better than ever'.

What Cleave's comments hint at, other than the obvious widespread use of psychotropic drugs, was an unravelling of the consensus in the pop single charts. The idea that good music was popular and popular music was good, and that the best groups should win, suddenly seemed to have come unstuck[61] – unsurprisingly, perhaps, at a time when increased personal entitlement fostered by education, a broader belief in social liberty, consumer goods, and a fondness for consciousness-expanding drugs were shattering so many long-held certainties.

Some musicians came to see the LP as a way of marking out their difference from the fly-by-night hit-singles-obsessed world of 'ordinary' pop. Where we are used to the idea of dumbing down, many musicians in the late 1960s wanted to move up – and accordingly aspired to communicate with their similarly minded fans on LP. Part of this impetus could have been merely commercial prudence. By 1966, singles and albums had edged level in sales in the UK, with each format running at about 49 million

61 Only three months later, in March 1967, Christine and Wendy, two Walker Brothers' fans from Leeds, wrote to *Disc* and *Music Echo* with an ingenious proposal for righting the charts: 'The Walkers needn't worry unduly about their recent singles "failing to emerge" in the top ten. One has only to look at the top twenty to see the present record-buying public has little appreciation of good music. A new top twenty should be organised for true artists like the Walker Brothers, Stevie Winwood, Beach Boys, the Tamla Motown sound, Cat Stevens, and leave the present one for the boring unoriginal artists like Ken Dodd, Engelbert Humperdinck, Monkees and Val Doonican.'

units. Though of course you could reverse this, and argue that as pop artists started to make more interesting LPs – or at least ones with less filler and nicer sleeves – they represented better value and were a more compelling purchase.

There was a World Cup on. London was swinging. New drugs were on the loose. And at this moment, people felt pretty good about what Harold Wilson later christened 'the pound in their pocket'.

Like jazz, pop too would come to want to assert its own aesthetic standards, ones that were not entirely dictated by the old benchmark, a place in the charts. Henceforth albums would become the territory in which 'artists' expressed themselves, as pop music gained a buoyant 'underground'.

Those loveable moptops, like others, now aspired to make art and not pop. Or some combination of the two.

Mick Jagger, crediting the Beatles' *Revolver* as 'the 'beginning of an appeal to the intellect', informed the *NME* in 1967 that: 'Once you could tell how well a group was doing by the reaction to their sex appeal but the days of the hysteria are fading and for that reason there will never be a new Stones or a new Beatles. We are moving after "minds" and so are most of the new groups.'

Pete Townshend of The Who (one such new group), having twice been pipped to the number one spot, first by the Seekers and then by Jim Reeves, vented his anger in *Disc and Music Echo* just a few weeks before Cleave's piece. '[T]he stuff people like Ken Dodd do is fantastically old fashioned at a time when most of us musicians are trying to make strides forward.'

Two months later, the collective Who 'brain', by then regularly gorging itself on LSD, unveiled plans for a 'pop opera'. A two-LP, twenty-five-act 'sound experiment', all about 'a man whose wife dies and he leaves his home and travels and become involved in wars, revolutions and gets killed'. What strides indeed.

Townshend, a graduate of Ealing Arts School, had originally ridden to fame stating that The Who stood for 'pop-art music' and maintained that 'albums were what you got for Christmas' and that he only believed in 'singles, in the Top Ten records and pirate radio'. Like many others, he was now expanding his canvas.

The title track of *A Quick One*, their next LP released in December 1966, was an enchanting mini-opera that recounted the unlikely amorous difficulties of a young woman, her absent-but-soon-to-be-returning lover and Ivor, an engine driver she's dallied with in between.

At Ealing, Townshend had attended lectures by Gustav Metzger, the exponent of Auto-Destructive art. The Who guitarist had appropriated Metzger's theories for the band's instrument-smashing stage act, and he was now among a slew of art school educated pop acts who were beginning to use pop as a means of self-expression and social criticism rather then mere entertainment.

As early as 1964, Ray Davies of the Kinks, who studied at Hornsey and Croydon, told *Rave* magazine that 'being a Kink was an art, only I am dabbling in sounds, not pictures'. And in March 1966, he informed the *NME*, 'I play at 33 1/3 rpm now'. Later that year saw the release of *Face to Face*, an album that had been the work of several months' labour in the studio. Casting aside the R&B trappings and covers of their previous two Kinks LPs, it was a thoughtful and thematically arranged self-penned album. The pop equal of *Darling* or *Cathy Come Home*, it was world-weary beyond its years. Satirical numbers like 'Dandy', 'Session Man' and 'House in the Country' explored its creators disdain for the giddy circus of Swinging London, while the plaintive, harpsichord-drenched 'Too Much on My Mind' touched on Davies' own mental breakdown. It was said by *Disc and Music Echo* to contain 'the most way-out Ray Davies comment compositions yet recorded.' In an otherwise positive review in *Crawdaddy*, Paul Williams complained that it was 'an overly arty LP'. He hadn't seen anything yet . . .

Davies' ambitions – which were broad enough to encompass a move into 'things like Christmas pantomimes' when 'Waterloo Sunset' topped the charts in 1966 – would for some time be thwarted by Pye, his record company. Pye Nixa was a power-house of often brilliant short-order pop, novelty singles, American blues and soul imports, and budget classical and easy LPs. The label had been responsible for the first LP to 'chart' in Britain. It had put the *Lonnie Donegan Showcase* out in December 1956 – a 10-inch album that made the singles list as there was no separate LP chart at the time. In the 1960s, Pye was home to Vince Hill, Jim Dale, the Searchers, Petula Clark, Sandie Shaw, Donovan Leitch (England's weird-chinned answer to Dylan) and, er, Freddie Lennon, John's dad. But Pye was behind the curve in the latter half of the 1960s when the pop market matured and increasingly embraced the 'rock' album as its format of choice. (The company passed on Led Zeppelin, signing instead the distressingly profitable Max Bygraves for Singalonga Max after Singalonga Max LP.) Davies had to sit back while Pye devalued his hard-fought attempts to make sustained statements on LPs like *(The Kinks Are) The Village Green Preservation Society*, by bunging out compilation albums of old singles on its bargain-bin March Arch offshoot.

The guitarist Eric Clapton, who as a member of high-octane supergroup Cream enjoyed a far easier transition into critically lauded and bestselling LPs, subsequently expressed his distaste for making anything other than sonically invigorating albums like *Fresh Cream* and *Disraeli Gears*: 'Single sessions are terrible, I can't take them at all.'

Scott Walker was another pop star growing weary of the whole business of having to have hit singles. By 1969, he wouldn't be having hit albums either, but, as he told Jonathan King in 1967, 'What I have to offer is not the sort of thing that can be sold in large quantities.'

Walker was the brooding, Garbo-esque front man of the London-based American orchestral popsters the Walker Brothers. None of them were related, nor were any of them named Walker – Scott was born Noel Scott Engel. And as the notes from the group's second LP, *Portrait*, imply, Walker's eventual separation from his bandmates and the flimflam of pop seem all but inevitable. 'Scott', the jacket states, 'lives too hard because it is the only way he knows how. The Existentialist who knows what it means and reads Jean Paul Sartre . . . The Loner who haunts late night London scenes and immerses his mind in the unfathomable depths of modern jazz.' John, meanwhile, is described as 'more affably American than most', owned two Alsatians and dreamed of retiring 'to a place called Laguna on the Californian coast'. And as for Gary . . . 'The Humourist who plays Russian Roulette with cartons of cream cakes – first one sick is out!'

Going solo in 1967, Walker announced that he was 'tired of people on my back about being commercial. I am not out to get anything in the chart anymore. What I have to SAY will be on albums in future . . . I can't say anything on singles . . . And I have so much to say musically.'

Walker's own views about ignoring the charts seem here to be at one with his most loyal admirers, letter-writers like our Christine and Wendy in *Disc*. Having already smuggled tunes involving tree-charming Greek gods into the nation's living rooms, Walker pursued a singular musical odyssey over the course of his next four LPs. Lushly orchestrated torch songs about lonely transvestites called Louise who were hefty. Pounding covers of Jacques Brel numbers where protagonists waited in line to catch the clap off dragoon-servicing prostitutes. Numbers critiquing neo-Stalinist regimes. Tributes to Danish cities and Swedish arthouse films. It was magnificent stuff, but somehow he possibly failed to carry even Christine and Wendy along with him: *Scott 4* bombed. In a television interview for the BBC in 2006, perhaps not entirely in earnest, he blamed the almost exclusive use of 3/4 time on *Scott 3* for scaring people away. Whatever the reason, ostensibly a number of years in the easy listening wilderness were to be his fate.[62]

The tension between wanting to strike out for new ground and the fear of alienating an existing audience was sometimes strongest in those acts who had done most to expand people's ideas about pop music. Interviewed by Ray Coleman in 1966 on the eve of *Revolver*'s release, Paul McCartney admitted: 'We'll lose some fans with it.' Then quickly added, 'But we'll also gain some. The fans we'll probably lose will be the ones who don't

---

62 Sleeved in post-punk grey, Julian Cope's 1981 compilation *The Godlike Genius of Scott Walker* helped to revive Walker's fortunes.

like the things about us that we never liked anyway, and those we'll gain are the ones who want to hear us breaking into new things.'

When the group progressed to *Sgt. Pepper's Lonely Hearts Club Band*, there were worries they might have gone too far. According to Barry Miles, Beatles' manager Brian Epstein 'was scared. He thought it might not sell and it might destroy their careers and his percentage.' And at least some of the motivation for giving the album such a lavish package – the now near-immortal 'crowd collage' of Peter Blake's sleeve, the cut-out figures on an inlay, the gatefold sleeve, printed lyrics, a tone only dogs could hear and a lulling mantra on the run-out groove – was to provide fans with 'the best value album ever'. Paul McCartney told the illustrator Alan Aldridge that 'the idea was to do a complete thing, that you could make what you liked of a little presentation – a packet of things inside the record sleeve'.[63]

Among those who were often most eager to hear – and see – the group breaking into new things were their immediate peers. An atmosphere of inquisitive and healthy competition flourished. As Roger McGuinn of The Byrds recalled, 'we transmitted messages across the Atlantic via records, which is really a lot of fun . . . we did actually have a nice kind of interaction where we all did influence each other for a while there.' Such interaction was, of course, only occurring among a relatively small clique – one that would become increasingly narcissistic and self-

63 In stark contrast to their debut *Please Please Me*, done in a day and for £400 in 1963, four years later *Sgt. Pepper* took four months and cost an unprecedented £25,000 to record. Those costs have, in the long run, been amply recouped: in November 2006, the album came second in a poll of bestselling British albums of all time (or that time, really), having shifted 4.8 million copies.

absorbed as the decade ebbed – but it yielded commercial, as well as artistic dividends in spades.

LPs were serving as transatlantic jungle drums, each new beat inspiring another in turn.

On first hearing the Beatles' *Rubber Soul* in a haze of pot smoke, Brian Wilson couldn't believe his ears. 'They put only great stuff on the album', he remembered in 1991. (The version he listened to was, in fact, different from the one that the Beatles had themselves meticulously prepared – Capitol in their customary wisdom had elected to re-jig the tracks to ride the folk boom, leaving off the beatier 'Drive My Car' and 'Nowhere Man', for instance.[64]) When the record was over, he ran into his kitchen and told his wife that he was, 'going to make the greatest album. The greatest rock album ever made.'

And he had a damned good try. But getting his ideas past the rest of the group, or the record company who had set notions on what the Beach Boys' fans would like was another matter. Wilson, who after a breakdown, no longer toured with the group, had become an avid pot smoker. As he wrote in his autobiography, 'pot made the music grow in my head'. He found writing and recording the whole of the second side of the Beach Boys' *Today* album under its influence had opened up whole new musical horizons. Progressing to LSD in 1965, he'd seen God. God, as deities who address partially deaf Californian musicians are wont to do, had plans for Brian. Those plans first involved a symphonic ode to the female form in the Golden State. All the snake and apples stuff was finally over and done with, it appeared. 'California Girls', acid-laced as it was, remained a sunny anthem that fitted the Beach Boys' blueprint. Cousin Mike

64 Never ones to pass on a trend, Jan and Dean in 1966 recorded their *Folk 'n' Roll* LP – a record that boasted their rather unconvincing cover of the already ersatz protest anthem 'Eve of Destruction'.

Love, worried that Brian was 'fucking with the formula', could get behind that. Chicks, oh yeah! And Love felt more vindicated in his belief that the Beach Boys were about Fun, Fun, Fun, when the *Beach Boys' Party!* – a just-add-a-six-pack mock party/jam session LP of covers and old hits knocked out for Christmas – outsold *Summer Days (Summer Night)*, that summer's studio LP.

But *Rubber Soul* had pointed the way for Brian. If Love's 'priority was getting airplay', Wilson's from now onwards was (like his British contemporaries) 'about making art'. He dreamed of creating an album of what he called 'spiritual music'. Calling in Tony Asher, an ad agency copywriter who'd penned such gems as 'You Can Tell It's Mattel – It's Swell', to devise lyrics while the group was away on a Far Eastern tour, songs like 'Wouldn't It Be Nice' and 'God Only Knows' and 'Don't Talk (Put Your Head On My Shoulder)' fell into place. By the time the rest of the group returned, much of the LP was complete. Love castigated it as 'ego music'. According to Wilson, during one session, he snapped: 'Who's gonna hear this shit? The ears of a dog?' – a rebuke Wilson volleyed back by naming the LP *Pet Sounds*. When finished, the LP, a *Wunderkammer* of exquisite layered vocal harmonies and unorthodox instrumentation, joyous, wistful and melancholy by turn, would close with the noise of a clanking train and Wilson's own dog, Banana, barking.

Capitol hated the record. They considered shelving it but opted instead to treat it with less than benign neglect. Doing their best to bury it, they rush-released a *Best of the Beach Boys* compilation LP. But even a sleeve that left many thinking the group had a bit of a weird thing about goats could not kill it off. In England it became a *cause célèbre* . . . a signpost in itself of where music might go next. The album was premiered in London at an elite listening session at the Hilton Hotel attended by Marianne Faithfull, John Lennon and Paul McCartney – the Beatle songsmiths adjourned to

McCartney's *pied-à-terre* once it was over to instantly commence writing 'Here, There and Everywhere'. 'THIRTEEN TRACKS of Brian Wilson genius', was Penny Valentine's verdict in *Disc*. In an article in the *Melody Maker* headed 'Pet Sounds, the Most Progressive Pop Album ever OR as sickly as Peanut Butter', Eric Clapton maintained that 'Ginger, Jack and I [of Cream] are absolutely completely knocked out by *Pet Sounds*. I consider it to be one of the greatest pop LPs to ever be released.' Expounding on the album in the same paper, a little later Wilson commented: 'If you take the *Pet Sounds* album as a collection of art pieces, each designed to stand alone yet which belong together, you'll see what I was aiming at.' Whatever his intentions for *Pet Sounds*, the British record-buying public, in contrast to their American peers who largely cold-shouldered it in favour of the *Best of . . .*, did take it to their hearts and to number two in the album charts. In the *NME*, meanwhile, the Beach Boys were hailed as the World's number one group.

Where this 'genius', Brian himself, would go next was a matter of wild speculation and great anticipation. A follow-up LP, advertised in the press and titled *Smile* was eagerly awaited. ('*Look! Listen! Vibrate! Smile!*' ran one campaign. 'It's Brian, Dennis, Carl, Al and Mike's greatest ever. Contains 'Good Vibrations', their all time biggest selling single, other new and fantastic Beach Boys songs . . . and . . . an exciting full colour sketchbook, look inside the world of Brian Wilson.') The eager, sadly, would have a long wait. Wilson would not complete the record until 2004.

He'd been through a lot in the interim, spending what felt like twenty-five years variously on drugs, overweight, in a sand box, wearing firemen's helmets, insane, in bed, looking unwell in a sketch with John Belushi and Dan Ackroyd, or in the clutches of some gold-digging quack. It seemed churlish for some to point out that whatever he did, *Smile* never, ever would be found now.

Its absence had become it existence. Its loss never nearer than when 'it' was finally to hand. Brian Wilson's *Smile* with the Wondermints was just another cruel reminder of what had not been. Perhaps the 1960s would never have ended if it had been finished and released in 1967. Or could its non-appearance in 1967 be the very reason why we never seem entirely able to break free of the 1960s? *Smile* is a loose tooth, an itch, something we continually have go back to and poke or scratch. It remains a cultural counterfactual that even its creator can't solve for us, however nice it is to have him back and well.

When Paul McCartney was interviewed about the making of *Sgt. Pepper* for the *South Bank Show* in 1997, he was asked about *Pet Sounds* and confessed to being 'really blown away with how clever it was and how intriguing the arrangements were . . . because of the work they'd done, it didn't seem too much of a stretch for us to get further out than they'd got; so it was very influential.'[65]

And looking back from this vantage point, what is most startling is the speed with which musicians and their fans retooled their desires for and expectations of an LP – even their demands for an LP full stop. Basic aspects like their length and what were fit subjects or styles for pop albums, taken as read today, suddenly came up for grabs in this period. What Beatles

---

65 Barry Miles, who was witness to *Sgt. Pepper*'s creation, recalled that: 'Everybody was fascinated by the Beach Boys. People used to sit around and try and count the edits in 'Good Vibrations', which apparently had 38 or whatever it has and some of them you could detect. But it was the very idea that you could compose a piece of sound in different layers. All of these things were fascinating – now it's utterly mundane but at the time when the Beach Boys were doing this, EMI was still in four-track studios – and really obsolete stuff that they had built themselves, it all looked like it came out of a Lancaster bomber.'

producer George Martin latterly characterised as 'an era of trying things out like mad in the studio, the era of almost continuous technological experimentation,'[66] only succeeded because they had such purpose and resonance with a growing audience for whom being unconventional – 'doing your own thing', in the parlance of the period – was in itself starting to be held in greater esteem.

That change did come on remarkable quickly. In April 1966, for instance, Mick Jagger could confidently boast in this mood of thrusting sonic experimentation that the Stones' new LP, *Aftermath*, would 'probably be the longest pop LP ever produced'. What Jagger had not reckoned upon was the almost simultaneous arrival of rock's first two double albums in that same year: Bob Dylan's *Blonde on Blonde* (seventy-one minutes!), closely followed by Frank Zappa and The Mothers of Invention's aptly entitled *Freak Out!* – an hour of . . . whatever it was – dada art, doo-woop parodies, strung-out blues, weird jams, satirical skits and the Dylanesque 'Trouble Every Day', a spot-on barb about the Watts Riots from the annoyingly self-righteously sober (control) freak and his cohorts.[67] One contemporary reviewer

66 'There is no doubt that their experience of taking drugs, and in particular LSD, was one of the main reasons that the Beatles, as George Martin himself has written, 'moved the pop song away from the old three-minute rock 'n' roll formula to a much more experimental, much freer musical form.'

67 This 'look at the length of my LP' pose seems to tally with Mick Farren's recollections of the machismo that surrounded the supposedly enlightening consumption of acid: 'Many of my peers', Farren wrote in his memoir *Give the Anarchist a Cigarette*, 'treated LSD as a spiritual rite of passage with distinctly macho overtones, and even though they sequestered themselves in their room with their water, brown rice and copy of *Blonde on Blonde*, a definite vibe could be felt that you weren't a real man until you'd taken your righteous trip.'

stated, 'it's all because the sounds they make are so weird that make it worth listening to a double LP'. Which, while damning in its faint praise, at least acknowledges that 'weirdness' might be a motivating factor in listening to an LP – and, specifically, a double one at that.

Aftermath, by comparison, would in the end seem almost short at fifty-three minutes and, by comparison, tame. (It was also still only the first Stones album to be comprised solely of Jagger/Richards songs.) Sugaring some of Mick and Keith's more bitter pills – not least by adding a marimba to the irredeemably misogynist 'Under My Thumb' and the smug push-off of 'Out of Time' – was Brian Jones, whose sitar- and dulcimer-playing on the record also reflected the era's rising fascination with all noises Eastern. George Harrison, introduced by the Byrds to records by the sitar player Ravi Shankar, had slipped the instrument onto 'Norwegian Wood', Lennon's post-fling Post-it note to Cynthia, while the second side of the Byrds' 1966 album *Fifth Dimension* jolted into previously

Frank Zappa's own prolixity eventually resulted in a contract-busting rift with his record company. In 1977, he handed Warner Bros *Läther*, an attention-deficient, challenging, double double LP. The label refused to release this four-sided, self-gratifying monster in its entirety, and lumps of it were eventually salami-sliced onto four separate albums. But in the ensuing legal fracas, Zappa responded by convincing a small Pasadena radio station to let him play the whole album on their show, encouraging listeners to bootleg it. 'This is Frank Zappa,' Zappa informed pop-pickers, 'as your bogus temporary disc jockey making it possible for you to run your little cassette machine and tape an album which is perhaps never going to be available to the public at large.' Among Zappa-ites who hadn't taped it, it acquired a mythic status as a lost masterpiece. When it appeared on CD in the 1990s, its mix of puerile humour and genre-hopping wack-outs inspired, in others, another word beginning with the letter M.

unreachable altitudes with the sitar-scaled 'Eight Miles High'.[68]

Preceding the release of the LP, the single 'Eight Miles High' was interpreted, not unreasonably as a drug song. In the UK, a young counsellor from Birmingham petitioned to have it banned.

The song was ostensibly an account of the culture-shock the group had experienced on their first trip to London in 1965 – 'the rain gray town, known for its sound', as they had it. Its modal instrumentation was derived from almost ceaseless daily exposure to a tour bus tape of John Coltrane and Ravi Shankar – the only single tape they had with them. But who were they kidding, really? On the LP, whose sleeve featured a shot of the group on a 'floating' oriental carpet, it joined tracks about alien visitations ('Mr Spaceman') and laying aside two-dimensional boundaries ('5D'), while Dave Crosby's questing 'What's Happening?!?!' waved goodbye to the conventions of punctuation as feverishly as any New Journalist on the trail of Ken Kesey's acid-dispensing International Harvester bus.

Like giggly schoolboys slipping notes past the teacher, slang and metaphor, traditionally deployed in popular song to refer to sex, was becoming preposterously druggy. (Hash brownie points were awarded for those, like 'Day Tripper' and 'She Said' that alludes to both.) Paul McCartney, given by sheer physiognomy to almost involuntary winks and nods anyway, explained to Barry Miles that in their 'psychedelic period', he and Lennon became 'interested in winking to our friends and comrades in arms, putting in references that we knew our

---

68 The who-did-it-first of white boys and sitars in pop is hotly contested, but the Kinks' 'See My Friends', a top ten single in July 1965, which has a sitar-like humming twelve-string guitar line, usually wins out in pub music quizzes.

friends would get but that the Great British Public might not.'[69]

On *Aftermath*, in a possibly rare moment of sensitivity, the Stones had presented a neat inversion of this with 'Mother's Little Helpers', a song that drew attention to the largely un-acknowledged, prosaic narcotic habits of a larger portion of the Great British Public.

At the time when the Beatles were chastising day trippers for their lack of commitment to alternative realms of consciousness, McCartney, while a dedicated pothead, had not yet taken LSD himself, and well into 1966, the acid scene in England remained confined to an elite clique (artists, writers, musicians, boutique owners, students, dentists, etc.). Arguably, since even at the height of its popularity in the years to follow acid was pre-dominantly the preserve of middle-class college-educated kids – or middle-class college kids who'd turned on, tuned in and dropped out of college – it was only ever confined to an elite clique. The comfort of that type of upbringing was frequently reflected in the range of illusions allegedly inspired by the drug that were culled from comfortably middle-class children's books about anthropomorphised rabbits with watches, or moles and rats running frightfully oikish weasels and stoats off country piles. (This was a nice change in some respects, since they did at least briefly abandon, or under LSD's influence were unable to

69 Accordingly, on *Sgt. Pepper*, listeners would be invited to take some tea on 'Lovely Rita', dig some weeds on 'When I'm Sixty-Four' and be advised that Ringo, in a possible nod to a misunderstanding in the Delmonico Hotel some years earlier, got high with a little help from his friends. The BBC would nevertheless deem 'A Day in the Life', with its 'woke up, had a smoke and I'd love to turn you on bag', a drug reference too far and banned it from their airwaves. 'Lucy in the Sky with Dia-monds', on the other hand, was obviously merely an innocent misunder-standing over a drawing of a schoolmate by young Julian Lennon.

sustain, the pretence of being sharecroppers from the Delta or wherever. Though much of the music remained amped-up-to-11 blues.)

Over in California, the psychedelic scene was a little more belligerent. The novelist Ken Kesey was pivotal in spreading the psychedelic word. His bestselling *One Flew Over the Cuckoo's Nest* had given him the funds to buy a ranch in La Honda near San Francisco where he gaily dished out trips to free thinkers, Beat poets and Harley-riding hoods. Buying an old school bus and recruiting Neal Cassady – the man who had chauffeured Jack Kerouac and been immortalised as Dean Moriarty – to do the driving, Kesey and his cohorts, now christened The Merry Pranksters, took acid On the Road. Kesey's immediate converts were in the Bay Area. Here, the Pranksters put on acid-soaked 'Trip Festivals' with music from 'switched-on' local groups like The Grateful Dead, Jefferson Airplane, Big Brother and the Holding Company, and Moby Grape. The run-down Victorian neighbourhood of Haight-Ashbury became the nucleus of this new 'hippy' movement; embracing communal living and committed believers in the liberating potentials of mind-expanding drugs – LSD but in the main, marijuana – the hippies, at their most optimistic or naive, believed that they were paving the way for a social revolution.

Some of this was down to sheer demographics. By 1966 there were more people in America under the age of twenty-five than over it, resulting in a widespread belief that an older minority hellbent on pursuing a war in Vietnam despite mass youth protest, was out of touch and its authority illegitimate. They were also a generation better educated than their forebears, with 85 per cent of baby-boomers born from 1947 to 1951 completing high school as opposed to just 38 per cent of their parents. And more than half of those went on to college – a figure unimaginable a decade or so before.

Though it's easy to trivialise now, this psychedelic expansion of the visual and aural palate was hugely important to the LP. Songs stretched to unprecedented lengths, sometimes filling entire sides of LPs: 'Revelation' on Love's *Da Capo*; the eponymous side-two track of Iron Butterfly's *In-A-Gadda-Da-Vida*; the nine-minute-long jam, 'Spare Chaynge', on Jefferson Airplane's *After Bathing at Baxter's*

Psychedelised musicians were making music on drugs that was good to take drugs to. Country Joe and the Fish's *Electric Music for the Mind and Body* LP was deliberately programmed to sound more stoned as each side went on. The first band to formally bill themselves as psychedelic – besting the Grateful Dead by some two weeks – were The 13th Floor Elevators. Their debut album *The Psychedelic Sounds Of . . .* , released in 1966, was Timothy Leary on LP: oddly scrawny, magnetic and a tad frightening. Wild-eyed vocalist Roky Erickson's howling vocals and some in-need-of-a-good-tuning electric guitars seem to spend the entire album trying to drown out a disquieting and insistent gurgling noise. The LP's liner notes, while asking 'What is that funny little noise?' (a jug, actually), spelt out the chapter and verse of their psychedelic vision:

> Recently, it has become possible for man to chemically alter his mental state and thus alter his point of view, that is, his own basic relation with the outside world which determines how he stores his information. He can then restructure his thinking and change his language so that his thoughts bear more relation to his life and his problems, therefore approaching them more sanely.
>
> 'It is this quest for pure sanity that forms the basis of the songs on this album.

Naturally, madness wasn't far away. Erickson, already diagnosed as schizophrenic, tried to beat a drugs charge by pleading insanity and ended up in a criminal mental institution in 1969.

But the Elevators' proselytising sleeve shows the greater interest in – and the control groups were exerting over – their own album sleeves. In the Grateful Dead's case, the whorling, blissed-out covers on their first three LPs were infinitely more exciting than their contents.

In the UK, having commissioned a friend, Terry Quirk, to conjure up a design for their final, deliciously choral LP, the Zombies opted to change the title of the album rather than lose the trippy sleeve when it was discovered that Quirk had rendered 'Odyssey and Oracle', 'Odessey and Oracle'.[70]

The Fool, jobbing Dutch psychedelic designers to the stars, having decorated John Lennon's Roller and supplied the sleeve

---

70 The band called it a day after the album and the singer Colin Blunstone was forced to take a job in an insurance office to make ends meet.

for the Incredible String Band's *5,000 Spirits Or the Layers of the Onion*, actually recorded an LP themselves.

Like the brightly coloured clothes worn to indicate an 'on' outlook, the jacket fast became the place to advertise the adventurousness of the musicianship inside. As commerciality in pop became suspect, so old standards about the commercial criteria of jacket design fell away. Band mugshots and names fell off. Abstract designs proliferated. Trippy imagery to enhance the tripping listener's pleasure proliferated. Gatefold sleeves and time-defying double LPs grew, their covers and contents intended to accompany dope smoking and facilitate skinning-up. The Small Faces' *Ogdens' Nut Gone Flake*, which along with trying the patience of all but the most monged by having an entire second side dominated by gobbledygook merchant Stanley Unwin, came with a sleeve that was a round facsimile of a tobacco tin.

In England, Harold Wilson's decision to keep Britain out of Vietnam made the war a less pressing concern. And LSD, for a time dished out by Leary associate Michael Hollingshead from the World Psychedelic Centre in Pont Street, Knightsbridge, was initially most enthusiastically adopted by a set of affluent Chelsea Bohemians with ties to both the Beatles and the Stones. Their reference points were De Quincey, Blake and Edward Lear. And the English acid scene would always be flavoured with an Arcadian edge, the Eastern mysticism somehow mingling with thoughts of India, the Empire and pink blotches lost from the map. (The soon *de rigeur* military dress sold by the Portobello Road shop I Was Lord Kitchener's Valet could almost be seen as a posh kid's joke at the expense of the parka-sporting working-class mods.)

Orbiting around the then down-at-heel Notting Hill, the UFO club and the Indica Gallery and Bookshop, and with *International Times* as its in-house magazine, the London underground's leading groups were the jazz-loving Soft Machine and The Pink Floyd Sound. Floyd's leader, the elfin former Camberwell art student Syd Barrett, guzzled acid as if there was no tomorrow. Their heavily improvised live sets at the UFO owed as much to avant-garde composers Cornelius Cardew, John Cage and AMM as the Byrds and Love.

Describing one of their early shows, Barry Miles reported in *International Times* that they were taking 'musical innovation further out than it had been before, walking out on incredibly dangerous limbs and dancing along crumbling precipices, saved sometimes only by the confidence beamed at them from their audience sitting a matter of feet away at their feet.'

The word 'sitting' says it all, really, doesn't it?[71]

The group were managed by Peter Jenner, who had only stumbled upon them after his approaches to a New York band, the Velvet Underground, had fallen through. The Velvets, for reasons best known to themselves, had signed up with Andy Warhol instead, who foisted the icy chanteuse Nico upon them. Her place in the group's pecking order was neatly defined by the title of their first LP, *The Velvet Underground and Nico*.

Brian Eno once famously quipped that hardly anyone bought that first Velvets album, but (perhaps in constrast to the horizontal Floyd-heads) those who did all formed bands. Seemingly 'the product of a secret marriage between Bob Dylan and the

---

71 But its significance shouldn't be underestimated. Robert Wyatt of the Soft Machine has stated that the supine state of the crowds at the UFO club greatly influenced his band's musical direction: 'the atmosphere created by an audience sitting down was very inducive to playing, as in Indian classical music, a long gentle droning introduction to a tune. It's quite impossible', he argued, 'if you've got a room full of beer-swilling people standing-up waiting for action . . . but if you've got a floor full of people . . . they're quite happy to wait half an hour for the first tune to get off the ground.'

Marquis de Sade', as the journalist Richard Goldstein put it, the Velvet Underground offered the flip-side to the acid scene: their trips were bad and downright dirty. If others, at least, spouted the rhetoric of love and peace, the Velvets looked at the world through a glass darkly. And then took that glass, smashed it and ground the shards into the face of a speed freak who had probably just finished sucking a cock for the price of another spike. A woman in leather boots, possibly chastising a commercial traveller with a bullwhip, might well be looking on. A-a-ah-ndy or one of his lackeys would be on hand to film it all. (If this was New York, no wonder everyone was going to San Francisco . . .[72])

Where drugs continued in many quarters to be spoken of in coy, or allegorical, terms, the Velvet Underground and Nico came right out and said yes to heroin. As Elliot Murphy, on his sleeve notes for the 1969 *Velvet Underground Live* LP asked, rhetorically: 'What goes through a mother's mind when she asks her fifteen-year-old daughter, "What's the name of that song

---

72 In the 1960s and on into the 1980s, until Oliver Stone and Val Kilmer helpfully rammed home what a total cock Jim Morrison was in their biopic, the Doors from LA were perceived as the Velvets' musical and spiritual peers on the West Coast. 'Spiritual' is probably the wrong word, but Joan Didion in her book *The White Album* gives an account of a visit she made to what she quaintly describes as 'a sound studio' to see them recording an LP in 1968. 'I had already heard', she wrote, 'about acid as a transitional stage and also about the Maharishi and even about Universal Love, and after a while it all sounded like marmalade skies to me . . . but The Doors were different, The Doors interested me. The Doors seemed unconvinced that love was brotherhood and the Kama Sutra. The Doors' music insisted that love was sex and sex was death and therein lay salvation. The Doors were the Norman Mailers of the Top Forty . . .' They still, however, managed to idle away hours of studio time with the best of the loved-up mob. 'It would be some weeks', Didion concluded, 'before The Doors finished recording this album. I did not see it through.'

you're listening to??" and her daughter replies, "Heroin".'
Exactly how many fifteen-year-old girls were listening to the
Velvets back then might be a moot point, but the album,
nevertheless, was included in a *Disc and Music Echo* alphabetical
Christmas round-up in December 1967.[73]

'Very Vinyl. Beautiful' was Warhol's gnomic statement at the
time. And in 1967, 'beautiful' was the word of the moment—well, apart
from 'love'. Around the time his *Sunshine Superman* LP appeared,
Donovan informed television viewers that: 'My job is writing
beautiful things about beauty. You see, my life is beautiful?' An issue
of the *NME* reported an exchange between Donovan and Sandie
Shaw, notable for Shaw's endearing down-to-earth bemusement.

> Donovan: 'I think you are beautiful. I love beautiful minds.'
> Sandie: 'Uh?'
> Donovan: 'I like beautiful people. I would like to write a book
> about your beautiful mind.'
> Sandie: 'Yeah?'
> Donovan: 'Beauty is beauty.'
> Sandie: 'Thanks.'

All of this was a million miles from the 'will it be a soaraway
smash?' mentality of only a year or so earlier. Derek Taylor, who
has deservedly earned his place in pop history as the writer of
some of the finest album-sleeve notes ever penned, later reflected
that pop 'after 1967 became slightly, ever so slightly serious –
now there was surrealism, seriousness of purpose, earnestness,

73 'V', the entry ran 'is for "Velvet Underground and Nico" which John Peel
    and his many followers can tell you all about (Fontana 33s 6d); "Vanilla
    Fudge" who came and went leaving behind a controversial debut album
    (Atlantic 32s 7d); and Vaughan, as in Frankie with the "Frankie Vaughan
    Song Book" (Philips 38s)'

even? dare we say it? silliness in the attempted sending of messages or social import or in search of change.'[74]

A sense of that growing seriousness is provided in the opening issue of *Rolling Stone,* first published in 1967, which its founder Jann Wenner described then as 'sort of a magazine and sort of a newspaper' which would be 'not just about music, but also about the things and attitudes that the music embraces'.

This was, of course, only one side of the story.

Thousands lavished as much affection – and money – on Dionne Warwick's *The Windows of the World,* Engelbert Humperdinck's *Release Me,* Tom Jones' *Green, Green Grass of Home, A Drop of the Hard Stuff* by the Dubliners, *This is James Last, The Sound of Music* and *Fiddler on the Roof* as the blissed-out flower children back from their trips to Morocco and Afghanistan did on *The Hangman's Beautiful Daughter.*

In post-pub revels LP sleeves were no doubt used as beer mats and hats, and stared at longingly as frequently as they were skinned up on. Shopping lists and betting tips were surely scribbled on Emitex cleaning cloth advertising inner sleeves as regularly as poems, star charts or runic symbols. And biroing

74 Taylor, who helped set up the Monterey Pop Festival, was all too aware of that silliness and message-sending. As the American correspondent for *Disc,* his columns for the paper during the height of the psychedelic period for a time became little more than coded accounts of drug taking. Describing a visit paid by Paul McCartney to Brian Wilson and the Byrds, he wrote: 'Paul in LA was as easy and open and settled as a child at play. He has, and not without conscious thought, reconstructed his attitudes to eliminate anger, intolerance, malice and spite (and as there was never any envy, greed, sloth or hatred, nor was there any of the pressure which might induce lust). Paul McCartney, free of any deadly sins, lopes with superb élan through a world which for the most part rejoices in his belonging to it. (The same goes for Mal Evans, a very beautiful product of an incomparable scene.) Far out, man.

stars beside favourite tracks was probably a universal practice.

But, for good and ill, the weight invested in LPs by late 1960s musicians and their fans would have lasting consequences for the music industry – and the format. The LP had a primacy and an importance in pop it had not previously enjoyed.

In some circumstances, the very thing that had once supplied artists with the only chance to make an LP (i.e. a hit single) became in fact a barrier to critical or commercial success. Commercial success, for its own sake, became suspect. As Frank Zappa told an industry conference in 1969, 'a lot of underground acts don't care about making a hit record. They're interested in artistic expression. The underground sounds are raw. But the record industry should remember that the music sounds that way because of the environment the kids live in . . . Some of their bodies are chemically altered, and they have leisure-time activities that would be very foreign to record company executives. They have a concept of music as an art.'

By this time, of course, it was dawning on some record companies that this form of pop music, could, if marketed appropriately, be enormously commercial. As Joe Smith, an executive at Warner Brothers reflecting on the period recalled in *Rolling Stone* in 1971: 'We learned that there were other ways to sell records, like sponsoring a free concert in Detroit. We learned you don't have to be on Top 40 radio, that there's a whole market in underground FM. We learned that posters mean something, that billboards mean something.'

For what the hipper (or hippier) record consumer now wanted were records that at least appeared to arrive from outside the pop mainstream and possessed notable signs of artistic expression and – as student violence flared in Paris, the Soviet troops moved into Czechoslovakia and cities in America burned following the assassination of Martin Luther

King - political content. For many then (and since), that was only possible to achieve and perceive across the breadth of a whole, hopefully 'freaky' album.

Profane Culture, Paul Willis's sociological study of the hippy scene in 'a large industrial city' in England in 1969, provides some rather priceless illustrations of how widely and deeply that attitude had penetrated. Willis maintained that an interest in LPs rather than singles was actually a fundamental characteristic of the hippies he met. One of his interviewees, Les, expressing his disdain for singles among his social milieu, remarked, 'I just don't know anybody that's got a 45 record.'

Les argues that some of his albums would 'mean fuck all to anybody who isn't turned on', while another subject, Stuart, suggests that certain LPs have helped him to transcend such humdrum considerations as space and time.

If you've been on some good smoke, and you're really out of your head, these, especially these LPs that are out now, where there's sort of half an LP, or an LP that's just one record, time becomes completely irrelevant . . . Once you've got into it, if somebody should switch it off, and say, "How long has that record been playing?", you wouldn't be able to say if it's been playing ten minutes, two minutes, five minutes, a week.

A week? This, by anyone's definition, was a long-playing record. But at the close of the decade, the chance for getting lost in music,

literally as well as metaphorically, had increased inordinately.

Exemplifiying the pitfalls of the era, Syd Barrett of Pink Floyd can almost be heard being escorted from the group on 'Jug Band Blues', the last track on their second LP, *Saucerful of Secrets*. And after unleashing two solo LPs, he disappeared in a drug-induced haze, leaving only a breadcrumb trail of rumours about his madcap antics for fanatics to nibble upon. (A prize showing during the recording of 'Shine on You Crazy Diamond' in 1975.) Occasionally sighted around Cambridge looking fat, bald and mildly demonic, a *Stars in Their Eyes* Aleister Crowley, photos of him and salacious accounts of a supposedly tragic life story would keep bottom-feeding tabloid news editors in 'THIS EVIL DRUG MENACE' stories until his death in 2006.

However, the activities and attitudes of a more genuine devil – almost summoned up by the titles of the first two (almost contiguous) albums by hard-rocking, Satan-spouting Brummies Black Sabbath, *Black Sabbath* and *Paranoid* – would also reveal the awful and unintended consequences of scattering sly allusions across your LPs.[75]

Charles Manson was just another 'glib, grubby little man with a guitar scrounging for young girls using mysticism and guru babble' on the Haight who wanted to make it as a rock star. He befriended the Beach Boy Dennis Wilson, giving him the song 'Never Learn Not to Love' (aka 'Cease to Exist') that sat nestling, like a viper, on the Beach Boys' *20/20* LP. Displeased with the

---

75 Evil or 'black' magic was in the air – British former bluesman Graham Bond recorded his ode to the old gods, 'Holy Magick', around the same time, while the Stones had already presented their sub-*Sgt. Pepper, Their Satanic Majesties Request* and asked the devil for sympathy on *Beggar's Banquet*.

progress of his music career and convinced he'd found correlations to his wacked-out Neo-Nazi beliefs in the lyrics (and even the cover) of the Beatles' *White Album*, he dispatched his acolytes to conduct a killing spree that resulted in the death of the actress Sharon Tate and her unborn child and four others. Using their victims' blood, the murderers daubed references to songs from the album on the walls. Manson himself would make an album, *Lie*, to drum up funds when the case went to trial, while Trent Reznor would record his bestial, techno-goth album *The Downward Spiral* at the murder scene.

Despite that that 1960s ended on a high note for Richard Williams of the *Melody Maker*. Accidentally sent a test disc bearing a single tone along with John Lennon and Yoko Ono's experimental *Wedding Album*, Williams gamely did his best to convey a sense of this record for his readers in November 1969. '[C]onstant listening', he wrote, revealed 'a curious point' to the tone. 'The occillation produces an almost subliminal uneven "beat" which maintains interest.

'You could', he went on to suggest, 'have a ball by improvising your very own rags, plain-song or even Gaelic mouth music against the drone.' But in conclusion, perhaps sensing something may have gone slightly awry, wrote: 'This album will make interesting listening in twenty years' time. What will we think of us then?' A question probably best left unanswered now, in the light of what was to follow on LP . . .

Chapter Nine

STACKS OF TRACKS

'I would say a lot of the time I spent in America in the seventies is really hard to remember', David Bowie remarked in 1997. 'I listen to *Station To Station*', he added, 'as a piece of work by an entirely different person.'

It's a hoary old cliché but no one is supposed to remember the 1960s. There's even a quote about it that no one can remember who to attribute it to.

I can't remember it off hand now, obviously . . .

And yet, those who were *there* seem to have had remarkable powers of recall; certainly once a publisher's advance has entered the equation, anyway. The bibliography in Shawn Levy's panoramic study of swinging London, *Ready Steady Go*, runs to over fourteen pages. It lists memoir upon memoir from movers and shakers whose undisputed theresness should by rights make them the most forgetful people of their age.

But what about the 1970s? Surely this is when things really start to go missing?

Albums, double albums, triple albums, whole careers, taste, trousers, minds, tunes, time constraints, perspective, flying inflatable pigs, all went missing in the 1970s – only later to be reclaimed.

Like the 1950s, which it in turn expended some energy remembering, as a musical decade the 1970s remains both one of the most keenly forgotten and over-remembered of the post-war era.

Having spent so long trying to forget it, it is almost as if we forgot to forget and then couldn't remember what we'd forgotten. And then, when it came down to it, all we had left were the LPs, even if they – or some of them – had never truly gone away.

Still, who can remember forgetting the 1970s now?

The 2007 BBC drama *Life on Mars*, a time-travelling cop show set in 1973, was one of the biggest television hits in years. And current musical trends ape the scratch and sniff of 1979, the twig-wielding singing strummers of 1971, the German experimentalism of 1973 and so on . . .

Irony of ironies, when it comes down to it, some of the era's most memorable LPs – the good, bad, ugly, awful, the ones we clung to, the ones we tried to forget, the ones we forgot to remember to forget – are but a blur to their creators . . . Or were lost to us for a time. And it's still a wonder that they ever got made. Because the 1970s also specialised in forgetting. It slashed and burned its own past as it went along, something that we've largely forgotten how to do thanks to Google, iTunes and twenty years of comprehensively liner-noted reissues.

Back in 1992, on the song 'The Osmonds', Lawrence Hayward of Denim sang: 'In the seventies there were Osmonds, there were lots of Osmonds, lots of little Osmonds everywhere, everywhere'. 'And I should know, 'cause I was there', he added for good measure, lest anyone wish to quibble the ubiquity of that large toothy Mormon pop clan in an era then still decried as the era that taste forgot. Aerated by the elongated vowels of Hayward's West Midlands accent, the words 'there' and 'everywhere' rang truer for sounding like the singer was expressing grievances rather than making statements of fact. Only a man who, as a child, personally experienced – and remembered – power cuts, the three-day week, man-made fibre tank-tops, the Bull Ring Shopping Centre and *Crossroads* could probably muster such a drear tone.

Anticipating Jonathan Coe's nostalgic novel *The Rotters' Club* by nearly ten years, 'The Osmonds' was a trip back to Birmingham in the 1970s – covering 'leftover hippies everywhere', the pub bombings, Hughie Green, skinheads, Lee Perry dub, Jeremy Thorpe's resignation, George Best's retirement and the moment 'Lieutenant Pigeon hit the scene'. With a square of Old Jamaica Rum and Raisin standing in for the Proustian madeleine, the song's finale (and it is over eight minutes long) was a glam rock-style terrace chant where Hayward simply reeled off a list of 1970s brand names, TV shows and fashions: star jumpers, bell records, side pockets, nelson house, orange hand, the Persuaders, Mungo Jerry etc., etc.

'The Osmonds' was the centrepiece of *Back in Denim*,[76] an LP that was, to all intents and purposes, a concept album about the 1970s. *A Song for Europe*, Leo Sayer, The Glitterband, middle of the road American rock and Thunderclap Newman – voted the great hope for the 1970s by readers of *Melody Maker* in 1969 – are all in there somewhere. While not quite reaching the dizzying meta-fictional heights of, say, a concept album about 1970s concept albums, *Back in Denim* nevertheless used the format dearest to the era – an era that was obsessed with revivals – as a means of holding a séance with the recent past.[77]

The early 1970s, as Denim remind us, was a period of fragmentation and musical polarisation with AOR, MOR and rock (progressive, heavy et al) on one side and what was derisively called 'teeny pop', often played by teenagers, or even pre-teens in the case of Our Kid and Little Jimmy Osmond, on the other.

The distinction was made more explicit by the decision of some acts to abdicate from singles entirely and concentrate solely on LPs. The trend, started in the 1960s, that if you wanted to be taken seriously, you made albums (preferably ones that seemed to be serious about something) only accelerated in the early years

76 On vinyl it's the last track on side one, but on CD – the medium on which I first encountered it – its length and scope make it feel much more like the wheelhub from which the rest of the songs on the album spoked.

77 We can possibly imagine Beryl Reid, combining her roles as the medium in *Psychomania* and Adrian Mole's Brummie gran, residing over the Ouija board glass in the studio.

of the 1970s.[78] In Feburary 1970, the *Melody Maker* carried a piece headed: 'Singles, Who Buys Them Today?', which questioned the viability of 45s, noting that their sales had fallen by

some 20 per cent while albums were up by 40 per cent. Where a mere 17 million LPs had been sold in Britian in 1962, by 1972, 84.5 million had been bagged up and taken home.

78 Even the Osmonds had a go in 1973, producing a religious 'rock opera' concept album, *The Plan*, which extolled the wonders of Mormonism. 'The Beatles', Alan Osmond writes on the Official Osmonds website, 'had their "Sergeant Peppers" album, and other groups had theirs with thought-provoking ideas. *The Plan* was ours . . . *The Plan* was our way to creatively share our thoughts and feelings about, "Who we are", "Why we are here", and "Where we are going". We expressed important principles that we believe, with a cue to our listeners to "don't take it too easy" . . . that there was something here that we wanted them to think about and know. It was quite a difficult task without seeming "preachy" which we did not want to do.'

That they had to rewrite the whole album from scratch after a fire destroyed a notebook containing the only draft of the project almost makes it all the more progtastic. Almost.

This was, in many respects, a magnificent period for the LP – possibly its greatest. As a physical object and arguably as an art form, it reached peaks and nadirs of quite startling disparity that it would never quite match again. And in tune with widening trousers and lapels, LPs and stadium concerts would expand exponentially.

In notable comparison to the 1960s, where broadly speaking there was a solid consensus of popular and critical opinion around an act like the Beatles, the 1970s would be marked by widely divergent styles and a profusion of new subgenres.

Robert Christagu of the *Village Voice* noted in 1969, 'times have changed: The fourteen-year-olds are richer (they buy albums) and more demanding (they buy art). Today the performers have their hunches, which they call their style or thing and invest with an almost lugubrious intensity of belief. Such faith is necessary, for the adolescent fan will accept only what he senses the performers believe in.'

Led Zeppelin and Pink Floyd were among the first flank of groups who made unwillingness to sully themselves with 45s a potent symbol of their musical integrity and intensity. 'Singles', Peter Grant, Led Zeppelin's bruiser of a manager once informed Simon Napier-Bell, 'are like races, they are competitive, they hit or they fail. If you want to avoid failing don't release them. Let the kids buy albums instead.' On *Led Zeppelin IV*, the band played cryptic games by issuing a cover that contained no information at all, just four runic symbols in its inner sleeve. Pink Floyd's *Atom Heart Mother* came with a photograph of a cow, conjured by the sleeve wizards Hipgnosis.

Of course, this was now a commercial option because there was a substantial audience who was willing and able to devote time to LPs.[79] As the academic and Mercury music prize judge Simon Frith

---

79 Jimmy Page from Led Zeppelin's penchant for applying a violin bow to his guitar was sent up gloriously by Christopher Guest in *Spinal Tap* in a scene when Nigel Tufnel delights the crowds by scraping a fiddle across

has maintained, the Floyd's fans, like the group itself, 'were . . . determined to be different from ordinary pop people and they realised this through superior consumption'. 'I think it's time you bathed your ears in something really nourishing', a character in Hanif Kureishi's 1970s-set novel *The Buddha of Suburbia*, remarks, as he slips a copy of *Ummagumma* onto the turntable.[80]

the strings of his Gibson Flying V. But a greater understanding of the sort of latitude afforded to indulgent musicians in the 1970s is found in Led Zeppelin's 'classic' concert film *The Song Remains the Same*. In the intervening years, I'll grant you, attention spans have withered. We are flibbity-gibbets, long since accustomed to grazing on music in a multi-track, online, on-demand world. There were fewer distractions back then. Possibly. Dope isn't what it was. Quaaludes can't be had for love nor money. Well, probably for money somewhere. But they certainly aren't £3 a tablet like they were in the early 1970s. Still, the sight of paying punters urging Jimmy Page to solo on and on and on, lapping up every additional note he can squeeze out of his guitar is almost intolerable now. As a style of virtuosity it seems divorced from even what the group are good at. Or what we find to admire about them these days. Which, I'll admit is not the same thing. But . . . The songs. The energy. The riffs. The beats. And, okay, the solos, to a point. The group as an ensemble, a sound if you like. Whereas the live solos seemed to speak of a need in everyone concerned to believe that this was art, this was jazz, this was significant musically. Was it enjoyable? Ah, man, you had to be there . . . and have gobbled four 'ludes. Sorry, I digress . . . By 2007, when the remaining members of Led Zep gave a rare concert, being there was far more important than the music. The music was almost a distraction, a coda to the real business of the difficulty of obtaining tickets.

80 The view that Pink Floyd were peddling something a little more refined was reinforced in the contemporary press. A nice example is found in Michael Wale's 1972 book *VoxPop*: 'Immediately', Wale writes, in his preamble to an interview with Roger Waters, 'one does not want to call them a "pop" group because they are light years away from other groups who challenge for positions in the charts.' Despite his obvious admiration, the album *Meddle* is referred to as *Medal* throughout the piece.

Gentle Giant, meanwhile, told purchasers of their *Acquiring the Taste* LP that 'From the outset we have abandoned all preconceived thoughts on blatant commercialism. Instead we hope to give you something more substantial and fulfilling.'

Such bands and their audiences were also being catered for by the emergence of similarly minded independent labels like Charisma, Chrysalis, Island and, slightly later, Virgin. Several of these had grown up and out of the 'underground' and college gig circuits. Tony Stratton-Smith, a former sports journalist, concert promoter and lifelong *bon viveur*, exemplified the new breed of aesthete-entrepreneur who flourished in this era. Explaining the let-it-all-hang ethos of his label on a sleeve note for the compilation *Charisma Disturbance*, he wrote:

> A recording label is the sum of its artists.
>
> What Charisma has required of its artists is material, performance, and the ability to 'get it on' with an audience.
>
> Artists have required of Charisma a situation in which they could 'happen'.

Genesis, Van Der Graaf Generator, Lindisfarne and The Nice, would, as it were, 'happen'. (In more recent times, Peter Gabriel, formerly of Genesis has confessed: 'We'd always tried to avoid writing hits, which may sound a really dumb thing. Actually now, I think it was really dumb . . . We did have these very high ideals about trying to do things a different way.')

Island was run by Chris Blackwell, a well-to-do white Jamaican. Set up in Jamaica and moving to the UK in the early 1960s, Island specialised in West Indian ska and American R&B. The roster expanded to embrace indigenous folk and prog acts (Jethro Tull, Fairport Convention and King Crimson). Reflecting on Robert Fripp and King Crimson in the late 1960s, Blackwell once observed that 'at this time there was more of the well-educated university types coming in as musicians and band members. So you were starting to have a different input into the music.' Since the numbers of university students had doubled since the war, there was an immediate fit between the musicians and punters. In 1972, though, Blackwell succeeded in selling Bob Marley and the Wailers as, essentially, a rock act in Britain.

*   *   *

Although the arrival of the SS Windrush from Jamaica in 1948 is often cited as triggering a wave of West Indian migration to Britain, the influx was modest and incremental. Crucially, Lee Gopthal, the founder of Trojan records was a passenger on the ship. And Jamaicans made up the largest proportion of Carribbeans moving to Britain in the 1950s and early '60s. With them came the sound systems and dance parties . . .

In the aftermath of the Second World War, imported American R&B and boogie-woogie records rather than live groups had gradually come to provide the main musical accompaniment to lawn dances in the cash-strapped shanty towns of Kingston. As the 1950s wore on, an often violently competitive culture of DJs and sound systems emerged and the hunt for fresh tracks to keep the crowds coming and jumping was intense. To best their peers, some of the leading DJs, Duke Reid, Prince Buster and Clement 'Sir' Coxone began employing local musicians to cut records – solely to play on their own systems, to begin with. But the result bequeathed a new style of music that drew equally on the percussive elements of folk music and American R&B. (Subsequent economic hardships would lie behind the creative flowering of dub or version reggae: unable to bankroll as many new recordings as they would have liked, producers put their energy into reworking old tracks and getting DJs to chat or toast new lyrics over the top. In so doing, they laid the foundations for

DJ remixing, sampling and rapping, thus inadvertently shaping the global development of hip hop and dance music.)

It was under Blackwell's exegesis that ska first made its mark on the British charts in 1964, when the Jamaican teenager Millie recorded a version of 'My Boy Lollipop'. Imported ska and blue beat singles were by then frequently played alongside soul and R&B in mod clubs.[81] By the end of the 1960s, the UK was the largest single consumer of Jamaican music. In 1968 the first Trojan *Tighten Up* compilation album was released.

However, a certain penchant among some labels to go for novelty songs to secure quick and easy hits, its primary existence on 7-inch single (at a time when the LP was becoming *the* thing) and its widespread adoption by the first wave of skinheads conspired to put many rock fans off reggae.

'There's nothing nice about the skins', Charlie Gillett wrote in

81 'They played Tamla stuff and R&B. They could have been perfect if they'd played Blue Beat as well', Jimmy, the protagonist of *Quadrophenia*, comments at one point in the 'story' on the album's sleeve.

Rock Files in 1972, 'and likewise there's nothing nice about their taste in music. They completely reject the music of the counter-culture. Nothing is more loathsome to them than the junk of Progressive Rock. Music is for dancing to, music is for getting off with birds to. And the best music for that, they have decided, is Reggae and Tamla Motown.'

Arguably, it was the release of Perry Henzell's film *The Harder They Come*, released in that same year, that did most to change many people's preconceptions of the music.

Shot, *vérité*-style, on location in the shanty towns and recording studios of Kingston, and largely eschewing professional actors, *The Harder They Come* starred the singer Jimmy Cliff as Ivan O. Martin, an innocent country boy who moves to the city seeking fame and fortune as a reggae star. A grittily real portrait of ghetto life, it opened a window onto a Jamaican music scene dominated by gun-toting hustlers and Rastafarian prophets. The action was powered along by a killer reggae soundtrack mixed by Chris Blackwell, who had also co-produced the film. Along with four numbers from Cliff himself ('You Can Get It If You Really Want', 'Sitting In Limbo', 'Many Rivers To Cross' and 'The Harder They Come'), Toots and The Maytals' 'Pressure Drop', Desmond Dekker's '007' and The Melodians' 'River of Babylon' all featured.

A huge hit in its native land, it was first screened in the UK at the ABC in Brixton Hill and quickly gained an audience in Britain far outside the West Indian community. Cliff had previously been signed to Island, but if Blackwell had any plans to capitalise on the film's success, these were now dashed when the singer signed a new deal with the major EMI. (Cliff's 1973 album, *Unlimited*, contains some magnificent and less than veiled rails against exploitation, with 'Commercialization' and 'Rip Off' hinting at a degree of acrimony with some (unnamed) former business accociates. The needle is hardly in the groove of side one before a decidedly grumpy Cliff starts spouting off about funds owed. 'Yes, as I was saying', Jimmy spits, 'I like to work you know, but when I work I must get paid'.)

Blackwell would put his energies into Bob Marley and the Wailers instead. Cliff had, in fact, given Bob Marley his recording break when he was an A&R scout for producer Leslie Kong a decade earlier. And Island had released Marley's first record, 'One More Cup Of Coffee', in the UK back in 1962.

The Wailers, having teamed up with the 'Upsetter' producer Lee 'Scratch' Perry in the late 1960s had already recorded two formative reggae albums, *Soul Rebel* and *Soul Revolution*, which had been highly admired locally. But in 1971, having been promised a slot on a European tour with the Jamaican-based American soul singer Johnny Nash, Marley and co. had decamped to London. The tour, however, never materialised. As winter drew in, and Nash headed off to the States, Marley and his band found themselves kicking their heels, skint, in chilly old Harlesden. When the police intercepted a package from Kingston containing a little herb to lift their spirits, they were busted as well.

As luck would have it, a meeting with Blackwell at Island's Notting Hill offices in December 1971 dramatically transformed their fate. Blackwell agreed to bankroll an album in Jamaica for £8,000. Chief in Blackwell's mind, if not Marley's as well, was the desire (perhaps fostered with Cliff) to break the group in among rock – for which read white – music fans. To this end, when Marley returned to London with the tapes, Blackwell made the decision to substantially retool the tracks. With the Wailers' consent, additional lines by keyboard player John 'Rabbit' Bundrick and guitarist Wayne Perkins were added to the album, supplying a 'rockier' feel to the final mix of *Catch a Fire*. A pedal steel guitar, for example, gently weeps on 'Stir It Up, while a clavinet – the keyboard that also makes that clunk-de-dunk noise on Stevie

Wonder's 'Superstition' – beefs up 'Concrete Jungle' and 'No More Trouble'. The *pièce de résistance*, however, was the cover. Trumping the Rolling Stones' *Sticky Fingers* for sheer tactile fiddliness, the whole sleeve of *Catch a Fire* was done up like a Brobdingnagian-sized flip-top Zippo lighter. Unfortunately, invariably the 'lid' tore after more than a few goes (a shot of Bob lodging a smouldering Kingston carrot in his gob eventually replaced it). The artwork, like the music, served as the kindling to the first sparks of Marley's international acclaim.

It was another, earlier Island charge, Steve Winwood, who'd also set what in the early 1970s was an all-out trend for rustic recording. Having left the Spencer Davis Group, Winwood, at Blackwell's suggestion, had retreated to a cottage in Berkshire with his new group Traffic and created the 'getting it together in the country' LP *Dear Mr Fantasy* in 1967.

Around this time most major English labels had been establishing 'progressive' imprints of their own. Decca's Deram, advertised with the tagline 'Deram is Different',[82] was one of the first and was briefly joined by the more out-there Nova label. Harvest (home to Pink Floyd) was established within EMI in 1968 and Philips' Vertigo, Pye's Dawn and RCA's Neon followed in quick succession. These bucolic-cum-space-age label names seemed remarkably in tune with an urge on the part of musician both to get out of it and to get out of the cities – an idea that had become far more advanced in the States. The Elektra label had established a remote country recording facility for its groups in the woods of northern California, and it encouraged Beaver and Krause to record a side of *Gandharva*, their moog synthesiser-riddled 'score from a non-existent film' in Grace Cathedral in San Francisco.

But Charisma 'artists' like Genesis were spirited away to Luxford House, Stratton-Smith's Tudor pile in Crowborough in Sussex, to compose their 'masterpieces' (well, *Nursery Cryme*, anyway). Reputedly haunted, the house appeared on the inner sleeve of Van Der Graaf Generator's *Pawn Hearts* LP. The band are pictured in infa-red goofing about as psychedelic Nazis (black shirts, white ties and arms aloft) in Luxford's sumptuous grounds.

Released in the fall of 1971, *Pawn Hearts* represents, for some, the apex of the vogue so enjoyed by Stuart, our time-travelling listener in the last chapter, for filling up an entire side of an LP with one track (see also 'Echoes' on Pink Floyd's 1971 effort, *Meddle*). 'A Plague of Lighthouse Keepers' is a ten-part maelstrom of sax, organ, clattering drums and din-pin wired synthesisers that dominates the LP. As Roy Hollingworth perhaps rightly opined in *Melody Maker* that December, 'It is dreadfully

82 It would be so different by 1981 that the label would release the *Strength through O!* compilation, an LP of kick-your-head-in skinhead punk.

hard to explain "Lighthouse Keepers". If I told you', he went on, 'it was a film on album, a nightmarish film we might get somewhere . . . its theme is ancient – the wrath of the seas. It reminds one of the old sepia prints of shipping disasters of Cornwall.' *Record Mirror* were less easily charmed: their reviewer stated: 'I have to confess complete ignorance of what Van Der Graaf Generator are trying to achieve.'

Like many progressive groups in Britain and beyond, Van Der Graaf Generator had an essential and unlikely ally in the BBC. 'There is a new public of young people with money to spend and many thousands of them despise the success factor and the "corny" product', Robin Scott, the first controller of Radio 1 and 2, argued in 1969. Catering for their needs was part of the station's public service remit and John Peel's *Top Gear* programme, in Scott's words, was 'uncompromising in its devotion to, and enthusiasm for, new sounds'.

That need for new sounds was also fuelled by the rapid depletion of 1960s stars. By 1971, Janis Joplin, Jimi Hendrix, and Jim Morrison were all dead. (Just a week before Morrison's demise was announced, the *Melody Maker* ran a coruscating review of the Doors' last album, *LA Woman*, declaring it 'their nadir' and 'a spunkless sterile effort'.) 'The dream is over', a bitter John Lennon told *Rolling Stone* that spring. 'I'm not just talking about the Beatles, I'm talking about the generation thing. It's over, and we gotta – I have personally gotta – get down to so-called reality.'

Whatever residual optimism there had been about the 1960s finally ebbed away in a slew of violence and hard drugs. The Rolling Stones, after the murder of a fan at Altamont in 1969, retreated into a cocoon of coke and morphine. (Keith Richards once boasted, 'While I was a junkie, I still learned to ski and I made *Exile on Main Street*'.) On *Sticky Fingers* – their first album of the decade and the first to be released on their own label – they shoehorned references to narcotics into almost every song. Leaving aside 'Brown Sugar', the racially dubious ode to cunnilingus-cum-tribute to Mexican heroin, there was 'Sister Morphine' and a host of lyrics elsewhere drawling on about 'cousin cocaine', 'speed freak hives' and 'cocaine eyes'. The album's extravagant sleeve – a shot of a male crotch in jeans with a working zipper fly, designed by Andy Warhol – peddled sex rather than drugs. (The zipper, unfortunately, sometimes gouged into the vinyl when copies of the record were stacked and shipped.) But its serial number, COC – 39105, was as flaky as it got.

Also encapsulating that dissipating mood were albums by Sly Stone, who moved from the euphoric *Stand* to the blistering coke-addled *j'accuse* of *There's A Riot Going On*. But Sly Stone's appearance on the Dick Cavett chat show should perhaps have alerted others to the dangers of cocaine. Stumbling onto the couch after performing 'Thank You (Falettin Me Be Mice Elf Agin)' and audibly slurring his words, Sly, exuding the self-love of a heavy coke-sniffer, told viewers, 'I look in the mirror when I write'. Soon the writing fell victim to the mirror, coke and a blade. The fatalism of a cover version of 'Que Sera Sera' on 1973's *Fresh* spoke of a man giving in to his drugs, while the titles of abject follow-ups to 1974's *Small Talk*, *Heard Ya Missed Me, Well I'm Back* (1976) and *Back on the Right Track* (1979) fooled no one and only confirmed what had been squandered in the interim.

The grubbier realities of the street trade in the drug had been dramatised, and to an extent glamorised, in the movie *Superfly*, released two years earlier. A popular Blaxploitation flick in the *Shaft* vein, the film was accused of 'increasing the popularity of the drug', according to *Time*. But its soundtrack by Curtis

Mayfield, a number one album in 1971, was in fact stridently moral. Mayfield had cut sixteen albums with The Impressions as a performer, writer, producer and, finally, record company boss, taking the group from the gospel R&B of 'Gypsy Woman' and 'It's All Right' to the politically impassioned soul of 'Choice Of Colours' and 'Mighty Mighty (Spade And Whitey)'. Going solo in 1970, Mayfield's eponymous debut LP featured 'Move On Up', a hit single whose stabby violins and clattering percussion helped to define the palate of funky, seventies soul, and the six-minute-long 'We The People Who Are Darker Than Blue'. Its follow-up, *Roots*, contained the black rights anthem 'Keep On, Keeping On' and saw tracks grooving out to over seven minutes in length. Mayfield had responded to the honesty of *Superfly*'s script and turned in a set of songs that addressed the poverty of life as a dealer as much as an addict. Mayfield told *Let It Rock*, 'We hope to make people see that this is not really where it's at. We don't want to show people what is going on but give an effective message against it.' 'Little Child Runnin' Wild', 'Pusherman' and 'No Thing on Me (Cocaine Song)' were powerful anti-drug vignettes about ghetto life.

Meanwhile, Gaye's *What's Going On* (statement rather than question) from 1971 was an LP of astonishing beauty and hard-hitting social commentary, belied by Gaye's sweet falsetto – a case of a fist in a velvet glove. Gaye had to fight tooth and nail to convince Motown head Berry Gordy to let him make it; Gordy, to paraphrase Mike Love, seeing no reason to fuck with his winning formula just because a load of hippies were making albums. (The *Melody Maker*, nevertheless, did ask 'Is Motown dead?' in 1968.)

Gaye, however, having enjoyed enormous success with 'I Heard It Through the Grapevine' in 1968, endured personal tragedy with the death of his singing partner Tammi Terrell in

1970 (Terrell died of a brain tumour at just twenty-four) and become rather fond of drugs, wanted something more. *What's Going On* was it. Executed in a fog of marijuana, and after much autonomous studio experimentation (the Detroit Lions, having popped by to say hello, guested on the title track), the album was disparagingly referred to as a 'protest album' by Gordy. The label boss tried to find any excuse not to release it but when Gaye threatened never to record for Motown again, he relented and the LP made the top ten.

For his next album, *Let's Get it On*, Gaye would turn from the social to the sexual and the personal, and in this, too, he would be acutely in step with his times – as he would again with the contractual kiss-off divorce album *Here My Dear* in 1978 (Gaye had married Berry Gordy's sister, and the LP called time on this marriage along with his association with the Motown label). If the 1960s were about helping to change the world, the early 1970s, with some notable exceptions, would be mainly about changing the self. In what Tom Wolfe disparaged as the 'Me-Decade', individual fulfilment would increasingly take precedence over the greater collective good.

Symbolising that phenomon for many was the appearance of James Taylor on the cover of *Time* in March 1971. Taylor was a rangy, brooding, posh kid in his early twenties who sang gentle, strangely consoling, self-revelatory tales of woe. He wore denim. Only denim – or so it seemed. Maybe corduroy now and again. A moustache came and went. He had a history of heroin abuse and mental instability. But apart from looking a little gaunt, you couldn't really tell. And after all, this was 1971, pre-Aids, and such scars only added to his charm. (How many acoustic-guitar-strumming junkies, after all, sang Bert Jansch's 'Needle of Death' and/or Neil Young's 'Needle and the Damage Done' with a smidgen of look-how-self-destructive-I-am pride?) The title of his million-selling 1970 album, *Sweet Baby James*, summed it up. 'I wish', he once confessed 'I were really part of the environment, part of the land instead of a successful Caucasian.' Fatalism and inevitability were other Taylor watchwords. He had a head of lanky, sometimes frightfully oily dark hair that glanced across his face whenever he intoned and picked away on an acoustic guitar. Willowy girls – and even their mothers – got tingles in their fingertips and had to prevent themselves from reaching out to adjust the errant strands.

But as an album, *Sweet Baby James* probably felt like a dose of vitamin C after a few bum trips. Conveniently coinciding with a widespread drift away from the mad talk about revolutions and barricades, and on towards the wire baskets full of soya beans and macrobiotic health food shops, the LP inaugurated a profitable era for solipsistic singer-songwriters. And for solo artists in general, actually. Several of the more successful were friends of Taylor, and lived in the now-fabled Laurel Canyon area of Los Angeles – home to David Crosby, Stephen Stills and Neil Young. He married Carly Simon in 1972. And he recorded with Linda Ronstadt and Carole King.

The Band's *Music from Big Pink* (an album so slow that it's like listening to mogadon), Bob Dylan's *John Wesley Harding* and the Byrds' country-rock *Sweetheart of the Rodeo* albums in 1968 had already offered simpler, rootsier things. Simon and Garfunkel and the supergroup Crosby, Stills, Nash and (Young), meanwhile, had poured out sweet harmonies as a bromide for troubled times. The shooting of four students protesting about the American invasion of Cambodia at Kent State University had provided the inspiration for CSNY's song 'Ohio'. And considering Joni Mitchell's debut LP in 1969, Paul Williams had written: 'What's really important? McCarthy, riots in Germany, spy ships in Korea, the demise of the LA Oracle, an auto accident in

Kansas, the looting and fires in Chicago, new evidence on who the assassin of Kennedy or King might really have been, a report on the price of milk in Britain? It's impossible to guess what really matters, and you can't avoid the dull suspicion that it's really none of the above. And when you get into such items as who's in love with whom, or what's a good book to read, or what should I do in the summer, it's hard to remember what anything feels like at all.'

Mitchell, having left Graham Nash and indulged in a brief fling with his bandmate Stephen Stills, was dating Taylor at the time of his meteoric ascendance, and her album *Blue* in 1971 took autobiographical songwriting to another plane, exposing in intimate detail her thoughts about several romantic entanglements. Unlike Sinatra or Billie Holiday, who relied on other people's words and tunes to express their anguish, Mitchell spoke directly for herself. For Mitchell, 'the most important thing [was] to write in your own blood'.

The considerable market for albums about the complexities of personal relationships tallied with a shift in attitudes toward sex, marriage and family life. The year 1970 saw the publication of two of the touchstone works of feminist literature: Germaine Greer's *The Female Eunuch* and Kate Millett's *Sexual Politics* and in 1971, an all-girl rock group called Fanny were dubbed 'Lib Rock' by the *Melody Maker*. The number of women entering the workforce doubled in the 1970s. In England, the Divorce Reform Act of 1971 made it much easier for couples to divorce by introducing the principle of 'irretrievable breakdown' and in America, between 1965 and 1975 divorce rates doubled.

The transformation of Carole King from one half of the Brill Building husband-and-wife songwriting hydra Goffin-King into the cross-stitching earth mother of *Tapestry* was certainly an advert for the liberating possibilities of divorce (and remarriage).

Since separating from Gerry Goffin, with whom she penned 'The Loco-Motion' for Little Eva and 'Pleasant Valley Sunday' for the Monkees, King had moved to the West Coast. She sang and played piano on *Sweet Baby James* and Taylor, in due course, would record King's 'You've Got a Friend' on his next album *Mud Slide Slim and the Blue Horizon* and generally encourage her to sing her own songs. With *Tapestry*, her sophomore album in 1971, she spun pure gold. The LP stayed in the *Billboard* charts for six years. 'My Way' meets mother earth, it was a record that exuded a loved, lost and survived maturity, dispensing sisterly wisdom from the heart of the hearth. As the title song suggested, the fabric of her life had taken a prick or two to achieve its lustrous weave, but having frayed a little of late, was looking forward to a fresh darn. The LP's *coup de grâce* was to reprise two of her cherished tin pan alley tunes. By slowing 'Will You Love Me Tomorrow' to a funereal pace, a song that was about finally submitting to Biff's persistent advances in the drive-in when sung by the Shirelles in 1961 became a here-we-go again statement from a woman who knew the score all too well. '(You Make Me Feel Like) A Natural Woman' was an I'm-getting-a-good-shafting belter in Aretha Franklin's hands, but King's piano-driven version is spare as twigs, leaving an impression that the words could easily have been uttered following a tender coupling on a rug before some smouldering logs.

Or at least that's what the cover suggested.

For in one of the most iconic sleeves ever produced, King sits denim-clad and barefoot on a knotty-wooded window ledge in her Wonderland Avenue home. She toys with some piece of decorative cloth. Her hair is centre-parted, long, curly and untameable (on her *Rhyme and Reason* LP a year later, the mane had grown beyond the confines of a single sleeve and entwines itself around the back cover as well). Beside her sits what must have been one of the biggest-headed cats ever bred – in the foreground, and appearing to be playing a stare-out game with the photographer, the beast's cranium looks larger than King's. The portrait conveyed an air of rustic domestic solitude that divorcées, independent girls in bedsits and couples could all get behind. This was the perfect album to mix and match with the latest handmade-looking pine furniture from Habitat.[83]

The oeuvre of lone troubadours, who were everywhere – from Neil Young, John Denver, Cat Stevens and early Elton John to Jimmy Webb, Harry Nilsson, Randy Newman, Dory Previn, Kris Kristofferson – dominated the first quarter of the 1970s. Theirs was a music ideally suited to listening to on LP in intimate domestic spaces. The words were meant to be heard. Most of it was pastoral and, though much less sonically jarring, shared a similar intensity of purpose and earnestness as elements of prog rock.

If the miso-gorging, singer-songwriter idiom had risen to prominence in reaction to some of the excesses of acid-fried rock, the genre would nonetheless succumb to similar pitfalls. Growing increasingly self-regarding and bloated as the Vietnam War receded, cocaine use soared and multi-track recording came on in leaps and bounds.

---

83 Along with settings agrarian or sylvan, pets really come into their own on singer-songwriter LP sleeves in the 1970s. Neil Young, a spit for the wild-eyed cowboy actor Jack Elam in his chequered shirt, stands over his trusty mutt Art for the cover of *Everybody Knows This Is Nowhere*. Stephen Stills serenades a knitted giraffe on his eponymous debut solo LP – a dig at his Buffalo Springfield CSNY buddy's pet sounds? While James Taylor's *One Man Dog*, a loose, jazzier, rather exuberant album with a ten-song cycle on one side, has a cover in which the singer-songsmith and his dog go boating.

New technology was by the early 1970s transforming not only how albums sounded, but also where they were being heard. Back at the dawn of rock 'n' roll, the AM transistor radio had allowed the first teenagers to wrestle control of the radio dial away from their parents. For a couple of decades music had therefore escaped the confines of the home, moving into cars and onto beaches. Here, if high school flicks of the period are to be believed, surprisingly physically-mature-for-their-years 'honeys' in bikinis delighted in games of volleyball under blistering suns.

By the late 1960s, AM 'pop' radio though had ossified into Top Forty format shows. In 1967, Tom Donahue, a San Francisco DJ and concert promoter, was becoming frustrated by dissonance between the freaky new sounds he was hearing at the Fillmore and what he was able to play on the radio. By bypassing traditional advertisers and taking slots from local concert promoters, Donahue was able to start broadcasting what he called 'free form radio' from a local stereo FM station. He would play album tracks and line up three or four songs in a row without talking in between them – something of a novelty in an era when the motor-mouthed DJ reigned supreme. In his memoir, *Radio Waves*, fellow FM pioneer Jim Ladd recounts an occasion at the station when he plopped 'Dark Star' by the Grateful Dead on and sauntered out onto the fire escape to smoke a joint. The door slammed behind him leaving him locked out of the studio. Fortunately, the Dead track he'd chosen from the LP *Live Dead* lasted for a full side of the album, allowing just enough time for him to clamber back into the building before the record ran out. By the close of the 1960s, there were 'album-orientated' FM stations across America aimed at young adults, often college students, rather than teenagers.

It is while fondling a new AM/FM radio that his travelling companion, the '300-pound Samoan' attorney, has purchased that Hunter S. Thompson in *Fear and Loathing in Las Vegas* finds that they are truly wired for sound. 'I picked up the radio', he writes, in a tone implying more out-of-touch high-court judge than bombed gonzo, 'and noticed that it was also a tape recorder – one of those things with a cassette-unit built in.' (What will they think of next?) Flipping over the tape at the behest of the Samoan, who is desperate to hear 'White Rabbit' by Jefferson Airplane ('I want a *rising* sound'), Thompson makes another discovery. 'The volume was so far up that it was hard to know what was playing unless you knew "Surrealistic Pillow" almost note for note . . . which I did, at the time, so I knew "White Rabbit" had finished: the peak had come and gone.'

Since *Fear and Loathing . . .* , published in two instalments in *Rolling Stone* in November 1971, is a freewheeling threnody to the 1960s, Hunter's turn of phrase is especially pointed. Given that much of the action in the narrative occurs in cars, and purportedly high on drugs, it seems rather appropriate that they should be listening to a tape. A leading factor in the development of consumer cartridge tape systems was a desire to invent something that played in cars. (RCA undertook trials with a compact automobile record player in the late 1950s, but as Irwin Tarr of the company put it in 1969: 'It failed because discs proved a nuisance in a vehicle and didn't play long enough.')

Cassette tapes were introduced by the Dutch firm Phillips in 1963. The first pre-recorded cassettes were on the market a year later. But there were big problems with 'hiss' and the sound quality was pretty low-fi. In 1966, Decca in London equipped their recording studios with the Dolby noise-reduction system. This was soon adopted universally on commercial tapes and players, the quality of cassettes improving with the use of chrome etc. as the 1970s progressed.

Almost contiguously, Bill Lear of the Lear Jet Company hired a company to come up with a tape player for his planes. The result was a cartridge that contained four sets of paired stereo tracks that ran on a continuous loop. Lear approached Ford with the design and, teaming up with Motorola and RCA, in 1966 the car manufacturer began installing eight-track stereo tape players as a top-of-the-range option on all their models. The cartridge was ideal for drivers, since it could be slotted into the player with one string-back gloved hand, and tracks easily changed at the push of a button. Sporting a fresh cashmere sweater in almost every scene, Warren Oates as GTO, the wired Pontiac driver who challenges James Taylor (yes, Baby James) and Dennis (Beach Boys) Wilson to a race in *Two Lane Blacktop* (1971), spends chunks of the film forcing his eight-track collection upon unwitting hitchhikers ('What kind of sounds you like . . . rock, soul hillbilly . . . western . . . what's your taste?'). 'These are groovy records,' Laurie Bird, clutching a handful of his tapes, comments at one point. Primarily a photographer rather than an actor, Bird delivers the line so impassively it's hard to tell if she's being sardonic or is merely bored or stoned. Either possibility works, really, since Oates enthusiastically suggests, 'Play one'.

Though usually lumped in with those other bested formats Betamax video and laserdisc, Stereo 8 Tapes were a huge success – in 1969 alone, a total of about $300 million worth were sold. The last ones, believe it or not, were produced in 1988 (Chicago's *Chicago XIX*, Fleetwood Mac's *Greatest Hits* and Michael Jackson's *Bad* were among them).

For record companies – and possibly musicians too – the Stereo 8 had one distinct advantage over the cassette. It was, as RCA noted in 1969, 'a tape turntable . . . a playback-orientated system as opposed to a system orientated to self-recording'. In other words, you got what you were given. Like vinyl LPs, you couldn't record onto them or copy them as such, only play them.[84]

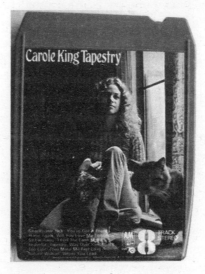

Though offering greater flexibility – Hunter could have jabbed onto 'White Rabbit' in seconds with a Stereo 8 – they were subject to fluctuations in sound quality, 'wows and flutters', and

84 Palm-sized tablets of plastic with beveled corners and edges, Stereos 8s were also rather pleasingly tactile objects. Their casings came in a range of sludgy colours. From this distance, it looks as if economic conditions demanded that even colour was put on a three-day week in the early 1970s. Everything from Austin Allegros to new polyurethane bathroom suites seemed to share a palette comprised almost exclusively of vermilion, avocado, mushroom and brown. Stereo 8s were no exception. To mimic the record sleeve, Stereo 8s came in little cardboard slipcases – jerkins, possibly, rather than jackets – bearing a miniaturised image of the cover. A copy of this was also pasted onto the tape itself – and they really did look almost like wallpaper pasted on (but then so did the labels on pre-recorded cassettes at the time).

had a lower dynamic range than LPs. This inhibited their success in bungalow range-style homes. But it seems to have enhanced their appeal to teenage stoners in cars. Stereo 8s were reported to sound particularly good if you were on Quaaludes. ('[I]t's worth noting, historically,' Thompson writes elsewhere in *Fear and Loathing* . . . , 'that downers came in with Nixon.') And interestingly, the drug and the format were at their most popular between 1970 and 1974.

A convincing argument can also be made for the eight-track's broader influence on the jalopy-friendly, roof open, sunglasses on, laid-back, cocaine-on-the-brain-I-forgot-my-mantra, American rock produced in the 1970s. In 1973, David Geffen, the thirty-year-old president of Elektra-Asylum Records, the label that had virtually copyrighted the white-as-wonderbread, sun-kissed sound of LA with the Eagles, explained how he personally sourced fresh talent: 'I have the demonstration records of new artists converted to eight-track tape for my car stereo,' he told a journalist, 'so I can audition while I drive.'[85]

85 Gene Clark, one of the founding members of the Byrds, stood on the brink of a major comeback in 1974. Signed to David Geffen's Asylum Records on the strength of his contributions to an otherwise abysmal Byrds reunion album for the label, Clark began burning through money and studio time as his ambitions for this record swelled. Whether 'From a Silver Phial' from *No Other* was a blatant reference to cocaine is a matter of dispute. Clark reputedly composed the album's songs under the influence of Mescal – a fact possibly borne out by the presence of lines where 'change' is rhymed with 'cosmic range'. But what was interpreted at the time as a nod to old hokey cokey didn't do the album any favours. Notching up studio bills of $100,000, *No Other*'s excesses were universally attributed to the drug. Whatever the reality, when Clark and his producer Thomas Jefferson Kaye came to present the record to Geffen, the LA music mogul threw a fit. Played eight ponderous songs lasting over six minutes each that drifted along in elaborate symphonic suites

Eight-tracks were also closely tied up with another rather less successful audio innovation of the 1970s: quadraphonic sound.[86]

Stereophonic sound, which came on to the market in 1958, imitates binaural human hearing. By making twin recordings from the same source, then playing them back across two speakers, it creates the illusion of depth and space. Quad – four channel sound – aimed to improve on this by recreating the three-dimensional experience of sound as it is in the world, the idea being that it would surround you with four walls of sound. The first types of quad LP discs were manufactured in Boston in 1968, but there were technical difficulties in encoding four channels onto a vinyl disc. At least three different systems, all using incompatible quad LPs eventually emerged in the early 1970s, which only confused potential punters.

Quad on eight-track tape was less problematic – technically and systems-wise – and the first quad eight-tracks, Q8s, hit the shops in 1970. Aside from the expense of having to fork out for additional speakers and new bits of frequency-decoding hardware, quadrophony as a whole had other drawbacks. It was difficult to get the 'full effect', or even an effect that worked. Positioning the speakers was nigh on impossible. If they were slightly out of whack, or the listener was in the wrong place, odd dead spots of sound were experienced, dubbed 'phantom centres'.

which shifted through a heady brew of funk, gospel, honky tonk and psychedelicised country, Geffen immediately pulled the plug. Clark and Kaye had planned to record another five tracks, but Geffen was unwilling to throw good money after bad and *No Other* crept out as it was. It vanished almost on release, becoming one of the most notorious lost albums of the 1970s.

86 Another even less successful 1970s innovation was Dynaflex Records, these were a bendier, cheaper brother to vinyl, adopted by RCA among others, they never caught on.

Quad in cars actually worked better, to a point, since any potential audience could move around a little, even confined to their bucket seats. Worse, however, was that many people simply found hearing in quad disorientating and rather unpleasant. An effect that was supposed to put them at the heart of an orchestra or band felt to many like being assailed from all sides by instrument-wielding muggers.

Quad was done and dusted by about 1978, and the eight-track not long afterwards, ostensiby. But as attempts at sonic advancements in listening, they were of a pace with those in recording. The first sixteen-track recording facilities opened in 1969, with twenty-four-track arriving just three years later. Goldfish, it is claimed, grow in proportion to the size of their ponds. Rock musicians given more tracks to play with responded in kind.

Reviewing *In the Wake of Poseidon*, Richard Williams was compelled to observe in the *Melody Maker* that if Richard Wagner was still alive he would be working with King Crimson. Delusions of classical grandeur would become *de rigeur* as progressive rockers, keen to display their musical virtuosity and studio nous, purloined symphonic tropes on ever more elaborate LPs. The foundations were laid in the late 1960s, with the Moody Blues' *Days of Futures Passed*, the Nice's *Five Bridges* and Deep Purple's *Concerto for Group and Orchestra* – a trio of pop-meets-classical LPs covering, respectively, a day in the life of an ordinary man, Newcastle Upon Tyne and pretty much what you'd expect to get when you let Deep Purple loose with the Royal Philharmonic Orchestra. But such adventures paled against the heights and depths achieved in the 1970s by Emerson, Lake and Palmer, Yes, and Rick Wakeman – though the latter has, perhaps, done more than most to atone for his sins simply by being more amusing/self-deprecating about them after the fact.

Comprised of Keith Emerson, a classically trained pianist who had played with the Nice, former King Crimson guitarist Greg Lake and the drummer Carl Palmer, ELP weren't shy of bombast.

Faced with the trio's live version of Mussorgsky's 'Pictures At An Exhibition', the legendary music journalist Lester Bangs wrote: 'Compared to this, the conceit and tastelessness involved in Jon Lord's Gemini Suite or the "Concerto For Rock Group and Orchestra" he and Deep Purple performed with the Royal Philharmonic were nothing, the modest work of quiet craftsmen.'

Making a speciality of amped-up organ and moog-fried versions of classical pieces, their debut LP fired into life – or burned up on entry, depending on your taste – with 'The Barbarian', a full-pelt take on Bartok's 'Allegro Barbaro'.

Tarkus, their next studio offering, included bits of Bach. The title track was a side-long meditation on the futility of war . . . or something. The message was wrapped up in an involving tale about an iron armadillo with tank-tracks instead of legs. An adaptation of Albert Ginastera's First Piano Concerto, Fourth Movement on its follow-up *Brain Salad Surgery* delighted its composer. However, *Karn Evil 9*, a demonic tripartite sci-fi epic about man's Manichean struggle with technology that came with a forest- depleting cardboard cover designed by H.R. Giger showed their gild-a-sprout tendencies were in full steam.

In October 1973, as a result of the ongoing Yom Kippur war between Israel and its Arab neighbours, the Arab oil-producing countries slapped an embargo on supplies to America. Oil prices rocketed, imposing extra costs on consumers and businesses across the world and seriously depleting stocks of vinyl for records. None of which seemed to have any impact on ELP, who responded to the growing economic uncertainty by putting out a sprawling live triple LP set. *Welcome Back My Friends to the Show That Never Ends* feels every inch as long as its title implies. One of the fastest selling albums in the States in 1974, it did at least shut them up for the next three years.

And then there was Yes.

When it came to brow-furrowingly 'evolved' rock, Yes were a triumph of pretentious gobbledygook, meandering time signatures and studio wizardry – the ornate title track of their *Close to the Edge* album required over forty tape splices to perfect. And dressed in Roger Dean's sleeves, with their fantastical depictions of otherworldly landscapes and scaly beasts, notions of sorcery of one kind or another were hard to shake off – and were greatly admired by the army of pimply male adolescent Tolkien aficionados who made up much of their fanbase. The glittery cape keyboard player Rick Wakeman flounced about in on stage didn't help. Nor did lyrics from singer Jon Anderson that attempted to invoke the spirit of the shastras and went on about velvet sailors. Or stories about the band filling the studio with cardboard cut-outs of animals and trees to create the right ambience.

In *The Rotters' Club*, his tender, comic valentine to this period, Jonathan Coe parodied a schoolboy review of Yes's four-suite double LP *Tales from Topographic Oceans*. Neatly skewering the album's cod-mysticism, he has his would-be Charles Shaar Murray write at one point: 'Hailing from Accrington, Lancs, Anderson has always had an affinity with Eastern spiritualism and philosophy.'

Coe's efforts, wonderful though they are, if anything underplay the purple prose the band seemed to inspire at the time. 'Yes', gushed one contemporary commentator in 1974, 'builds textures like an incoming tide inexorably playing over an oyster bed. Rather than hit the listener with a toe-tapping melody and then repeat it until it is ingrained, Yes builds from the smallest motifs, altering and mutating them into bright aural mosaics.'

Ponderous, yes; pretentious, certainly; but not uncommon then.

Here is Roger Waters of Pink Floyd explaining *Dark Side of the Moon*, an LP whose sonic palette was invigorated by a newly installed sixteen-track desk at EMI's Abbey Road studio:

> There are a number of things that impinge upon an individual that colour his view of existence. There are pressures that are capable of pushing you in one direction or another and these are some of them and whether they push you toward insanity, death, empathy, greed, whatever, there's something about the Newtonian view of physics that might be interesting and it is what this album is about.

The Dark Side of the Moon, in fact the title of a flop LP by the group Medicine Head only the previous year, succeeded in part because its central themes – life, death, getting older, going mad – were, unlike Anderson's, expressed with the earnest simplicity of an acoustic guitar-wielding singer-songwriter. An album about coping with the approach of middle age, the shock of having bones that needed warming by fires, etc., its angst was naively adolescent enough to keep the kids on side. Waters himself would later confess that the lyrics were 'so lower sixth' that he was surprised he got away with them. The LP would, of course, tarry in the US charts for over 724 weeks. It was accepted wisdom at my school in the 1980s that there was an entire factory somewhere in Germany devoted to pressing copies of *Dark Side* . . . I never did discover if it was true or not. The LP's sheer ubiquity made it sound convincing enough not to need to probe any further.

Though it has weathered less well – or at least badly enough to be given away free with the *Daily Mail* in April 2007 – Mike Oldfield's *Tubular Bells* was heralded as a masterpiece upon its release. (Where side one builds into a twisted Ennio Morricone western theme with Vivian Stanshall of The Bonzo Dog Doo-Dah Band's fruity tones leading a cavalcade of instruments that concludes in chiming bells, a chorus of voices and plangent acoustic guitars, side two has some unfortunate troglodyte impersonations to endure. Signing off with 'The Sailor's Hornpipe' also means that the disc ends on a kind of 'That's all, folks' comic note that rather punctures the preceding atmosphere.)

The album was predominantly self-played and involved Oldfield meticulously layering track upon track – over 2,000 recordings – to create two side-engulfing symphonic pieces; a practice that was then highly unusual, if not unique. Oldfield had had a troubled childhood – his mother was an alcoholic – and music was an escape and a source of comfort, so from a young age he taught himself to play an assortment of instruments, deploying twenty-two on *Tubular Bells*. Only nineteen when he made the

LP, he had already cut a folk album with his sister when he was fifteen and played with The Whole World on Kevin Ayers' *Shooting at the Moon* LP. Tubular Bells was among the first batch of LPs to be released on Richard Branson's new Virgin record label –Faust's *The Faust Tapes* (retailing, as a sweetener, for just 48p), *Gong's Flying Teapot*, and a live jam session album featuring various Virgin artists at the company's Manor studios were the others. Oldfield's magnum opus could easily have sunk without trace. Richard Branson nearly put an early spanner in the works by questioning the need to spend £20 on a set of said bells. But sponsorship by John Peel was its saving grace. Peel was so entranced by the album that he played it in its entirety on his radio show – a practice Radio London, where Peel was then a DJ, had pioneered with *Sgt. Pepper* some six years before. 'You'll never forget this', those who'd tuned in were duly informed.

Readers of the BBC's *The Listener* were treated to a further dose of Peel evangelising about *Tubular Bells*, an LP he called 'a new recording of such strength, energy and real beauty that to me it represents the first breakthrough into history that any musician regarded primarily as a rock musician has ever made'.

This was still an era when 'breakthroughs' were deemed possible, welcome even. (As Peel said of another Virgin signing, the German band Faust – his notice from *Disc* was included on the sleeve of the *Faust Tapes* – 'It is not often you hear a band that is heading off in a totally new direction – and it's surprising that when you do many of those bands are from the continent.')

The profits that poured into Virgin's coffeurs from *Tubular Bells* allowed acts like Gong, Henry Cow and Hatfield and the North to indulge artistic whims that other labels – even at this point in the 1970s – may have considered commercially suicidal.

It is, therefore, thanks to Mike Oldfield that we have *Angel's Egg*, *Unrest* and *The Rotters' Club*.

But Peel presaged his own comments about *Tubular Bells* with this rather astute proviso:

On the all too frequent occasions when I'm told that a record by a contemporary rock musician is a work of "lasting importance" I tend to reach for my hat and head for wide open spaces', he maintained. 'Today these experts would probably tell you that in twenty years' time collectors will still be enthusing over the records of such weighty bands as Yes and Emerson, Lake and Palmer. I'm ready to bet you a few shillings that Yes and ELP will have vanished from the memory of all but the most stubborn and that the Gary Glitters and Sweets of no lasting value will be regarded as representing the true sound of the 1970s.

*　　*　　*

In a rather glorious quirk of fate, a photograph of the awning at the Labour conference in Blackpool in 1973 shows the political party sharing the billing with drag star Danny La Rue. That year, the apex of Glam, La Rue announced his retirement, only to return some eighteen months later. Ziggy Stardust and his

Spiders from Mars appearing at the Hammersmith Odeon that July would stage a more permanent farewell.

Rejecting dowdy naturalism in favour of dressing up, glam was, in Charles Shaar Murray's opinion in 1977, 'the first real *pop* thing that happened in the seventies'. At its most boorish it was a three-chord trick on the cheesecloth shirt and Gandalf's pikestaff mob, if you like. It was doubly effective to begin with, since the movement's lodestar was Marc Bolan, a former mod turned petted-elfin fixture of the Hobbit-loving underground. In a volte face as shocking to some – well, to a couple of Afghan-coated potheads in Covent Garden's Middle Earth, maybe – as when Dylan went electric, Bolan plugged in a Gibson Les Paul and transformed himself from a hippie strummer into a corkscrew-haired superstar. Booked for TV's *Top of the Pops* to promote T-Rex's first number one single 'Hot Love', a lively twelve-bar, he let his publicist Chelita complement his already flamboyant garb by smearing glitter under his eyes. Such was the paucity of anything else for teenagers to do in Heath's Britain, the glitter look was abroad by the following day.

T-Rexstasy was compact and for a while bijou. But the Bolan look and his crunchy toe-tapping sound would be purloined to outright parody by a legion of glam rock chancers: The Sweet, Gary Glitter, Mud, Alvin Stardust and the rather loveable one-time skinheads Slade, whose foot-stomping singalongs, poor spelling and home barbered hairstyles proved surprisingly winning.

Bolan's problem was that having landed upon a hit formula, he couldn't quite get beyond it. After two solid chart-topping T-Rex LPs, *The Electric Warrior* and *The Slider*, the powder was, if not dry, then certainly drying up. Or, perhaps, more accurately, going up his nose.

Tony Visconti, his producer, recalled that by 1973 when they parted company, he 'could set up a Marc Bolan sound for you on the desk, or a Marc Bolan mix, within five minutes. There were certain earmarks to our productions that hadn't changed for a few years. I tried to change Marc's direction, but by that time, he was unchangeable.' Bolan's tragedy, in Visconti's view, was that he 'never did get around to making anything . . . on a grander level'. Where plans were laid for an album called *Children Of Rarn* that was going to be their '*Tommy* or *Sgt. Pepper*', whenever Visconti got Bolan in the studio, he would just start 'knocking out these three-minute ditties as he'd done previously'. Ironically, albums had been the most important thing to Bolan back when he'd formed the bongos-and-guitar Tyrannosaurus Rex in 1969: 'I didn't want to do any singles,' he recalled in 1972, 'I just wanted to do an album.'

We can only speculate about what Bolan possibly would have done. But if he was afflicted by stasis, endlessly remaking the same songs, the same singles and never quite . . . well, quite getting up to 33 1/3 speed, his friend and rival David Bowie earned himself a place in the record books for the breadth and sheer variety of his LPs, and his longevity was shored up by a back catalogue of albums.

When fame belatedly came with the LP *Ziggy Stardust and the Spiders from Mars*, fans were able to investigate reissues of *David Bowie* (or *Space Oddity*, as it was retitled), *The Man Who Sold the World* and *Hunky Dory*. This not only prevented them from becoming bored of a single LP, and by extension Bowie, it arguably prepared them for the idea that he would move on to other things (Philadelphia soul on *Young Americans*, coke-frazzled, white-magic-infused, demon-dispelling groove rock on *Station to Station*, the ethereal, synthesiser-laced *Low* and *Heroes* during the come-back-to-earth years in Berlin, and so on, until *Tin Machine*.)

With the possible exception of the unearthing of 'Laughing Gnome', a sub-Syd Barrett skeleton in his cupboard from 1967 that embarrassed the singer by going on to sell over 250,000 copies in 1973, his back catalogue was both similar enough to and different enough from his latest records that a continuum could be traced. Unlike Bolan, for example, where the difference between *My People Were Fair and Had Sky in Their Hair . . . But Now They're Content to Wear Stars on Their Brows*[87] and, say, *The Slider*, was as jarring as stepping out of a horse and cart and into a Jensen Interceptor.

Bowie, like Bolan, was an ex-mod, and similarly he had moved from publicity-hungry ace-face to free festival mystic – in his case decamping to Scotland to become a Tibetan Buddhist, setting up a mime troupe and forming something called an Arts Lab above a pub in Beckenham. Re-entering the fray in time for the moon landings, he had a hit single with the stylophone-infused 'Space Oddity'. A melancholy album of largely folk-tinged Dylan cum Roy Harper[88] songs about shoplifting tins of stewing steak,

87 An idea of the album's contents is conveyed in a sleeve note by John Peel: 'Tyrannosaurus Rex', Peel wrote, 'rose out of the sad and scattered leaves of an older summer. During the hard, grey winter they were tended and strengthened by those who love them. They blossomed with the coming of spring, children rejoiced and the earth sang with them. It will be a long and ecstatic summer.' *My People* . . . was for a long time credited with possessing the lengthiest album title ever foisted upon the world. In 1999, though, Fiona Apple trumped it with *When the Pawn Hits the Conflicts He Thinks like a King What He Knows Throws the Blows When He Goes to the Fight and He'll Win the Whole Thing Fore He Enters the Ring There's No Body to Batter When Your Mind Is Your Might So When You Go Solo, You Hold Your Own Hand and Remember That Depth Is the Greatest of Heights and If You Know Where You Stand, Then You'll Know Where to Land and If You Fall It Won't Matter, Cuz You Know That You're Right.*

88 Vocalist on Pink Floyd's 'Have A Cigar', inspiration for Led Zeppelin's 'Hats to (Roy Harper)' and accompanying Kate Bush on 'Breathe', Harper is, either in spirit or in person, on plenty of albums that loads of people who have never heard a Roy Harper album own.

writing letters to ex-girlfriends and not washing followed. The wild-eyed boy was dreaming of more than free festivals and free clouds, though. Warhol and the Velvet Underground and its New York demi-monde were on his mind. Aided and abetted by his bisexual American wife, Angie, he slipped into dresses and by January 1972 Bowie was telling Michael Watts of the *Melody Maker* he was gay ('and always have been') and stood poised to unleash an LP about a hermaphrodite rock star from outer space. Forget 'Life on Mars', planet earth would never be quite the same again.

Bowie's public confession of homosexuality was the first of its kind.[89] But Watts, for one, saw it for what it was: a pose, an image. 'He's gay, he says. Mmmmmm,' Watts writes, adding, 'there's a sly jollity about how he says it, a secret smile at the corner of his mouth. He knows that in these times it's permissible to act like a male tart, and that to shock and outrage, which pop has always striven to do throughout its history is a ball breaking process.' Watts also notes, wisely, that: 'The expression of his sexual ambivalence establishes a fascinating game: is he or isn't he? In a period of conflicting identities he shrewdly exploits the confusions surrounding the male and female roles.'

If feminism by the early 1970s was starting to unpick long static assumptions about gender, then it was complemented by an increasingly vocal gay rights movement. The Sexual Offences Act of 1967 had decriminalised homosexual acts in private for consenting adults over twenty-one in England and Wales, though it continued to be an offence for serving soldiers, sailors, airmen, merchant seamen and if 'witnesses' were present. (*Scary Monsters* would be in shops before Scottish gays were afforded the

89 Although he may have been just pipped to the post by Dusty Springfield, who'd confessed to running on alternating and direct current a little earlier.

same freedoms.) While it was a landmark piece of legislation, discrimination remained widespread and arrests for importuning continued much as before. In order to change this, the Committee for Homosexual Equality was formed in Britain in 1969. Over in New York, however, where homosexuality was still illegal, a brutal police raid on the Stonewall Inn, a gay bar in Greenwich Village, had led to a riot. Fired by the injustice of their situation, gays in the city established the Gay Liberation Front. The following year, the first Lesbian and Gay Pride march was held in New York to commemorate Stonewall. On this side of the pond, the London Gay Liberation Front was founded in 1970, and a march to protest against the inequality of the ages of consent was held in 1971.

These events illustrate the shifting cultural attitudes to sexuality that were broadly in sync with seeking greater fulfilment in relationships full stop. For every *Scenes from a Marriage*, there would be a *Wife Swappers* or an *Adventures of a Taxi Driver*, but the sexual revolution had removed the veil of secrecy from the bedroom. Homosexuality and bisexuality were now common enough topics in mainstream books and films, as the widespread popularity of Bob Fosse's epoch-defining film *Cabaret* in 1972 attested.[90]

Bowie's androgyny, nevertheless, was shocking enough that the cover image of his hardish rocking 1970 LP, *The Man Who Sold the World* – an epicean Mr Davy Jones, dolled up like Veronica Lake in a silken 'man's' dress, reclines on a chaise longue tossing playing cards hither and thither – was replaced in

90 Two decades on, Bowie would confess to Suede's Brett Anderson that they were 'very miffed that people who'd never seen *Metropolis* and had never heard of Christopher Isherwood were actually becoming glam rockers'. (That 'miffed' is prime Bowie vocab, isn't it? Up there with the 'not much cop' lyric on Kooks.)

the US by a cartoon of a man in a cowboy hat. Reissued by RCA in 1972, it was Ziggyfied, with the dress swapped for a more recent shot of Bowie high-kicking in his glitter jumpsuit. Continuing to ring in the sexual 'Changes' – the single was a Tony Blackburn record of the week, incidentally – Bowie, with his hair pulled back and slightly rouged lips, looked not unlike Greta Garbo on the sleeve of *Hunky Dory*. The tinted shot possessed shades of Warhol's celebrity screen prints. A quieter album than its predecessor, the LP had a dressing-up-box eclecticism about it. The 'actor', as he was referred to on the back cover, was exploring his range, in preparation for his biggest role. Rock 'n' rollers were warned to look out.

In addition to its cover, *Hunky Dory* was also hardwired by Warhol's theories about art in an age of mass production. When he was working on the LP, he told Steve Peacock in *Sounds*: 'I'd rather retain the position of being a photostat machine with an image, because I think most songwriters are anyway. I don't think there are many independent-thinking songwriters, they are all heavily influenced, far more than in any other form of writing . . . because it's a disposable medium.'

Bowie and Angie had earlier befriended the cast of Warhol's *Pork* during their spell at the Roundhouse in Camden in the summer of 1971. And a few months later, Bowie had paid his respects to Warhol, Lou Reed and Iggy Pop in New York at Max's, the 17th Street New York bar that was a home from home to the factory set and a lively assortment of elite hipsters, drug dealers and drag queens.

Back in Beckenham, and perhaps, after the excesses of the Bowery, feeling not unlike a visitor from outer space here on the fringes of South London, the inspired notion of a sexually ambidextrous, drug imbibing, rock god alien came to him.

A composite of a then little known Brit rocker, Vince Taylor (who lost his mind to drink and drugs sometime in the mid-1960s), Syd Barrett, Iggy, Bolan and Bowie himself, Ziggy Stardust inevitably became a monster whose creator would never be able to contain him. (His successor, Aladdin Sane, would be a kind of musical wooden stake by which Bowie finally tried to lay Ziggy to rest.)

The album itself was an audacious and brilliantly realised pop concept.[91] Seemingly set in the five years before an imminent apocalypse, it's a work of speculative fiction that charted, in numerous voices, the life and times of a doomed superstar. As an LP, it was as much about rock 'n' roll as it was rock 'n' roll. A futuristic fantasy, it was a hymn to rock's past. Ziggy, as perhaps the telephone box on the back cover suggested, was Doctor Who with an electric guitar. (The Time Lord, with uncanny synchro-nicity, was suffering a lengthy exile on earth in the body of Jon Pertwee during this period. In between tussles with the Daleks in the company of the diminutive if shapely Jo Grant, Pertwee recorded the single 'I am the Doctor' that materialised in 1972.) And the sleeve implied that this Starman, a harbinger of doom from days to come, was actually standing right here and now outside a furrier's on a litter-strewn Haddon Street lined with parked Austin 1100s.

A month after the release of *Ziggy Stardust and the Spiders from Mars*, a live review by Ray Coleman appeared in the *Melody Maker* under the banner 'A Star is Born'. The headline,

---

91 Naturally, as with all good ideas, there were precedents. The Kinks' *Lola vs the Powerman & the Money-Go-Round* from 1970 had a song about the Warhol transsexual Candy Darling (Lola) and painted a grim portrait of life in a rock and roll band. However, since Ray and the Kinks had been through the mill, these acidic vignettes about the invidiousness of the music biz came all too transparently from the heart.

reprising the title of Judy Garland's infamous comeback film from 1954, spoke volumes, especially as Coleman crowned Bowie 'the undisputed king of Camp rock' in the piece. 'Bowie', Coleman observed, 'is a flashback in many ways to pop star theatrics of about ten years ago, carrying on a detached love affair with his audience, wooing them, yet never surrendering that vital aloofness that makes him slightly untouchable.'

Bowie's avowed sexuality set him apart from his rock peers. Not as much as Jobraith, who was, well, gay and glam. But enough to matter.

One of his more vocal critics was Cliff Richard, who in 1973 condemned Bowie as a corrupter of the young. 'Here's a genuine, married man', Cliff vented, 'dressing up as a woman. The impact is not on people like myself, or those in my age group but on the youngsters who will be tomorrow's people. What will those ten and-eleven-year-olds think of someone who's a man dressing up as a woman at a pop show? . . . He upsets me as a man.'

Interviewed again by Michael Watts, a year and a half after his initial gay 'confession' and after Ziggy, Bowie expressed, perhaps rather disingenuously, his surprise at the reaction. Nobody, he'd apparently reasoned, was going to be offended by it because 'everybody knows most people are bisexual'. 'The only thing it ever did', he strenuously maintained, 'was sell albums.' But of course, he had done a lot more than that. To an army of teenage outsiders, unlike Cliff, he made being a little different a lot more acceptable and created a cult of Bowie-imitating individualists in the process. For the confused, the certain and the simply curious, he represented a haven from orthodoxy. Boys and girls identified with and adored him in equal measure; breaking down barriers between, and ideas about, gender as never before.

**Most rock groups would be better off
listening to Iggy and the Stooges
mixed by David Bowie**

James Osterberg alias Iggy Pop, the committed pioneer of all the correct distilled debauchery, the Master of Self-immolation via his demoniacally masochistic on-stage acrobatics, the very essence of mordant energy, returns after a protracted absence to savage tender ears and upset musical biscuit. Despite the backstage presence of that disconcerting cornucopious of the moving currents David Bowie, the rough edged mason intact as the reformed line-of Stooges provide a menacing wall of sound behind our hero's own brand of affirmative body-odour boogie. Praise Lucifer and pass the crushed glass in aspic.

"Raw Power celebrates. A magnetism in one snarling beat it strips away the layers of commercial compromise that hem - apart from a few rare occasions - defused the whole essence of rock.
...Iggy and chums play as if this was the first and last gig. Living for the moment, with no thought of the past or the present, they have come up with the first real rock album of the seventies.'
Roy Carr, New Musical Express

**Iggy and the Stooges,
'Raw Power.' Rock as it's meant
to sound. On CBS 65586.**

By collaborating on LPs with artists he admired, like Iggy Pop and Lou Reed, he not only presented himself as a man of particular tastes and discretion but also used his success to open people's ears to other music. In Iggy Pop's case, the results were mixed. Bowie is still held culpable for ruining the Stooges' *Raw Power* album and derailing Pop's career. *Transformer*, on the other hand, changed Lou Reed's fortunes and provided another disc filled to the brim with singalong tales of speed freaks and transvestite hookers for the kids to enjoy at home. 'There's a lot of sexual ambiguity in the album', Reed told *Disc and Music Echo* in 1972, 'and two outright gay songs from me to them, but they're carefully worded so the straights can miss out on the implications and enjoy them without being offended.'

When one of Reed's roadies was asked if Lou, like David Bowie, was bi, he replied: 'Bi? The fucker's quad.' No better description, perhaps, sums up the sounds of the epoch.

Chapter Ten
BACK TO THE FUTURE

Rather like Ziggy, Roxy Music crashed into 1972 looking and sounding like visiting aliens. Aliens whose knowledge of the earth came from TV and radio signals that had taken light years to reach them. (You could almost imagine that they were the last of a lost space civilisation who'd set out to colonise the world believing it to be populated by Gene Tierney lookalikes.) With backgrounds in art school, soul bands and experimental 'scratch orchestral' ensembles, the group spun rock 'n' roll through a pop art, postmodern mangle. Singer Bryan Ferry crooned in a strange, sneering vibrato that somehow brought Marlene Dietrich and Gene Vincent to mind. Possessing sultry, matinee idol good looks, an oiled quiff and eyebrows ever quivering above silvery-green lids, he was a vision of the 1990s from the pages of *Dan Dare*. The egg-headed Brian Eno, unleashing an unholy whorl of cosmic noise from the banks of his button-encrusted VCR3 synthesiser, was practically the Mekon in glittery eye make-up and feathers. Honking away on oboes and saxophones, Andy Mackay was a one-man *Star Wars* bar-band four years early. Phil Manzanera played a guitar whose notes appeared only to emerge after being beamed back from a communications satellite. Drummer Paul Thompson, meanwhile, pounded away, a Morlock among Eloi. (Bass players seemed interchangeable; and they were.)

Retro futurists or future revivalists, their songs oozed a robotic energy while simultaneously seeming to mourn the decline of Brylcreem, black and white moving pictures, evening dress, the cocktail hour and the hourglass figure. Simon Puxley caught their out-of-time aesthetic ('hi-fi or sci-fi, who can tell') immaculately, in his sleeve notes for their first LP:

> Piccadilly, 1972: taking a turn off mainstreet, away from cacophony and real-life relics & into the outer spaces myriad faces & sweet deafening sounds of rock 'n' roll. And inner space . . . the mind loses its bearings. What's the date again? (it's so dark in here) 1962? Or twenty years on?

And twenty years on, people would still not be quite sure.

But if Roxy's homage to the past was radical, their glorying in the frivolity of the cheap glamour of yesteryear, underpinned by the practice of contemporary art, rock was already entering into a deeply nostalgic phase.

One of the UK's bestselling albums of 1972 was Don McLean's *American Pie*. Its eponymous title number was a rhyming-couplet-laden *A la recherche du temps perdu* for the rock 'n' roll generation. The song is hung upon McLean's own wistful memories of 3 February 1959, the day when Buddy Holly, Big Bopper and Ritchie Valens were killed in a plane crash – 'the day the music died', as the lyric has it. A heartfelt lament for lost youth and innocence, McLean uses the tragedy as a springboard to reflect on the decade that followed. Charting its highs and disillusioning lows, the song is a roll call of oblique (and direct) references to sock hops, the Monotones, Marty Robyns, Elvis, Dylan, Janis Joplin, Woodstock and Altamont.

'The song', McLean recently observed, 'was written as my attempt at an epic song about America, and I used the imagery of music and politics to do that. Also, I was really influenced by the *Sgt. Pepper* album, and the *American Pie* album was my attempt to do that, but the song totally overshadowed the album.' The 'sergeants played a marching tune' in the lyric is taken by some to be a nod to the Beatles.[92]

The song and the LP – a pleasant enough early seventies singer-songwriter job containing McLean's requiem to Van Gogh, 'Vincent' – expressed a widespread yearning to escape a more troubling present. And beating the *American Pie* LP in terms of cash sales in 1972 were K-Tel's *20 All Time Hits Of The 50s* and K-Tel's *25 Rockin' and Rollin' Greats*.

There had always been budget-priced compilation LPs, of course. Among the most notorious in Britain in the late 1960s and 1970s were the *Top of Pop* records from Hallmark and Music for Pleasure's *Hot Hits*. Sold through Woolworths and all manner of now long defunct corner shops and supermarkets (Liptons, Keymarkets, God knows), these albums contained competent versions of current hits recorded by jobbing session men or cash-strapped would-be pop stars. (Elton John, or Reg

---

92 McLean was a paperboy in 1959 and in the song shivers while delivering this bad news to every doorstep. It's wild speculation but . . . 'A Day in the Life' from *Sgt. Pepper* – whose lyrics were based on Lennon's rather literal reading of a page from the *Daily Mail* – begins with the words: 'I read the news today, oh boy.' Lennon was a Holly fanatic and 'Oh Boy' was one of the Lubbock singer's biggest hits. Just a thought.

Dwight, as he still was at the time, contributed more than his fair share to the knock-off canon.)

Each volume was blessed with a scantily-clad go-go girl on the cover and at around seventy-five new pence a punt, gave the purchaser a grab bag of chart songs for little more than the price of two actual singles. In a land where the ersatz was second nature – in an earlier era, teams of BBC light orchestras had toiled selflessly to recreate contemporary American dance songs for English broadcasts – these LPs were phenomenally successful. Their relationship to 'real' chart pop or rock, however, wasn't far off that of, say, Camp or Mellow Birds to fresh coffee or Stork margarine to butter: same aisle but worlds apart. Just as Bruce Forsyth in those days seemed to devote hours of good golfing time to prowling about supermarkets challenging timorous pensioners to eat slabs of Mother's Pride coated in oily great drifts of yellowy marge without prejudice, so Music For Pleasure's *Hot Hits*, seemingly in all honesty – or with bare-faced cheek – also asked: 'Can you tell the difference?' Erm, it usually wasn't hard.

But rather like *Stars in Their Eyes*, points were awarded for effort and the listeners felt sufficiently flattered if they were simply able to recognise the song. This was the 1970s, after all, when, much as today, tuneless club singers were beamed into the nation's living rooms on TV talent shows like *New Faces* and *Opportunity Knocks*.

However, in August 1971, the BBC relaxed their rules on allowing budget-priced LPs into the official charts. And lo and behold *Hot Hits 6*, adorned by a summery image of a babe in a bikini and . . . er . . . cricket pads, stole pole position. It was quickly followed by *Top of the Pops 18*, an LP boasting rip-roaring sound-not-alikes of The Who's 'Won't Get Fooled Again', T-Rex's 'Get It On' and Middle of the Road's 'Chirpy

SIDE 2
1. THREE STEPS TO HEAVEN
2. STAND BY YOUR MAN
3. WOMBLING WHITE TIE AND TAILS
4. AUTOBAHN
5. SEND IN THE CLOWNS
6. I WANNA DANCE WIT CHOO

Chirpy Cheep Cheep'. The sight of it lording it over T-Rex's *Electric Warrior*, Carole King's *Tapestry* and John Lennon's *Imagine* was more than some industry types could bear. When *Top of the Pops 20*, an LP whose croaky-oke of Rod Stewart's 'Maggie May' was one of its chief selling points, knocked the pineapple-haired rocker's own *Every Picture Tells A Story* off the top spot that November, the major record companies cried foul. The cheapies were subsequently banished to No-Hitsville UK.

Their removal from the main charts, of course, did nothing to dim their sales, which had never depended on industry gongs anyway. The *Top of the Pops* albums lingered on until 1985, notching up a staggering ninety-two volumes over a seventeen-year lifespan. What their brief storming of the citadel showed, however, was just how huge the market for compilations might be. By the summer of 1972, a slew of new companies had entered the record game with a new line in albums of recent hits. Advertised on television and produced by firms whose names – K-Tel, Ronco, Arcade – inferred a cosier familiarity with battered lock-ups and pub fruities than HMV and Denmark Street, the major difference with these LPs was that they featured original versions instead of covers. There was a polite time-lag between a single's big chart run and its inclusion on such LPs, naturally. And a few of the songs used on K-Tel's *20 Dynamic Hits*, Arcade's *20 Fantastic Hits* or Ronco's *20 Star Hits* were either positively ancient or fillers – middling hits rather than soaraway smashes. But they were an immensely attractive proposition to price-conscious shoppers. K-Tel's *20 Dynamic Hits* spent eight weeks at number one and was the biggest selling LP of 1972. By 1976 these compilations accounted for 30 per cent of all albums sold.

K-Tel was canny enough to twig that LPs of old hits, if packaged and promoted in the same fashion, would sell too. Regular TV viewers tended on the whole to be older – teenagers were out kicking phone boxes in – and back catalogue material had the added bonus of, at that point, being cheaper to license. K-Tel's *20 All Time Hits of the 1950s* enjoyed a total of eleven weeks at number one and picked up the silver to *Dynamic Hits'* gold in the year's sales. *All Time Hits* was a moonlight memories selection with the balladeers Johnny Ray, Eddie Fisher and Frankie Laine helping to turn back those hands of time. They followed it with *25 Rockin' and Rollin' Greats* – an LP whose rather baggy definition of rockin' and rollin' greats went from Bill Haley's 'Shake Rattle and Roll' and Carl Perkins' 'Blue Suede Shoes' to 'Surfin' USA' by the Beach Boys and 'Glad All Over' by the Dave Clark Five.

Sheer demographics certainly played their part in the success of these albums, brazenly unsophisticated though they were, but a revival of the 1950s was on the loose. Nik Cohn, in the 'Afterthoughts' of his book *AwopBopaLooBopaLopBamBoom*, admitted: 'More and more, I have retreated into the past and immersed myself in fifties rock 'n' roll.' His response was fuelled by a feeling that 'a new solemnity and piety' had crept into pop, and he mourned the 'loss of energy and honesty and humour'. Cohn's book, first published in 1969, along with Charlie Gillett's *The Sound of the City* were among the first – and remain the best – to trace the story of rock 'n' roll. After the heady rush of developments in the 1960s, there was a sense that rock, like jazz before it, had an untapped or overlooked history worth exploring. *Let It Rock*, a short-lived monthly founded in 1972 and edited by Gillett was an early forerunner of magazines like *Mojo*, in that it included lengthy articles on 1950s doo-wop, R&B, girl groups, the jukebox in a caff on Chatsworth Road, etc., alongside pieces on contemporary acts.

To meet a growing demand from new twentysomething connoisseurs and old Teds who perhaps now had more spare cash, old labels like Sun, Speciality, Chess and Roulette stepped up their reissue programmes on LP. Roulette, who owned the masters of a number of New York R&B labels of the late fifties, offered a nineteen-volume *Golden Oldies* series, and complete albums by groups like the Teenagers and the Chantels, complete with their original track listings and sleeves – which was still a rarity then. The idea of LPs of rock 'oldies' had itself stemmed from the 1950s. Art Laboe was a DJ in Hollywood who hosted a popular radio show dedicated to playing old-ish doo-wop and rock 'n' roll – what he dubbed 'oldies but goodies'. In 1959, he pressed up the compilation album *Oldies But Goodies in Hi-Fi* and watched in astonishment as it entered the *Billboard* charts, where it stayed for the next three years.

The musical *Grease*, beginning its New York run in 1972 and the films *That'll be the Day* and *American Graffiti* – both of which opened in 1973 – confirmed a popular mainstream appetite for the era. Ray Connelly's *That'll be the Day* was the first major British film to consider the era. Starring David Essex and Ringo Starr, its soundtrack LP was produced by Ronco and blessed with the immortal rejoinder 'As Seen on TV'. George Lucas's *American Graffiti* was set in 1962 – an indicator, perhaps, of just quite how long the 1960s took to get going before the Brits piled in with 'Love Me Do's and long hair. Brought instantly to life by the snap of the snare drum from Bill Haley's 'Rock Around the Clock', the picture's heartbeat is rock 'n' roll and as it pours out of car radios tuned, to a man, to the Wolfman Jack[93] show, it bathes practically every scene, effortlessly, if a touch manipulatively, evoking the period.

The combination of a nostalgia-inducing soundtrack, a coming-of-age story and a summer setting would now become a Hollywood mainstay. Richard Linklater's valentine to the 1970s, *Dazed and Confused*, in which obtaining tickets to see *Toys in the Attic*-era Aerosmith is a key motif, is one of *American Graffiti* more respectable descendants.

American Graffiti's soundtrack LP was a bestseller and ultimately paved the way for similar albums from the films of *Grease* and *Saturday Night Fever* as well as opened the door to *Happy Days*, which began broadcasting the following year. And Showaddywaddy, too, probably. 'Rock Around the Clock' re-entered the charts and the world seemed to spin into a 1950s timewarp for a while. 'In affluent circles,' opined *Time* around this period, 'there are Fabulous '50s parties: the debutantes rigged out in calf-length skirts and open-toed, high-heeled numbers, and their dates in narrow ties and pink shirts and trousers that bag at the ankle.'

The mood was infectious. The Band had begun life in the late 1950s as the Hawks, the hot-rocking backing group to 'Toronto's answer to Elvis', Ronnie Hawkins. Like most jobbing acts back

93 A homage to Wolfman Jack can also be found on Todd Rundgren's expansive/sprawling/inspiringly wilful double LP *Something/Anything* from 1972.

then, the Beatles in Hamburg included, they were a walking jukebox and were expected to turn their hand to whatever songs would please hoofers, diners and drinkers. On *Moondog Matinee*, the group took a trip back to their roots with an album of 1950s and 1960s covers. Trade adverts for the LP in *Cashbox* – *Billboard*'s main rival – announced 'The Band Remembers The Hawks'. Named in honour of the Cleveland DJ Alan Freed, whose *Moondog's Rock and Roll Party* sent the kids crazy, man, crazy, the LP was supposedly programmed to resemble a club set and was a mixed bag of rockers and ballads: Chuck Berry's 'The Promised Land', Fats Domino's 'I'm Ready', Sam Cook's 'A Change is Gonna Come', the Bobby Blue Bland's 'Share Your Love with Me'.

Slap bang in the middle (i.e. at the end of side one) was a we'll-be-right-back-folks break number, their version of the *Harry Lime Theme* from *The Third Man*.

The LP, while bemusing some and not selling especially well, seemed to trigger a wave of nostalgic cover LPs. Everyone seemed to have a go. Asking 'Where Have All the Good Times Gone?' in 1973 was David Bowie, who recorded a selection of his 'favourites from the '64–67 period of London'. Unfortunately, *Pin Ups* is largely an example of someone hurting what they most love. Singing like Deanna Durbin on the Easybeats' *Friday on My Mind* and Cookie Monster on Syd Barrett's *See Emily Play*, Bowie's oft-parodied vocal mannerisms and penchant for effects get the better of the material.

For his first solo album in 1974, Bryan Ferry cast his net for covers a little wider. Though looking like a 1950s greaser on the sleeve, with the quiff, black T-shirt and jewellery seeming to anticipate John Travolta's Tony Menero look, Ferry's *These Foolish Things* dipped into the 1930s and '40s. It even somehow managed to transport the Stones' 'Sympathy for the Devil',

Dylan's 'A Hard Rain's a-Gonna Fall' and Smokey Robinson's 'The Tracks of My Tears' into some future-past matinée idol age where silver screens and cigarette smoke were all the rage. Which in the 1970s, they were. (Tom Wolfe's The Man Who Always Peaked Too Soon in *Mauve Gloves & Madmen, Clutter & Twine* gets into 'wing collar shirts and double breasted waist-coats and senior service cigarettes and martinis and short-hair slicked back like the patent leatherkid's' in 1973.)

John Lennon, once inadvertently unnerving journalists with avant-garde albums of tone noises, was similarly in throwback mode. Having spent much of his time with the Beatles voicing a desire to go back to making old fashioned rock 'n' roll records that would recapture the thrill of Hamburg, by 1973 he too was at work on an album of oldies.[94]

However, the project had arisen not from simple sentiment but from a need to settle a lawsuit from Chuck Berry's publisher, Morris Levy. Lennon had pilfered the riff on 'Come Together' from Berry's 'You Can't Catch Me' and to square things he'd agreed to record an album of rock standards that would include a smattering of songs Levy controlled. It was an inauspicious start. If Lennon had a desire to get back to basics, his producer, Phil Spector, now at ease with albums – even triple albums by George Harrison (*All Things Must Pass*) – did not share it. As the relationship between Lennon and Spector soured, the sessions for

94 A month-long bender with Harry Nilsson in 1974 resulted in another album of covers for Lennon, when the pair collaborated on their drunken, drug-addled postcard from LA album, *Pussy Cats*. On the record, Nilsson rasps as a man accustomed to cleaning his teeth with whisky possibly might. Lurching from Nilsson's own compositions to 'Subterranean Homesick Blues', 'Loop de Loop' and 'Rock Around the Clock', it's an LP whose internal logic only comes into its own late at night and after a jar or five.

the album descended into drunken chaos. Spector, already exhibiting a worrying fondness for firearms, discharged a pistol into the studio's ceiling during one particularly fraught day of recording and eventually made off with the master tapes. The dissonance between the relative innocence of the late fifties and early sixties, and the excesses of the 1970s, was being laid horribly bare. A black and white portrait of Lennon taken by Jurgen Vollmer in Hamburg 1961 was chosen for the cover of *Rock n Roll* when it finally appeared in 1975. A ton-up kid in a leather jacket slouching in a doorway, Lennon exudes all the truculence of youth. Nothing, however, could disguise the fact that the album inside was the product of duelling egos and had required a team of lawyers to negotiate its release.

The Who's 'I Can't Explain' and 'Anyway, Anyhow, Anywhere' were among the 1960s mod faves Bowie had had a stab at on *Pin Ups*. But their author Pete Townshend remained more acutely aware than most of the changes in rock music since they'd been composed. While Lennon and others sought to recapture the past by primitive acts of homage or imitation, Townshend would want to use his memories to probe the transition from then to now – now being 1973. It had taken under three and a half minutes for Townshend to sum up 'My Generation' in 1965. *Quadrophenia*, his *memento mori* to mod, was a synthesiser-laced, operatic double LP lasting eighty-two minutes that came with a fully illustrated photo booklet containing the lyrics and an outline of the story. Townshend later commented, 'It could have been written in a simple song like 'My Generation', if I could still write a song like 'My Generation' in 1973.'

All the simple things, it's fair to say, had got complicated for Townshend by 1973, as *Quadrophenia* – an album about a young mod called Jimmy who is a double schizophrenic, hence quadrophenia – attests. (Although the development of quadraphonic sound was largely the catalyst for this conceit, technical difficulties meant the album was never released in quad.)

The album's working title was *Rock is Dead – Long Live Rock* and as songs like 'The Punk and the Godfather' make plain, it was Townshend's attempt to analyse if it was still feasible, or even desirable, to keep on rocking as one grew up and grew older.

Rock's mid-life crisis would affect others rather differently. The Rolling Stones brazened it out with the statement LP *It's Only Rock and Roll* in 1974. For the Beach Boys, the past would become their present and their future. The group's 'All Summer Long', dating from 1964, had been featured on the closing credits of *American Graffiti*. 'Surfin' Safari' had also been used in the film.

Since the late 1960s, Brian Wilson's consumption of drugs had left him a physical and mental mess. The beach boy had bloated to the size of a whale and rarely left his bed, and then only to play the Ronettes' 'Be My Baby' on constant rotation. Now led by youngest brother Carl, the band had recruited some new members, and bolstering whatever crumbs Brian gave them with their own compositions, had matured into a much more autonomous live and recording act.

Perhaps only the Beach Boys could decamp to the Netherlands to record and compose an album and come back with a record that was almost entirely about California. But the resulting *Holland* LP, with its epic 'California Saga', a musical triptych complete with poetry recital – was heralded as a triumphant development on its release in January 1973. 'I expect more from The Beach Boys than anyone else', Richard Williams stated in the *NME*. '*Holland* has the goods.'

Even the fact that Brian's lengthiest contribution to the album was a wacky fairy tale about a magic radio, that to the benefit of all concerned was relegated to a separate 7-inch EP bagged up with the final LP, couldn't spoil the sense of renewal about the Beach Boys' endeavours. Unfortunately, all this would be scuppered by *American Graffiti*. Much of the Beach Boys' output was out of print when the film first opened, so to satisfy the sudden clamour of interest in the early hits that the picture generated, their old record company Capitol banged together a compilation of pre-*Pet Sounds* car, surf and honey numbers. Cleverly packaged and evocatively titled, *Endless Summer* was a testament to a large portion of the American public's need to have something . . . anything . . . nice to enjoy after Watergate. 'Don't Worry Baby', these extraordinary voices from yesteryear helpfully counselled. And who could resist?

The album went to number one, and stayed on the *Billboard* chart for the next three years. Within a year it was joined by two further Beach Boys compilations, *The Spirit of America* and *The Good Vibrations*. The omnipresent past weighed heavily on the band. The Beach Boys didn't make another new studio album until 1976. By then the group would remain lashed for ever more to the mast of their own back catalogue. From then on, every step forward was followed by three steps back as the group settled for the easy wins of life on the oldies circuit – while new LPs seemed built like hot rods from shop-soiled leftovers and spare parts.

The inner gatefold of *Endless Summer* seems to contain a spooky premonition of what would come to pass. On the sleeve, there's a cartoon tableau of a beach scene and at its centre is an overweight figure clearly intended to be Brian. The Wilson avatar stands in front of a hot dog stand. Assailed to his left by a crashing ocean wave carrying a surfer and a sailboat and to his right by a bodybuilder, Brian is vending balloons and wears a straw boater with a 25c price tag tucked into its brim. He is the mad hatter – and one of the balloons he clutches actually has the word 'loon' in mirrored letters emblazoned on it – with the goodies. Instead of carrying him up into the sky, his wares appear to root him to the ground. He looks miserable and as if he would dearly love to be elsewhere. But until every last one of the balloons is gone, the image seems to imply, Brian is going to be stuck here on the sand.

Chapter Eleven

GOD BLESS YOU LESTER BANGS AND THE GREATEST ALBUM EVER MADE

How bad, exactly, were things around, say, 1975–6?

George Orwell was fond of mentioning that until AD1800, no one had noticed that the sea appeared blue. And in the aftermath of punk, many things that had looked, you know, fine really, or at worst tolerable, suddenly acquired completely different hues.[95] The onset of millennial irony and the passing of time, of course, has subsequently altered those colours too. LPs cast as bloated and grandiloquent during the punk era might be relished for those very qualities, their appeal heightened by the idea that they were supposed to be swept away. The ability of Pink Floyd, for instance, to vex some old punks – which endures to this day if the Clash-loving poet Attila the Stockbroker's spot on Radio 4's

---

95 'Once I'd heard this stuff there was no going back', Julian Cope recalled in his memoir *Head On*. 'For about a year after October 1976, the Doors sounded muso, the Velvets sounded reasonable. Can sounded like hippies.'

Saturday Live in 2006 is to be believed – soon became as good an excuse as any to play their LPs. Not that those buggers ever went away anyway . . . But inevitably that kind of punkier than thou intransigence came to seem as unenlightened and reactionary as someone in flares insisting that Rick Wakeman's *No Earthly Connection* was really where it was at may have done at the spittle-flecked 100 Club in 1976.

A random selection of LPs released in 1975 perhaps looks less horrifying than it once did: *Sabotage* by Black Sabbath (marks for the terrible cover, a lopsided group shot); *Neu! 75* by Neu (certainly in the Influential German Electronic albums you should own, or pretend to own, camp); *Funky Kingston* by Toots and the Maytals (by any standards one of pop/reggae's best LPs); *Katy Lied* by Steely Dan (not *Aja* or *Pretzel Logic* but up there as jazz rock staples go); *Piece of the Sky* by Emmylou Harris (respectable country rock); Bob Dylan's *Blood on the Tracks* (a small claim perhaps, but did Dylan make a better album in the 1970s?), Curtis Mayfield's *There's No Place Like America Today* (damning indictments of racial inequality have seldom sounded better); *Shamal* by Gong (Anglo-Gallic pothead pixies go fusion jazz – nice!); *Spartacus* by Triumvirat (as German progressive rock concept albums about slave gladiators leading the rebellion against the Roman Empire go . . .); *One of these Nights* by the Eagles (um, well, *The Hitchhiker's Guide to the Galaxy* would have lacked its theme tune without 'Journey Of The Sorcerer' from this one); and *The Myths and Legends of King Arthur and the Knights of the Round Table* by Rick Wakeman . . . (okay, point taken). *We All Had Doctors' Papers* by Max Boyce (enough, already!)

Punk's demolition job was necessary but could never be entirely sufficient. Arguably, what Peter York categorised as its 'self-conscious simplicity' was difficult to sustain and could never be repeated. But it did succeed in performing an 'emperor's new clothes' manoeuvre, revealing the indulgence, callowness and smug complacency of a lot of what was going on elsewhere on the music scene. Not that many of the public – or the indulgent, smug or complacent – probably thanked them for it, or took that much notice. Here they were, after all, selflessly toiling away on boundary breaking LPs of medievalist rock for grateful sixth formers and undergraduates, bagging, in the case of Gentle Giant on their *Free Hand* (1975) and *Interview* (1976) albums, 6/8 and 7/8 time signatures for popular-ish song. Or staying up all night to record on consecutive full moons just to get the right vibes, as Steve Hillage did on *L* (1976) – an album dedicated to 'all optimistic visions of the future'.

But new age-y optimism was in short supply in the wake of the oil crisis. And punk, with its 'no future' schtick, would have no truck with any of that – not for a short while, at least . . .

At the close of 1975, Queen's six-minute long epic single 'Bohemian Rhapsody', from their baroque album *A Night at the Opera*, was at the top of the charts. On its release, *A Night at the Opera* was reputed to be the most expensive album ever recorded. Overblown in every conceivable sense of the word – 'Bohemian Rhapsody' alone, with its cod-operatic interludes and preposterous shifts in musical style, took over seventy hours to record – the album was a pompous, self-important masterpiece of high camp. It remains today as insufferable and overbearingly silly as it is breathtaking – as any LP that includes a rebuff to a sacked manager, a love letter by the drummer to an Alfa Romeo car, a ponderous strumalong about Einstein's theory of relativity and an arrangement of the English national anthem probably should do.

But while Freddie Mercury was breezily singing about 'no escape from reality', the imperial grandiosity of these records was starting to strike some as out of step with increasingly straightening economic circumstances. (Having said that, it's hard not to feel that some of their middle-to-late 1970s singa-longs – 'We Are the Champions' from 1977's *News of the Word*, for example – weren't fulfilling some desperate need for chest-swelling, morale boosters in the Vera Lynn 'We'll Meet Again' vein, as both the economy and England's chances of qualifying for the World Cup in Argentina went on the skids.)

Led Zeppelin, perhaps at their creative peak as heavy rock's marauding visigoth gods with their diverse double album *Physical Graffiti* and a five-night sell-out run at Earl's Court, were now tax exiles. Part of a burgeoning elite of Starship jet-chartering stadium rockers, they, and groups like them, lived as pampered adolescents, contemptuously indulging their whims in stratospheres as remote to their fans as Jupiter and Mars. But that was what many expected/wanted of their 'rock stars' – and a bombastic double album replete with swirling headbangers conjuring up the mystical East was a welcome escape from drudgery. But the sense that millionaire rock stars were 'no longer part of the brotherly rock fraternity which helped create them in the first place', as the journalist Caroline Coon would observe a little later, was growing among music fans.

By this time, unemployment in Britain had risen to over 1.1 million, the highest since 1940 and inflation was standing at 24 per cent. Over in America, meanwhile, New York had been teetering on the brink of bankruptcy. Initial petitions for federal assistance by the city's burghers were rejected by President Gerald Ford and a front-page headline in the *Daily News* ran: 'Ford to City: Drop Dead'.

Whatever the underlying economic currents, the music indus-try had, by now, become a global business dominated by multinationals. Just two years earlier, *Time* had reported that sales of records and tapes had spiked to nearly $2 billion, and $3.3 billon worldwide, making music 'the most popular form of entertainment in America'. 'With such sales', the piece continued, 'no wonder the conglomerates are conglomerating in the record business. From film studios to breakfast-food makers to rent-a-car companies – everyone is trying to buy up a label and go from wax to riches.' At the end of that year, seven majors (CBS, Capitol, MCA, Warners, Polygram, RCA and A&M) whose corporate portfolios ran from film companies and cemeteries to TV stations and gift stores had consolidated their grip on the record industry. Two giants, CBS and Warners, by then accounted for nearly 40 per cent of all the records produced in the US. Similarly, by 1975, six multinational companies (EMI, CBS, PolyGram, Warners, RCA, and Decca) were bagging over two-thirds of the British record market.

With albums by established artists now selling in their millions – Elton John's *Captain Fantastic and the Brown Dirt Cowboy* shifted 1.4 million copies in the first four days of its release in America – these firms thought big. Walter Yetnikoff of the CBS group informed the press around this time that 'if an artist can only sell 100,000 records . . . then this company is not interested in pursuing that artist. We are looking for the major, major breakthroughs'.

The oil crisis slightly earlier had, if anything, only hurried this attitude on. Out of financial prudence, record companies favoured pressings of surefire sellers over untested acts. And they reduced the accumulation of new groups accordingly, but continued to dole out generous multimillion-dollar deals and recording budgets to their superstar cash cows.

In the world of pop, it was business as usual. Nineteen seventy-five was the year of Rollermania as the Tartan-clad

Bay City Rollers spent six weeks at number one, and disco *à la* 'The Hustle' by Van McCoy and the Soul City Symphony and KC and the Sunshine Band's 'That's the Way I Like it' tumbled out of gay clubs and onto the high street. 'Love to Love You Baby', the title track of Donna Summer's second LP produced by Giorgio Moroder was one of the more significant records in the disco field. Lasting over sixteen minutes, with Summer moaning in convincing imitation of a highly aroused sexual state over a synthesiser backing, it filled one whole side of the album, becoming by default an early dance 12-inch.

Disco, in a sense, wasn't so dissimilar to punk in that its ethos was that everyone could join in; as Neil Bogart, Donna Summer's label boss, observed, people were 'tired of guitarists playing to their own amplifiers . . . they wanted to be the star'. Though one usually needed more than the urge to strut your stuff, and an ability to skip over the uncollected garbage then littering Manhattan streets, to gain entry into Studio 54.[96]

But rumbling discontent about the gigantism of rock was rising beyond the discotheques. In a run-down Lower East Side club called CBGBs (Country Blue Grass Blues – Other Music For Uplifting Gormandizers, to give it its full name), groups such as the Ramones, the Dictators and Television were already regularly performing a fresh strain of fast, dirty guitar music.

---

96 As even Nile Rogers and Bernie Edwards of Chic were to discover when they were refused entry to the club – despite the fact that the musicians could clearly hear its patrons stomping away to their yowser, yowser, yowser anthem, 'Dance, Dance, Dance'. Returning to Rogers' apartment, fuelled by rage, they picked up their instruments and started to jam around the phrase 'fuck off', later substituting 'freak' for 'fuck' and 'out' for 'off' in what became 'Le Freak', a massive hit and one that wound up on the impeccable *C'est Chic*, their second and bestselling LP.

Meanwhile, in London, a back-to-basics pub rock scene had sprung up. Hailing from the outer 'burbs of London and Essex and playing no-frills, drainpipe-trouser-straight sixties R&B in boozers such as the Hope and Anchor in Islington, groups like Kilburn and the High Roads (featuring Ian Dury), Eddie and the Hot Rods and Dr Feelgood presented a welcome antidote to the excesses of English prog. The Feelgoods sported short hair, ties and suits and looked like low-rent gangsters. Their guitarist, Wilko Johnson, whose severe pudding-bowl fringe and wild, staring eyes made him a dead ringer for Lurch from the Addams Family, seemed to prowl the stage as if dodging a hit man's bullets.

Keen to capture the unvarnished, crunchy vitality of their gigging sound, Dr Feelgood's debut album, *Down by the Jetty*, was mixed in mono. Mick Farren, reviewing one of their Dingwalls gigs in the *NME*, commented that they were 'a far cry from the pseudo-faggot glitzies or urban cowhands who seem to be the current norm in rock and roll'.

This pub rock circuit not only provided the springboard (and later the support slots) for up-and-coming English punk rockers including Joe Strummer of the Clash, who cut his musical teeth in the West London squat rockers the 101ers, it also birthed a new breed of street-savvy cottage industry record labels.

Chiswick, founded by Ted Carroll and Roger Armstrong in 1975, was one of these, and Stiff, a concern established shortly afterwards by pub rock promoters Dave Robinson and Andrew 'Jake Rivera' Jakeman, on a £400 loan from Lee Brilleaux of Dr Feelgood, was another.

Carroll was a record dealer who sold vintage rockabilly and sixties-beat 45s to many on the pub rock and nascent punk scene. He supplied Vivienne Westwood and Malcolm McLaren with the 7-inch fodder for the jukebox at their *That'll be the Day* clothes-supplying emporium Let it Rock on the King's Road.[97] John Lydon, who auditioned for the Sex Pistols by singing Alice Cooper's 'Eighteen' in front of *that* machine in *that* shop, wrote in his memoir, *Rotten: No Irish, No Blacks, No Dogs*, that the song was chosen because he 'knew practically none of the records inside Malcolm's jukebox' as 'it was full of all that awful sixties mod music that I couldn't stand'.

Both Chiswick and Stiff, in opposition to some of the indulgences of the era, pursued a policy of cutting records, mainly 7-inch EPs, cheaply and cheerfully with local scenesters – an enterprise that proved a vital component in English punk.

With that in mind, it's worth pausing to acknowledge that to talk about punk and albums might seem positively perverse, facetious – antithetical, even. And it probably is. As Al Clark, a press officer for Virgin records when the Sex Pistols' *Never Mind the Bollocks* LP was released told Pistols biographers Fred and Judy Vermorel, 'the whole idea of making an LP was counter-revolutionary' to some at that time. Singles were the things. Albums were 'part of the then-generation'.

The rallying cry of punk,was supposed to be 'do something *now*'. Do it yourself. As a three tab-chord laden missive in the Stranglers' fanzine *Sideburns* counselled: 'This is a chord, this is another chord, this is a third. *NOW FORM A BAND.*'

Every moment was precious. Speed, snorted and shot up – and contemporary Super 8 material, most of it from the DJ Don Letts, shows a shocking level of casual needle use on the punk scene – was of the essence.

97 The 'little interest displayed' with the Aireon company's LP jukebox in 1949 (noted in chapter one) had not really changed with the arrival of prog rock and concept albums; it would take the arrival of CDs to put whole LPs into bars and pool halls.

True to that spirit, bands, fans and critics would, out of necessity, desire, personal preference, prejudice and a need for things not to be Yes, fetishise the 7-inch 45.

It was, after all, the single 'Anarchy in the UK' that EMI employees refused to pack.

It was the single 'God Save the Queen' that urinated on the delusional parade of the Jubilee and was accordingly banished from the airwaves, banned from Woolworths, WHSmith and Boots and effectively barred from assuming its rightful place at the top of the charts.

It was the Buzzcocks' self-produced and released *Spiral Scratch* EP[98] that helped to demystify the process of putting out records.

So any attempt to write about punk and albums is going to be a little cock-eyed.

But, of course, the Sex Pistols *did* make an album – a full fat-sounding, dog's bollocks of an album that even had its own semi-official bootleg, *Spunk* (another *Great White Wonder?*) – and one that, because of its Bollocks title, resulted in a court case that along with swearing on the telly and spitting has gone down in the mythology of punk as *so* punk.

By then, of course, punk albums were no longer a rarity. The Clash and the Damned all had long-players under their studded belts before the Sex Pistols. And soon enough, yobbo johnnies like the Lurkers with Fulham Fallout would be testing the waters (muddying them?) with such long-haired and flared-trouser faves as (horror of horrors) gatefold sleeves . . .

Albums of various kinds unavoidably had their roles to play in punk, both as sword carriers on the sidelines and as lead actors on centre stage. So however ludicrous, pointless and counter-intuitive it might be, and before this sounds like protesting too

98 While a 7-inch, it did, however, revolve at 33 1/3 rpm.

much, we'll make no further bones about proceeding in an LP-orientated mode.

In retrospect, whatever his reasons, Lydon's choice of an Alice Cooper number for his Sex Pistols audition proved especially apposite. One of the earliest uses of the term 'punk' in the British music press appeared in a review of Alice Cooper's *Love to the Beat* LP in 1971. The *Melody Maker* declared it 'an album for the punk and pimply crowd' – managing to peg the Sex Pistols, who would tour under the pseudoynym the Spots, and their fellow acne-scarred travellers at a single stroke.

The term 'punk', as this dismissive notice suggests, was pejorative – one usually reserved for American hoodlums, goons, finks, no-goods and all round violators of decency. Clint Eastwood was bandying it around in the then contemporary *Dirty Harry* films, while more significantly for punk rock, William Burroughs had deployed it in his semi-autobiographical cult novel *Junky* in 1953. ('I always thought a punk was someone who took it up the ass', Burroughs maintained, long after the expression had become synonymous with the Ramones, bondage trousers and Sid Vicious.[99])

The word and its quasi-literary life, however, are important. Like heavy metal (which I'll admit we've rather skimped on in this book) and many other phrases that come to be applied to specific musical-cum-aesthetic genres, 'punk rock' was coined by a music writer – in this instance, Dave Marsh in *Creem*, who in the early 1970s was busy using it to describe the ragged glories of the Velvet Underground, Iggy and the Stooges, the MC5, the New York Dolls and a slew of nearly forgotten sixties garage bands. But what made punk different – and until then quite unusual – for a genre was the extraordinary number of interactions and crossovers between journalists, fanzine writers and performers; especially, but not exclusively, in its Stateside incarnation.

The arguments, about who, what and where punk started, exhausted by bad television documentaries, tend to descend into those pointlessly nationalistic squabbles that still bubble about Newton and Leibniz's seemingly simultaneous discovery of the calculus. The transatlantic cross-pollinations were numerous and extensive, fortunately for us extending further than Malcolm McLaren's far from negligible but disastrous spell in Manhattan managing the New York Dolls (or conversely the New York Dolls' appearance on the BBC's *Old Grey Whistle Test*), and they involved the odd frisbee of a 12-inch 33 rpm vinyl into the bargain.

If one were, by chance, looking for a reasonable bridging figure between the pre-punk punk of the Velvet Undergound and the MC5, and the punk that surfaced at CBGBs, Patti Smith, although older than Iggy Pop is not a bad candidate. We could also go with Johnny Thunders of the New York Dolls and the

99 In 1965, Burroughs himself recorded an LP of his readings from *Naked Lunch* in Paris. Entitled *Call Me Burroughs*, it was eventually issued on the free jazz label ESP.

Heartbreakers, who toured the UK with the Pistols, or Patti's future husband, Fred 'Sonic' Smith, who was in the MC5 and Television – and she probably wouldn't be everybody's first choice, either.

John Lydon, pogoing at the 100 Club on the same night that Patti and her band had played a show at the Roundhouse in London, pronounced Smith's debut LP, *Horses*, 'horseshit' and the band 'hippies'.[100] 'Is she as overrated as Springsteen?' ran a byline to that particular gig in the *NME*. (And illustrating the other rather dismal stuff people were into then, the remaining live music picks of that week were Gallagher and Lyle, the New Seekers and Hall and Oates, while back-page clothing adverts suggested 'Look Scandinavian – Continental Clogs' and offered cheesecloth shirts for £2.80.)

100 Robert Hull, reviewing the first album by Lydon's post-Pistols Public Image Ltd in *Creem* in 1978 found time in between declaring that the album was 'the rotting corpse of Johnny Rotten' to complain about 'the terrible Jim Morrison/Patti Smith poetry' on the track 'Religion I'.

But in the opinion of whip dancer to the Velvet Underground, Gerald Malanga, Smith 'was a punk true to heart, right from the start'. Smith had an acutely tuned fix (fixation even) on the trash glamour of Andy Warhol, free verse, William Burroughs' cut-up prose and, particularly, rock and roll as a democratic art form. As she told the *Los Angeles City Beat* newspaper in July 2007:

> I was very concerned about the state of rock 'n' roll. It might seem presumptuous, but in that period of my life I loved rock 'n' roll probably more than anything, and I didn't want to see it get so decadent. Basically, I just wanted to be some clarion call and to remind the new guard to take over rock 'n' roll. It's the people's art, and I really felt that we needed to step up and not let it get into the hands of corporations and big business and merchandising and rich rock stars.

A published and performing poet and a music journalist, Smith contributed to *Creem* and *Rolling Stone*.[101] She shadowed (stalked, by some accounts) the Warhol crowd in Max's Kansas City, and gave readings at venues like the Mercer's arts centre, where the New York Dolls frequently played. She also dated Todd Rundgren, the, multicolour-haired, multi-talented, multiple-double-album-penning solo star,[102] and fader slider on the

101 Smith's reviews had much the same musical cadence as her poetry and subsequent lyrics. Reviewing Television, the equally arty lodestars of American punk, whose guiding lights Richard Meyer and Tom Miller adopted the stage surnames 'Hell' and 'Verlaine' in tribute to French symbolist poets, Smith wrote in June 1974: 'Television's wings are a little twisted but the way they play is nearly perfect. Creating infinite space. Trobbing you over and over like sex. And sexy as hell.' Transplendent. Obviously.

102 And what double double albums they were too, with *Todd* containing a song about the foolishness of making albums ('An Elpee's Worth of Toons') and *Something/Anything* boasting a side that played sonic games with the idea of listening to albums on headphones.

Dolls' first LP, Steve Hillage's *L* and Meatloaf's *Bat Out of Hell*.

Smith's musical career really got going, however, after fellow critic, Village Oldies' record store clerk and musician Lenny Kaye began accompanying her recitals/performances on his guitar. (Smith's earlier readings had, on occasion, involved flinging chairs against walls, something that endeared her to a young Joey Ramone.) The poet and the guitarist's friendship had in fact been sparked by a piece Kaye had written about *a cappella* groups. And it was also Kaye's acuity as a pop archaeologist that produced an LP of paramount importance to punk.

Before getting the chance to make records with Smith, Kaye had assembled a double LP of rare garage-sale garage band singles called *Nuggets*. This record celebrated the music created by US bands in the aftermath of the British invasion, when the Beatles, the Stones, the Animals, the Dave Clark Five, Herman's Hermits and so on all stole into the US charts. Suddenly reacquainted, via their English imitators, with the blues and early rock 'n' roll, thousands of white American teenagers were inspired to form 'beat' groups, forging – almost by Chinese whispers – a style of their own. Characterised by easy three-chord riffs played on cheap distorted guitars, bellowed vocals with the odd bit of harmonica and a wheezy organ here and there, these combos, often recording with small local labels, enjoyed bright, if frequently brief careers in the mid-1960s.

To an extent, the *Nuggets* album did for American punk what Harry Smith's Folkways compendium had done for the folk revivalists a decade earlier: it helped to open a generation's ears to this lost (or briefly misplaced, at any rate) vein of American music. The continuum seems all the more striking when we consider that not only did it feature one single ('No Time Like the Right Time' by the Blues Project) originally issued by Folkways, but for a time Smith (Harry) and Smith (Patti) were neighbours, living in the legendary Bohemian fleapit, the Chelsea Hotel.[103] (Immortalised in song by Leonard Cohen, the Chelsea would also go on to host punk's most famous murder, providing the backdrop for Sid Vicious's alleged stabbing of Nancy Spungen.)

Possibly illustrating the pace of change in the 1960s and the shrinking distance between obsolescence and revival since Harry Smith's *American Folk* in 1952, when Kaye's map to 'another world' appeared in 1972 the oldest track on it ('Open My Eyes' by Nazz, who included one Todd Rundgren among their ranks) was actually only four years old. (Can we even conjure that? Ah yes, I remember 2004 . . . whatever happened to Pete Doherty and all those TV talent-show winners that were so popular back then?)

But Kaye, like Smith, was using the long-playing format to salvage the neglected, and pulling off an arresting curatorial job too. Although he protested that the LP was merely 'designed as a listening album' (I am not quite sure what other kind there is, but the anti-manifesto drift is plain), the arrangement or 'programming' of the tracks and his annotations and notes did, however, mount a cohesive case for the joys of adventuring in amateuristic rock.

As Kaye explained, many of the groups featured were young, 'decidedly unprofessional, seemingly more at home practising for a teen dance than going out on national tour'. 'The name', he went on, 'that has been unofficially coined for them is "punk rock" ' – which he felt was 'particularly fitting in this case, for if nothing else they exemplified the berserk pleasure that comes with being on-stage outrageous, the relentless middle finger drive and determination offered only by rock and roll at its finest'.

Though Smith and Kaye's own music would be a little more studied, on-stage outrageousness, middle-finger drive and the

---

103 And there was also CBGBs, the Patti Smith Group, Television, Talking Heads, the Ramones and so on's venue of choice.

give-it-all fearlessness of these 1960s bands was the cornerstone of their aesthetic – and of punk on either side of the Atlantic. But where most of the acts on *Nuggets* had 'relied on the old ways of thinking – the emphasis on hit singles to make or break a group', the Patti Smith Group announced their intentions to the world at large on LP.[104]

Horses (John Lydon's snide horseshit gibe aside) was an album that made a splash. 'It was wonderful. Like something from another planet', Tony Wilson, future Factory records impresario and a flag-waver for punk on Granada Television in Manchester wrote in his novelisation of *24 Hour Party People* in 2002.

Again joining up the intergenerational dots, the LP was produced by John Cale. But the former Velvet had by then already serviced the Stooges, Jonathan Richmond and the Modern Lovers and his old Velvet cohort, Nico. Cale's own

104 All right, there is the minor matter of an independently pressed single that assisted in securing them their major record deal, but what did Arista, their label, expect? An album, naturally. Bloody hippies.

prestigious output of solo LPs was marred (sabotaged?) only by some of the most atrocious album artwork of the 1970s.[105])

Employing, with Cale's encouragement (insistence, really), the literary cut-up techniques of William Burroughs, *Horses* was an LP that wedded Smith's avant-garde poetics to a bare if languorous garage rock backing from Kaye and co. Making able use of the loud/quiet, wander-somewhere-else-for-a-while-come-back-with-gusto song structure of, say, the Doors' *The End* on tracks like 'Birdland', and a bouncy, reggae-ish lilt on 'Redondo Beach', it's dominated by Smith's vocal delivery. Buttonholing the listener like a deranged Times Square street preacher from the off, Smith's opening line on the record is the stark declaration that, 'Jesus died for somebody's sins but not mine'. A striking black and white photo on the cover, shot by (former boyfriend) Robert Mapplethorpe, topped off this

105 *Helen of Troy?* A photo of Cale dressed in a straitjacket, leather trousers with turn-ups, socks and sandals, crouched on an elaborate throne, above him a gaudy gilt mirror that holds the reflection of some imploring, bejewelled harridan. *Slow Dazzle?* Cale in glittery, electrified sunglasses and a leather jacket with the collar turned up . . . Somehow, the sleeves on these records continue to be so mystifyingly wrong.

Not wrong in quite the same manner as Mickey Jupp's *Juppanese*. This cracking album of post-pub rock from the Southend rocker also boasts (like Cale's *Helen of Troy*) the talents of Chris Spedding on guitar, but its cover makes the Vapours' ode to masturbation, 'Turning Japanese' and the film *Lost in Translation*'s views of Japanese people seem positively respectful. Jupp, a lampshade cresting the top of his head, is pictured surveying a table laden with oriental food (courtesy of the Sukhothai Restaurant, as the menu on the corner shows). In a pose (possibly) intended to convey inscrutability or (more likely) in imitation of a certain Eastern physical characteristic that once got Prince Philip's goat, his index fingers test the corner of his eyes, giving them a slightly angled cast, shall we say. (On the back cover the table is bare and Jupp is looking the worse for wear after his indulgences.) No, Cale's sleeves are not wrong in that way. They just look wrong. Terribly wrong.

musical package. Smith, androgynous in a man's white dress shirt and with a jacket slung over her shoulder, seems to challenge the viewer, gaze for gaze, to have a go if they think they're hard enough.

The critical froth the LP generated simultaneously upped the level of attention paid to CBGBs and the other bands that gigged there, including Wayne (later Jayne) County, Television and the Ramones.

Julian Cope confessed in his memoir *Head On* that when he first heard the Ramones' debut LP, he thought they were 'just cartoony' and reminded him of the Banana Splits. But it was that very quality that chimed so precisely with two comic-book-loving aspiring writers and cartoonists, Legs McNeil and John Holstrom, who adopted the Forest Hills foursome as their own. And it was McNeil and Holstrom who also finally tagged (lumbered?) the whole CBGBs scene with the label 'punk' when they used the word for the name of their fanzine. They had, however, been inspired to start this publishing venture by an album from another group entirely, the Dictators, who did play at CBGBs but were, on the whole, far more peripheral to the main scene – though ahead of their time in many respects.

As McNeil explained in his oral history of punk, *Please Kill Me*, their magazine, *PUNK*, was intended to be 'a Dictators album come to life'. He and Holstrom had spent much of the summer of 1975 listening to *Go Girl Crazy*, the Bronx-based band's numb-nuts, proto-punk hymn to beer, White Castle hamburgers, chicks, pro-wrestling and B-movies.[106] The project had really been conceived as a good ruse to hang out with the

---

106 Its poor showing elsewhere led to the group being dropped, but as another example of transatlantic punk traffic, Sandy Pearlman, who co-produced them and the Blue Oyster Cult, later attended to the Clash's second album, *Give them Enough Rope* – a disc that rocks like an American army tank, to the dismay, in 1978, of some of the Clash's 'I'm So Bored with the USA' supporters.

Dictators, but in the event, other CBGBs acts caught their fancy, and their first issue, put together at the fag-end of 1975 and trailed by a flyposting campaign that proclaimed 'Watch Out! Punk is Coming', was dominated by their coverage of the Ramones – four glue-sniffing, trick-turning misfits who adored junk food, bubblegum pop, the Ronettes, the New York Dolls and the Stooges. A couple of years later, Holstrom provided a Loony Tunes-style portrait of the group for the sleeve of their *Road to Ruin* LP.

The cover star for this opening issue of *PUNK*, however, was not some newcomer in torn sneakers but Lou Reed, his image (naturally) rendered in cartoon by Holstrom. Spying Reed in CBGBs, where they'd gone to see the Ramones play, the pair had commandeered the singer for an interview.

Reed, a decade older than the Ramones, was seemingly casting an eye over this whippersnapper scene with the jaded, aviator-shaded eyes of a man who, short of nailing his penis to an amplifier on stage, had in effect been there and done it all, and then done it some more on smack, on speed, in nail polish, with David Bowie, with an iron cross shaved into the side of his head, and with a guy called Rachel. Reed's punk credentials in 1975 were, however, at their zenith. The Velvets' frontman had only recently released *Metal Machine Music*, an album that one reviewer classed as 'understandable only as an act of artistic suicide' but that others felt wasn't far off the sound of a man nailing his penis to an amplifier on stage. Well, if he wasn't actually going the whole hog and nailing the thing down, he was certainly pulling it out and doing something pretty unpleasant with the flex.

At *PUNK*'s offices, Holstrom, according to McNeil, had been playing the record for weeks before their fortuitous encounter in CBGBs. Something that even its creator, if the sleeve notes were to be believed, had avoided doing. 'No one I know has listened to it all the way through,' Reed wrote, 'including myself. It is not meant to be.'

In Victor Bockris's biography of Reed, Frank O Donnell, a marketing executive at the musician's record label, RCA, recalled first hearing the album: 'About twenty of us were seated around a vast mahogany conference table for a monthly new-release album meeting', O Donnell stated. 'The A&R representative at the meeting put the tape on and the room was filled with this bizarre noise. Everyone was looking at everyone else; people were saying, "What the hell is that?" Somebody voiced the question and the answer came back, "That's Lou Reed's new album, *Metal Machine Music*. His contract says we've got to put it out." '

Coming on the heels of *Sally Can't Dance*, a top ten album and the biggest seller of his career, *Metal Machine Music* consisted of four sixteen-minute sides of ear-splitting feedback. The fourth side had a locked groove, so the album, if you chose not to yank the needle off, would play ad infinitum. Denounced as 'a jab of contempt' that 'sounds like the tubular groaning of a galactic refrigerator' by James Wallcott in *Rolling Stone*, the album divides opinion to this day. On the one hand, there are those who hear method, even beauty in its madness. It can be seen both as a continuation of the atonality of songs like 'Black Angel Death Song' and 'Sister Ray' and thus saluted as an early instantiation of industrial and ambient music, and as a witty, ironic comment on avant-garde methodologies, 7-inch-single-collecting journalists, quad, bloated progressive rock double albums and Mantovani all rolled into one.[107]

107 Certainly on the 'ambient' front, while admittedly much more abrasive in its challenge to the listener to find monotony interesting, *MMM* isn't so far away from Brian Eno's adventures in the field at that time. The rather apocryphal-sounding story of how the future Talking Heads and Television producer Eno first came up with the notion of 'ambient music' was recounted on the back of his 1975 album, *Discreet Music*, the title track of which lasts for over half an hour and is accommodated on one single side by the deployment of narrower (and therefore quieter) grooves.

Then there are those who regard it as just a really annoying noise. Q magazine ranked it as one of their fifty worst records ever made. But really, *Californication* by the Red Hot Chili Peppers was in their top 100 of Best Albums Ever Made. On

'In January this year', Eno wrote, 'I had an accident. I was not seriously hurt, but I was confined to bed in a stiff and static position. My friend Judy Nylon visited me and brought me a record of eighteenth-century harp music. After she had gone, and with some considerable difficulty, I put on the record. Having laid down, I realised that the amplifier was set at an extremely low level, and that one channel of the stereo had failed completely. Since I hadn't the energy to get up and improve matters, the record played on almost inaudibly. This presented what was for me a new way of hearing music – as part of the ambience of the environment just as the colour of the light and the sound of the rain were parts of that ambience. It is for this reason that I suggest listening to the piece at comparatively low levels, even to the extent that it frequently falls below the threshold of audibility.'

Nylon, however, remembered things a little differently. Interviewed by Bart Plantenga for *3AM* in 2003, she maintained, 'So it was pouring rain in Leicester Square, I bought the harp music from a guy in a booth behind the tube station with my last few quid because we communicated in ideas, not flowers and chocolate, and I didn't want to show up empty-handed. Neither of us was into harp music. But I grew up in America with ambient music. If I was upset as a kid I was allowed to fall asleep listening to a Martin Denny album . . . I think it was called *Quiet Village*. The jungle sounds, played very softly made the room's darkness caressing instead of empty as a void. Pain was more tolerable. Brian had just come out of hospital, his lung was collapsed and he lay immobile on pillows on the floor with a bank of windows looking out at soft rain in the park on Grantully Road on his right and his sound system on his left. I put the harp music on and balanced it as best as I could from where I stood; he caught on immediately to what I was doing and helped me balance the softness of the rain patter with the faint string sound for where he lay in the room. There was no "ambience by mistake".'

If only one could buy LPs of harp music from a booth in Leicester Square tube today.

release, *MMM* was thought a poor and rather arrogant joke from an egomaniac who'd planned it as a 'fuck you' to both the fans who'd dared to buy its annoyingly popular predecessor and the record company that had the audacity to make him make it. Which, at the end of day, might obviously make it all the more . . . punk.

Well, it is all of those things. And more. And less. Which is possibly why it's still available to this day. That and the fact that Reed immediately followed it with *Coney Island Baby*, a gentle, rather wistful album of sensitive songs dedicated to a guy named Rachel that people bought before he pissed everyone off again with his disco album *The Bells*, gained forgiveness with *The Blue Mask*, pissed everyone off again with *New Sensations* and so on.

Bockris is not alone, however, in dubbing the album 'the progenitor of New York punk rock'. This might be overdoing it just a tad, but then it was nothing when compared to Lester Bangs, who christened it 'the Greatest Album Ever Made'. If, he argued, tongue teasing his droopy moustache if not his cheek, 'you ever thought feedback was the best thing that ever happened to the guitar, well, Lou just got rid of the guitars'. Bangs quizzed Reed about the album, which he rather eloquently described as sounding like: 'ZZZZZZZRRRRRRRREEEEEEEGGGGGGG-GGRRRRRAAAAARRRRRRRGGGGGGGGGGHHHHHHNN-NNNNNNNNNNNIIIIIIIIIIIEEEEEEEEERRRRRRRRRRRRRR . . .' And Reed, possibly in jest but then possibly not, maintained there were 'all kinds of symphonic rip-offs in there, running all through it, little pastoral parts . . . Like Beethoven's Third or Mozart . . .'

Seek and ye shall find, I suppose.

Whatever *Metal Machine Music* did for punk, *PUNK* gave it a glowing review, but the Ramones would represent punk's immediate future. One of their greatest assets at this juncture was simply their youth. The discovery that the band are '23, 24' is met by *PUNK* interviewer Mary Harron with an enthusiastic, 'Oh that's us!' underlining her delight at actually finding a band so close to the magazine staff's own age.

McNeil, recalling his first Ramones gig at CBGBs, wrote: 'I really thought I was at the Cavern Club in 1963 and we had just met the Beatles. Only it wasn't a fantasy, it wasn't the Beatles, it was *our* band – the Ramones.'

The Ramones' surname, uniformly adopted by Tommy, Dee Dee, Johnny and Joey was a tribute to Paul McCartney, 'Ramone' being one of Macca's many pseudonymns. And just as the Beatles had galvanised many of the American 'punks' on Kaye's *Nuggets* LP, the Ramones would now return the favour, with their debut album in particular having an unprecedented effect on English punk.

Aside from on the Lower East Side of New York, the Ramones were more warmly received in Britain than practically anywhere else. Most Americans (and plenty of Brits too), chose in any case to devote 1976 to filling the coffers of another Limey, the curly-haired 1960s survivor Peter Frampton, whose double live LP, *Frampton Comes Alive* spent ten weeks at number one and eventually sold 6 million copies in the States alone.

But if sales of the Ramones' self-titled debut LP were modest – it failed to chart on either side of the Atlantic – its impact wasn't.

As Tony James of Generation X and later Sigue Sigue Sputnik told Joe Strummer's biographer Chris Salewicz, 'The Ramones were the single most important group that changed punk.' He maintained that 'When their album came out, all the British groups tripled speed overnight. Two-minute-long songs, very fast. The Pistols were the only group who stuck to the Who speed.'

'Buzzsaw' is one of those words that tend to be over-deployed to describe the sound of the Ramones, but then the to-the-bone sinewy version of three-to-four-chord rock that they played at breakneck pace *was* rather saw-like. The longest song on their debut album, 'I Don't Wanna Go Down to the Basement' lasts only two minutes thirty-five seconds, and the shortest, 'Judy Is a Punk', lasts one minute thirty. The whole LP, fourteen songs, lasts less than twenty-eight minutes in total.

It is so brief that it almost feels like an album pretending to be a single. Just as Lou Reed's *Metal Machine Music* feels like a single noise pretending to be a four-sided album. At a point when Pink Floyd and Fleetwood Mac were taking two years to compose their albums and nuturing recording budgets of phenomenal proportions, it was a model of thrift. One that even the money-conscious President Gerald Ford (and the new leader of the Conservative party, Margaret 'Milk Snatcher'[108] Thatcher) could well have approved of.

Made on a budget of around $6,400 and released on the

108 A punk band name begging to be used, I think.

independent label Sire (who would snap up Talking Heads and the Dead Boys from the CBGBs crowd, and some years later Madonna), *Ramones* was recorded in less than a week in February 1976, at a studio in the heart of New York's Radio City Music Hall. Its cover, a shot of the band taken for *PUNK* by Roberta Bayley, caught the group standing in front of a heavily graffitied brick wall, looking every bit the street hustlers who'd turn a trick to cop money for drugs that they were, and became an almost instantaneous punk icon.

The album was released in the UK on 23 April 1976, when if you felt so inclined, you could have taken in the Sex Pistols and the 101ers, the squat pub rock band then still fronted by Joe Strummer, at the Nashville in West Kensington.[109]

One possible reason why the Sex Pistols may have remained so impervious, as Tony James suggested, to the Ramone's frenetic bpm was that guitarist Steve Jones had been so staunchly loyal to the New York Dolls' first album. In their formative months, he'd ceaselessly striven to improve his technique by dropping a black bomber each morning and practising for hours on end to the LP in the band's Denmark Street rehearsal rooms.

However, later recruit Sid Vicious, who cited the Ramones as his favourite band, had 'mastered' the bass with the aid of their LP. His friend Keith Levene, fleetingly a guitarist in the Clash and later a member of PIL, recalled in 2003, 'One night he played the first Ramones album non stop, all night, then next morning, Sid could play the bass – that was it, he was ready!' ('I don't understand why people think it's so difficult to learn to play guitar. I found it incredibly easy', Vicious himself told *Sounds* in October 1976. 'You just pick a chord, go twang, and you've got

109 Explaining why he broke up the 101ers, Joe Strummer told Caroline Coon in 1977, 'I saw the Sex Pistols . . . and decided to move into the future.'

music.') But since Vicious hardly added an audible note to any of the Sex Pistols' records, and there was a distinct paucity of new material written after the original bassist Glen Matlock was ousted, the steady velocity established by Jones and Matlock never wavered – nor did it really need to, since Lydon's manic stage persona and his habit of spinning lyrics in mannered Old Man Steptoe yelps and hasty clusters provided the giddiness to songs that otherwise just chugged along in a pretty pedestrian manner.

One of the earliest reviews of the Sex Pistols to appear in the *NME* was actually printed around the time that the Ramones were ensconced in Radio City undertaking their blink-and-you'll-miss-it recording sessions. But if anything, it only emphasises the similarities, rather than the differences, between the two bands. Neil Spencer, catching the last few numbers of their set before pub rockers Eddie and the Hot Rods took to the stage, summed up the Sex Pistols as 'a quartet of spiky teenage misfits from the wrong end of various London roads, playing sixties-styled white punk rock as unselfconsciously as it is possible to play it these days i.e. self-consciously'. Spencer ended his piece with a quote from one of the Pistols, saying: 'We're not into music . . . We're into chaos' – a line that could only have come from Lydon. But without wishing to cast doubt on the twenty-year-old's commitment to chaos back then, the singer's autobiography confirms that he did, of course, care deeply about music, as attested by his scrawling the words 'I Hate' onto a Pink Floyd T-shirt.

'Music was a big thing at age fourteen,' he writes at one point. 'I started buying records that would be my most fun, not actually going out anywhere, but just sitting indoors playing my records to myself.' What he liked was predominantly on LP: Keith Hudson; *Fun House* by Iggy and the Stooges; *Tago Mago* by Can ('It's stunning, my fave'); *Bitches Brew* by Miles Davis ('I loved that album'); and Captain Beefheart. What he didn't like, other than Pink Floyd, was university students who 'thought they knew it all with their Emerson, Lake and Palmer albums'.

By the summer of 1976, Rotten wasn't alone in feeling that ELP and their ilk had had their day. Many punks pictured themselves in some kind of Manichean battle for the soul of music – a contest not unlike the one then being waged at the cinema between Luke Skywalker and the rebel forces against Darth Vader and the Evil Empire in *Star Wars*.

Mick Farren, himself a veteran of the 1960s underground, part of the *Oz* magazine team and a member of the anarchic hippy rock band the Deviants, wrote a lengthy diatribe against the rock dinosaurs in the *NME* under the headline 'The Titanic Sails at Dawn'. It is 'time for the seventies generation to start producing their own ideas', he argued, 'and to ease out the old farts who are still pushing tired ideas from the sixties'.

As a couple of responses to the piece in the paper's letters pages showed only too well, some of those tired ideas from the 1960s were not going to be edged out quite so easily. 'Some of us', Hubin from Romford wrote, 'are working flat out to achieve a new direction – shitting on the old money and constant hassles like money and plastic people. There are many people who have fled from the big smoke to the West Country in the last few years. The West Country has become a hot house of creativity – the Trentishoe Earth Fayre was ample proof of that.'

Back in 1969, the Radio 1 DJ John Peel's show had been described as 'uncompromising in its devotion to, and enthusiasm for, new sounds'. And seven years on, the man who'd once penned hippy dippy sleeve notes for Tyrannosaurus Rex about the earth singing, scattered leaves of old summers and children rejoicing (in Trentishoe, probably) now proved just how uncompromising that devotion was when he began airing tracks from the Ramones' LP on his show.

With Peel's posthumous reputation enduring as the bloke many would have loved as a dad and playing the most wonderfully obscure and eclectic stuff imaginable, this might not seem especially avant-garde; however, it was a very different matter then. That isn't to say he wasn't playing wonderfully electic stuff back then. He was. Stackridge, National Health, Michael Chapman, Graham Parker, Bridget St John, Thin Lizzy, Deaf School and Ivor Cutler all did studio sessions for Peel in 1976. And even after the punk era, most would return. It's just that many fans of 'evolved' rock – 'heads', as they were known – regarded Peel as one of their own.

Only a few months before filling the airwaves with 'Judy Is a Punk' Peelie had, after all, kindly bathed their ears in *Ommadawn*, Mike Oldfield's far-out follow-up to *Tubular Bells*. And not long after that played the whole of the new Dylan album, *Desire*. All fifty-five minutes of it – to the exclusion of practically everything else. And while he had added reggae and pub rock to the roster, and was already beginning to voice some impatience with the more corpulent efforts around (Queen, for one) his audience tuned in with a good idea of what they were going to hear – the idea that they would hear good things that they liked. Unfortunately, for some regulars, punk would turn the 'good' to 'bad' and the 'liked' to 'hated'.

The tastes, expectations and predjudices of Peel's regulars around this period are best illustrated by the records they voted into the first festive fifty later that year. While the Modern Lovers' two-chord marvel 'Roadrunner' creeps in at the respectable position of thirty-three, the run-down is dominated by classic rock staples and at the top of the heap, just above Derek and the Dominos' 'Layla' is Zeppelin's 'Stairway to Heaven'. Perhaps more surprising is that 'Layla's placing seems to have been entirely unaffected by a drunken outburst Eric Clapton made at a gig in Birmingham in August that year. Addressing the audience to urge them to back the right-wing MP, Enoch Powell,

Clapton is reputed to have said: 'I think Enoch's right . . . we should send them all back. Throw the wogs out! Keep Britain white!' His comments led to the formation of the Rock Against Racism organisation. (And moving the clock forward just two years, it's gratifying to find Derek down to number thirty-one, with Buzzcocks' 'Moving Away from the Pulsebeat' above him.)

Peel's conversion to punk via the Ramones' LP was especially fortuitous for the English punk milieu. Where the daytime Beeb tried to give punk a wide berth, especially after the Sex Pistols' infamous contretemps with Bill Grundy on Thames TV's *Today* programme on 1 December 1976,[110] Peel defended it, played the records as they appeared (during the BBC's ban of 'God Save the Queen' he continued to air the song) and pretty early on, opened

110 What still remains most mystifying about the *Daily Mirror*'s 'The Filth and the Fury' front-page piece on the incident is how casually the reactions of one James Holmes, lorry driver, 47, of Beechfield Walk, Waltham Abbey, Essex were reported. Holmes, outraged that his eight-year-old son, Lee, had been exposed to such appalling language, 'kicked in the screen of his TV'. Holmes was then quoted as saying: 'I am not a violent person, but I would like to have got hold of Grundy.' The Sex Pistols and their entourage, who included Siouxie Sioux and Steve Severin of the Banshees, had only ended up on the *Today* show because Queen, another EMI act, had pulled out. As Fred and Judy Vermorel point out, the art/performance/industrial band Throbbing Gristle had appeared on Grundy's show in October 1976 – a good month before the Pistols. The group's invitation stemmed from the outrage their used-tampon-scattered Prostitution exhibition/event – attended, incidentally, by Siouxie Sioux and Steve Severin – had caused in the tabloids. As the Vermorels put it, 'Suspecting that Grundy wanted them to be provocative, TG perversely went out of their way to be charming, decent and respectable . . . If TG had beeen more obliging', they mused, 'would they have sat in the Pistols' throne?' And from our point of view, would *Second Annual Report* be nestling at the top of those 'best albums' polls?

the doors of the corporation's Maida Vale studios to bands like the Vibrators and the Damned. For the latter, he received a soiled piece of bog paper in the mail from 'some bloke in Manchester'.

The Peel sessions were to prove particularly important to the 'independent' groups thrown up once most of punk's vanguard (the Sex Pistols, the Clash and so on) had had their year zero and were either imploding, splitting up, forming new groups or, in the words of some, selling out.

In at number six in Peel's (self-selected) festive, er, thirteen in 1977, for instance, was 'Smokescreen' by the Desperate Bicycles. Recorded in three hours for the princely sum of £153, this debut single from a group who had two songs and had never played together before hitting the studio concluded in the rallying cry: 'It was easy, it was cheap – go and do it'. For their follow-up, *The Medium Was Tedium* – 'an amateurish record in praise of amateurism' in Graham Lock of the *NME*'s opinion, the sleeve contained a breakdown of the costs of the single and explained how to put out a record yourself. Thriving in a network of small record shops (Bonaparte on the Pentonville Road, Rough Trade in Notting Hill, Small Wonder in Walthamstow, Probe in Liverpool, Graphiti in Glasgow), fanzines and word of mouth, and exposure from John Peel, the group were dogged in their commitment to remaining outside the main music biz. 'The Desperate Bicycles have a refreshingly left-field attitude to the music business – and, one suspects, some influence in encouraging others to follow their DIY example' was Lock's accurate conclusion. The spirit of Tom Lehrer, dormant for a little while, was on the loose again.

All of this was happening at a Ramones-esque rate. The Damned had only released the 'first' English punk single in October 1976. Always the jokers in the pack, and having adopted wacky stage clobber (vampire garb, nurses' outfits, pilot shirts, nudism, etc) and such dole-snoop evading stage names as Rat Scabies and Captain

Sensible, they were easily as cartoonish as the Ramones if not more so – a cartoon of a cartoon, but a good one at that.

From the phoney Yank-accented spoken intro parodying the Shangri-Las to the if-Status-Quo-had-developed-a-taste-for-Methedrine bar-blocked guitars, 'New Rose', issued on Stiff Records, was a very British riposte to the American 1-2-3-4 buzzzzzzzzzzzzzsawwwww blueprint. Forest Hills via Forest Hill, or, more accurately, Queens via Croydon, and a blast of gleeful (artificial) energy that doesn't sound capable of lasting the full two minutes forty-six seconds claimed on the label.

Fuelled by 'cider and sulphate', according to bassist Captain Sensible (Ray Burns), English punk's first long-player, *Damned, Damned, Damned* was settled up in little more than seven days and issued on 18 February 1977 with the injunction 'Play it at Your Sister'.

In contrast to the J.G. Ballard-inspired tower blocks and grubby alleyways that would become a cliché of punk album art, on the front sleeve, the band appeared post-food fight, smeared with the remains of a large, what must have been heavily iced birthday cake.

However, on the back of growing press coverage (outrage), music paper and fanzine coverage, the support of John Peel and independent record shops and punters who were desperate for something that wasn't Yes, its ability to make the top thirty confirmed that UK punk on LP was a viable – if still not for some entirely welcome – development.

Where the Damned were comedic – and, unable to coax Syd Barrett[111] out of hiding, the wacky funsters did employ Nick

---

111 Captain Sensible, as was revealed at the Syd Barrett tribute concert at the Barbican in 2007, gives very good Barrett himself. As, for that matter, does his punk peer, the journalist turned performer, Pretender Chrissie Hynde.

Mason, the drummer of Pink Floyd, to produce their second album only to see it sink – the Clash were committed. It was a reputation they obtained by a mixture of genuine intent, default, wish-fulfilment on the part of other people (not least journalists), grave error and the singer Joe Strummer's long-standing association with London's collectivist squats.

For a while, they seemed to own the copyright on being photographed underneath the Westway looking like a gang of dole-boy toughs, despite having relatives in the diplomatic service and spells at art school in their collective personal portfolios.

The Clash, not unsurprisingly, in the more fervent political atmosphere of the mid-1970s, disappointed impassioned fanzines like *Sniffin' Glue* and even Joe Strummer's ex-girlfriend's Paloma/Palmolive and her Slits bandmates when they opted to sign a deal with the major label CBS in January 1977. 'The Clash', *Sniffin' Glue* griped, rather astutely as it turned out, 'represent something which those in power have seen before, and can be easily assimilated, controlled, dealt with and even incorporated into existing structures.' Further burying the knife, they added, 'There's always a place for a token revolutionary.'

Their approach to recording their first LP was, however, punk to the letter. After a week in the studio, they delivered the master tapes to CBS on 3 March 1977,[112] their debut single 'White Riot'

---

112 Delivering tapes was never quite so painless for the Clash. In 1979, a set of demos of work in progress, recorded at the Vanilla studio in Pimlico, went missing after the roadie Johnny Green asked to take them to the producer Guy Stevens and ended up leaving them on a tube train. Missing for twenty-five years, a copy of the tape eventually turned up in a box in the guitarist Mick Jones' house.

('catchy enough to sing in the bath' in the *Melody Maker*'s opinion) was in the shops fifteen days later and the long-player, *The Clash*, was released on 8 April.

By this point, the Sex Pistols had only managed one single and were record deal-less, having lost contracts with EMI and A&M. They had also earned the enmity of the establishment at large and an assault or two from 'vigilantes'.

Malcolm McLaren, the rag-trade revolutionary, wannabe art terrorist and Sex Pistol Svengali, Fagin to Rotten's Artful Dodger, would latterly glue these events into some grand pre-conceived text. But in the summer of 1977, the Sex Pistols were running out of options and only very reluctantly hitched up with Richard Branson's 'hippie' label, Virgin. 'The Sex Pistols needed a record company and Virgin needed a sensation' Tom Bower notes in *Branson*, his fine, scabrous hatchet job on the entrepreneur. (Gong and David Bedford were not, it appears, sensational enough for Branson.) He adds, 'McLaren was not surprised by the absence of any records in Branson's house except for one Reader's Digest collection of Mozart.'

The Pistols' association with the label would, at least, result in the creation of an LP – one that thirty years later they'd play in concert, just like Pink Floyd with *The Dark Side of the Moon*. Until its release, if you had been really, really impatient for a Sex Pistols album, there had already been a dodgy live LP. Entitled *No Fun*, this inside-someone's-anarchist-symbol-scrawled-sports-bag recording of a gig at the Lesser Free Trade Hall in Manchester sadly lived up to its name. But on 28 October 1977, *Never Mind the Bollocks* officially crashed into the world.

Although if you happened to visit a few select outlets – for example, Rough Trade on London's Portobello Road (within spitting distance of Virgin's offices) – a week or three earlier, you could nab an LP – nay, an *album* – that sounded the spit of the Sex Pistols.

It didn't actually say 'Sex Pistols' on the cover or anything. In fact, it didn't say very much on the cover at all. There *was* no cover, per se. This was punk nihilism at its finest. The label at the centre of the disc carried a cartoon of a pop-gun and the name 'Blank', and an act called Spunk were credited with the twelve numbers listed, with the producer named as P. Dickerson. But exposure to no more than twenty seconds confirmed that this was Lydon and his cohorts, and that the unfamiliar sounding titles 'Nookie', 'No Future' or 'Lots of Fun' were none other than 'Anarchy in the UK', 'God Save the Queen' and 'Pretty Vacant'.

For some, it was too good to be true. 'All in all, and despite the fact that it's a bootleg and illegal and everything,' Chas de Whalley wrote in *Sounds*, 'Spunk is an album that no self respecting rock fan would turn his nose up at. I've been playing it constantly for a week'. Then he added, surely the finest compliment from a music reviewer, 'and I'm not bored yet.'

The mystery nevetheless remained of how kosher studio recordings – albeit demos recorded with Dave Goodman – had escaped from the Sex Pistols' lair just as their eagerly anticipated album was about to be released.

Had a roadie left them on a tube train?

In *Sounds*, de Whalley confided: 'Seasoned Pistols observers suggested that Malcolm McLaren might have been behind the Blank Label.' This was, of course, firmly denied. But since McLaren 'retained the full rights' to these recordings, the pop-pistol on the label looked like smoking gun. Especially as McLaren publicly confessed to preferring these demos to the finished album. However, to this day he still claims not to have been involved. But further circumstantial evidence – a last-minute fiddling with the running order and the demand for 'Submission' to be added to the finished album (an act many, not least the Pistols' biographer, Jon Savage, believe was a delaying tactic to allow time for contrabanded records to reach the shops) – all adds fuel to the fire. In the end, both an eleven-track – with 'Submission' on a 7-inch single – and a twelve-track version of *Never Mind the Bollocks* slunk out.

Back then, any punk band worth its salt got bootlegged. In a subculture that made a virtue of the ragged and the ripped, served by small independent shops and where posters, fanzines and record sleeves were all churned out on office photocopiers and the Desperate Bicycles were singing 'Xerox Music's Here at Last!', the bootleg had unimpeachable samizdat cool.

For the punks who wanted *Never Mind the Bollocks* but were worried it was counter-revolutionary as it wasn't a 7-inch single, or it was passé or overproduced, or that after being razored on the streets of Highbury on an almost daily basis, the Sex Pistols had gone soft or had sold out, *Spunk* was the credible, untamed twin they could buy with a clear conscience. With this LP, they knew that they were sticking it to the man. The man with the little beard and nice line in jumpers, at the very least.

Seeing the degree of amusement/annoyance/excitement/confusion that the incident caused Virgin, the Sex Pistols were not only honoured by bootlegs but also given a spoof 'lost' live album in the *NME* on April Fool's Day in 1978. The story, written by one April

Fule, gave the low-down on *Anarchy in the USA*, a low-fidelity live LP that Virgin had purportedly got cold feet over. Its release had, 'apparently' also been delayed to avoid hurting the sales on the new Tangerine Dream album, Cyclone. A company spokesman was 'quoted' as saying: 'Most Pistols fans groove on the Tangs'.

However, there was nothing low-fidelity about *Never Mind the Bollocks*, with Rotten/Lydon's dog-straining-at-the-leash vocals delivering lyrics about abortion, Belsen and the stupidity of the Queen against the ship-sinking crashes of Steve Jones' heavy, riffing guitars. Jones, incidentally, was also credited with coming up with the album's title, which led to the famous court case: in a heated debate about what they should call the record, Jones allegedly grew so exasperated that he shouted, 'Oh fuck it, never mind the bollocks of it all.' Which they all agreed would do very nicely.

The title, in and of itself, might (possibly) have passed without too much incident. This was still the Sex Pistols, after all – the police were never going to greet it with the same polite indifference as that year's other releases, like Supertramp's *Even in the Quietest Moments*, *Thunder in My Heart* by Leo Sayer, Godley and Creme's almost suicidal triple album *Consequences* (a record expressly designed to show off the Gizmo, a violin-mimicking gadget they'd invented) or Donna 'I Moan in Ecstasy from Time to Time Rather Suggestively' Summer's *I Remember Yesterday*. Or even Fleetwood Mac's *Rumours*, the break-up album to end all break-up albums, whose cover features Mick Fleetwood dressed in a jerkin and britches, appearing to bare his balls – velvet (leather?) balls, admittedly, but they're in the right place (ish).[113]

113 Could the Sex Pistols, just possibly, have been cocking a snook at the Macs? After all, in 1977, *Rumours* with its, er, ballsy cover was number one for months on end and eventually spent 477 weeks in the British charts.

But Jamie Reid's fluorescent yellow ransom-note-style art-work for the album's sleeve (described by Lydon as 'the simplest and ugliest thing we could come up with') did not exactly go quietly into the night. Especially not when reconfigured for 9-foot-by-6-foot window display posters.

Today, it's quite acceptable to wander around in a T-shirt whose brand logo is 'fuck' with a couple of letters swapped around. I am also free, here, to type the word 'fuck' without recourse to blush-saving asterisks. But this was 1977 and even the *Melody Maker*, bless them, opted to blot out the word 'bollocks' in adverts for the album in their pages, while two national newspapers resorted to sticking dots over it.[114]

Naturally WHSmith, Woolworths and Boots, peddlers of girlie mags, pick 'n' mix sweets and over-the-counter drugs to the nation, all refused to stock the LP. Despite this, it still managed to top the album charts.

On 5 November, however, the manager of the Nottingham branch of Virgin Records was arrested under the 1899 Indecent Advertising Act, after a policewoman, Julie Dawn Storey, investigated the store's window displays.

Virgin Records and the Sex Pistols were arraigned in court on 24 November. Branson employed John Mortimer QC to defend their case. Mortimer, creator of Rumpole of the Bailey, had successfully defended the underground paper *Oz* against pornography charges in 1970.

Mortimer's chief witness was Reverend James Kingsley. A former Anglican priest and a fellow of the Royal Academy, Kingsley was Professor of English Studies at Nottingham

114 In the let-it-all-hang-out 1960s, the nude photo of John Lennon and Yoko Ono on their *Two Virgins* LP and the plethora of naked women on Jimi Hendrix's *Electric Ladyland* were banned in some shops or sold only in brown paper bags.

University. Under questioning, Kingsley charted the proud and lengthy history of the word 'bollocks'. He argued that it had long been used as a term for nonsense and as a nickname for clergymen, who were known for speaking nonsense. (Asked at one point if the 'words fuck, cunt and shit also appeared in the Dictionary of Slang from which he had quoted', Kingsley replied, 'if the word fuck does not appear in the dictionary it should'.)

Summing up, Mortimer, who also asked the magistrates to consider if the good citizens of Maidenhead had any reason to feel ashamed of their town's fine name, appealed to their patriotic duty: 'What sort of country are we living in', he queried, 'if a politician comes to Nottingham and speaks here to a group of people in the city centre and during his speech a heckler replies "bollocks", are we to expect this person to be incarcerated, or do we live in a country where we are proud of our Anglo Saxon language? Do we wish our language to be virile and strong or watered down and weak?'

Against their better judgements, the panel let them off. 'Much as my colleagues and I wholeheartedly deplore the vulgar exploitation of the worst instincts of human nature for the purchases of commercial profits by both you and your company', the chairman stated, 'we must reluctantly find you not guilty of each of the four charges.'

For the Sex Pistols it was a hollow victory; the group were spent artistically and ultimately, so was punk. Seized upon by a legion of beer-boy imitators, enslaved by their own bondage trousers, its motifs of rebellion were fast becoming clichés. Or so the cliché goes. But at least things were beginning to get interesting for the LP.

Punk, to begin with, had always been about fresh ideas and many of the original punk stars spread their wings on LP. John Lydon formed Public Image Ltd with Keith Levene and Jah

Wobble, and produced a series of harshly industrial, discordant albums that were fed by their mutual love of dub reggae, the German experimentalists Can and boredom with the persistence of jobbing rock.

In the States, though, before *Never Mind the Bollocks* had a title, Television, aided by Brian Eno, were unfurling eleven-minute songs, pared-down prog with guitar solos as taut as cheese wire, on their debut album *Marquee Moon*. And Talking Heads produced three preppy, cerebral and oddly funky albums, *77*, *More Songs About Buildings and Food* and *Fear of Music*, in the time it had taken Sid Vicious to move from the 100 Club to the Chelsea Hotel.

But though the haircuts might have been shorter, the trousers and ties narrower and the guitar solos thinner-sounding, some old habits would return, just as the old guard – ELO, Elton John, Supertramp and even Yes – weren't that easily swept away in the end.

Howard Devoto left the Buzzcocks to form Magazine and plough an intense, brainy furrow, creating some of the most striking albums of the era . . . but wasn't history repeating itself, with ranks of synthesisers and gatefold sleeves . . . ? Meanwhile, his former bandmates would wind up falling for acid and crashed out of the 1970s in a rush of phased guitars on *A Different Kind of Tension*.

Even the Radio 1-friendly Stranglers were found to be composing concept LPs about Norse gods, while their bass player, Jean-Jacques Burnel, pursued a solo LP about a European super state.

The Clash, after finishing the double album *London Calling*, would prove that reggae-loving punk revolutionaries could be every bit as indulgent as Emerson, Lake and Palmer, when they unleashed *Sandinista*, their triple-dub, punk, rockabilly, gospel triple album to a critical mauling during a period of economic strife.

For despite it all, perhaps there really was something slightly un-punk about LPs. Even ones that began with a clumsy burst of the Moomins obviously taped off the telly by Chaos UK, or sleeved in newspaper-quality paper and issued by the anarchists Crass.

Once you've made one LP, you usually just can't help wanting to make more . . . and more of them. The Sex Pistols escaped by just making the one.[115] (But then they were always something of a one-off.) And the Manic Street Preachers, just over a decade later, rode to acclaim promising to do the same. Not that they kept to it, mind.

The Ramones avoided the trap by just making that ONE FIRST LP again and again. The sheer unwavering, 'finishedness' of their sound unnerved Phil Spector when he was producing their *End of the Century* LP. Largely dispensing with the group after three weeks – two weeks longer than they had ever taken to record any of their previous LPs – Spector spent six months mixing the album. Once he'd finished, he had – the odd string arrangement aside – something that sounded like a Ramones LP.

By the winter of discontent in 1978–9, the brick wall on the cover of their debut had been pinched by Pink Floyd and by Michael Jackson for his masterpiece *Off the Wall*.

The CBGBs band that would truly melt hearts, even those made of glass, were Blondie, whose album *Parallel Lines* wedded the straight-trouser, sixties garage sound to an utterly infectious disco beat and stole to the top spot of the UK charts. And sadly for Lester Bangs, who left this world with a copy of the Human

---

115 Punters were not satisfied, though, and Virgin was happyily dishing out floor-sweeping compilations, like *Flogging a Dead Horse* in 1980.

League's *Dare* on his turntable, the greatest album ever made, at least in terms of sales, would not be *Metal Machine Music* but the Eagles' *Their Greatest Hits*, which following its release in 1976 went on in the States to become the biggest-selling album of all time.

The ethos of punk would nevertheless live on in the scores of independent labels like Rough Trade, Factory and Mute that emerged in its aftermath. From the dour beauty of an LP like *Unknown Pleasures* from Joy Division, or the brittle folk of the Raincoats, the possibilities of who could make records were opened up then as never before.

By the spring of 1980, the *NME* had inaugurated separate LP and singles charts for disco, reggae, and independent labels. In 1982, an 'International Discography of the New Wave' was published, cataloguing over 16,000 records issued by 300 labels, few of whom had existed before punk. And the fields of journalism, stand-up comedy and film would be similarly emboldened by punk's have-a-go instincts.

But if 1977 represented punk's high watermark, it was also the centenary of the phonograph, and schemes every bit as canny as Malcolm McLaren's were now afoot to enact a year zero of sorts on that out-of-touch old fart, the long-playing record.

Chapter Twelve

TAKE UP THY STEREO
AND WALK, MAN

On 7 July 1979, the Boomtown Rats, the toast of the town for their second album of pub-closing-time singable pop-punk, *Tonic for the Troops*, opened the very first Virgin Megastore on London's Oxford Street. This nexus of Richard Branson and Bob Geldof in the first few months of Mrs Thatcher's premiership seems almost an omen from the gods – a portent for what the 1980s were to hold: shopping, old hippies coining it in, old punks forgetting their generational hang-ups and getting into Pink Floyd (or, in Bob's case, getting into films based on Pink Floyd double albums, anyway), the big charity rock concert, international flights, world music and a lot of oversized jackets with the sleeves rolled up.

As a pre-emptive strike for new consumer culture, however, the Megastore was a little premature, since a sharp rise in oil prices again triggered a global recession. (An indication of those straightening times could be found in a 1980 interview by Mike Stand in *Smash Hits* with XTC at Branson's Manor House Studios, as the group prepared for the release of their *Black Sea* LP and the single 'Generals and Majors'. 'Nobody', Stand noted, 'mentioned the war or the redundancies at Virgin itself earlier that week.'[116])

But the Megastore's moment would come again, just as Bob's would too. Refurbished by Terence Conran, the new and improved Virgin super shop was right on cue for Live Aid – and the CD of Dire Straits's *Brother's in Arms*.

In the interim, the record industry, having experienced virtually uninterrupted growth since the 1960s, would suffer, along with practically everyone else, a severe downturn. In the States, sales of LPs fell by a fifth in 1979.

Such a turn of events took the big record companies largely by surprise, especially since 1978 had been a bumper year for many. The soundtrack LPs from *Saturday Night Fever* and *Grease* had wiped the (multicoloured, flashing) floor with everything else. Based on a Nik Cohn story about a 1960s ace-face mod who lived for the weekends,[117] *Saturday Night Fever* was dismissed by *Time Out*'s Tony Rayns as the 'disco movie for people who don't go to discos'. Whether they did or not, the LP was to spend a total of eight weeks at number one in England in 1978. (Perhaps, as Rayns suggests, enabling those who were cautious of the real thing to juggle a can of Dulux, slip on a white suit and frug to the trilling falsettos of the Bee Gees without running the gauntlet of bouncers, Bianca Jagger on a horse or people who looked like the Village People adusting their tools, helmets and choppers in time to the beat.)

116 Another, rather happier indication was to be found that same year in the form of UB40's never-bettered debut LP, *Signing Off*, with its dole office form sleeve.

117 At the time when *SNF* was being produced, Paul Weller and the Jam, from Woking, London's graveyard, were busy digging up the ghost of weekending mods on their *In the City* LP.

Polygram, who had the soundtrack of *Saturday Night Fever* and that other Travolta vehicle, the 1950s high school musical *Grease*, on their books, became, in 1978, the first record company to top a billion dollars in sales.

Naturally it expected a hat trick and in the autumn of 1978 it shipped big on a soundtrack for a film musical version of the Beatles' *Sgt. Pepper* starring the Bee Gees and Peter Frampton. Here was a film of an LP. An LP, in effect, that would now have its own musical soundtrack LP – confirmation, if confirmation were needed, that the pop concept LP had truly come of age. Post-modernist pop had arrived. A callous new strain of marketing and 'film to musical' product synergy was on the loose. Or something. At the time, it probably did look like a sure thing.

The Bee Gees, playing the Pepper Band, appeared, despite the beards, the teeth, the jewellery and the trilling falsettos, unable to put a foot wrong. And Peter Frampton's *Frampton Comes Alive* album was still on the *Billboard* charts two years after its release. There were also cameos for Aerosmith (who, I confess, I have rather airbrushed out of our tale so far), Earth, Wind and Fire, Alice Cooper – the guy who, by default, had helped Johnny Rotten wangle his job in the Sex Pistols – George Burns and, er, Frankie Howerd.

But the film, which somewhat misguidedly casts the Bee Gees and Peter Frampton as besters of the evil music business in a show-and-tell-the-songs plot that forced them, Paul Nicholas and sundry others to wade all too literally through large chunks of *Sgt. Pepper* and *Abbey Road* for good measure, flopped. Catastrophically. As, rather obviously, did the accompanying album causing almost landfill levels of bulk returns. Produced by George Martin ('who', as *Rolling Stone* pointed out, 'steered the source LP through its 700 studio hours in 1967'), it was greeted by outright dismay. As *Rolling Stone* put it, 'It sounds exactly like those once-ubiquitous $1.98 collections of Greatest Hits from the Sixties performed by anonymous artists for the South American market . . . Is this reprehensible version of *Sgt. Pepper's Lonely Hearts Club Band* the epitome of soulless Ultimate Product?' they asked in conclusion, before replying: 'Unquestionably.' (Perhaps even more damning was another call and response elsewhere in the review that ran: 'Is Peter Frampton really this bad? Yes.')

The album, like the film, was – and is – truly dreadful (trust me, you only need to hear George Burns' 'Fixing a Hole' or Dianne Steinberg and Stargard's 'Lucy in the Sky with Diamonds' once). However, it did serve as a tipping point of sorts. Sales of albums would not reach the dizzy heights of *Saturday Night Fever* or *Grease* again now until the arrival of Michael Jackson's *Thriller*.

Whatever unfavourable economic conditions were affecting the record business were only exacerbated by the sudden arrival of a range of new gadgets. Records, once the predominant pocket money wasters for teenagers and young adults, were having to fight their ground against arcade Space Invaders – whose blips and bloops provided the accompaniment to and the title of a jolly instrumental on the Pretenders' debut LP in 1980. And if that wasn't bad enough, TV Atari gaming consoles and video recorders were increasingly occupying pole postion in lounges and dens, edging out those spare hour-with-an-album moments. Or, so some industry types, liked to claim, at least some of the cash previously devoted to them – and not unreasonably, since Atari notched up $513 million worth of sales in 1980.

Of more pressing concern to the record companies, though, was the home taping of LPs. By 1980, one in two American homes were estimated to have a cassette machine. And at a point when some FM stations in America were still in the habit of slinging an album on, then perhaps wandering out onto the fire escape and sparking up, Jack Reinstein, treasurer of Elektra/Atlantic, calculated that 400 million albums were taped off the air in 1980 'without any compensation to the artist, the songwriters and publishers, the musicians, the record company'. A CBS report on home taping from the same year put the loss to the industry at 20 per cent.

The industry's gripes culminated in a concerted advertising campaign headed up by the slogan 'Home Taping Is Killing Music' that boasted a logo casting the cassette as a skull in a reworking of the pirate standard. This image was soon stamped onto the back of LP covers and inner sleeves, in the (probably) rather vain hope of guilt-tripping punters during those last few seconds as they un-sheathed AC/DC's *Back in Black* or Motorhead's *Ace of Spades* and prepared to jolly roger their monsters of rock.

Swash and buckling really was something of a craze in the opening years of the 1980s. The first year of the decade marked the centenary of *The Pirates of Penzance* and a rocked-up musical version of the light opera *Papp's Pirates* opened on Broadway with Linda Ronstadt and Kevin Kline in its cast – an original cast LP duly followed. The show later transferred to London, with Tim Curry of *Rocky Horror* fame splicing the mainbraces in the West End. Malcolm McLaren and Vivienne Westwood, on the hunt for new things after punk and the Sex Pistols, seemed to have seized on the idea of pirates. *The Rock and Roll Swindle*, the Pistols film which opened in 1980, had closed with a cartoon of the band performing a nautical ditty about masturbation, 'Friggin' in the Riggin'', on a sinking pirate ship. Now advising Adam and the Ants, McLaren (and Westwood) evidently wanted to take the whole 'Yo ho ho' bag to another level. As Adam Ant recalled in his autobiography, 'Malcolm kept trying to get me to read stuff about pirates (it was going to be Vivienne's new look, he said)'. In the end, McLaren spirited away Adam's Ants, teaming them up with Annabella Lwin, a fourteen-year-old Burmese-born girl he'd discovered singing in a launderette. Christening the new group Bow Wow Wow, he penned the lyrics for their first release, 'C30, C60, C90', an ode to home taping that was only released on cassette. It was the first 'cassingle', and one side of the tape was left deliberately blank, presumably so that listeners could put the song's message into action themselves, to the chagrin of their own record label, EMI, who was at the forefront of the campaign to stamp out piracy.

Bow Wow Wow's eight-track 'cassette' album, *My Cassette Pet*, similarly saluted a format whose sales by the end of the decade would outstrip those of vinyl long-players. In America in 1987, they accounted for 63 per cent of all albums sold. At their peak in 1989, sales of pre-recorded tapes reached 83 million.[118]

When pre-recorded cassettes had first appeared in the 1960s, at £2 a go they had been, despite their comparative infidelity, more expensive than records. As late as 1976, Decca's *Rock Roots*

---

118 I find encountering these dinky plastic efforts now an oddly emotive experience. For me they are hideously timebound, in my case timebound to a moment in the 1980s when my mother forbade me from buying any more records. Somewhat reluctantly I resorted to cassettes, which could be smuggled into the family home inside a jacket pocket. Some albums – *Zen Arcade* by Hüsker Dü and *Psychocandy* by the Jesus and Mary Chain, to name but two – although repurchased later on vinyl and CD, have never sounded quite as good as they did then. Savoured sly fag out of the bedroom window-style, on cassette and in defiance of a parental ban, they sounded all the sweeter for it. Though I didn't indulge in this myself, preferring to construct my own inserts using cuttings from music magazines for any albums I taped off friends, one of the effects of home taping was a widespread shoplifting of cassette covers. This in turn meant that in the local WHSmith or Boots there was always a selection of coverless cassettes at a knock-down price. Such bargains were difficult to resist. But after buying them, and as you snipped another homemade cover together, you would still be left wondering, other than the name neatly printed on the cassette, what more you had really gained over taping it off a mate . . .

compilation, for example, sold for £1.50 on LP but £1.99 on cassette. But prices dropped over the next couple of years, with albums on cassette tending to be around 50p cheaper than their vinyl peers by around 1980. But where three Ferros C90s could be had in, say, Boots for £2.40 in October 1980, their album of the month, Supertramp's *Paris*, cost £4.99. And those were only the advertised high street prices – there were always cheaper blank cassettes available down the market from your local Arthur Daley. (*Minder*, the TV show that charted the adventures of Daley, the ultimate cashmere- coated dodgy wheeler-dealer and his bodyguard, Terry, serves as an interesting barometer of Thatcher's entrepreneurial, aspirational Britain, since it was first broadcast just a few months after she came to power.[119])

---

119 Dennis Waterman, who starred as Terry, did of course sing the theme tune to *Minder* – a piece of information widely disseminated by the sketch show *Little Britain*. He also cut LPs. *Waterman*, recorded and released in 1977, finds the former Sweeney star dishing up a convincing country rock version of 'It Ain't Easy' and, in a similar idiom, such self-penned numbers as 'The Cockney Cowboy', with the assistance of Shadows Brian Bennett and Hank Marvin.

The quality of cassettes had also come on: in 1979, the 3M company introduced their Metafine brand of chrome tapes. But it was really the arrival of the Sony Walkman that same year which completely changed the fortunes of tape, and by extension, the LP.

The idea of taking your *own* music, your own albums, with you, had gained ground throughout the 1970s with eight-tracks and portable stereo radio-cassette players. An ad in the *NME* headed 'Outdoor Concert', for a Superscope stereo tape player that in 1979 still looked like a hulking great suitcase, ran: 'Listen to the Eagles in the Highlands, the Police on Dartmoor, Traffic in the middle of nowhere, the Stones on Salisbury Plain. All in Stereo.'

But Akio Morita, Mr Sony, couldn't help being struck by the sheer cumbersomeness of these players. His company had produced some of the sleeker models around. But a reasonably compact portable player like the Sony CF still weighed over 12 lbs *sans* batteries in 1978. A workaholic, Morita's entire schedule was arranged over a year in advance, but he was also fanatical about art, music and sports and tessellated his four passions with alacrity, blurring the distinctions between them. To use more contemporary jargon, Morita was a highly accomplished exponent of multi-tasking.

Seeing friends and family members constantly lugging monster-truck-sized stereos to the beach and listening to music on cassettes in their cars, he asked Sony's engineers to create a portable cassette player that could be used 'while doing other things'. The speakerless Walkman with headphones was the result.

Launched in Tokyo in June 1979, it was expected to do well with busy salarymen types, but when the first 30,000 produced were gone by August, Morita knew he had a bigger hit on his hands. Its success outside Japan was more muted to begin with. And it wasn't only due to the $199.98 price tag. Though inspired by the popular Hollywood film *Superman*, Sony America, apparently, didn't like the name. The Walkman had therefore first appeared in the US as the Soundabout and, obviously intent on mining the McLaren/Westward vogue for things piratical and maritime, in Britain as the Stowaway. (Tape is spliced as frequently as mainbraces, I suppose, so there is another kind of lexical link in there somewhere.)

Just as people will always call 30 St Mary Axe in London the Gherkin, and that statute in Birmingham the floozy in the jacuzzi rather than whatever it was actually christened, the better name will always out. (For this reason, the Bee Gees will be always be Les Tossers, and Snickers bars Marathons to me.) And on business trips to the States and Europe, Morita found people routinely calling the 'Soundabout' and the 'Stowaway' a 'Walkman'. At the earliest opportunity, he reinstated its original name across the board and watched as sales flew upward.

By 1981, 'Walkman' was already listed in the French dictionary *Le Petit Larousse*, arriving in the *Oxford English Dictionary* five years later. A decade after its launch, Sony had offloaded over 50 million Walkmans. By 1992, they'd doubled that figure to 100 million. The iPod would reach that same figure in less than five years, but the Walkman was the trailblazer, the first in a line of small but groundbreaking items that would offer the chance to listen to more, more often. And on the go.

Like Hoover, it became a brand name applied universally to millions of portable cassette players that sprang up in its wake. The Walkman arrived with remarkable timing and possibly helped stoke the craze for jogging and street-cred sportswear

– the outward displays of fitness, mobility and technology being at one with the ideals espoused by both the emerging yuppies and the style of kids on the block.

Along with concerned reports from doctors that heavy usage would turn people deaf were academic articles about 'the Walkman effect', discussing how it was changing listening habits. 'The pleasure of Walkman', claimed S. Hosokawa in the journal *Popular Music, 4,* 'can be found in the way that listening is incidentally overlapped by and mixed up with different acts: as a listening act, it is not exclusive but inclusive, not concentrated but distracted, not convergent but divergent, not centripedal but centrifugal.'

A humanised Walkman, with a cassette tape for a head and a jack and lead for an arm, marching ever onwards, appeared on the cover of the *NME* cassette compilation *C81*. It was the first release from the independent label Rough Trade's new tape cassette catalogue – a catalogue that would soon be offering Scritti Politti's *Songs to Remember*, Cabaret Voltaire's

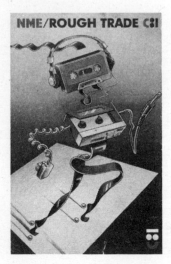

Voice of America and the Young Marble Giant's *Colosssal Youth* on tape and issuing 'cassette only' collections and live albums from Wire and the Raincoats. You couldn't have everything taped unless you went for at least *some* cassettes.

But for the kind of small independent groups on *C81*, the cassette offered a cheap and easy way to produce, distribute and sell their 'albums'. Daniel Johnston, the spinner of heartbreaking songs of

372

unrequited love and battles with the devil would conduct most of his 'outsider' career on cassette, MTV, and at times from secure mental institutions. Now, as never before, some albums were *only* available on cassette.

For if Walkmans where changing how and where music was listened to, then boom boxes and cassettes were also vital components in how a whole new musical genre that was emerging around that time – hip hop and rap – would escape from the Bronx and conquer the world.

The Last Poets, who had issued their righteous debut LP containing the broadsides 'Run Nigger' and 'Wake Up Nigger' in 1969 were among the originators of the rap style continued on Hustler's *Convention* LP and developed by Gil Scott Heron on *The Revolution Will Not Be Televised* in the 1970s.

Campaigning for election in 1976 and 1980, both Jimmy Carter and Ronald Reagan gave TV press conferences from the Bronx to highlight their commitments to improving the plight of the urban poor. And it was in Bronx and Harlem, against this background of deprivation in the 1970s, that hip hop was essentially born, when resourceful local party DJs began to blend snippets of records and different tracks together to form new songs. This form of mixing wasn't dissimilar to the techniques employed in dub reggae and one of the pioneers, Kool Herc (Clive Campbell) was Jamaican born and moved to the States in 1967.

As Herc span platters, he would call out to crowds and draft friends in to 'toast' or 'rap' as he went along, a practice that other Bronx DJs like Afrika Bambaataa and Grandmaster Flash also adopted until each had their own crews of rappers and dancers. This was party music and DJs would use anything to hand to keep the punters dancing. And so it was that virtually dormant

James Brown live album cuts,[120] obscure soundtrack LPs, heavy rock and electronica from the German group Kraftwerk began to form musical collages that came to life during the heat of the night.[121]

A novelty instrumental album by Michael Viner's the Incredible Bongo Band called *Bongo Rock* that contained a version of the Shadows' 'Apache' and Iron Butterfly's 'In-A-Gadda-Da-Vida' became the unlikely Rosetta Stone for early hip hop, its tappy-tap drum sounds finding their way onto pratically every early rap record released.

Before rap made it onto record, however, it was carried beyond the Bronx on tape. As Jeff Chang writes in his history of hip hop, *Can't Stop Won't Stop*, 'Live bootleg cassette tapes of Kool Herc, Afrika Bambaataa, Flash and the Furious 5, the L Brothers, the Cold Crush Brothers and others were the sound of the OJ Cabs that took folks across the city. The tapes passed hand-to-hand in

---

120 Back in 1962, Brown had forked out the $5,000 to produce his first live album, *Live at the Apollo*, when his label refused to back it.

121 *Radio On*, Christopher Petit's prophetic British film from 1979, pretty much opens with the arrival of an envelope containing three Kraftwerk cassettes and charts a mysterious existential voyage from London to Bristol in the company of Robert, a taciturn DJ (he is what he plays). Shot in luminous black and white, the film is a glimpse of a Britain teetering on the brink of terminal but exquisitely beautiful decay. Robert drives to a glacial soundtrack of Berlin-era Bowie, Devo and of course Kraftwerk, along twisted vernacular roadways through a blasted industrial wasteland. He meets a psychopathic squaddie, a teenage dope peddler, a German woman who has lost her child, and Sting, who is living in a decrepit caravan beside a petrol pump and sings old Eddie Cochran numbers. A collision of contemporary futuristic sounds and a cold decaying present, redemption here, as with hip hop, seems to reside in salavaging bits of the past.

the Black and Latino neighbourhoods of Brooklyn, the Lower East Side, Queens and Long Island's black belt.'

As Afrika Bambaataa has observed elsewhere: 'Cassette tapes used to be our albums before anybody recorded what they called rap records.' In fact, there's a compelling symmetry between rap and cassettes in that this most eclectic form of music, composed in an 'I like that bit' fashion, is simply a more extreme/creative version of the compilation tapes that people were now readily able to put together themselves. (If Nick Hornby hadn't got there first I'm sure I would have some devastating insights to offer on mix-tape etiquette, but anything I'd offer now would inevitably feel derivative so let's draw a veil over the idea and move on.) Both the cassette and rap, though, irreparably smashed the idea that you get what you are given. From their inception, everyone could be their own DJ or create an album in their bedroom if they so wished.

But according to Chang, Grandmaster Flash, for one – though he was not alone – didn't believe that anyone would want to buy an actual *record* of people rapping along to records. It therefore came as a shock when in October 1979, a record by a crew no one on the scene seemed to have heard of had a smash with a fifteen-minute freestyle over Chic's 'Good Times' entitled 'Rapper's Delight'. The Sugarhill Gang were a prefab job put together by Sylvia Robinson, 1950s R&B singer turned would-be record mogul, who'd been intrigued by rap after hearing the tapes her kids played.

'Rapper's Delight' showed the genre's commercial potential and soon enough Afrika Bambaataa and Grandmaster Flash and the Furious Five (who posed with their beat boxes on the cover of *The Message* LP) had acquired record deals. But Kurtis Blow, managed by Russell Simmons, the subsequent founder of Def Jam records, was the first to secure a major label deal. His debut album, *The Breaks*, is one of 'old skool' rap's earliest LPs and its title track, a huge single, was voted *Village Voice*'s record of the year in 1980. The LP also featured an unusual cover version of Bachman-Turner Overdrive's 'Takin' Care of Business', a rock/rap crossover that foreshadowed what Blow's sometime DJ Joseph 'Run' Simmons would pull off in Run DMC – and Run DMC would, in 1982, bag rap's first gold LP.

(Before we get too excited, we should bear in mind that in 1982, REO Speedwagon's *Hi Infidelity* shifted 6 million copies, becoming, at the time, the second-largest selling album in their record company's history.)

However, in a rather paradoxical fashion, although rap and dance culture broke through to the mainstream on cassette, the DJ culture continued to rely on vinyl, at least as a raw creative material, and its patronage of the format contributed to keeping vinyl production alive in the West at a time when in some parts of the Arab world and Africa, where international (for which read Western) copyright conventions were not enforced, cassettes almost immediately ousted LPs. In India, which went on to become the second-largest manufacturer of cassettes in the world, vinyl records had virtually disappeared by the end of 1982. It was an early indication that the format might perhaps have a sell-by date after all, but since record companies had lost most of their trade in places like Ghana to dubious cassette-copying shops, a cassette-only future scarcely seemed the ideal solution to their troubles. No, the solution would come, like the Sony Walkman, in the form of another small but groundbreaking item that also seemed to offer the chance to listen to more . . .

As Sony president Norio Ohga commented in 1993, 'At the time we developed the compact disc, the LP market was saturated and the cassette was beginning to slow down so we needed a new carrier.' If the LP and the cassette were analogue, working off those good vibrations to do their job, the CD would be coolly digital. And like the LP before it, its chief selling point was its quality of sound and its possibilities in terms of length.

The move into digital sound began at the recording end. The development of computer micro-processing chips that ate up information in binary codes allowed sound to be captured 'digitally' by the 1970s. Digital sound is not reproduced, as in analogue signal, but sampled; so whereas on vinyl a physical groove is etched into the record, mimicking the sound wave, with digital the waveforms of a squealing guitar or pounding drums are bundled up into a pack of numerical information, then reconstructed as a near-as-perfect replica. Or that was the idea. In its infancy, much like the computer game graphics of the period, the low sampling resolution rates resulted in rather blocky replicas: think of the Cylons in the original *Battlestar Galatica* in the 1970s – tin-men with red beams of light for eyes – and the contemporary TV series remake where they are indistinguishable from humans, and the development of CD technology follows roughly the same trajectory.

By 1976, digital recording was of a high enough standard to be installed in studios. And three years later, the guitarist Ry Cooder is thought to be the first 'major' to use this new technology on a whole album when he made *Bop Till You Drop*, an LP of fifties and sixties covers, digitally. He was closely followed by Stevie Wonder, who on a fertile creative streak had produced three Grammy award-winning albums after another (*Talking Book, Innervisions* and *Songs in the Key of Life*) and

went on to unveil his serpentine, digitally recorded double album *Journey through the Secret Life of Plants* – simultaneously making a tribute to the natural world and a collection of oldies the earliest voyagers into this shiny new audio galaxy.

Around the same time as these recording breakthroughs were being made, Sony, in conjunction with the Dutch electronic company Philips, was developing a new digital disc – a carrier, in Ohga's words.

They originally planned to devise something that could hold an hour of music, and an 11-centimetre prototype digital disc was produced. There are conflicting stories, the most romantic of which maintains that its capacity was increased to accommodate

Norio Ohga's or his wife's favourite piece of music – Beethoven's Ninth Symphony – but the final CD was bulked out to 12 centimetres and lasted, then, for seventy-four minutes. (This story also serves as a neat continuum to that of the LP; Beethoven's 'Eroica' was one of the pieces it was expressly hoped the new long-playing format would accommodate.) However, in 2007, Jacques Heemskerk, a Philips engineer who had worked on the CD, stated that he believed the revised diameter been a mistake: 'I always wish we had stuck with the original plan for an 11-centimetre disc; it would have been more suited to the on-the-go age.'

Since yuppies managed to Filofax them into their schedules, the on-the-go-set of the 1980s didn't seem unduly bothered by their dimensions. At less than a quarter of the size of an LP, they were, well, compact discs. Not quite as top-pocketable as a cassette, but even so. That additional fourteen minutes, however, was a hefty add-on to a disc that would already have supplied, on average, twenty minutes more than a long-player.

Along with this extra time, there was of course the bonus of digital sound. With a higher dynamic range than the LP, CDs were capable of carrying frequencies of 96 decibels, as opposed to 70 on a vinyl album.[122]

The first public demonstration of the compact disc's capabilities was given at Eindhoven in March 1979, and two years later a

---

122 The breadth of sound on CDs has deteriorated radically since they were first introduced, as record companies started to gradually increase the volume on them. To do this, engineers have to further 'compress' the dynamic range to prevent the digital equivalent of distortion. In 2007, one engineer maintained:'From the mid-1980s to now, the average loudness of CDs increased by a factor of 10, and the peaks of songs are now one-tenth of what they used to be.' This increase in volume actually makes them more tiring to listen to.

formal press conference for the CD was held at the Salzburg Easter Festival for 200 journalists.

Since the economy was in recession, many doubted the wisdom of foisting a new audio format on the world at that time. Sony launched the CD in Japan at the Tokyo Hifi Show in October 1982, an *annus* so *horribilis* that at its close, *Gramophone* magazine observed that it 'might prove to be one of those years best forgotten' and was certainly 'a bad one for the record and audio industries'.

Landing in Europe in March 1983 and in America some five months later, the CD had the immaculate good fortune to coincide with a gentle upsurge, UK miners' strike excepted, in the global economy.

Although, technically, the first CD produced in Europe was Abba's *The Visitors* and in America it was a toss-up between *52nd Street* by Billy Joel and Glen Miller's *In the Digital Mood*, like the LP before it, the CD was purpose-built for classical music. (As if to ram the point home, by 1988 there were over seventy different versions of Beethoven's Ninth on CD.)

In a virtual replay of Compton Mackenzie's listening tests with LPs in the magazine some thirty-plus years before, the classical music organ *Gramophone* had its longest standing contributor, W.A. Chislett, put the new machine through its paces. Chislett had been writing for *Gramophone* since 1925, but confessed to being floored by the 'dazzling sonorities' of the compact disc: 'I find the absolute, almost uncanny stillness in silent bars most impressive of all. At times I found myself holding my breath lest I disturb it.'

History essentially repeated itself. Die-hard classical fans were prepared to invest in new equipment and even buy recordings they already owned because of the perceived improvement in sound quality. Much like baroque on LP several decades earlier,

previously recondite tastes like early music or modern minim-
alism, which were ideally suited to the 'uncanny stillness' of CD,
gained new audiences. *The Four Seasons*, which I think I may
have mentioned way back when, could now be appreciated as a
whole and its fortunes rose once again. There were also plenty of
now ageing baby-boomers who, having grown up with rock and
roll, wanted to show a bit of maturity, and impressed by what
they heard, were interested in obtaining a nuts and bolts set of
the classics. Since companies had stores of repertoire to draw
upon for reissues, the margin per disc was far greater and the
classics proved to be highly profitable.

However, one 1983 correspondent to *Gramophone* did question the quality to quantity ratio of these reissues: 'I should like
to suggest to your reviewers', wrote one Gilles David, 'to make it
a constant rule to mention the playing time of CDs reviewed: it
might deter the readers from buying partly blank records and the
companies from promoting a policy turned towards the past
rather than the future.'

For David, more seemed to be . . . well, more – a case of
quantity over quality, if you like – and you can hardly blame him
for that when a CD cost, on average, nearly twice as much as an
LP. And since they cost less if anything to make, record companies were widely accused of profiteering . . . which they were,
really. But what exactly were you were paying more for with a
CD? The sound? The length? Both? This in itself raised fundamental questions: for example, was the sound alone so much
better that it was worth replacing on CD something you already
owned on LP or cassette? In the end, the answer seemed to be yes.

In the mid-1980s, the average CD cost £12 – around £30 today
in real terms. At the time, though it was decried in some quarters,
this wasn't necessarily thought wildly exorbitant. Much like the
1950s when the LP came into its own, this was a period when

social aspiration was being expressed through conspicuous consumption. CDs were regarded as a luxury item and, like the early breeze-blocks that were mobile phones, modern.

In Japan, their sales had already passed those of LPs by early 1986 and did the same in America two years later, indicating that the public were willing to fork out for a 'premium product'. (After all, they *were* starting to buy bottled water.) And these babies were shiny and silver. They were also handy. They didn't scratch, per se, though early claims peddled by the BBC that you could smear them with jam and still play them proved wildly optimistic. Dust and fingerprints made them skip. Mind you, since the noise they made when they did was on a par with an orchestral stab from a Fairlight sampler (another new arrival in 1982), it was sometimes difficult to tell if the CD was broken or whether Laurie Anderson, say, or Prince, had got carried away again. During one passage in Brett Easton Ellis' novel, *American Psycho*, having completed a morning toilet of staggering complexity involving much detailing of the mineral deposits in his moisturisers, Patrick Bateman, the eponymous protagonist, has to cope with a sticking Talking Heads CD (a rare foray on his part into music that isn't instantly hateable). 'The laser lens', he notes, 'is very sensitive, and subject to interference from dust or dirt or smoke or pollutants or moisture, and a dirty one can inaccurately read CDs, making for false starts, inaudible passages, digital skipping, speed changes and general distortion.'

Skipping aside, though, there was a widespread consensus that CDs did sound better. Despite that slightly antiseptic quality they brought to the table, that bell-like 'ringing of a bedpan dropping in a hospital corridor' quality felt strikingly . . . new at the time. (For what it's worth, my own personal memory of the advent of the CD is of a trip during a school lunchtime to the local Rumbelows, where Roxy Music's 'Avalon' was serving as the demonstration disc. While my own musical tastes at that time erred towards the more abrasive, there was no denying that Bryan and the boys were coming out Queen Ann crystal clear, or so it seemed back then.)

There was also the extraordinary novelty of being free to play the tracks you liked, edit out the ones you didn't, put it on to 'random', program it to play 'I Will Always Love You' or 'Don't Worry Be Happy' 400 times or whatever you wanted to drive the neighbours insane. These things were of no small significance. The sky was the seventy-four-minute limit – or more, even, if you kept the player on repeat or had invested in a multi-disc machine.

On the other hand, there *was* a lack of warmth to the sound. Everything appeared a little clinical – like coming face to face with a lover under a 100-watt electric bulb after spending an hour or two admiring them in candlelight. Everything you loved was there and more besides, but the brightness was disconcerting all the same.

After all, is it any coincidence that the designer-label-obsessed, anal, icy-hearted Patrick Bateman listens to all of his music on compact disc? Chunks of the novel are given over to his incessant analyses of Huey Lewis and the News and Genesis albums. All are rendered in a tone so deadpan in its Speak-Your-Weight machine mockery that rereading it today is to be reminded again of how refreshing, how necessary irony was in 1991. Without an arched eyebrow in sight, Bateman states, 'Genesis is still the best, most exciting band to come out of England in the 1980s.' Choicier still, about the instrumentals on Huey and co.'s *Small World* he muses, 'just because these tunes are wordless doesn't mean the global message of communication is lost, and they don't seem like filler or padding because of the implications of their thematic reprise'.

But in associating those little silver discs with Bateman, Bret Easton Ellis was surely on to something. Even just having

Bateman utter the words, 'and side one (or, on the CD, song number five)' says everything we need to know about the format. With CDs, it's always about the numbers.

The plastic boxes they came in were horrible too; Jewel cases as they were known. That was wishful thinking on someone's part. CDs may have been miniatures, but a casing of cracked plastic never made them seem any more precious. The covers were rubbish – album art shrunk to the size of a postcard – and they always got snagged by those annoying nobbly bits on the side that were supposed to hold them in place (cue very 1980s observational comedy routine from Ben Elton). They could never hope to match the sweep, the physical allure, the *sensuality* of an LP sleeve. In America, the phenomenon of the long-box – a kind of cardboard packaging elevator shoe used to bring this Lilliputian audio runt up to size in record shops – was an embarrassing admission of this failure. But it was an ecological disaster, since opening them usually involved destroying them, or certainly leaving a redundant card sheaf that played no further useful part in storing the CD since it also came in a jewel case (they were phased out in 1992).

The rituals of vinyl, too, were being swept away. The needle doing its damage to two sides. The etchings on the inner ring; the pressing plant codes; the little messages from masterers like Porky boasting of another prime cut. Then there were the grooves. Like ripples in the sand to a camel trader, to the trained eye, the distribution of grey to black lines thrown off by the vinyl's peaks and troughs tell a million little stories. Gone, too, was the chance of spinning the record backwards and finding out if Paul McCartney was dead, or if Led Zeppelin (always the ones with wide grooves, those boys) loved Satan, or if Pink Floyd's *The Final Cut* had a secret message telling you you'd found the secret message.

And in the 1980s, secret messages on LPs were suddenly of burning concern. The issue reared its head in 1982 when two

Republican senators, Robert Dorman and Phil Wyman, submitted a bill to Congress asking for warning labels to be placed on rock records that contained backward messages extolling the worship of Satan. To the *New York Post*, who reported on the bill, it remained a mystery just quite how the human brain went about sorting out from the multitude of sounds perceptible on a rock record being played forward a message that was both inaudible and backwards.

Three years later, two Judas Priest fans shot themselves in a suicide pact after listening to the group's *Stained Class* LP. While some might be willing to kill themselves rather than listen to a Judas Priest LP, it was alleged that backward messages on the record had persuaded Raymond Belknap and James Vance (who lingered for three years before dying of his injuries) to end their lives. The case was eventually dismissed. Satan, ever the wily one, would have to settle for subliminal messaging on CD.

But if some things were lost, others saw the gains. Dire Straits, whose *Brothers in Arms* became the first CD to sell a million copies, did so by trading on the benefits offered to the audience by the disc. In an astute sponsorship and marketing deal with the manufacturer Philips, the album was specially programmed for and promoted on CD. It was therefore, quite deliberately, an album where you got significantly less if you bought it on LP rather than on CD or cassette. Several of its tracks were clipped to fit onto a single LP, while they twanged around in the extra freedom offered on CD (and cassette). The album was also trailed by the single 'Money for Nothing', whose partially computer animated video was given constant play on MTV – and it was almost guaranteed to get shown for simply using (albeit slightly disparagingly) the MTV slogan in its lyrics, much as all songs about radio (with the possible exception of the Smiths' 'Hang the DJ') are basically guaranteed wide exposure on the airwaves. The combination of genuine old-school rockers in headbands doing-it-live, and the blocky microchip processor-generated workmen in the video encapsulated the mix of new and old technology that was embodied by the CD itself.

When MTV had first begun broadcasting in 1981, electronic music was on the ascendant. The dearth of videos meant it existed to keep art-electro geniuses Devo out of/in mischief and gave British synth pop acts such as Duran Duran and the Human League, whose *Dare* LP was the first to be composed using a digital microprocessor, a crack at the American charts. At that point, synthesizers, like video games, threatened to render anything that had gone before, obsolete.

In its opening issue of the decade, *NME* had invited its readers to 'Oscillate into the 80's', presenting a double number 'Guide to Electronic Music & Synthesised Sound' and offering a chance to 'Win a Wasp synthesiser'. In 1981, Kraftwerk's self-explanatory *Computer World* had painted a vision of an entirely cybernetic future, albeit one leavened by impish humour ('By pressing down a special key, it plays a little melody' they sang knowingly on 'Pocket Calculator'). Listings of the synthesisers used on the inner sleeves of LPs such as *Dazzle Ships* by OMD became endemic, a parody of what building by robots was doing to manufacturing jobs at the time. And the following year, when sales of electronic keyboards for the first and last time surpassed those of guitars, even quixotic country rocker Neil Young ventured into electronica on the much maligned but impressively adventurous *Trans* – an LP that had its origins in Young's attempts to communicate with his autistic son using a vocoder. *Rolling Stone*'s reviewer likened its diverse shifts in style to 'seeing a satellite dish sitting outside a log cabin' – which perhaps tells us how far we've travelled since then. Young's label boss David Geffen was not so taken with *Trans* and famously sued him for making a 'musically uncharacteristic' album. Signalling the importance of electro pop to dollar cash sales, at the Grammy Awards ceremony in 1985 Thomas Dolby, Herbie Hancock and Howard Jones conducted a synth jam session, but really, by then, the novelty had worn off. Videos with the rather more earthly Madonna and Michael Jackson had stolen the lead. Once MTV had finally agreed to play his videos, something they only undertook to do after his record company threatened to pull all their acts, Jackson was catapulted into the super league by MTV, with his 1982 album *Thriller* selling 40 million copies worldwide.

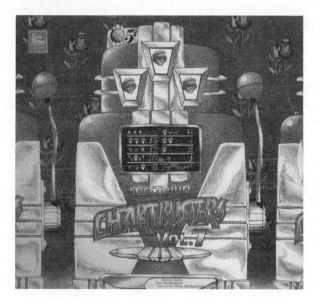

But Dire Straits couldn't have been further from a synth pop group if they'd tried. And while it could be argued that there was a more general shift after Live Aid – oh, and Bruce Springsteen's *Born in the USA* – when liking old rockers 'cause they could play' became far less of a fashion faux pas than it had been in, say, 1982 (perhaps it was Simon Le Bon singing off key at Wembley that did it?), the clarity of CD seemed to make 'proper' instruments sound more real. It could also carry every 'pop' and 'click' of the new Roland 808 digital drum machine, or 'clunk de clunk' of a DX7 digital keyboard. But it particularly impressed many by bringing the minute squeaks of, say, fingers moving up the guitar fret right up close. Michelle Shocked's *The Texas Campfire Tapes*, recorded with a Walkman, was cherished on CD because the sense of intimacy was so palpably unmediated (achieved, of course, by being highly technically mediated). And so as reissues of rock and pop classics got up to steam, the you-can-hear-Ringo-dropping-a-stick school of audio appreciation came on in leaps and bounds.

Accessing the CD of Fleetwood Mac's *Rumours*, in his 1987 book *Rock 'n' Roll on Compact Disc* David Prakel wrote:

> The advantages however are clarity in the multi-tracked vocals on "The Chain" and a sharpening of the propulsive drum smack; the famous bass guitar build-up is also tighter. The cymbal crashes which introduce "You Make Loving Fun" now jump right out of the speakers. The auditorium acoustic around voice and piano in "Songbird" is now vividly relayed. With the long production runs of LPs many copies of this album are in circulation that have a disappointingly dull sound. CD copies of *Rumours* have one great advantage in that they will not wear with the repeated playing this music deserves.

Vividly relayed auditorium acoustics and drum smacks, it appeared, were worth twelve quid of anyone's money in 1987. And they'd only be spending it on Beaujolais Nouveau and red braces otherwise. Just as vinyl, far more durable than shellac, had encouraged the idea of collecting records that would last, CDs were now sold on the basis of being 'unbreakable' and permanent.

Magazines like *Q* (established in 1986), with its comprehensive coverage of reissues, catered specifically for the slightly older, affluent rock music fan that was buying their music old and new on CD. (Jarvis Cocker of Pulp, when asked in their tenth birthday issue what *Q* meant to him, said simply, 'a CD player' – a put-down that they had the good humour to print.)

By 1992, back catalogue titles were accounting for more than 40 per cent of all CDs sold. During the same period, contemporary pop culture that used samplers and engaged in a cycle of revivals that commenced in the late 1970s when the Jam, the Specials, the Soft Boys and Dexy's Midnight Runners embarked on their respective courses through mod beat, ska, psychedelia and soul, was itself turning to older records for inspiration.

Initially to help persuade people to buy what they already had, many reissues were equipped with 'bonus' tracks, alternative takes and all manner of whatever was going spare, often with little regard for the sequence of the original album: the value-for-money issue overstepping the integrity of the piece as an entity. When several of David Bowie's albums from the 1970s (*The Man Who Sold the World*, *Diamond Dogs*, and co.) were reissued on CD for the second time in 1990, extra tracks were added to help persuade even those people who'd already replaced LPs with CDs to replace their CDs as well. Later editions on CD, however, then stripped the albums back to their original tracks.

The possibility of repackaging and repackaging again, coupled with the extra length of the CD, played merry hell with the 'Greatest Hits' albums. The concept was started by Mitch Miller, scourge of Frank Sinatra, when he collected Johnny Mathis's smashes onto one LP. In a long, distinguished and hit-filled career it is always possible that a group might have more than one greatest hits album, but it would ordinarily be something like a greatest hits of greatest hits – the Blue and Red collections from the Beatles, perhaps, or

Madonna's *Immaculate Collection*. *Legend* by Bob Marley would stand the test of time. Queen's *Greatest Hits*, released in 1981, though subsequently receiving supplementary volumes was confirmed as the UK's bestselling album of all time in 2006.

When Simon and Garfunkel's *Greatest Hits* came out in 1972, the LP had fourteen tracks. Since it first appeared on CD in the 1980s with those same fourteen tracks, however, there have been a further six greatest hit packages. *The Best of Simon and Garfunkel* contains twenty songs, as does *The Definitive Simon and Garfunkel*; *The Very Best of Simon and Garfunkel* is a two-disc CD with forty tracks, while *The Essential Simon and Garfunkel*, another two-CD job, has only thirty-three. And then there are *The Collected Works*, *The Columbia Studio Recordings*, and so on.

Most obviously, the first thing the CD changed about albums was to meld those two sides into a continous whole. On Kate

Bush's *Hounds of Love*, released in 1985 but clearly composed with vinyl's 'a' and 'b' sides in mind, the distinct moods of the separate sides – entitled 'Hounds of Love' and 'The Ninth Wave' – blurred into one another on the CD. However, its 1989 follow-up, *The Sensual World*, boasted an extra (bonus?) track exclusively on the CD. Like *Brothers in Arms*, this penalised the vinyl purchaser but also suggested that either the CD was the 'proper' version of the album and the others were incomplete, or that it didn't really matter either way and this was a musical doodle, afterthought, that on vinyl would have been banished to a limited edition 7-inch so it didn't get confused with the main tracks.

In the pre-CD era, around forty-five minutes was long for a single LP. Simon and Garfunkel's *Parsley, Sage, Rosemary and Thyme* is under half an hour; *Pet Sounds* is just over thirty-five minutes, as is *Kimono My House* by Sparks, and Stevie Wonder's *Talking Book* is only around ten minutes longer. There was a natural stretching out during the double album prog years, but after punk things settled down to around thirty-five to forty minutes again, though brevity rather got the better of LA punks the Circle Jerks on *Group Sex*, which comes off, as it were, rather fittingly in just over fifteen.

As the 1980s moved into the 1990s, lengths started to creep up. Prince, who stuggled to contain his output as it was, can be forgiven for the odd one-hour-and-twenty-minute album. And the Magnetic Field's *69 Love Songs*, requiring three CDs to contain the it-does-what-it-says-on-the- jewel-case high conceptual 173-minute long feat showed how it could – if it should – be done. Or vice versa.

What might be thought of as fairly unassuming albums, however, are into the fifty-plus-minute mark – the Stereo MCs' *Connected*, for instance, or Sinead O'Connor's *I Do Not Want What I Haven't Got*, Rage Against the Machine's

Rage Against the Machine, *Doggystyle* by Snoop Doggy Dogg or the Prodigy's *The Fat of the Land*. Fine albums one and all but . . . two hours of Smashing Pumpkins? Wasn't the album getting rather long?

The cycles of production also grew similarly elephantine: *Loveless* by My Bloody Valentine would take five years to produce, with the whole of 1990 spent recording the basses alone. Kate Bush managed to make the Blue Nile look like the Ramones. The second coming would seem more likely than the Stone Roses' second LP. And by the time it arrived, LPs had all but gone.

A year after Axl Rose entered the studio to begin recording *Chinese Democracy* (The Most Expensive Album Never Made and as yet still incomplete and unreleased), vinyl LPs represented just a single per cent of the world's music sales. As a representative from the Tower records chain told the press when this fact was announced: 'You just don't think about LPs. They're just not there.'

EPILOGUE

In 1977, the centenary year of Edison's phonograph, the first two Voyager probes were launched on their missions to Jupiter and Saturn. Along with the instruments that would beam signals back to Earth as they spun through the solar system, both craft were carrying very special cargo. Inside each Voyager were a 12-inch gold-plated copper disc, cartridges and a player. To aid any extraterrestrial fortunate enough to find them, there was a diagram explaining how to play the record. The disc itself contained an extensive range of sounds (and analogue-encoded images) from the Earth. There were salutations in Sumerian and Wu dialects, thunderclaps, birdsong, Peruvian panpipes, Gregorian chants, initiation songs from Zairian Pygmy girls, Chuck Berry playing 'Johnny B. Goode,' Louis Armstrong performing 'Melancholy Blues' and Glen Gould giving it his all on the Prelude and Fugue from Bach's *Well-Tempered Clavier.*

Carl Sagan, the scientist who assembled the record, commented that, 'The spacecraft will be encountered and the record played only if there are advanced spacefaring civilisations in interstellar space.'

I was reminded of Voyager only the other afternoon while standing in Rough Trade Records, off Brick Lane. My hand had glanced upon a vinyl copy of Hawkwind's *In Search of Space*. Fingering the familiar sleeve, I became lost in memories of 'real' space odysseys from the 1970s. (It was a dull, cold January day - what can I say . . .)

On reflection, the thought of sending a record, even a gold-plated copper one, into space just seemed comic. What had once been the future now struck me as hilariously archaic. And the idea that only an 'advanced spacefaring civilisation' could tackle a disc, a rather arrogant presumption. I had an image of some dome-headed green-skinned super-math from a distant galaxy. I pictured them hauling the disc out and contemptuously tutting, 'How Very Primitive', in a tongue that, although entirely unknown in this solar system, was the spit of Noël Coward. Casting the disc aside, the creature would no doubt jab white headphones into each of its three ears, scroll through its playlists, select Zarga Zarg's 89th millennia hit, 'Yes I Know You're There Baby, But Really You Aren't Worth the Bother,' and wander off to grab a smoothie blended from asteroids.

But then the Voyager space mission was only supposed to last five years. Over thirty years on and the little fellows are, a quick Google search later confirmed, continuing to send information back to Earth, though they are currently further away from us than we are from Pluto. And in Rough Trade there were, against all the odds, and despite countless death knells from now defunct retailers, young pretenders and old detractors, still plenty of 12-inch long-playing records. Racks of them, in fact.

On that day I spied 180-gram monos 'cut from the original masters' of *The Notorious Byrd Brothers*, Big Star's *3rd* on vinyl 'for the first time since its debut in 1978', limited edition pressings of Harry Smith folk compendiums, and platter upon platter of Out Rock!, Free Noise, the lot.

Vinyl, for years a dead man walking in the aftermath of the CD, Napster and the iPod, was seemingly back. An article discussing its renaissance in *Wired* magazine in October 2007 was actually headed 'Vinyl May Be Final Nail in CD's Coffin.' A quarter of a century since music went properly digital, who could really have predicted that?

Many times in 'record' shops over the last year or so, I've caught myself thinking, I can remember when all of this (or certainly most of this) was CDs. Shops called Mr CD (or was it Mister CD?) have definitely gone. The interior of the new-ish Rough Trade is, tellingly, much more like an art gallery (in that reborn-industrial-building way) than a record shop of old – regardless of the vinyl. The café, the pristine white fittings, slumber bags, and banks of help-yourself-Net stations, land it somewhere between the orgasmatron lounge in Woody Allen's *Sleeper* and the White Cube.

During that visit, staff armed with clipboards scurried around purposefully, noting shortages of Wooden Shjips albums, managing in the process to pull off a look that was hip slacker and efficient Teuton all in one. In comparison with the old store in Covent Garden, which was a standing-room only subterranean lair heady with the aroma of trainers from Slam City Skates above, this shop offers a journey into . . . well, some serious space. And customers are encouraged to treat it as *a* space. A poster advertising an in-store DIY T-shirt printing and badge making workshop linked it in spirit to its wilted fanzine, polythene-sleeved disc and CD rack-stuffed ancestor. But it also hinted at the way record shops have to provide experiences and services beyond the stock to compete with downloading and online sales.

'Hear every album in full and effortlessly order from our members area', advised a sign on a listening post promoting their monthly bespoke Rough Trade Album Club. You never got any of that in Portland Records when I was growing up. All requests to the patron, Ron, a stoaty, chain-smoking rocker with a thinning, grimy quiff, to play an album before buying it were met with an ingrown-toenail intransigence. As for attempting to return any LP that was later discovered to be faulty . . . not a chance. 'You've scratched that, son, I can't take that back now', he'd say, even if it was obviously warped or mis-pressed.

Browsing was barely tolerated. You'd be there half-an-hour, more or less, long enough for the brain to get its bearings after the sugar rush of the first few bins: What was new? What did you have already? What could you afford today? What was worth coming back for? Next week? Next month? Next year? Next life? What was worth a punt, after an inky weekly review, a friend's recommendation, a spot on *Whistle Test* or *The Tube*? Would it fit into that perfect collection, an unobtainable total library that always lurked somewhere just out of reach?

All the while you'd also be soaking up the stories on the sleeves, the information seeming to pass via your fingertips by osmosis, as you flicked through records. Who is this? What the hell is that? What label is it on? Who's on this one? (Does Phil Collins playing drums on it, if only as a session man, put it utterly beyond the pale even if it is by John Cale?) Who produced it? Who did the cover? Before long, though, these reveries were inevitably interrupted by a barked question from across the counter: 'So, you going to buy anything today?'

Ashamed as I am to say it now, it was a relief when a new Our Price opened in town. It was duller, the range was less rangy, but they'd order stuff in for you and were happy to let you idle hours away in there. Portland suffered enough to close down.

Record shopping is easier these days. It can, after all, be done from home or while barrelling along the street with a mobile phone. Typing these words, Wifi-ed to the web, I can't help feeling ever so slightly mocked for spending so much of my youth scouring bargain bins and tramping from shop to shop. Practically the whole musical canon is only a mouse click or two away – and a good deal of it is completely free. But Rough Trade, unlike Portland or Tower, is obviously alive and well. And pressing plants like Hayes, mothballed by EMI in 2000 are, according to the *Financial Times*, turning out 20,000 records a week. A far cry from 250,000 a day in the early 1970s, but a sign, for the moment at least, that people have a hunger for vinyl.

But how long will it last? Albums that I bought in Portland Records are now older than *Sgt. Pepper* was back then. And yet today's technology means none of us have to listen to or make music in that time-honoured and time-constrained fashion ever again. Unless we want to, which for now, some of us seem to. Though if we are honest with ourselves, those of us who revere the concept of the album (and, on occasion, concept albums) will probably concede that we are far more likely to hear discs (new and old) on the hoof these days, often slightly distractedly, while doing something else. And iPhones, Blackberries and Facebook pokes ensure that we are practically never without distractions.

The LP, and really the album itself, has only survived this long because it met the needs and fed the desires of its times. And however fashionable vinyl might be at the moment, it remains a niche interest – one that will appear anachronistic to anyone suckled on downloading and the instant availability of everything. (A factor, no doubt, to some in its appeal.)

Stumbling upon a set of wall frames for LP sleeves for sale in Rough Trade, I had a slightly queasy moment-cum-premonition. The LP had been turned into an arcane curio, an artefact to be put under glass on a wall. To me, to frame an LP sleeve is to put it out to pasture rather than on a pedestal, implying that its working life is at an end. But I guess we all have our own ways of paying respect. Another might be admitting it's time to let go or at least to accept that paradigms do shift and the historical urgency of the album may have passed. And yet . . .

Only a year or so ago, I read about Mingering Mike. Mike was a Vietnam veteran who in the 1970s dreamed about becoming a soul star and duly made fifty albums of his own. Mike did not, as it happens, have a record contract nor did he have access to a recording studio or a pressing plant. He simply fashioned all of his records from bits of leftover cardboard. Paying homage to soul and Blaxploitation albums of the period, Mike painstakingly pencilled the illustrations for the jackets, drew fake grooves on the cardboard discs and wrote sleeve notes for a non-output of such fantasy funk gems as 'Boogie Down at the White House,' 'Let's Get Nasty' and his righteous anti-Vietnam effort 'I've Got the Battlefield Blues.'

Until 2003, when a box of Mike's 'albums' turned up at a Washington flea market, they had languished in storage for over twenty-six years. Their discovery and subsequent fame as the lost albums of the soul singer who never was, seemed to sum up both the imaginative power of the LP format and to illustrate its limitations. Today, surely, Mike would very probably have his own Myspace page, and the means to put the tunes in his head out into the world on the Web.

But what Mingering Mike's efforts also suggested to me was that, actually, anything we want can be an LP. Vinyl, cassette, CD and download, the carrier no longer matters. With crayons and cardboard, perhaps a guitar or with the garage band software, we can all make our own albums, just as those that we listen to have made us. After sixty years, there's more than enough out there – real and imagined – to keep us spinning for a good while yet.

SOURCES

This book, if we are looking for a clunky metaphor (and hell, why not?), feels more like a compilation tape than an album per se. It could not have been written without the aid of numerous other books, articles, sleeve notes, documentaries, films, fanzines, websites, and late night conversations in bars with fanatics.

The sources below hopefully give credit where credit is due. As an avid reader of the music press since my teens and a voracious consumer of musical biographies, in recent years, on a professional basis, the list is probably far from complete. But it and the select bibliography below should point those who want to read more in the right directions.

Sleeve Notes

David Byrne's comments on downloading appeared in the *Montreal Gazette*, 2 October 2006.

The *New York Times* article discussing the death of the album was 'The Album, a Commodity in Disfavour', Jeff Leeds, 26 March 2007.

The findings from Dr Adrian North's study of Downloaders were reported in the *Guardian* in 'Are downloads creating apathy?' Charles Arthur, 12 January 2006.

Paul William's review of *(The Kinks Are) The Village Green Preservation Society* was published in *Rolling Stone*, 14 June 1969.

Chapter One: Speed Wars

For much of the background, the story of the LP's creation and the subsequent battle of the speeds, see *From Tinfoil to Stereo: Evolution of the Phonograph*, Oliver Reed and Walter L. Welch (Indianapolis: Bobbs-Merrill, 1976), *The Fabulous Phonograph, 1877-1977*, Roland Gellatt (New York: Macmillan, 1977), *Where Have All The Good Times Gone? The Rise and Fall of the Record Industry*, Barfe, Louis (London Atlantic, 2004), *America on Record: A History of Recorded Sound*, Andre Millard (Cambridge: Cambridge University Press, 1995), *The Label: The Story of Columbia Records* Gary Marmorstein. (New York: Thunder's Mouth Press, 2007), *45 RPM: The History, Heroes & Villains of a Pop Music Revolution*, Jim Dawson and Steve Propes (San Francisco, Calif.: Backbeat, 2003.) and William S. Paley's *As It Happened: A Memoir* (Garden City: Doubleday, 1979).

Peter Goldmark's autobiography is *Maverick Inventor: My Turbulent Years at CBS* (New York: Saturday Review Press, 1973). For Edward Wallerstein's version of events see: 'Creating the LP Record', *High Fidelity*, April 1976. The same issue of *High Fidelity* also contains John Mullan's recollections of Nazi broadcasts and material on V-Discs. But also see: *V-Discs: A History and Discography* Richard S. Sears (Westport: Greenwood Press, 1980).

John Culshaw's widely quoted account of dubbing from 78s is in *Putting the Record Straight: The Autobiography of John Culshaw* (London Secker & Warburg, 1981).

For Alex Steinweiss and the LP sleeve see: *For the Record: The Life and Work of Alex Steinweiss* by Jennifer McKnight-Trontz and Alex Steinweiss introduction by Steven Heller. (New York Princeton Architectural, 2000).

Chapter Two: Four Seasons on Two Sides

For the impact of The Lonely Crowd see Todd Gitlin's introduction to the 2001 edition, *The Lonely Crowd: A Study of the Changing American Character*, David Riesman with Nathan Glazer and Reuel Denney (New Haven: Yale Nota Bene, 2001).

Sigmund Spaeth's views on record lovers are in his foreword to *How to Build a Record Library: A Guide to Planned Collecting of Recorded Music*, Paul Affelder (New York: Dutton, 1947).

For the expansion of classical repertoire on LP and much else see *A Century of Recorded Music: Listening to Musical History*, Timothy Day (New Haven; London: Yale University Press, 2000). Some of Barzun's observations about record buyers are quoted in Day but also see his preface to *Pleasures of Music: An anthology of writing about music and musicians* Ed. Jacques Barzun (London: Cassell, 1977).

For Culshaw on Wagner's Ring Cycle see *Ring Resounding: The Recording in Stereo of Der Ring des Nibelungen* (London: Secker & Warburg, 1967, 1971).

For Vivaldi's *Four Seasons* see: 'The Masterpiece That Took 200 Years to Become Timeless' by Jeremy Eichler, *New York Times*, 27 February 2005. And for the popularity of Baroque music see also Glenn Gould's essays from the 50s and 60s in *The Glenn Gould Reader*, edited by Tim Page (London: Faber, 1987, 1984).

For recording and the controversy over tape splicing, Legge and Gaisberg et. al. see *The Recording Angel: Explorations in Phonography*, Evan Eisenberg (New York: McGraw-Hill, 1987) as well as *The Music Goes Round*, Fred Gaisberg (New York: Macmillan, 1942) and *On and Off the Record: A Memoir of Walter Legge*, Elisabeth Schwarzkopf with an introduction by Herbert von Karajan (London: Faber, 1982).

On Glenn Gould and the Goldberg Variations see: *Glenn Gould: A Life and Variations*, Otto Friedrich (London: Methuen, 1990, 1989), *Wonderous Strange: The Life and Art of Glenn Gould*, Kevin Bazzana (New Haven: Yale University Press, 2004) *Glenn Gould: Music & Mind*, Geoffrey Payzant (Toronto: Van Nostrand Reinhold, 1978), *Glenn Gould: The Ecstasy and Tragedy of Genius*, Peter Ostwald (New York: W.W. Norton, 1997), *Conversations with Glenn Gould*, Jonathan Cott

Boston: Little, Brown, 1984 and *The Glenn Gould Reader*, edited by Tim Page (London: Faber, 1987, 1984).

Chapter Three: Cunning Linguists and Extended Pleasures

A lot of the biographical data is drawn from the back issues of contemporary magazines, *Time*, *Life* and *High Fidelity*, and, especially in the case of the stars of easy listening augmented by material from liner notes ancient and modern.

For Lieberson and Murrow see, again, both *The Label: The Story of Columbia Records*, Gary Marmorstein (New York: Thunder's Mouth Press, 2007) and *The Recording Angel: Explorations in Phonography*, Evan Eisenberg (New York: McGraw-Hill, 1987).

A profile of the Caedmon girls is in the November 1953 issue of *High Fidelity* magazine.

For the easy listening boom see the peerless *Elevator Music: A Surreal History of Muzak, Easy-Listening and other Moodsongs*, Joseph Lanza (London: Quartet, 1995). Also *Making Easy Listening: Material Culture and Post-war American Recording*, Tim J. Anderson (Minneapolis: University of Minnesota Press, 2006).

Jackie Gleason's forthright directive to his musicians, quoted in Lanza, appears in William A. Henry III's *The Great One: The Life and Legend of Jackie Gleason* (New York: Doubleday, 1992) from which other Gleason gems were also gleaned.

For Lyman and Co. also see *The Book of Tiki : the Cult of Polynesian Pop in the Fifties*, Sven A. Kirsten (London: Taschen, 2000).

Colin MacKenzie's loving, and comprehensive *Mantovani: A Lifetime in Music* (Ely, Melrose Book Company, 2005) proves that the Maestro has fans (one at the very least) left in the world.

For Emory Cook see 'Sounds of Our Times', *Time*, 15 November 1954 and 'Sounds from the Caribbean', *Time*, 27 February, 1956.

Chapter Four: Blowing Hot and Cold

Whitney Balliett's comments appear in *The Sound of Surprise: 46 pieces of Jazz* (Harmondsworth: Penguin Books, 1963).

Aside from Ned Polsky's *Hustlers, Beats and Others*, for Beats and jazz see *The Hip: Hipsters, Jazz and the Beat Generation*, Roy Carr, Brian Case, Fred Dellar (London: Faber, 1986), *Birth of the Cool: Beat, Bebop, and the American Avant-Garde*, Lewis MacAdams (New York: Free Press, 2001), John Leland's *Why Kerouac Matters: the Lessons of On the Road (They're Not What you Think)* (New York: Viking, 2007) and his excellent, *Hip, the History* (New York: Ecco 2004), *Blows like a Horn: Beat Writing, Jazz, Style, and Markets in the Transformation of U.S. Culture*, Preston Whaley, Jr. (Cambridge: Harvard University Press, 2004) and Norman Mailer's 'The White Negro: Superficial Reflections on the Hipster', (1957) which is reproduced along with Kerouac's 'Essentials of Spontaneous Prose' in *The Portable Beat Reader*, edited Ann Charters, (London: Penguin, 1992).

For Kerouac on Lester Young and jazz see 'Jazz of the Beat Generation' (1955) and 'The Beginning of Bop', both are in *The Portable Kerouac*, edited by Ann Charters (New York: Viking Penguin 1996) plus *Nights in Birdland: Jazz Photographs, 1954-1960*, Carole Reiff, (London: Simon & Schuster, 1987).

Kerouac's letter to Cassady on the Charlie Christian LP is from *Jack Kerouac: Selected Letters, 1940-1956*, ed. Ann Charters (New York: Viking, 1995).

The effect of the *Life* magazine piece on Kerouac is discussed in some detail in Ann Charters' *Kerouac: A Biography*, Ann Charters (London: Deutsch, 1974) but for other biographical material see *Memory Babe: A Critical Biography of Jack Kerouac*, Gerald Nicosia, (New York: Grove, 1983), *Jack Kerouac, King of the Beats: A Portrait*, Barry Miles (London: Virgin 1998), *Jack Kerouac: a Biography*, Tom Clark (London: Plexus, 1997) and *The Beat Book: Writings from the Beat Generation*, edited by Anne Waldman, foreword by Allen Ginsberg (Boston: Shambhala, 1996).

For the birth of jazz and the effects of recording see *The Jazz Scene*, Francis Newton, (Penguin: London 1961), once again, *The Recording Angel: Explorations in Phonography*, Evan Eisenberg, (New York:

McGraw-Hill, 1987), *Capturing Sound: How Technology Has Changed Music*, Mark Katz (Berkeley: University of California Press, 2005), *Jazz, New Orleans, 1885-1963: An Index to the Negro Musicians of New Orleans*, Samuel Charters (New York: Da Capo Press, 1983) and *New Orleans: Playing a Jazz Choru*s, Samuel Charters (New York: Marion Boyars, 2006).

For bebop, modern jazz and the (less than immediate) effects of the LP on jazz, see *Giant Steps: Bebop and the Creators of Modern Jazz*, Kenny Mathieson (Edinburgh: Payback Press, 1999), *A New History of Jazz*, Alyn Shipton, (London: Continuum, 2007), *Profiles in Jazz: from Sidney Bechet to John Coltrane*, Raymond Horricks (New Brunswick: Transaction Publishers, 1991), *Swing to Bop: an Oral History of the Transition in Jazz in the 1940s*, Ira Gitler (Oxford: Oxford University Press, 1985), *Jazz Masters of the Forties*, Ira Gitler, (London : Collier Macmillan, 1974), *Jazz Masters of the Fifties*, Joe Goldberg (London: Collier-Macmillan, 1965) and *A Guide to Longplay Jazz Records*, Frederic Ramsey, Jr. (New York: Da Capo, 1977).

Also see *The 101 Best Jazz Albums: A History of Jazz on Records* (New York: Morrow, 1980) by Len Lyons, invaluable throughout this chapter.

Thomas Pynchon's reminiscences appear in *Slow Learner: Early Stories*, (London: Picador, 1985).

For Blue Note's metal mastering etc., see *Blue Note Records: The Biograpy, Richard Cook*, (London: Secker & Warburg, 2001) and *The Blue Note Label: A Discography*, Michael Cuscuna and Michel Ruppli, (New York: Greenwood Press, 1988).

Newton's (aka Hobsawn's) observations about jazz fans appear in *The Jazz Scene* (Penguin: London 1961) but he along with Iris Murdoch's jazz-loving art student are referred to in Simon Frith's *Art Into Pop* (London: Methuen, 1987).

For Norman Granz and the Jazz at the Philharmonic see Whitney Balliett, *The Sound of Surprise: 46 pieces of Jazz* (Harmondsworth: Penguin Books, 1963) and *Collected Works: A Journal of Jazz, 1954-2000*, (London: Granta, 2001).

For Coltrane and the Blue Train LP, see again *Blue Note Records: The Biography*, Richard Cook (London: Secker & Warburg, 2001) plus *Chasin' the Trane: The Music and Mystique of John Coltrane*, J.C.

Thomas (London: Elm Tree Books, 1976) and *As Serious as Your Life: John Coltrane and Beyond*, Valerie Wilmer (London: Serpent's Tail, 1992). The latter has material on Ornette Coleman too.

For Pacific Jazz and Brubeck see *West Coast: The Los Angeles Jazz Scene of the 1950s*, Robert Gordon (London: Quartet, 1986) and *The Melody Lingers on: Scenes from the Golden Years of West Coast Jazz*, Jo Brooks Fox and Jules L. Fox (Santa Barbara: Fithian Press, 1996).

For Charles Mingus see *Mingus: A Critical Biography*, Brian Priestley (London: Paladin, 1985).

For Miles Davis see *It's About that Time: Miles Davis On and Off Record*, Richard Cook (London: Atlantic Books, 2005), *Miles: the Autobiography*, Miles Davis with Quincy Troupe (New York: Simon and Schuster, 1989), *'Round about midnight: A Portrait of Miles Davis*, Eric Nisenson (New York: Da Capo Press, 1996) and his *The Making of Kind of Blue: Miles Davis and His Masterpiece* (New York: St. Martin's Press, 2001), *The Miles Davis Companion*, edited by Gary Carner (London: Omnibus, 1996), *Kind of Blue: The Making of the Miles Davis Masterpiece*, Ashley Khan (London: Granta, 2001) and, also, *The Label: The Story of Columbia Records*, Gary Marmorstein (New York: Thunder's Mouth Press, 2007).

For Ornette Coleman see *Ornette Coleman: The Harmolodic Life*, John Litweiler (London: Quartet, 1992) and *Ornette Coleman: His Life and Music*, Peter Niklas Wilson (Berkeley: Berkeley Hills Books, 1999).

Larkin's last rites for jazz can be found in *Jazz Writings: Essays and Reviews 1940-84*, edited by Richard Palmer and John White, (London: Continuum, 2004).

Chapter Five: To Be Frank

For Gerry Wexler's observation about rock 'n' roll and LP buyers see *High Fidelity*, April 1976.

David Thomson's verdict on Sinatra appears in his *New Biographical Dictionary of Film*, 4th ed., (London: Little, Brown, 2002).

For Sinatra's life and times, glorious tittle tattle and all, see *His Way: The Unauthorised Biography of Frank Sinatra*, Kitty Kelley (London: Bantam,

1986), *Sinatra: the Man Behind the Myth*, J. Randall Taraborrelli (Edinburgh: Mainstream, 1997), *All or Nothing at All: A Life of Frank Sinatra*, Donald Clarke (London: Pan, 1998), and *All the Way: A Biography of Frank Sinatra*, Michael Freedland (London: Weidenfeld & Nicolson, 1997).

On Sinatra's artistic significance, see *Sinatra the Artist and the Man*, John Lahr (London: Phoenix, 1999) and *Why Sinatra Matters*, Pete Hamill (Boston: Little, Brown, 2000).

For the films, the songs, singing and recording techniques see *Frank Sinatra at the Movies*, Roy Pickard (London: Hale, 1994), *The Complete Guide to the Music of Frank Sinatra*, John Collis, edited by Chris Charlesworth (London: Omnibus, 1998) and *Sessions with Sinatra: Frank Sinatra and the Art of Recordings*, Charles L. Granata (Chicago: A Cappella, 1999).

Sinatra's account of selecting the songs for his LPs is in *Sinatra*, Robin Douglas Home (Michael Joseph: London, 1962).

Mitch Miller's quotes are from 'How the Money Rolls', *Time*, 20 August 1951 but for Miller's stranglehold on the pop charts also see Donald Clarke's *The Rise and Fall of Popular Music* (London: Viking, 1995).

For Sinatra and his clan, see Shaun Levy's *Rat Pack Confidential: Frank, Dean, Sammy, Peter, Joey & the Last Great Showbiz Party* (London: Fourth Estate, 1998) and Gay Talese's 'Frank Sinatra Has A Cold' in *The Gay Talese Reader: Portraits and Encounters* (Walker & Company: New York 2003). For Sinatra's fateful falling out with the Kennedys also see Richard Williams' 'Frank's Place' in *Granta* Magazine 76: Music (London: Granta 2002).

Chapter Six: And Now for Something Completely Different

Michael Billington made his comments about the *Beyond the Fringe* LP in an interview with *The Bookseller* magazine on 20 September 2007 but also see his *State of the Nation: British Theatre since 1945* (Faber: London 2007).

For *Beyond the Fringe* see *The Complete Beyond the Fringe*, Alan Bennett et. al.; with an introduction by Michael Frayn (London: Methuen, 2003), *That was Satire That Was: Beyond the Fringe, the Establishment Club, Private Eye and That Was The Week That Was*, Humphrey Carpenter (London: Victor Gollancz, 2000), *From Fringe to Flying Circus: Celebrating a Unique Generation of Comedy 1960-1980*, Roger Wilmut; preface by Bamber Gascoigne (London: Eyre Methuen, 1980) and *Beyond the fringe . . . and Beyond: A Critical Biography of Alan Bennett, Peter Cook, Jonathan Miller and Dudley Moore*, Ronald Bergan (London: Virgin, 1989).

For American satire see The Sickniks, *Time* magazine, 13 July 1959, *Seriously Funny: The Rebel Comedians of the 1950s and 1960s*, Gerald Nachman (New York: Pantheon Books, 2003) and *Revel With a Cause: Liberal Satire in Post-war America*, Stephen E. Kercher (Chicago: University of Chicago Press, 2006).

For Tom Lehrer also see 'Time Out from Thinking' in *Time* magazine, 4 January 1954.

Mort Sahl's memoir is *Heartland* (New York: Harcourt Brace Jovanovich, 1976) but for the importance of his LPs and the stand-up scene also see *The Unruly Life of Woody Allen*, Marion Meade (London: Weidenfeld & Nicolson, 1999).

For Goldman's thoughts on comedy LPs and beatnik pads and much more on Lenny Bruce see *Ladies and Gentlemen, Lenny Bruce!*, Albert Goldman from the journalism of Lawrence Schiller (London: Pan Books, 1976). Also see (and hear, since it comes with a CD), *The Trials of Lenny Bruce: The Fall and Rise of an American Icon*, Ronald K.L. Collins and David M. Skover (Naperville: Sourcebooks MediaFusion, 2002).

Chapter Seven: Beat Less

Barry Miles 'leap of the imagination' is from *The Beatles Diary: an Intimate Day-by-Day History* (London: Omnibus, 1998) which along with *The Complete Beatles Chronicle*, Mark Lewisohn (Pyramid Books 1992), *The Complete Beatles Recording Sessions: The Official Story of the Abbey Road Years* (London: Hamlyn, 1988), also Lewisohn, and *The Ultimate Beatles Encyclopedia*, Bill Harry (London: Virgin 1992), was never far from hand when this chapter was written. Nor for that matter was Ian MacDonald's *Revolution in the Head: The Beatles' Records and the Sixties* (London: Pimlico, 2005) source of his 'coolly unromantic new age' quote.

For other Beatles' biographical information see: *Shout!: The True Story of the Beatles*, Philip Norman (London: Pan, 2004), *The Beatles*, Hunter Davies (London: Cassell, 2002), *The Love You Make: An Insider's Story of the Beatles*, Peter Brown and Steven Gaines (New York: McGraw-Hill, 1983), *John, Paul, George, Ringo & Me: The Real Beatles Story*, Tony Barrow (London: Andre Deutsch, 2005), *The Beatles: the Complete Illustrated Story*, Terry Burrows (London: Carlton, 1996), *The Rough Guide to the Beatles*, Chris Ingham (London: Rough Guides, 2003), *The Beatles*, Jon Ewing (London: Orion, 1994), *The Day John Met Paul: an Hour-by-Hour Account of How the Beatles Began*, Jim O'Donnell (New York: Routledge, 2006), *The Beatles Come to America*, Martin Goldsmith (Hoboken: John Wiley & Sons, 2004), *A Day in the Life: the Music and Artistry of the Beatles*, Mark Hertsgaard (London: Macmillan, 1995).

Also for some of the background see *The Beatles and Some Other Guys: Rock Family Trees of the Early Sixties*, Pete Frame (London: Omnibus, 1997) and *Beat Merchants: The Origins, History, Impact and Rock Legacy of the 1960s' British Pop Groups*, Alan Clayson (London: Blandford, 1995), *1960s Pop*, Bob Brunning (Oxford: Heinemann, 1998) and *Flowers in the Dustbin: The Rise of Rock and Roll, 1947-1977*, James Miller (New York: Simon & Schuster 1999). The latter supplies Miller's comment about 'four characters'.

Both Lennon's remarks about preferring to stay in rather than see Harry Secombe and hating Cliff Richard appear in *Love Me Do: The Beatles' Progress*, Michael Braun (Harmondsworth: Penguin, 1977).

For Lennon also see *John Lennon in his Own Words*, compiled by Miles, designed by Pearce Marchbank (London: Omnibus Press, 1980), *The Lives of John Lennon, Albert Goldman* (London: Bantam, 1988), *John Lennon*, Ray Coleman (London: Pan 2000), *Days in the Life: John Lennon Remembered*, Philip Norman (London: Century, 1990).

McCartney's 'whacky chaps' line appears in *Paul McCartney: Many Years from Now*, Paul McCartney and Barry Miles (London: Secker & Warburg, 1997) for Macca also see *McCartney*, Chris Salewicz ,(London: Futura, 1987), *Paul McCartney: The Definitive Biography*, Chris Welsh

(Proteus: London, 1984) and *McCartney: Yesterday and Today*, Ray Coleman (London: Boxtree, 1996).

For Hamburg, Sutcliffe and those haircuts see *The Beatles' Shadow: Stuart Sutcliffe & His Lonely Hearts Club*, Pauline Sutcliffe with Douglas Thompson (London: Pan, 2002) and *Hamburg Days*, Astrid Kirchherr & Klaus Voormann; compiled by Ulf Kruger (Guildford: Genesis, 1999).

For the Beatles and Larry Parnes see *Johnny Gentle and the Beatles: First Ever Tour: Scotland 1960*, Johnny Gentle & Ian Forsyth (Runcorn: Merseyrock, 1998).

For Joe Meek see *The Legendary Joe Meek: The Telstar Man*, John Repsch (London: Cherry Red, 2000).

For Epstein see *A Cellarful of Noise*, Brian Epstein (New English Library: London, 1965), *The Brian Epstein Story*, compiled and written by Deborah Geller; edited by Anthony Wall (London: Faber, 2000) and *Brian Epstein: the Man Who Made the Beatles*, Ray Coleman (London: Penguin, 1990).

For the Beatles' Parlophone deal and the cutting of the first LP see *All You Need is Ears*, George Martin with Jeremy Hornsby (New York: St. Martin's Press, 1994) and *Abbey Road: The Story of the World's Most Famous Recording Studios*, Brian Southall, Peter Vince, Allan Rouse; foreword by Paul McCartney; preface by George Martin (London: Omnibus, 2002).

Cliff Richard's admission that he copied Elvis is taken from *My Story*, Cliff Richard (England: s.n., 1973). For Cliff also see *The Cliff Richard Story*, George Tremlett,
(London: Futura Publications, 1975), *Cliff in His Own Words*, compiled by Kevin St. John (London: W.H. Allen, 1981), *Cliff Richard: The Biography*, Steve Turner (Oxford: Lion, 1994), and *Driftin' with Cliff Richard*, Jet Harris and Royston Ellis (London: Charles Buchan's Publications, 1959).

For the King himself see *Elvis Presley: A Complete Reference*, compiled by Wendy Sauers (Jefferson: McFarland, 1984), *Careless Love: The Unmaking of Elvis Presley*, Peter Guralnick (London: Abacus, 2000), *The Complete Guide to the Music of Elvis Presley* by John Robertson, edited by Chris Charlesworth (London: Omnibus Press, 1994), *Down at the End of Lonely Street: The Life and Death of Elvis Presley*, Peter Harry

411

Brown and Pat H. Broeske (London: Heinemann, 1997) and *Aspects of Elvis: Tryin' to Get to You*, edited by Alan Clayson and Spencer Leigh (London: Sidgwick & Jackson, 1994).

For Loog Oldham's '1963' et. al. see *Stoned*, written and produced by Andrew Loog Oldham; interviews and research by Simon Dudfield, edited by Ron Ross (London: Secker & Warburg, 2000). And for the Stones also see *The Stones*, Philip Norman (London: Elm Tree, 1984), *The Rolling Stones Story*, George Tremlett (London: White Lion Publishers, 1976), *The Rolling Stones: Off the Record*, Mark Paytress (London: Omnibus, 2003.) and *The Early Stones: Legendary Band in the Making 1963-1973*, photographs by Michael Cooper, foreword and commentary by Keith Richards, text by Terry Southern (London: Secker & Warburg, 1993)

For Jools Holland on Ray Charles' twist LP see 'My Groovy Hero', *Guardian*, 21 January 2005.

For George Melly's theory about the Twist and his comments about the first two Beatles LP see *Revolt into Style: the Pop Arts in Britain* (Harmondsworth: Penguin, 1972).

For Cleave's 'Ooo' see *The Beatles Book*, Norman Parkinson, with words by Maureen Cleave (London: Hutchinson, 1964).

Walter Shenson discusses United Artists' scheme for a soundtrack LP in an interview on the DVD of *A Hard Day's Night* (Walt Disney Studios Home Ent, 30 September 2002) which also boasts interviews with director Dick Lester, among others.

For Hugh Mendel on the recording of 'New Orleans Joys' see 'Go Lonnie Go', Billy Bragg, *Guardian*, 21 June 2004. I am also grateful to Louis Barfe who generously supplied me with a transcript of his interview with Mendel. For Skiffle and trad jazz also see *Skiffle: The Definitive Inside Story*, Chas McDevitt (London: Robson, 1997), *The Skiffle Craze: a Popular Music Phenomenon of the 1950s*, Michael Dewe (Aberystwyth: University of Wales, 1999) and *The Quarrymen*, Hunter Davies (London: Omnibus, 2001). For Harrison's comment on Donegan see *Fifty Years Adrift*, Derek Taylor, edited by George Harrison (Guildford: Genesis in association with Hedley New Zealand & Hedley Australia, 1984).

For the different Beatles LPs see *The Beatles Album File and Complete Discography*, Jeff Russell (London: Blandford, 1989), *All Together Now:*

The First Complete Beatles Discography, 1961-1975, Harry Castleman and Walter J. Podrazik (Ann Arbor: Pierian Press, 1975), *The Beatles' Story on Capitol Records*, compiled by Bruce Spizer, foreword by Alan Livingston (New Orleans: 498 Productions, L.L.C, 2000) and Spizer's *The Beatles Records on Vee-Jay* (New Orleans: 498 Productions, L.L.C, 1998).

Lou Reed's account of songsmithing to order appears in *Lou Reed: The Biography*, Victor Bockris (London: Hutchinson, 1994).

For surf music and California see *Surf City, Drag City*, Rob Burt (Poole: Blandford, 1986), *The Illustrated Discography of Surf Music, 1959-1965* ,John Blair (Riverside: J. Bee, 1978), *Waiting for the Sun: Strange Days, Weird Scenes and the Sound of Los Angeles*, Barney Hoskyns (London: Bloomsbury, 2003) and for Tom Wolfe on Dick Dale, *The Kandy-Kolored Tangerine-Flake Streamline Baby* (London: Picador, 1981).

Brian Wilson's statements about the potential of the surfing fad are made in *Wouldn't it be Nice: My Own Story*, Brian Wilson with Todd Gold (London: Bloomsbury, 1992).

For the Beach Boys see *Heroes and Villains: The True Story of the Beach Boys*, Steven Gaines (New York: Da Capo Press, 1995), *The Beach Boys and the California Myth*, David Leaf (New York: Grosset & Dunlap, 1978), *The Nearest Faraway Place: Brian Wilson, the Beach Boys and the Southern Californian Experience*, Timothy White (London: Macmillan, 1996), *Catch A Wave: The Rise, Fall & Redemption Of Brian Wilson*, Peter Ames Carlin (Emmaus: Rodale Press 2006), *The Beach Boys: The Musical Evolution of America's Band*, Robert G. Anstey (Sardis: West Coast Paradise Pub., 2004), *Brian Wilson and The Beach Boys: The Complete Guide to their Music* Andrew G. Doe and John Tobler, (London: Omnibus, 2004) and *Surf's Up!: The Beach Boys on Record* 1961-1981, Brad Elliott (Ann Arbor: Pierian Press, 1982).

Ian MacDonald's assessment of Dylan and the Beatles' songwriting prowess appears in *Revolution in the Head: The Beatles' Records and the Sixties* (London: Pimlico, 2005).

For the Folk revival see *When We Were Good: the Folk Revival*, Robert Cantwell (Cambridge: Harvard University Press, 1996), *Which Side Are You On?: An Inside Story of the Folk Music Revival in America*, Dick

Weissman (London: Continuum, 2005), *Folk Music USA: The Changing Voice of Protest*, Ronald D. Lankford, Jr. (London: Schirmer, 2005) and *Positively 4th Street: the Lives and Times of Joan Baez, Bob Dylan, Mimi Baez Fariña, and Richard Fariña*, David Hajdu (London: Bloomsbury, 2001).

For the Folkways Label see *Folkways Records: Moses Asch and His Encyclopedia of Sound*, Anthony Olmsted (New York: Routledge, 2003), *Making People's Music: Moe Asch and Folkways Records*, Peter D. Goldsmith (Washington: Smithsonian Institution Press, 1998).

Quotes from Samuel Charters are from an author interview, 10 October 2006 but also see *The Country Blues* (London: Jazz Book Club, 1961), *The Legacy of the Blues: a Glimpse into the Art and the Lives of Twelve Great Bluesmen: an Informal Study* (London: Calder and Boyars, 1975) and *Walking A Blues Road: A Selection of Blues Writing 1956-2004* (New York: Marion Boyars, 2005), all by Samuel Charter.

For Harry Smith and the folk anthology see 'American Folk', Greil Marcus in *Granta* Magazine 76 Music (London: Granta, 2002), as above for *Folkways*, and again, *Positively 4th Street: the Lives and Times of Joan Baez, Bob Dylan, Mimi Baez Fariña, and Richard Fariña*, David Hajdu (London: Bloomsbury, 2001). The latter is also where the quote about the air conditioning at Columbia and Joan Baez can be found.

For Dylan see *Chronicles* (New York: Simon & Schuster, 2004), *Dylan: Behind the Shades*, Clinton Heylin (London: Penguin, 1992), *No Direction Home: The Life and Music of Bob Dylan*, Robert Shelton (New York: W. Morrow, 1986), *Down the Highway: The Life of Bob Dylan*, Howard Sounes (London: Black Swan, 2002), *The Bob Dylan Encyclopedia*, Michael Gray (London: Continuum, 2006), *Chimes of Freedom: The Politics of Bob Dylan's Art*, Mike Marqusee (New York: New Press, 2003), *Dylan: Behind Closed Doors: the Recording Sessions 1960-1994*, Clinton Heylin (London: Penguin, 1996), *The Rough Guide to Bob Dylan*, Nigel Williamson (London: Rough Guides, 2006) and *Dylan on Dylan: The Essential Interviews*, edited by Jonathan Cott (London: Hodder & Stoughton, 2006). Also see Cott's anthology for a taste of Weberman's garbage raiding missives on Dylan.

For Dylan's first trip to London see 'Flash-back', Caspar Llewellyn Smith in the *Observer*, 18 September 2005.

Toby Thompson's Gonzo-esque Dylan-odyssey is *Positively Main Street: an Unorthodox View of Bob Dylan* (London: New English Library, 1972).

For the Great White Wonder and Co., see *Invisible Republic: Bob Dylan's Basement Tapes*, Greil Marcus (London: Picador, 1998), *Bootleg: the Secret History of the Other Recording Industry*, Clinton Heylin (New York: St. Martin's Press, 1995), *The Bootleg Guide: Classic Bootlegs of the 1960s and 1970s*, Garry Freeman (Lanham: Scarecrow Press, 2003) and Avery Koler's 'Great White Wonder: The Morality of Bootlegging Bob' in *Bob Dylan and Philosophy: It's Alright, Ma (I'm Only Thinking)*, edited by Peter Vernezze and Carl J. Porter (Chicago, Ill. : Open Court, 2006).

Chapter Eight: Pop Goes Pop!

Much of the material in this chapter is drawn from the contemporary music press – back issues of *Disc* and, as it later became, *Disc and Music Echo*, in particular.

For The Who also see *Before I Get Old: The Story Of The Who*, Dave Marsh (London: Plexus Publishing, 1989) and *The Who On Record: A Critical History 1963-1998*, John Atkins (Jefferson: McFarland, 2000).

Ray Davies' comments to *Rave* magazine are quoted in Jon Savage's *The Kinks: The Official Biography*, Jon Savage (London: Faber, 1984). For Pye see *The Story of Pye Records*, Jim Irvin, (Sequel Records, 1998) and also see *The Kinks Are the Village Green Preservation Society*, Andy Miller (London: Continuum, 2004).

Eric Clapton's distaste for single sessions is quoted in Simon Frith's *Art Into Pop* (London: Methuen, 1987).

Barry Miles on Epstein and Sgt Pepper etc., are from an author interview Sept 2006.

Paul McCartney remarks to Alan Aldridge about making Sgt. Pepper a package are quoted in *It Was Twenty Tears Ago Today*, Derek Taylor (London: Bantam, 1987) as are Roger McGuinn's observations about transmitting messages via records.

Brian Wilson's recollections about *Rubber Soul* appear in *Wouldn't it Be Nice: My Own Story*, Brian Wilson with Todd Gold (London: Bloomsbury, 1992). For this section see sources for earlier surf section, plus *I Just Wasn't Made for These Times: Brian Wilson and the Making of Pet Sounds*, Charles L. Granata (London: Unanimous, 2003), *The Beach Boys' Pet Sounds: the Greatest Album of the 20th Century*, Kingsley Abbot (London: Helter Skelter, 2001), *Smile. The Story of Brian Wilson's Lost Masterpiece*, Dominic Priore (London: Sanctuary Publishing, 2005).

Extracts from McCartney's interview for the *South Bank Show* appear in *It Was Twenty Tears Ago Today*, Derek Taylor (London: Bantam, 1987). Martin's era of trying things out is from *Summer of Love: The Making of Sgt. Pepper*, George Martin with William Pearson (London: Macmillan, 1994).

For the Californian psyche scene see *The Haight-Ashbury: a History* by Charles Perry (New York: Random House, 1984), *Beneath the Diamond Sky: Haight Ashbury 1965-1970*, Barney Hoskyns (London: Bloomsbury, 1997), *Eight Miles High: Folk-rock's Flight from Haight-Ashbury to Woodstock*, Richie Unterberger (San Francisco: Backbeat, 2003) and *Fuzz, Acid and Flowers: a Comprehensive Guide to American Garage, Psychedelic and Hippie Rock* (1964-1975), Vernon Joynson (Telford: Borderline, 1993).

Taylor's observations about the seriousness and silliness of pop post-Monterrey appear in *It Was Twenty Tears Ago Today* (London: Bantam, 1987) which also does an excellent job of comparing and contrasting the UK and US strands of the hippy movement. But for UK scene etc., also see *In the Sixties*, Barry Miles (London: Jonathan Cape, 2002), *Pink Floyd: The Early Years*, Barry Miles (London: Omnibus, 2006), *All Dressed Up: the Sixties and the Counter-Culture*, Jonathan Green (London: Pimlico, 1999), *Days in the Life: Voices from the English Underground 1961-1971*, Jonathon Green (London: Pimlico, 1998), and *Ready, Steady, Go!: Swinging London and the Invention of Cool*, Shawn Levy (London: Fourth Estate, 2002).

For the Velvets see *Up-tight: The Velvet Underground Story*, Victor Bockris and Gerard Malanga (London: Omnibus, 1983), *The Life and Death of Andy Warhol*, Victor Bockris (London: Fourth Estate, 1998), and *Lou Reed: The Biography*, Victor Bockris (London: Hutchinson, 1994).

Frank Zappa's bands-want-to-make-art shtick is immortalised in the *Complete Report of the 1st International Music Industry Conference* (1969 APR: NASSAU).

Joe Smith's remarks to *Rolling Stone* are quoted in *American Popular Music and Its Business From 1900-1984*, Russell Sanjek (Oxford: OUP, 1988).

Les losing track of time and space is from *Profane Culture*, Paul E. Willis (London: Routledge and Kegan Paul, 1978).

For Manson see *The Family: The Story of Charles Manson's Dune Buggy Attack Battalion*, Ed Sanders (St. Albans: Panther, 1973), *The Nearest Faraway Place: Brian Wilson, the Beach Boys and the Southern Californian Experience*, Timothy White (London: Macmillan, 1996) and *Waiting for the Sun: Strange Days, Weird Scenes and the Sound of Los Angeles*, Barney Hoskyns (London: Bloomsbury, 2003).

Chapter Nine: Stacks of Tracks

Typically (or fittingly) I have lost the precise source of Mr Bowie's confession . . .

Simon Napier-Bell recalls Peter Grant's remarks in *Black Vinyl, White Powder*, Simon Napier-Bell, (London: Ebury, 2002).

Frith's comments on Floyd fans appear in Art Into Pop, (London: Methuen, 1987).

For Gabriel see *Mojo* magazine article, 'Pink Floyd & The Story of Prog Rock', July 2007.

Blackwell's comments about students are quoted in *Rockin' in Time: a Social History of Rock and Roll*, David P. Szatmary (Englewood Cliffs: Prentice-Hall, 1987) Charlie Gillett's profile of skinheads for *Rock File* appears in *The Faber Book of Pop* edited by Hanif Kureishi and Jon Savage (London: Faber, 1995). For the Harder They Come and Marley etc, also see *Bass Culture: When Reggae was King*, Lloyd Bradley (London: Viking, 2000), *The Rough Guide to Reggae*, Steve Barrow and Peter Dalton (London: Rough Guides, 2004), *Bob Marley*, Chris Welch (London: Orion, 1994), *Catch a Fire: The Life of Bob Marley*, Timothy White (London:

Omnibus, 2006) and *Flowers in the Dustbin: the Rise of Rock and Roll, 1947-1977*, James Miller (New York: Simon & Schuster, 1999). That latter has much that is germane for Stone, Gaye et al.

Robin Scott's description of Peel's uncompromising commitment to new sounds appears in the *Complete Report of the 1st International Music Industry Conference* (1969 APR: NASSAU).

For Keith Richard's comments on skiing and *Exile on Mainstreet* see *The Stones*, Philip Norman (London: Elm Tree, 1984).

For Sly, Mayfield and Gaye see *All Music Guide to Soul: the Definitive Guide to R&B and Soul*, edited by Vladimir Bogdanov (San Francisco, Calif.: Backbeat, 2003), *Curtis Mayfield: People Never Give Up*, Peter Burns (London: Sanctuary, 2003), *There's a Riot Goin' On*, Miles Marshall Lewis (London: Continuum, 2006), *Trouble Man: The Life and Death of Marvin Gaye*, Steve Turner (London: Penguin, 1999), *Marvin Gaye: What's Going On and the Last Days of the Motown Sound*, Ben Edmonds (Edinburgh: Mojo Books, 2001) and Mick Brown's obituary, 'Marvin Gaye: Heart and Soul', *Guardian*, April 1984.

James Taylor's comments about wishing to be part of the environment were reported in *Time*, 'One Man's Family of Rock', 1 March 1971. For the Laurel Canyon set see *Hotel California: Singer-songwriters and Cocaine Cowboys in the LA Canyons 1967-1976*, Barney Hoskyns (London: Harper Perennial, 2006) also see *Joni Mitchell: Both Sides Now: the Biography*, Brian Hinton (London: Sanctuary, 2000), *Joni Mitchell: Shadows and Light*, Karen O'Brien (London: Virgin Books, 2002) and *Shakey: Neil Young's Biography*, Jimmy McDonough (Toronto: Random House Canada, 2002). For Carole King also see 'Will You Still Love Me Tomorrow?', Rachel Louise Snyder at Salon.com 19 June 1999, *The Words and Music of Carole King*, James E. Perone (Westport: Roundhouse 2006).

For Jim Ladd's account of playing 'Dark Star' see *Radio Waves: Life and Revolution on the FM Dial* (New York: St. Martin's Griffin, 1992).

Hunter S. Thompson quotes from *Fear and Loathing in Las Vegas: a Savage Journey to the Heart of the American Dream*, Hunter S. Thompson, illustrated by Ralph Steadman (London: Harper Perennial, 2005).

For Irwin Tarr on the car record player see *International Music Industry Conference* (1969 APR: NASSAU).

For cassettes and 8-tracks etc., see *Playback: From the Victrola to MP3, 100 years of Music, Machines, and Money*, Mark Coleman (New York: Da Capo Press, 2004) *Platforms: A Microwaved Cultural Chronicle of the 1970s*, Kennedy and Pagan (New York: St. Martin's Press, 1994) and *8-Track Mind Magazine* at http://www.8trackheaven.com.

David Geffen's account of using an 8 track to audition new acts is culled from his interview in *Time*, 'Geffen's Golden Touch', 25 February 1974.

For Prog see, *The Tapestry of Delights: the Comprehensive Guide to British Music of the Beat, R&B, Psychedelic and Progressive Eras 1963-1976*, Vernon Joynson, Jon Newey and John Reed (Telford: Borderline, 1995), *Listening to the Future: the Time of Progressive Rock 1968-1978*, Bill Martin (Chicago: Open Court, 1998), *Progressive Rock Reconsidered*, edited by Kevin Holm-Hudson (New York: Garland, 2001) *Mojo* magazine, 'Pink Floyd & The Story of Prog Rock', July 2007, *Emerson, Lake & Palmer: the Show that Never Ends: a Musical Biography*, George Forrester, Martyn Hanson, Frank Askew (London: Helter Skelter, 2001).

Roger Waters on Newtonian physics and *The Dark Side of the Moon* is quoted in *Pink Floyd: The Early Years*, Barry Miles (London: Omnibus, 2006).

For Oldfield and *Tubular Bells* see *The Making of Mike Oldfield's Tubular Bells: the Story of a Record Which Has Sold over 15,000,000 Copies and Helped to Found the Virgin Empire*, Richard Newman (Ely: Music Maker, 1993), *Richard Branson: The Inside Story*, Mick Brown (London: Headline, 1994), *Branson*, Tom Bower, (London: Fourth Estate, 2000) and Peel's remarks are taken from *The Listener* magazine 1973.

Charles Shaar Murray's comment about glam being the first pop phenomenon of the 1970s is quoted in Barney Hoskyn's *Glam!: Bowie, Bolan and the Glitter Rock Revolution*, (London: Faber, 1998). Bolan on just wanting to do an album is from *Voxpop: Profiles of the Pop Process*, Michael Wale (London: Harrap, 1972).

For Glam and Bowie also see England is Mine: *Pop Life in Albion from Wilde to Goldie*, Michael Bracewell (London: HarperCollins, 1997), *Glam!: An Eyewitness Account*, Mick Rock (London: Omnibus, 2005), *Bowie in his Own Words*, compiled by Miles, designed by Perry Neville (London: W.H. Allen, 1982), *Alias David Bowie: a Biography*, Peter and Leni Gillman (Sevenoaks: New English Library, 1987), *The*

David Bowie Story, George Tremlett (London: Futura Publications, 1974) and, for material on Stonewall see *Rockin' in Time: a Social History of Rock and Roll*, David P. Szatmary (Englewood Cliffs: Prentice-Hall, 1987).

Bowie's interview with Michael Watts is anthologised in *The Faber Book of Pop*, edited by Hanif Kureishi and Jon Savage (London: Faber and Faber, 1995).

Cliff's remarks on men dressing up as women appears in *Cliff in His Own Words*, compiled by Kevin St. John (London: W.H. Allen, 1981).

For 'the fucker's quad' see *Lou Reed: The Biography*, Victor Bockris (London: Hutchinson, 1994).

Chapter Ten: Back to the Future

For Roxy Music see *Roxy Music: Style with Substance - Roxy's First Ten Years*, Johnny Rogan (London: Star Books, 1982), *Re-make/Re-model: Becoming Roxy Music*, Michael Bracewell (London: Faber, 2007) and also the interviews with Ferry et. al, in *The Nineties: When Surface was Depth*, Michael Bracewell (London: Flamingo, 2002).

Don McLean's thoughts on 'American Pie' appear on his official website http://www.don-mclean.com.

For budget albums' run on the charts see the entries in *The Mojo Collection: The Ultimate Music Collection*, edited by Jim Irvin and Colin McLear (Edinburgh: Canongate, 2003) and *Collins Complete British Hit Albums*, Graham Betts (London: Collins, 2005).

For Nik Cohn's steps back in time see his *Awopbopaloobop alopbamboom: Pop from the Beginning* (London: Pimlico, 2004). For *American Graffiti* see *Flowers in the Dustbin: The Rise of Rock and Roll 1947-1977*, James Miller (New York: Simon & Schuster 1999).

For The Band see *Across the Great Divide: The Band and America*, Barney Hoskyns (London : Pimlico, 2003).

For Lennon's battles with Phil Spector see *Lennon*, Ray Coleman

(London: Pan, 2000), *Phil Spector: Out of His Head*, Richard Williams (London: Omnibus, 2003) and *Tearing Down the Wall of Sound: the Rise and Fall of Phil Spector*, Mick Brown (London: Bloomsbury, 2007).

Townshend's observation about all the simple things getting complicated appear in *Before I Get Old: The Story Of The Who*, Dave Marsh, (London: Plexus Publishing, 1989).

For the Beach Boys see sources from Chapter Seven plus Nick Kent's portrait of Brian Wilson in *The Dark Stuff*, (London: Penguin, 1994). John Cale's 'Mr Wilson' from *Slow Dazzle*, also lent a helping hand, if obliquely.

Chapter Eleven: God Bless You Lester Bangs and The Greatest Album Ever Made

Peter York's assessments of punk appear in *Style Wars* (London: Sidgwick & Jackson, 1980) and *Modern Times* (London: Futura, 1985).

The UK unemployment figures are quoted in Jon Savage's *England's Dreaming: Sex Pistols and Punk Rock* (London: Faber, 2001) – an inspiration as much as a source for much else in this chapter. For the record industry's drift toward surefire cash cows in the wake of the oil crisis see *American Popular Music and Its Business from 1900-1984*, Russell Sanjek (Oxford: OUP, 1988) also the source of Neil Bogart's quote.

For pub rock see Savage plus *No Sleep till Canvey Island: the Great Pub Rock Revolution*, Will Birch (London: Virgin, 2000) and *Rock 'n' Roll London*, Max Wooldridge, foreword by Malcolm McLaren (London: New Holland, 2002).

Rotten's comments on the jukebox and his favourite albums et. al., are from *Rotten: No Irish, No Blacks, No Dogs: the Authorised Autobiography, Johnny Rotten of the Sex Pistols* John Lydon with Keith and Kent Zimmerman (London: Hodder & Stoughton, 1994).

Malanga's winning endorsement of Patti Smith as a true punk appears in *Please Kill Me: the Uncensored Oral history of Punk*, Legs McNeil and Gillian McCain (London: Abacus, 1997) also the source of McNeil's comments about the Ramones and so on. Tony Wilson's view that *Horses* was from another planet appears in *24-Hour Party People: What the Sleeve Notes Never Tell You*, Anthony Wilson (London: 4 Books, 2002).

Cope on the Ramones and Can can be found in *Head-On: Memories of the Liverpool Punk-Scene & the Story of the Teardrop Explodes 1976-82* (Great Britain: Magog Books, 1994).

Frank O'Donnell's account of the playback session of *Metal Machine Music* appears in *Lou Reed: The Biography*, Victor Bockris (London: Hutchinson, 1994). For Lester Bangs going ZZZZZRRRR and so on see *Psychotic Reactions and Carburetor Dung*, edited by Greil Marcus (London: Minerva, 1991).

Mary Harron's interview with the Ramones from the debut issue of *Punk* appears in *The Faber Book of Pop*, edited by Hanif Kureishi and Jon Savage (London: Faber, 1995) – this anthology also contains Neil Spencer's *NME* review of the Sex Pistols. For the Ramones also see *Hey Ho Let's Go: the Story of The Ramones*, Everett True (London: Omnibus 2002).

For Tony James on the Ramones and UK punk see *Redemption Song: the Definitive Biography of Joe Strummer*, Chris Salewicz (London: HarperCollins, 2006).

For John Peel and punk see *The Sex Pistols: The Inside Story*, compiled and edited by Fred and Judy Vermorel (London: Star Books, 1978) and *Margrave of the Marshes*, John Peel and Sheila Ravenscroft (London: Bantam, 2005). The former is germane for UK punk in general.

For the Damned see *The Book of the Damned: The Light at the End of the Tunnel: the Official Biography*, Carol Clerk (London Omnibus, 1987).

For punk background see, *1988, The New Wave, Punk Rock Explosion*, Caroline Coon (London: Orbach & Chambers, 1997), *'77: The Year of Punk & New Wave*, Henrik Bech Poulsen (London: Helter Skelter, 2005), *From the Velvets to the Voidoids: a Pre-punk History for a Post-punk World*, Clinton Heylin (London: Penguin, 1993), *The Album Cover Art of Punk*, edited by Burkhardt Seiler and friends, foreword by Malcolm McLaren (London: Collins & Brown, 1998), *The Clash 'Talking'*, Nick Johnstone (London: Omnibus Press, 2006) and *Encyclopedia of Punk Music and Culture*, Brian Cogan (Westport: Greenwood Press, 2006).

For Spunk see Savage and *Bootleg: The Secret History of the Other Recording Industry*, Clinton Heylin (London: Penguin, 1995).

For the Ramones and Spector see *True*, as above, and *Phil Spector: Out of His Head*, Richard Williams (London: Omnibus, 2003) and *Tearing Down the Wall of Sound: the Rise and Fall of Phil Spector*, Mick Brown (London: Bloomsbury, 2007).

Chapter Twelve: Take Up Thy Stereo and Walk, Man

For the Virgin Megastore phenomenon in the 1980s see *Time Travel: Pop, Media and Sexuality, 1976-96*, Jon Savage (London: Chatto & Windus, 1996).

For the carnage that was the Frampton and the Bee Gees' film/album of *Sgt. Pepper* see *Hit Men*, Frederic Dannen (New York: Random House, 1990) and *American Popular Music and Its Business from 1900- 1984*, Russell Sanjek (Oxford: OUP, 1988). The latter is also the source of Reinstein's calculations on home taping et. al.

For Adam Ant on Westward's pirate look see *Adam Ant: Stand & Deliver: the Autobiography* (London: Sidgwick & Jackson, 2006).

For Sony and the Walkman and compact discs see *Akio Morita and Sony*, David Marshall (Watford: Exley, 1995), *Made in Japan: Akio Morita and Sony*, Akio Morita with Edwin M. Reingold and Mitsuko Shimomura (London: Collins, 1987), *Sony: the Private Life*, John Nathan (Boston: Houghton Mifflin, 1999), *The Sony Vision*, Nick Lyons (New York: Crown, 1976) plus *Playback: From the Victrola to MP3, 100 years of Music, Machines, and Money*, Mark Coleman (New York: Da Capo Press, 2004) and *How Technology Has Changed Music*, Mark Katz (Berkeley: University of California Press, 2005).

For hip hop see Jeff Chang, *Can't Stop Won't Stop: A History of the Hip-Hop Generation* (London: Ebury, 2005), *Rap Attack 3: African rap to Global Hip Hop*, David Toop (London: Serpent's Tail, 2000), *Encyclopedia of Rap and Hip-Hop Culture*, Yvonne Bynoe (Westport: Harcourt Education 2005), *Hip-Hop Culture*, Emmett G. Price III (Santa Barbara: ABC-CLIO, 2006), *Born in the Bronx: a Visual Record of the Early Days of Hip Hop*, edited by Johan Kugelberg, foreword by Afrika Bambaataa, (New York: Rizzoli, 2007).

The Africa Bambaataa comment on cassettes is quoted in *Rockin' in Time: a Social History of Rock and Roll*, David P. Szatmary (Englewood Cliffs: Prentice-Hall, 1987).

Jacques Heemskerk's expressed his regrets over the length of the CD to BBC news online on 17 August 2007.

Patrick Bateman's difficulties over a stuck *Talking Heads* CD and so on are from *American Psycho*, Bret Easton Ellis (London: Picador, 1991).

For more on the long-box see *The Total Package: The Evolution and Secret Meanings of Boxes, Bottles, Cans and Tubes* by Thomas Hine (Little Brown, New York: 1995).

For heavy metal in the dock see *Minds on Trial: Great Cases in Law and Psychology*, Charles Patrick Ewing and Joseph T. McCann (Oxford: OUP, 2006) and *The Story of Judas Priest: Defenders of the Faith*, Neil Daniels (London: Omnibus, 2007) and *Ozzy: Unauthorised*, Sue Crawford (London: Michael O'Mara, 2003).

For Dire Straits and the CD see *Dire Straits*, Colin Irwin (London: Orion Books, 1994) and *Where Have All the Good Times Gone? The Rise and Fall of the Record Industry*, Louis Barfe (London: Atlantic, 2004).

The Tower Records representative is quoted in *Rockin' in Time: a Social History of Rock and Roll*, David P. Szatmary (Englewood Cliffs: Prentice-Hall, 1987).

Epilogue

For the *Voyager* LP see *Murmurs of Earth: The* Voyager *Interstellar Record*, Carl Sagan (London: Hodder and Stoughton, 1979).

And for Mingering Mike see *Mingering Mike*, Dori Hadar (New York: Princeton Architectural, 2007).

BIBLIOGRAPHY

A

Abbot, Kingsley, *The Beach Boys' Pet Sounds: the Greatest Album of the 20th Century*, London: Helter Skelter, 2001

Affelder, Paul, *How to Build a Record Library: A Guide to Planned Collecting of Recorded Music*, New York: Dutton, 1947

Akhtar, Miriam, and Humphries, Steve, *The Fifties and Sixties: a Lifestyle Revolution*, London: Boxtree, 2001

Allsop, Kenneth, *The Angry Decade: A Survey of the Cultural Revolt of the Nineteen-Fifties*, Wendover: Goodchild, 1985

Anderson, Tim J, *Making Easy Listening: Material Culture and Post-war American Recording*, Minneapolis: University of Minnesota Press 2006

Ant, Adam, *Stand & Deliver: the Autobiography*, London: Sidgwick & Jackson, 2006

Arnott, Jake, *The Long Firm*, London: Sceptre, 1999

Atkins, John, *The Who On Record: A Critical History 1963-1998*, Jefferson: McFarland, c. 2000

B

Balliett, Whitney, *Collected Works: A Journal of Jazz, 1954-2000*, London: Granta, 2001

— The Sound of Surprise: 46 pieces of Jazz, Harmondsworth: Penguin Books, 1963

Bangs, Lester, ed, Greil Marcus, *Psychotic Reactions and Carburetor Dung*, London: Minerva, 1991

Barfe, Louis, *Where Have All the Good Times Gone: The Rise and Fall of the Record Industry*, London: Atlantic, 2004

Barrow, Steve and Dalton, Peter, *The Rough Guide to Reggae*, London: Rough Guides, 2004

Barrow, Tony, *John, Paul, George, Ringo & Me: The Real Beatles Story*, London: Andre Deutsch, 2005

Barzun, Jacques, ed., *Pleasures of Music: An Anthology of Writing about Music and Musicians,* London: Cassell, 1977

Bazzana, Kevin, *Wonderous Strange: The Life and Art of Glenn Gould*, New Haven, CT: Yale University Press, 2004

Bennett, Alan, et. al., introduction, Michael Frayn, *The Complete Beyond the Fringe*, London: Methuen, 2003

Bergan, Ronald, *Beyond the fringe . . . and Beyond: A Critical biography of Alan Bennett, Peter Cook, Jonathan Miller and Dudley Moore*, London: Virgin, 1989

Billington, Michael, *State of the Nation: British Theatre since 1945*, Faber: London 2007

Birch, Will, *No Sleep till Canvey Island: The Great Pub Rock Revolution*, London: Virgin, 2000

Blair, John, *The Illustrated Discography of Surf music 1959-1965*, Riverside, CA: J. Bee, 1978

Bockris, Victor, *The Life and Death of Andy Warhol*, London: Fourth Estate, 1998

— *Lou Reed: The Biography*, London: Hutchinson, 1994

— and Gerard Malanga, *Up-tight: The Velvet Underground Story*, London: Omnibus, 1983

Bogdanov, Vladiamar, ed., *All Music Guide to Soul: The Definitive Guide to R&B and Soul*, San Francisco, CA: Backbeat, 2003

Booker, Christopher, *The Neophiliacs: the Revolution in English life in the Fifties and Sixties*, London: Pimlico, 1992

Bower, Tom, *Branson*, London: Fourth Estate, 2000

Boyd, Joe, *White Bicycles: Making Music in the 1960s*, London: Serpent's Tail, 2005

Bracewell, Michael, *England is Mine: Pop Life in Albion from Wilde to Goldie*, London: HarperCollins, 1997

— *The Nineties: When Surface was Depth*, London: Flamingo, 2002

— *Re-make/Re-model: Becoming Roxy Music,* London: Faber, 2007

Bradley, Lloyd, *Bass Culture: When Reggae was King*, London: Viking, 2000

Braun, Michael, *Love Me Do: The Beatles' Progress*, Harmondsworth: Penguin, 1977

Brown, Mick, *Richard Branson: The Inside Story*, London: Headline, 1994

— *Tearing Down the Wall of Sound: the Rise and Fall of Phil Spector*, London: Bloomsbury, 2007

Brown, Peter, and Steven Gaines, *The Love You Make: An Insider's Story of the Beatles*, New York: McGraw-Hill, 1983

Brown, Peter Harry and Pat H. Broeske, *Down at the End of Lonely Street: The Life and Death of Elvis Presley*, London: Heinemann, 1997

Brunning, Bob, *1960s' Pop*, Oxford: Heinemann, 1998

Burn, Gordon, *Best and Edwards: Football, Fame and Oblivion*, London: Faber, 2006

Burnett, Robert, *The Global Jukebox: the International Music Industry*, London: Routledge, 1996

Burns, Peter, *Curtis Mayfield: People Never Give Up*, London: Sanctuary, 2003

Burrows, Terry, *The Beatles: the Complete Illustrated Story*, London: Carlton, 1996

Burt, Rob, *Surf City, Drag City*, Poole: Blandford, 1986

Bynoe, Yvonne, *Encyclopedia of Rap and Hip-Hop Culture*, Westport: Harcourt Education 2005

C

Cantwell, Robert, *When We Were Good: the Folk Revival*, Cambridge: Harvard University Press, 1996

Carlin, Peter Ames, *Catch A Wave: The Rise, Fall & Redemption Of Brian Wilson*, Emmaus: Rodale Press 2006

Carner, Gary, ed., *The Miles Davis Companion*, London: Omnibus, 1996

Carpenter, Humphrey, *That was Satire That Was: Beyond the Fringe, the Establishment Club, Private Eye and That Was The Week That Was*, London: Victor Gollancz, 2000

Carr, Roy, Brian Case and Fred Dellar, *The Hip: Hipsters, Jazz and the Beat Generation*, London: Faber, 1986

Casteleman, and Walter J. Podrazik, *All Together Now: The First Complete Beatles Discography 1961-1975*, Ann Arbor: Pierian Press, 1975

Chang, Jeff, *Can't Stop Won't Stop: A History of the Hip-Hop Generation*, London: Ebury, 2005

Chapple, Steve and Reebee Garofalo, *Rock 'n' Roll is Here to Pay: The History and Politics of the Music Industry*, Chicago: Nelson-Hall, 1978

Charters, Ann, *Kerouac: A Biography*, London: Deutsch, 1974

— ed., *The Portable Beat Reader*, London: Penguin, 1992, [2006] printing

— ed., *The Portable Kerouac*, New York: Viking Penguin, 1996

Charters, Samuel, *The Country Blues*, London: Jazz Book Club, 1961

— *Jazz, New Orleans, 1885-1963: An index to the Negro musicians of New Orleans*, New York: Da Capo Press, 1983

— *The Legacy of the Blues: A Glimpse into the Art and the Lives of Twelve Great Bluesmen: An Informal Study*, London: Calder and Boyars, 1975

— *New Orleans: Playing a Jazz Chorus*, New York: Marion Boyars, 2006

— *Walking A Blues Road: A Selection of Blues Writing 1956-2004*, New York: Marion Boyars, 2005

Christgau, Robert, *Rock Albums of the 70s: Christgau's Guide*, London: Vermilion, 1982

Clarke, Donald, *All or Nothing at All: A Life of Frank Sinatra*, London: Pan, 1998

— *The Rise and Fall of Popular Music*, London: Viking, 1995

Clark, Tom, *Jack Kerouac: A Biography*, London: Plexus, 1997

Clayson, Alan and Spencer Leigh, eds, *Aspects of Elvis: Tryin' to Get to You*, London: Sidgwick & Jackson, 1994

Clayson, Alan, *Beat Merchants: The Origins, History, Impact and Rock Legacy of the 1960's British Pop Groups*, London: Blandford, 1995

Clerk, Carol, *The Book of the Damned: The Light at the End of the Tunnel: the Official Biography*, Carol Clerk , London: Omnibus, 1987

Coe, Jonathan, *The Rotters' Club*, London: Viking, 2001

Cogan, Brian, *The Encyclopedia of Punk Music and Culture*, Westport: Greenwood Press, 2006

Cohn, Nik, *Awopbopaloobop alopbamboom: Pop from the Beginning*, London: Pimlico, 2004

Coon, Caroline, 1988, *The New Wave, Punk Rock Explosion*, London: Orbach & Chambers, 1997

Cope, Julian, *Head-On: Memories of the Liverpool Punk-Scene, & the Story of the Teardrop Explodes 1976-82*, Great Britain: Magog Books, 1994

Coleman, Mark, *Playback: From the Victrola to MP3, 100 years of Music, Machines, and Money*, New York: Da Capo Press, 2004

Coleman, Ray, *Brian Epstein: The Man Who Made the Beatles*, London: Penguin, 1990

— *John Lennon*, London: Pan 2000

— *McCartney: Yesterday, and Today*, London: Boxtree, 1996

Collins, Ronald K.L. and David M. Skover, *The Trials of Lenny Bruce: The Fall and Rise of an American Icon*, Naperville: Sourcebooks MediaFusion, 2002

Collis, John, ed. Chris Charlesworth, *The Complete Guide to the Music of Frank Sinatra*, London: Omnibus, 1998

Cook, Richard, *Blue Note Records: The Biography*, London: Secker & Warburg, 2001

— *It's About that Time: Miles Davis On and Off Record*, London: Atlantic Books, 2005

Cooper, Kim and David Smay, eds., *Lost in the Grooves: Scam's Capricious Guide to the Music You Missed*, New York, London: Routledge 2005

Cooper, Michael, foreword and commentary by Keith Richards; text by Terry Southern, *The Early Stones: Legendary Photographs of a Band in the Making 1963-1973*, London: Secker & Warburg, 1993

Cott, Jonathan, *Conversations with Glenn Gould*, Boston: Little, Brown, 1984

— ed., *Dylan: The Essential Interviews*, London: Hodder & Stoughton, 2006

Crawford, Sue, *Ozzy: Unauthorised*, London: Michael O'Mara, 2003

Culshaw, John, *Putting the Record Straight: The Autobiography of John Culshaw*, London: Secker & Warburg, 1981

— *Ring Resounding: The Recording in Stereo of Der Ring des Nibelungen*, London: Secker and Warburg, 1967

Cuscana, Michael Michel Ruppli, *The Blue Note Label: A Discography*, New York: London, Greenwood Press, 1988

D

Daniels, Neil, *The Story of Judas Priest: Defenders of the Faith*, London: Omnibus, 2007

Dannen, Frederic, *Hit Men*, New York: Random House 1990

Dawson, Jim, and Steve Propers, *45 RPM: The History, Heroes & Villains of a Pop Music Revolution*, San Francisco: Backbeat 2003

Davies, Hunter, *The Beatles*, London: Cassell, 2002

— *The Quarrymen*, London: Omnibus, 2001

Davis, Miles with Quincy Troupe, *Miles: the Autobiography*, New York: London: Simon and Schuster, 1989

Day, Timothy, *A Century of Recorded Music: Listening to Musical History*, New Haven: Yale University Press, 2000

Dellar, Fred, *Where Did You Go To, My lovely?: The Lost Sounds and Stars of the Sixties*, London: Star Books, 1983

DeLillo, Don, *Great Jones Street*, London: Picador, 1992

DeRogatis, *Let it Blurt: the Life and Times of Lester Bangs*, London: Bloomsbury, 2000

Dewe, Michael, *The Skiffle Craze: A Popular Music Phenomenon of the 1950s*, Aberystwyth: University of Wales, 1999

Dimery, Robert, gen, ed.,*1001 Albums You Must Hear Before You Die*, London: Cassell Illustrated, 2005

Doe, Andrew G., and John Tobler, *Brian Wilson and The Beach Boys: The Complete Guide to their Music*, London: Omnibus, 2004

Dyer, Geoff, *But Beautiful: A Book About Jazz*, London: Abacus, 1998

Dylan, Bob, *Chronicles*, New York: Simon & Schuster, 2004

E

Edmonds, Ben, *Marvin Gaye: What's Going On and the Last Days of the Motown Sound*, Edinburgh: Mojo Books, 2001

Egan, Sean, ed., *100 Albums That Changed Music*, London: Robinson, 2006

Eisenberg, Evan, *The Recording Angel: Explorations in Phonography*, New York: McGraw-Hill, 1987

Epstein, Brian, *A Cellarful of Noise*, New English Library: London, 1965

Elliott, Brad, *Surf's Up!: The Beach Boys on Record 1961-1981*, Ann Arbor: Pierian Press, 1982

Ellis, Bret Easton, *American Psycho*, London: Picador, 1991

Ewing, Charles Patrick and Joseph T. McCann, *Minds on Trial: Great Cases in Law and Psychology*, Oxford: Oxford University Press, 2006

Ewing, Jon, *The Beatles*, London: Orion, 1994

F

Farren, Mick, *Give the Anarchist a Cigarette*, London: Jonathan Cape, 2001

Fisher, Marc, *Something in the Air: Radio, Rock, and the Revolution that Shaped a Generation*, New York: Random House, 2007

Forrester, George, Martyn Hanson and Frank Askew, *Emerson, Lake & Palmer: the Show That Never Ends: a Musical Biography*, London: Helter Skelter, 2001

Fox, Jo Brooks and Jules L. Fox, *The Melody Lingers On: Scenes from the Golden Years of West Coast Jazz*, Santa Barbara: Fithian Press, 1996

Frame, Pete, *The Beatles and Some Other Guys: Rock Family Trees of the Early Sixties*, London: Omnibus, 1997

Freedland, Michael, *All the Way: A Biography of Frank Sinatra*, London: Weidenfeld & Nicolson, 1997

Freeman, Garry, *The Bootleg Guide: Classic Bootlegs of the 1960s and 1970s*, Lanham: Scarecrow Press, 2003

Friedrich, Otto, *Glenn Gould: A Life and Variations*, London: Methuen, 1990

Frith, Simon, *Art Into Pop*, London: Methuen, 1987
— Will Straw and John Street, eds., *The Cambridge Companion to Pop and Rock*, Cambridge: Cambridge University Press, 2001
— *Sound effects: Youth, Leisure and the Politics of Rock*, London: Constable, 1983

G

Gaines, Steven, *Heroes and Villains: The True Story of the Beach Boys*, New York: Da Capo Press, 1995
Gaisberg, Fred, *The Music Goes Round*, New York: Macmillan, 1942
Galbraith, John Kenneth, *The Affluent Society*, Harmondsworth: Penguin Books, 1962
Gellatt, Roland, *The Fabulous Phonograph, 1877-1977*, New York: Macmillan, 1977
Geller, Deborah, ed Anthony Wall, *The Brian Epstein Story*, London: Faber, 2000
Gentle, Johnny and Ian Forsyth, *Johnny Gentle and the Beatles: First Ever Tour: Scotland 1960*, Runcorn: Merseyrock, 1998
Giddins, Gary, *Riding on a Blue Note: Jazz and American Pop*, New York: Da Capo Press, 2000
Gillman, Peter and Leni, *Alias David Bowie: A Biography*, Sevenoaks: New English Library, 1987
Gillett, Charlie, *The Sound of the City: the Rise of Rock and Roll*, London: Souvenir, 1996
Gitler, Ira, *Swing to Bop: an Oral History of the Transition in Jazz in the 1940s*, Oxford: Oxford University Press, 1985
— *Jazz Masters of the Forties*, New York: Collier Books, 1974
Goldberg, Joe, *Jazz Masters of the Fifties*, New York: Collier-Macmillan, 1965
Goldman, Albert, from the journalism of Lawrence Schiller, *Ladies and Gentlemen, Lenny Bruce!*, London: Pan Books, 1976
— *The Lives of John Lennon*, London: Bantam, 1988
Goldmark, Peter, *Maverick Inventor: My Turbulent Years at CBS*, New York: Saturday Review Press, 1973
Goldsmith, Martin, *The Beatles Come to America*, Hoboken: John Wiley & Sons, 2004
Goldsmith, Peter, D., *Making People's Music: Moe Asch and Folkways Records*, Washington: Smithsonian Institution Press, 1998
Gordon, Robert, *West Coast: The Los Angeles Jazz Scene of the 1950s*, London: Quartet, 1986
Granata, Charles L., *I Just Wasn't Made for These Times: Brian Wilson and the Making of Pet Sounds*, London: Unanimous, 2003

— *Sessions with Sinatra: Frank Sinatra and the Art of Recording*, Chicago: A Cappella, 1999

Granta Magazine 76: Music, London: Granta 2002

Gray, Michael, *The Bob Dylan Encyclopedia*, London: Continuum, 2006

Green, Jonathan, *All Dressed Up: the Sixties and the Counter-Culture*, London: Pimlico, 1999

— *Days in the Life:Voices from the English Underground 1961-1971*, London: Pimlico, 1998

Gruen, John, *The Party's Over Now. Reminiscences of the Fifties, New York's Artists, Writers, Musicians, and Their Friends*, New York: Viking Press, 1972

Guralnick, Peter, *Careless Love: The Unmaking of Elvis Presley*, London: Abacus, 2000

H

Hadar, Dori, *Mingering Mike*, New York: Princeton Architectural, 2007

Hajdu, David, *Positively 4th Street: the Lives and Times of Joan Baez, Bob Dylan, Mimi Baez Fariña, and Richard Fariña*, London: Bloomsbury, 2001

Hamill, Pete, *Why Sinatra Matters*, Boston: Little, Brown, 2000

Harris, Jet, and Royston Ellis, *Driftin' with Cliff Richard*, London: Charles Buchan's Publications, 1959

Harris, John, *The Dark Side of the Moon: The making of the Pink Floyd Masterpiece*, London: Harper Perennial, 2006

Harry, Bill, *The Ultimate Beatles Encyclopedia*, London: Virgin, 1992

Hennessy, Peter, *Having it So Good: Britain in the Fifties*, London: Allen Lane, 2006

Henry III, William A., *The Great One: The Life and Legend of Jackie Gleason*, New York: Doubleday, 1992

Hertsgaard, Mark, *A Day in the Life: the Music and Artistry of the Beatles*, London: Macmillan, 1995

Heylin, Clinton, *Bootleg: the Secret History of the Other Recording Industry*, New York: St. Martin's Press, 1995

— *Dylan: Behind the Shades*, London: Penguin, 1992

— *From the Velvets to the Voidoids: a Pre-Punk History for a Post-Punk World*, London: Penguin, 1993

Hibbert, Tom, ed., *The Perfect Collection*, New York: Proteus, 1982

Hine, Thomas, *The Total Package: The Evolution and Secret Meanings of Boxes, Bottles, Cans and Tubes*, New York: Little Brown, 1995

Hinton, Brian, *Joni Mitchell: Both Sides Now: the Biography*, London: Sanctuary, 2000

Holm-Hudson, Kevin, ed., *Progressive Rock Reconsidered*, New York: Garland, 2001

Home, Robin Douglas, *Sinatra*, Michael Joseph: London, 1962

Hornby, Nick, *High Fidelity*, London: Gollancz, 1995

— *31 Songs*, London: Penguin, 2003

Horricks, Raymond, *Profiles in Jazz: from Sidney Bechet to John Coltrane*, New Brunswick: Transaction Publishers, 1991

Hoskyns, Barney, *Across the Great Divide: the Band and America*, London: Pimlico, 2003

— *Beneath the Diamond Sky: Haight Ashbury 1965-1970*, London: Bloomsbury, 1997

— *Glam!: Bowie, Bolan and the Glitter Rock Revolution*, London: Faber, 1998

— *Hotel California: Singer-songwriters and Cocaine Cowboys in the LA Canyons, 1967-1976*, London: Harper Perennial, 2006

— ed., *The Sound and the Fury: a Rock's Backpages Reader: 40 Years of Classic Rock Journalism*, London: Bloomsbury, 2003

— *Waiting for the Sun: Strange Days, Weird Scenes and the Sound of Los Angeles*, London: Bloomsbury, 2003

Hoye, Jacob, ed., *VH-1 100 Greatest Albums*, New York: Pocket Books 2003

I

Ingham, Chris, *The Rough Guide to the Beatles*, London: Rough Guides, 2003

International Music Industry Conference, 1969 APR: NASSAU

Irvin, Jim and Colin McLear, eds., *The Mojo Collection: The Ultimate Music Collection*, Edinburgh: Canongate, 2003

Irwin, Colin, *Dire Straits*, London: Orion Books, 1994

J

Jones, Dylan, *iPod, Therefore I Am*, London: Weidenfeld & Nicolson, 2005

Johnstone, Nick, *The Clash 'Talking'*, London: Omnibus Press, 2006

— *Melody Maker: History of 20th Century Popular Music*, London: Bloomsbury, 1999

Jesmer, Elaine, *Number One With a Bullet: A Novel*, Elaine Jesmer, New York: Farrar Straus & Giroux, 1974

Joynson, Vernon, *Fuzz, Acid and Flowers: a Comprehensive Guide to American Garage, Psychedelic and Hippie Rock 1964-1975*, Telford: Borderline, 1993.

— Jon Neweyy and John Reed, The Tapestry of Delights: the Comprehensive Guide to British Music of the Beat, R&B, Psychedelic and Progressive Eras 1963-1976, Telford: Borderline, 1995

K

Katz, Mark, *Capturing Sound: How Technology Has Changed Music*, Berkeley, University of California Press, 2005

Kelley, Kitty, *His Way: The Unauthorised Biography of Frank Sinatra*, London: Bantam, 1986

Kennedy, Pagan, *Platforms: A Microwaved Cultural Chronicle of the 1970s*, New York: St Martin's Press, 1994

Kent, Nick, *The Dark Stuff*, London: Penguin, 1994

Kercher, Stephen E., *Revel With a Cause: Liberal Satire in Post-war America*, Chicago: University of Chicago Press, 2006

Kerouac, Jack, *On the Road*, London: Penguin, 1972, 2000 [printing]

— ed. Ann Charters, *Selected Letters, 1940-1956*, New York: Viking, 1995

Khan, Ashley, *Kind of Blue: The Making of the Miles Davis Masterpiece*, London: Granta, 2001

Kircherr, Astrid and Klaus Voormann, compiled by Ulf Kruger, *Hamburg Days*, Guildford: Genesis, 1999

Kirsten, Sven A., *The Book of Tiki: the Cult of Polynesian Pop in the Fifties*, London: Taschen, 2000

Kugelberg, Johan, photographs by Joe Conzo, foreword by Afrika Bambaataa, original flyer art by by Buddy Esquire, featuring a timeline by Jeff Chang, *Born in the Bronx: a Visual Record of the Early Days of Hip Hop*, New York: Rizzoli, 2007

Kureishi, Hanif, *The Buddha of Suburbia*, London: Faber, 1990

— and Jon Savage, eds., *The Faber Book of Pop*, London: Faber, 1995

L

Ladd, Jim, *Radio Waves: Life and Revolution on the FM Dial*, New York: St. Martin's Griffin, 1992

Lahr, John, *Sinatra: the Artist and the Man*, London: Phoenix, 1999

Laing, Dave et. al., *The Electric Muse: the Story of Folk into Rock*, London: Eyre Methuen, 1975

Lambert, Gavin, *The Slide Area: Scenes of Hollywood Life, a Novel*, Harmondsworth, Penguin Books, 1963

Lankford, Ronald D, Jr, *Folk Music USA: The Changing Voice of Protest*, London: Schirmer, 2005

Lanza, Joseph, *Elevator Music: A Surreal History of Muzak, Easy-Listening and other Moodsong*, London: Quartet 1995

Larkin, Colin, ed., *The Virgin Encyclopedia of Fifties Music*, London: Virgin 1998

Larkin, Philip, edited by Richard Palmer and John White, *Jazz Writings: Essays and Reviews 1940-84*, London: Continuum, 2004

Leaf, David, *The Beach Boys and the California Myth*, New York: Grosset & Dunlap, 1978

Lee, Martin A. and Bruce Shlain, introduction by Andrei Codrescu, *Acid Dreams: the Complete Social History of LSD, the CIA, the Sixties and Beyond*, London: Pan, 2001

Leland, John, *Hip, the History*, New York: Ecco 2004

— *Why Kerouac Matters: the Lessons of On the Road, They're Not What You Think*, New York: Viking, 2007

Levy, Shaun, *Rat Pack Confidential: Frank, Dean, Sammy, Peter, Joey & the Last Great Showbiz Party*, London: Fourth Estate, 1998

— *Ready, Steady, Go!: Swinging London and the Invention of Cool*, London: Fourth Estate, 2002

Lewis, Miles Marshall, *There's a Riot Goin' On*, London: Continuum, 2006

Lewis, Peter, *The Fifties*, London: Heinemann, 1978

Lewis, Roger, *The Life and Death of Peter Sellers*, London: Century, 1994

Lewisohn, Mark, *The Complete Beatles Chronicle*, Boynton Beach: Pyramid Books, 1992

— *The Complete Beatles Recording Sessions: The Official Story of the Abbey Road Years*, London: Hamlyn, 1988

Litweiler, John, *Ornette Coleman: The Harmolodic Life*, London: Quartet, 1992

Lydon, John with Keith and Kent Zimmerman, *Rotten: No Irish, No Blacks, No Dogs: the Authorised Autobiography*, London: Hodder & Stoughton, 1994

Lyons, Len, *The 101 Best Jazz Albums: A History of Jazz on Records*, New York: Morrow, 1980

M

Mabey, Richard, *The Pop Process*, London: Hutchinson Educational, 1969

MacAdams, Lewis, *Birth of the Cool: Beat, Bebop, and the American Avant-Garde*, New York ; London: Free Press, 2001

MacDonald, Ian, *The People's Music*, London: Pimlico, 2003

— *Revolution in the Head: The Beatles' Records and the Sixties*, London: Pimlico, 2005

MacKenzie, Colin, *Mantovani: A Lifetime in Music*, Ely, Melrose Book Company, 2005

Marcus, Greil, *Invisible Republic: Bob Dylan's Basement Tapes*, London: Picador, 1998

— *Lipstick Traces: A Secret History of the Twentieth Century*, London: Faber, 2001

Marmorstein, Gary, *The Label: The Story of Columbia Records*, New York: Thunder's Mouth Press, 2007

Marqusee, Mike, *Chimes of Freedom: The Politics of Bob Dylan's Art*, New York: New Press, 2003

Marsh, Dave, *Before I Get Old: The Story Of The Who*, London: Plexus Publishing, 1989

Marshall, David, *Akio Morita and Sony*, Watford: Exley, 1995

Martin, George, with Hornsby, Jeremy, *All You Need is Ears*, New York: St. Martin's Press, 1994

— with William Pearson, *Summer of Love: The Making of Sgt. Pepper*, London: Macmillan, 1994

Marwick, Andrew, *British Society Since 1945: The Penguin Social History of Britain*, London: Penguin, 2003

Mathieson, Kenny, *Giant Steps: Bebop and the Creators of Modern Jazz*, Edinburgh: Payback Press, 1999

Meade, Marion, *The Unruly Life of Woody Allen*, London: Weidenfeld & Nicolson, 1999

Melly, George, *Revolt into Style: the Pop Arts in Britain*, Harmondsworth: Penguin, 1972

McAleer, Dave, *Beatboom!: Pop Goes the Sixties*, London: Hamlyn, 1994

McCartney, Paul and Miles, Barry, *Many Years from Now*, London: Secker & Warburg, 1997

McDevitt, Chas, *Skiffle: The Definitive Inside Story*, London: Robson, 1997

McDonough, Jimmy, *Shakey: Neil Young's Biography*, Toronto: Random House Canada, 2002

McKnight-Trontz and Alex Steinweiss, introduction by Steven Heller, *The Life and Work of Alex Steinweiss*, New York: Princeton Architectural, 2000

McNeil, Legs, and Gillian McCain, *Please Kill Me: The Uncensored Oral History of Punk*, London: Abacus, 1997

Milano, Brett, *Vinyl Junkies: Adventures in Record Collecting*, New York: St Martin's Griffin, 2003

Miles, compiled by, *Bowie in his Own Words*, London: W.H. Allen, 1982]

Miles, compiled by, *John Lennon in his Own Words*, London: Omnibus Press, 1980

Miles, Barry, *The Beatles Diary: an Intimate Day by Day History*, London: Omnibus, 1998

— *In the Sixties*, London: Jonathan Cape, 2002
— *Jack Kerouac: King of the Beats: A Portrait*, London: Virgin 1998
— *Pink Floyd: The Early Years*, London: Omnibus, 2006
Millard, Andre, *America on Record: A History of Recorded Sound*, Cambridge: Cambridge University Press, 1995
Miller, Andy, *The Kinks Are the Village Green Preservation Society*, London: Continuum, 2004
Miller, James, *Flowers in the Dustbin: The Rise of Rock and Roll*, 1947-1977, London: Simon and Schuster, 1999
Morley, Paul, *Ask: The Chatter of Pop*, London: Faber, 1986
— *Words and Music: a History of Pop in the Shape of a City*, London: Bloomsbury, 2003
Morita, Akio, with Edwin M. Reingold and Mitsuko Shimomura, *Made in Japan*, London: Collins, 1987
Mulholland, Gary, *Fear of Music: The 261 Greatest Albums since Punk and Disco*, London: Orion, 2006
Murdoch, Iris, *The Bell*, Harmondsworth: Penguin, 1962
Murray, Charles Shaar, *Crosstown Traffic: Jimi Hendrix and Post-war Pop*, London: Faber, 1989
— *Shots from the Hip*, London: Penguin, 1991

N

Nachman, Gerald, *Seriously Funny: The Rebel Comedians of the 1950s and 1960s*, New York: Pantheon Books, 2003
Napier-Bell, Simon, *Black Vinyl, White Powder*, London: Ebury, 2002
Nathan, John, *Sony: the Private Life*, Boston: Houghton Mifflin, 1999
Newman, Richard, *The Making of Mike Oldfield's Tubular Bells: The Story of a Record Which Has Sold over 15,000,000 Copies and Helped to Found the Virgin Empire*, Ely: Music Maker, 1993
Newton, *The Jazz Scene*, London: Penguin, 1961
Nicosia, Gerald, *Memory Babe: A Critical Biography of Jack Kerouac*, New York: Grove, 1983
Nisenson, Eric, *The Making of A Kind of Blue: Miles Davis And His Masterpiece*, New York: St. Martin's Griffin, 2001
— *'Round About Midnight: A Portrait of Miles Davis*, New York: Da Capo Press, 1996
Norman, Philip, *Days in the Life: John Lennon Remembered*, London: Century, 1990
— *Shout!: The True Story of the Beatles*, London: Pan, 2004
— *The Stones*, London: Elm Tree, 1984
Nuttall, *Bomb Culture*, London: Paladin, 1970

THE LONG-PLAYER GOODBYE

O

O'Brien, Karen, *Joni Mitchell: Shadows and Light*, London: Virgin Books, 2002

O'Brien, Lucy, *She Bop: the Definitive History of Women in Rock, Pop and Soul*, London: Penguin, 1995

O'Donnell, *The Day John Met Paul: An Hour-by-Hour Account of How the Beatles Began*, New York: Routledge, 2006

Oldham, Andrew Loog, interviews and research by Simon Dudfield, ed. Ron Ross, *Stoned*, London: Secker & Warburg, 2000

Olmsted, Anthony, *For the Folkways Label see Folkways Records: Moses Asch and His Encyclopedia of Sound*, New York: Routledge, 2003

Ostwald, *Glenn Gould: The Ecstacy and Tragedy of Genius*, New York: W.W. Norton, 1997

P

Page, Tim, ed. *The Glenn Gould Reader*, London: Faber, 1987

Paley, William S., *As It Happened: A Memoir*, Garden City: Doubleday, 1979

Parkinson, Norman, with words by Maureen Cleave, *The Beatles Book*, London: Hutchinson, 1964

Paytress, *The Rolling Stones: Off the Record*, London: Omnibus, 2003

Payzant, Geoffrey, *Glenn Gould: Music & Mind*, Toronto: Van Nostrand Reinhold, 1978

Perone, James E., *The Words and Music of Carole King*, Westport: Roundhouse, 2006

Perry, Charles, *The Haight-Ashbury: A History*, New York: Random House, 1984

Pickard, Roy, *Frank Sinatra at the Movies*, London: Hale, 1994,

Polsy, Ned, *Hustlers, Beats and Others*, Harmondsworth: Penguin, 1971

Poulsen, Henrik Bech, *'77: The Year of Punk & New Wave*, London: Helter Skelter, 2005

Priestley, Brian, *Mingus: A Critical Biography*, London: Paladin, 1985, c1982.

Priore, Dominic, *The Story of Brian Wilson's Lost Masterpiece*, London: Sanctuary Publishing, 2005

Pynchon, Thomas, *Slow Learner: Early Stories*, London: Picador, 1985.

R

Rachlin, *The Encyclopedia of the Music Business*, New York: Harper & Row, 1981

Ramsey, Frederic, Jr, *A Guide to Longplay Jazz Records*, New York: Da Capo, 1977

Reed, Oliver, and Walter L. Welch, *From Tinfoil to Stereo: Evolution of the Phonograph*, Indianapolis: Bobbs-Merrill, 1976

Rees, Tony, *Vox Record Hunter: A Collector's Guide to Rock and Pop*, London: Boxtree, 1995

Reiff, Carole, *Nights in Birdland: Jazz Photographs, 1954-1960*, London: Simon & Schuster, 1987

Repsch, John, *The Legendary Joe-Meek: The Telstar Man*, London: Cherry Red, 2000

Reynolds, Simon, *Rip it Up and Start Again: Post-punk 1978-84*, London: Faber, 2005

Richard, Cliff, *My Story*, England: s.n., 1973

Riesman, David with Nathan Glazer and Reuel Denney, *The Lonely Crowd: A Study of the Changing American Character*, New Haven: Yale Nota Bene, 2001

Robertson, John, ed, Chris Charlesworth, *The Complete Guide to the Music of Elvis Presley*, London: Omnibus Press, 1994

Rock, Mick, *Glam!: An Eyewitness Account*, London: Omnibus, 2005

Rogan, Johnny, *Roxy Music: Style with Substance - Roxy's First Ten Years*, London: Star Books, 1982

Russell, Jeff, *The Beatles Album File and Complete Discography*, London: Blandford, 1989

S

Sagan, Carl, *Murmurs of Earth: The Voyager Interstellar Record*, London: Hodder & Stoughton, 1979

Sahl, Mort, *Heartland*, New York: Harcourt Brace Jovanovich, 1976

Salewicz, Chris, *McCartney*, London: Futura, 1987

— *Redemption Song: The Definitive Biography of Joe Strummer*, London: HarperCollins, 2006

Sanders, Ed, *The Family: The Story of Charles Manson's Dune Buggy Attack Battalion*, St. Albans: Panther, 1973

Sandbrook, Dominic, *Never had it So Good: a History of Britain from Suez to the Beatles*, London: Little, Brown, 2005

— *White Heat: A History of Britain in the Swinging Sixties*, London: Little,Brown, 2006

Sanjek, Russell, *American Popular Music and Its Business From 1900-1984*, Oxford: OUP, 1988

Sauers, Wendy, compiled by, *Elvis Presley: A Complete Reference*, Jefferson: McFarland, 1984

Savage, Jon, *England's Dreaming: Sex Pistols and Punk Rock*, London: Faber, 2001

— *The Kinks: The Official Biography*, London: Faber, 1984

— *Time Travel: Pop, Media and Sexuality*, 1976-96, London: Chatto & Windus, 1996

Schwarzkopf, Elisabeth, with an introduction by Herbert von Karajan, *On and Off the Record: A Memoir of Walter Legge*, London: Faber, 1982

Scott, Barry, *We had Joy, We Had Fun: The 'Lost' Recording Artists of the Seventies*, London: Faber and Faber, 1994

Sears, Richard S., *V-Discs: A History and Discography*, Westport: Greenwood Press 1980

Seiler, Burkhardt and Friends, eds., foreword by Malcolm McLaren, *The Album Cover Art of Punk*, London: Collins & Brown, 1998

Shelton, Robert, *No Direction Home: The Life and Music of Bob Dylan*, New York: W. Morrow, 1986

Shipton, Alyn, *A New History of Jazz*, London: Continuum, 2007

Smith, Giles, *Lost in Music: a Pop Odyssey*, London: Picador, 1995

Sounes, Howard, *Down the Highway: The Life of Bob Dylan*, London: Black Swan, 2002

Southall, Brian, Peter Vince and Allan Rouse, foreword by Paul McCartney; preface by George Martin, *Abbey Road: The Story of the World's Most Famous Recording Studios*, London: Omnibus, 2002

Spizer, Bruce, *The Beatles Records on Vee-Jay*, New Orleans: 498 Productions, L.L.C, 1998

— compiled by, foreword by Alan Livingston, *The Beatles' Story on Capitol Records*, New Orleans: 498 Productions, L.L.C, 2000

St John, Kevin, compiled by, *Cliff in His Own Words*, London: W.H. Allen, 1981

Strong, Martin C., *The Essential Rock Discography*, Edinburgh: Canongate Books, 2006

Sutcliffe, Pauline, with Douglas Thompson, *The Beatles' Shadow: Stuart Sutcliffe & His Lonely Hearts Club*, London: Pan, 2002

Szatmary, David P., *Rockin' in Time: a Social History of Rock and Roll*, Englewood Cliffs: Prentice-Hall, 1987

T

Talese, Gay, *The Gay Talese Reader: Portraits and Encounters*, New York: Walker & Company, 2003

Taraborrelli, J. Randall, *Sinatra: the Man Behind the Myth*, Edinburgh: Mainstream, 1997

Taylor, Derek, ed. George Harrison, *Fifty Years Adrift*, Guildford: Genesis in association with Hedley New Zealand & Hedley Australia, 1984

— *It Was Twenty Tears Ago Today*, London: Bantam, 1987

Thompson, Ben, *Ways of Hearing: a User's Guide to the Pop Psyche, from Elvis to Eminem*, London: Orion, 2001

Thompson, Hunter S., illustrated by Ralph Steadman, *Fear and Loathing in Las Vegas: a Savage Journey to the Heart of the American Dream*, London: Harper Perennial, 2005

Thompson, Tony, *Positively Main Street: an Unorthodox View of Bob Dylan*, London: New English Library, 1972

Thomas, J.C., *Chasin' the Trane: The Music and Mystique of John Coltrane*, London: Elm Tree Books, 1976

Thomson, David, *Biographical Dictionary of Film*, 4th ed., London: Little, Brown, 2002

Thorp, Viper: *The Confessions of a Drug Addict*, World Distributors: London, 1960

Toop, David, *Ocean of Sound: Aether talk, Ambient sound and Imaginary Worlds*, London: Serpent's Tail, 1995

— *Rap Attack 3: African Rap to Global Hip Hop*, London: Serpent's Tail, 2000

Tremlett, *The Cliff Richard Story*, London: Futura Publications, 1973

— *The David Bowie Story*, London: Futura Publications, 1974

— *The Marc Bolan Story*, London: Futura Publications, 1975

— *The Rolling Stones Story*, London:White Lion Publishers, 1976

True, Everett, *The Ramones*, London: Omnibus, 2002

Turner, Steve, *Cliff Richard: The Biography*, Oxford: Lion, 1994

— *Trouble Man: The Life and Death of Marvin Gaye*, London: Penguin, 2000

U

Unterberger, Richie, *Eight Miles High: Folk-Rock's Flight from Haight-Ashbury to Woodstock*, San Francisco: Backbeat, 2003

V

Vermorel, Fred and Judy, compiled and edited by, *The Sex Pistols: The Inside Story*, London: Star Books, 1978

Vernezze, Peter and Carl J. Porter, eds, *Bob Dylan and Philosophy: It's Alright, Ma, I'm Only Thinking*, Chicago: Open Court, 2006

Vollmer, Jürgen, *The Beatles in Hamburg*: Photographs, 1961, Düsseldorf: Schirmer/Mosel, 2004

W

Wakefield, *New York in the Fifties*, Boston: Houghton Mifflin Seymour Lawrence, 1992

Waldman, Anne, ed, foreword by Allen Ginsberg, *The Beat Book: Writings from the Beat Generation*, Boston: Shambhala, 1996

Wale, Michael, *Voxpop: Profiles of the Pop Process*, London: Harrap, 1972

Weissman, Dick, *Which Side Are You On?: An Inside Story of the Folk Music Revival in America*, London: Continuum, 2005

Welch, Chris, *Bob Marley*, London: Orion 1994

— *Close to the Edge: The Story of Yes*, London: Omnibus, 1999

— *Paul McCartney: The Definitive Biography*, Proteus: London, 1984

Whaley, Preston, Jr, *Blows like a Horn: Beat Writing, Jazz, Style, and Markets in the Transformation of U.S. Culture*, Cambridge: Harvard University Press, 2004

Whitburn, Joel, *Joel Whitburn's Top Pop Albums 1955-1996* compiled from *Billboard* magazine's pop album charts 1955-1996, Menomenee Falls: Record Research, 1996

White, Timothy, *Catch a Fire: The Life of Bob Marley*, London: Omnibus, 2006

— *The Nearest Faraway Place: Brian Wilson, the Beach Boys and the Southern Californian Experience*, London: Macmillan, 1996

Williams, Richard, *Phil Spector: Out of His Head*, London: Omnibus, 2003

Wilmer, Valerie, *As Serious as Your Life: John Coltrane and Beyond*, London: Serpent's Tail, 1992

Wilmut, Richard, preface by Bamber Gascoigne, *From Fringe to Flying Circus Celebrating a Unique Generation of Comedy 1960-1980*, London: Eyre Methuen, 1980

Willis, Paul, E., *Profane Culture*, London: Routledge and Kegan Paul, 1978

Willis, Tim, *Madcap: the Half-Life of Syd Barrett, Pink Floyd's Lost Genius*, London: Short, 2002

Wilson, Brian, with Todd Gold, *Wouldn't it be Nice: My Own Story*, London: Bloomsbury, 1992

Wilson, Peter Niklas, *Ornette Coleman: His Life and Music,* Berkeley: Berkeley Hills Books, 1999

Wilson, Tony, *24-Hour Party People: What the Sleeve Notes Never Tell You*, London: 4 Books, 2002

van Witteloostuyn, Jaco, trans. Antoon Hurkmans, Evelyn Kort-van Kaam & Shawm Kreitzman, *The Classical Long Playing Record: Design, Production and Reproduction: a Comprehensive Survey*, Rotterdam: A.A. Balkema, 1997

Wolfe, Tom, *The Kandy-Kolored Tangerine-Flake Streamline Baby*, London: Picador, 1981
— *Electric Kool-Aid Acid Test*, London: Bantam, 1972
— *Mauve Gloves & Madmen*, Clutter & Vine, London: Bantam, 1977
— *The Purple Decades*, London: Cape, 1983
Woodridge, Max, foreword by Malcolm McLaren, *Rock 'n' Roll London*, London: New Holland, 2002

Y

Yates, Richard, *Revolutionary Road*, London: Methuen, 1986
York, Peter, *Modern Times*, London: Futura, 1985
— *Style Wars*, London: Sidgwick & Jackson, 1980
Young, William H. with Nancy K. Young, *The 1950s*, Westport: Greenwood Press, 2004

Picture Acknowledgements

iv: Mike Jones. 20: Getty Images/Time & Life Pictures. 34: Columbia LP advertisement, 1948. 39: Fidelitone advertisement, 1958. 53: W. Schwann catalogue advertisement, 1953. 56: The Musical Masterpiece Society Inc advertisement, 1954. 62: Glenn Gould, photo Getty Images/Time& Life Pictures. 73 The Radio Craftsmen Inc *Assembly* Home Music System advertisement, 1953. 76: *Music for Two People Alone* The Melachrino Orchestra, 1954, RCA Victor LPM 1027. 91: *Skins!* A Bongo Party with Les Baxter (back cover), Capitol Records T 774. 95: Cook Laboratories advertisement, 1958. 103: *The Beat Generation* Readings by Jack Kerouac, Verve Records MGV 15005. 122: *Mingus at the Bohemia,* Debut Records DEB 123/Victor Musical Industries Inc. 126: *Jazz at the College of the Pacific,* The Dave Brubeck Quartet, Fantasy Inc 3-223, cover illustration by Arnold Roth, cover design by Ed Colker. 138: *European Holiday* produced exclusively for SAS Scandinavian Airlines System. 145: *Sinatra Sings Great Songs from Great Britain,* Reprise Records R 1006, cover photograph by Ray Manley-Shostal, Art Direction by Merle Shore. 151: *Beyond The Fringe,* Parlophone PMC 1145/EMI Records Ltd, photos by Lewis Morley. 156: Sleeve notes from back cover *Tom Lehrer Revisited,* Decca Record Company Ltd LK 4375. 158: *Tom Lehrer Revisited,* Decca Record Company Ltd LK 4375. 167: Brian Epstein, photo Rex Features. 193: *New Orleans Joys,* Chris Barber's Jazz Band and Skiffle Group, Decca Record Company Ltd LF 1198. 199: *The Mersey Sound,* Fidelio ATL 4108/ Delta Record Co Ltd. 207: *Surfin' U.S.A.,* The Beach Boys (back cover), Capitol Records Inc SM 1890/Capitol Industries EMI Inc. 212: Lightnin' Hopkins, photo Getty Images/Michael Ochs Archives. 214: *Easy Rider Leadbelly Legacy Volume Four,* Folkways Records and Service Corp FA 2034, album illustration by Ron Sibley. 224: *Duane Eddy does Bob Dylan,* Colpix Records SCP 494/ Columbia Pictures Corporation 1965. 239: *Sunny Afternoon,* The Kinks, Marble Arch MAL 716/Pye Records Ltd 1967, photography by Mike Leale Clareville Studios. 251: *Da Capo,* Love (back cover) Elektra Records EKL 4005. 259: *Hammond à Gogo Volume 3,* James Last and his Hammond-Bar-Combo Polydor Records Ltd Z 49304. 264: *Fresh,* Sly and the Family Stone, Edsel Records XED 232, cover design by John Berg, photographs of Sly Stone by Richard Avedon. 267: *In search of Space,* Hawkwind, United Artists Records UAG 29202, cover printed and made by the E.J. Day Group London and Bedford. 272: *Tighten Up,* Various Artists, Trojan Records TTL1, design by C.C.S. Advertising Associates Ltd, photography B.O.A.C. 275: 'Into Reggae' record shop, photo Getty Images. 288: *Tapestry* (8 Track Stereo), Carole King, Ode Records Inc/A&M Y8AM 2025, 1971, Art Direction by Roland Young, Design by Chuck Beeson, Photography by Jim McCrary.

295: *Dark Side of the Moon,* (sticker), Pink Floyd, Harvest SHVL 804B/EMI, 1973, sleeve design and photography by Hipgnosis, sleeve art and stickers art by George Hardie N.T.A. 296: Virgin Records advertisement, 1973. 306: CBS advertisement for *Raw Power,* Iggy and the Stooges, 1973, CBS 65586, photography by Mick Rock. 311: *Top of the Pops* (back cover) Hallmark Records SHM 905/Pickwick International Inc (GB) Ltd. 330: Record shop advertisement for *The Stranglers, 1978,* United Artists Records Ltd UAK 30222, sleeve design by Kevin Sparrow, cover photography by Ruan O Lochlainn. 332: Patti Smith, photo Mick Gold/Redferns. 336: *Nuggets Original Artyfacts from the First Psychedelic Era,* Elektra advertisement, 1973. 342: Advertisement for *Street Hassle,* Lou Reed, Arista Records Inc AB 4169/Columbia Pictures Inc, 1978. 355: Bootleg label for *Spunk,* Sex Pistols, 1977. 372: *NME Rough Trade* first release off Rough Tapes, catalogue number Copy 001. 376: *The Message,* Grandmaster Flash & The Furious Five, Sugarhill Records Ltd 1982 SH 268, photography front and back by Hemu Aggarwal, album design and production by A Q Graphics Inc. 378: Stevie Wonder, EMI/Tamla Motown advertisement, 1973.

387: *Motown Chartbusters Volume 7* Tamla Motown/EMI Records STML 11215, cover design by Andrew Christian, typography by Stephen Coelho. 390: *Dire Straits Live in 85,* Philips Compact Disc. 397: Mike Jones.

Text acknowledgements

The author and publisher would like to thank Random House for permission to quote from *The Bell* by Iris Murdoch on page 112 and *Slow Learner: Early Stories* by Thomas Pynchon on page 107. *On the Road* and *The Selected Letters of Jack Kerouac* on pages 101 and 102 reprinted by permission of SLL/Sterling Lord Literistic, Inc. Copyright 1957 by John Sampas, Literary Rep.

INDEX

INDEX

ng and I
inal Soundtrack..........W-740

Tamboo!
Les Baxter....................T-655

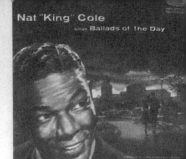

Ballads of the Day
Nat "King" Cole..............T-6

n Hi Fi
ny Goodman..............W-565

Oklahoma!
Original Soundtrack........SAO-595

Carousel
Original Soundtrack..........W-6

y in Spain
sic of the Bull Ring.....TAO-10022

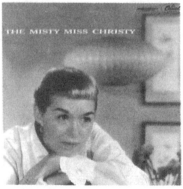

The Misty Miss Christy
June Christy..................T-725

Our Paris
Franck Pourcel..............T-100